WHISTLEBLOWERS, LEAKS, AND THE MEDIA

THE FIRST AMENDMENT AND NATIONAL SECURITY

PAUL ROSENZWEIG
TIMOTHY J. McNULTY
ELLEN SHEARER
EDITORS

Cover design by Anthony F. Nuccio/ABA Publishing.

Library of Congress Cataloging-in-Publication Data

Whistleblowers, leaks and the media : the First Amendment and national security / Edited by Timothy J. McNulty, Paul Rosenzweig, and Ellen Shearer.
  p. cm.
  Includes bibliographical references and index.
  ISBN 978-1-62722-825-1 (alk. paper)
1. Whistle blowing—Law and legislation—United States. 2. Freedom of speech—United States. 3. National security—Law and legislation—United States. 4. United States. Constitution. 1st Amendment I. McNulty, Timothy J. editor. II. Rosenzweig, Paul, editor. III. Shearer, Ellen, editor.
  KF3471.W48 2014
  342.73'068—dc23

                                                      2014028803

Contents

CONTENTS

CONTENTS

Preface

Let me thank the editors and authors for producing this outstanding volume on leaks, whistleblowers, and the media. The ABA Standing Committee on Law and National Security and the Medill School of Journalism at Northwestern University, through its National Security Journalism Initiative, have again collaborated to produce a timely, thoughtful set of essays on one of the mostly hotly debated issues of the day. How we understand, investigate, and prosecute leaks in this cyber age, where secrets are so hard to keep, has emerged as one of the central concerns of our democracy. The right to know and the right for the government to keep secrets address many of the ongoing tensions that have been with us since the birth of the republic. Recent developments, from WikiLeaks to reporter prosecutions to Assange to Snowden, have generated much commentary and strong public opinions. This volume not only sets the record straight and lays out the legal framework, but provides a forum for future discussions and ideas that warrant more exploration and elaboration. This book is just the type of collaboration that we need at the ABA as the debate concerning the First Amendment and the role of government in the realm of national security continues and intensifies. In short, I deeply applaud this effort—well done.

James R. Silkenat
President, American Bar Association
New York, New York
June 4, 2014

"Three may keep a secret, if two of them are dead."
—Benjamin Franklin, *Poor Richard's Almanack*

The Fundamental Tension: An Introduction

Paul Rosenzweig, Timothy J. McNulty, and Ellen Shearer

Manning, Assange, Snowden: Their names are by now familiar to most Americans and certainly familiar to every reader of this volume. Some think them heroes and patriots; others think them villains and traitors. This dichotomy reflects what we have come to think of, in creating this volume, as the fundamental tension—the perpetual and unsteady equilibrium between secrecy and transparency in American society.

We say "fundamental" because in many senses the tension is ineradicable and inherent in the structure of American government. It requires us to consider and reconcile two cherished values—limited government and effective government.

Americans value limited government because they value freedom—and they think that government is as much a threat to freedom as an enabler of it. And so we esteem an independent check on government excess so highly that the right to freedom of the press is enshrined in the First Amendment. The words are familiar to almost everyone—"Congress shall make no law . . . abridging the freedom . . . of the press." From the time of our founding Americans saw the press as a critical check on authority. Indeed, distrust of government is, boiled down to its essence, the foundational insight of the Declaration of Independence—an assertion that the rights to life, liberty and the pursuit of happiness are inalienable rights that belong to citizens by virtue of their humanity—and not, in any way, derived from or granted by governments. If you see government as subordinate to natural rights then, naturally, you see a need for ways to effectively check government abuse and overreach.

At the same time, however, we want a government that works and works well. The desire for order and government protection from threats stretches at least as far back as the Hobbesian concern that, without communal security, life is "nasty, mean, brutish, and short." That concern finds strong echoes in the constitutional preamble, which sets as one of the priorities for the new government that it "provide for the common defense."

American law is foundationally committed to a vision of freedom and transparency that sees the press as a crucial component of limited government—so much so that it is often called the "Fourth Estate," the fourth branch of government. At the same time, we recognize that, at some level, secrecy is essential in an increasingly dangerous world.

This fundamental tension is, in the end, best summarized by a quip and a quote. The quip is "Doctors bury their mistakes; government officials classify theirs." That reflects the skepticism with which we view official secrecy—it is as much a barrier to accountability as it is an enabler of effective action.

By contrast, the late Army Lt. Gen. Vernon A. Walters, former U.S. ambassador to the United Nations and deputy director of central intelligence, once wrote, "Americans have always had an ambivalent attitude toward intelligence. When they feel threatened, they want a lot of it, and when they don't, they regard the whole thing as somewhat immoral."[1] That, too, describes the fundamental tension—Americans want an effective government, but it has to be one that is circumscribed by law and policy.

In the end, we think the tension metaphor may present a false choice—that you can either have transparency and accountability or you can have secrecy and effectiveness. If we really were put to such a choice it would a difficult, indeed almost existential, question—but the choice is not real. The United States can, and indeed, does have both transparency and secrecy; both accountability and effectiveness. The goal should be to maximize both values to the extent practicable.

And that, at bottom, is the theme of this book. It's not about "resolving" the fundamental tensions that exist permanently in American democracy. It's about managing them, living with them, and accommodating the competing values to the maximum extent practicable. We all want to be safe; we all want an effective government that can provide national security; and we all want one that acts within the rule of law. We all want a government that is transparent and accountable, not despotic. And we all want a legal and policy structure that fosters our desires.

Sometimes the country gets the balance wrong. Far more often, as is to be expected in a pluralistic society, citizens simply disagree about precisely how to achieve the ends we seek. You will see much of that disagreement played out in these pages. But at its core, the discussion and even tensions in this book are emblematic of the value of competing ideas—legal analyses of a living, breathing aspect of a functioning democracy.

I. A CONSTITUTIONAL PERSPECTIVE

The concern for ineffective government action was an animating force behind the Constitutional Convention. The Articles of Confederation had proven to be inadequate to the task of enabling the federal government. The Constitution itself was, therefore, a reaction against an ineffective government and the chaos of an ungoverned society. Hence, the framers of the Constitution sought to create a stronger government—what Alexander Hamilton so famously called one possessing "energy in the Executive."[2]

And throughout U.S. history, Americans have confronted crisis with strong executive action—sometimes even action that trenches close to or crosses the line of the law. Examples abound, ranging from President Abraham Lincoln's unilateral suspension of the writ of habeas corpus to President Franklin Roosevelt's covert aid to Britain in World War II in contravention of the Neutrality Act. Most recently, of course, and more controversially, we have seen strong executive branch action in the wake of the events of September 11, 2001. Those activities have ranged from covert surveillance to the military response in Afghanistan and the subsequent conflict in Iraq.

But one thing unites all of these examples—the need, in some part, for secrecy in execution. Roosevelt's aid to Britain would have been stopped had it been widely known to a still isolationist Congress. And, manifestly, secrecy was essential to the successful operation targeting Osama bin Laden. Indeed, to cite an example from recent headlines, the disclosure by *The New York Times* that the National Security Agency (NSA) is capable of physical intrusions into computers in China[3] inevitably means that that program of covert surveillance will become less effective—with effects on American security that cannot be known or predicted. In short, secrecy is sometimes crucial to effectiveness.

But secrecy is likewise often a handmaiden to thwarting transparency and accountability. The case of the disclosure of the Pentagon Papers (involving the leak of a Defense Department analysis of the Vietnam War) reminds us that often governments use secrecy to conceal mistakes or misconduct (like the FBI's surveillance of Americans in the 1970s as part of its counterintelligence program, COINTELPRO), or simply to avoid embarrassment. And so secrecy and transparency are often in equipoise—too much secrecy threatens liberty; too much transparency threatens security.

We've recognized this tension since the dawn of democracy in America. Thomas Jefferson once said: "The natural progress of things is for liberty to yield and government to gain ground."[4] We must guard against this natural tendency. Though Jefferson was right that we must be cautious, philosopher John Locke was equally correct when he wrote: "In all states of created beings, capable of laws, where there is no law there is no freedom. For liberty is to be free from the restraint and violence from others; which cannot be where there is no law; and is not, as we are told, a liberty for every man to do what he likes."[5]

Thus, the obligation of the government is a dual one: to protect civil safety and security against violence and to preserve civil liberty. That dual obligation remains, at the core, the challenge of the secrecy/transparency debate.

II. JAMES ROSEN AND THE RESPONSE OF GOVERNMENT

We can see all of these different strands of concern play out in any number of recent cases—NSA leaker Edward Snowden, Private First Class Chelsea (formerly Bradley) Manning, and WikiLeaks founder Julian Assange are familiar to most readers these days.

Consider the case of James Rosen, a Fox News reporter. Rosen had written several stories regarding American policy and North Korea—at least one of which seems clearly to have been based on classified information that he received from a confidential source. On June 11, 2009, Rosen published a story in the midst of a U.N. Security Council debate as it considered its response to North Korean developments. Rosen's article addressed the question of how North Korea might react to a Security Council action. The story was significant in part because Rosen disclosed that the U.S. government thought that the North Korean regime would in all likelihood stage another nuclear test as a result of American action.

The source of the information for Rosen's story was, according to Rosen, information that "the Central Intelligence Agency has learned, through sources inside North Korea."[6] The story went on to say that "FOX News is withholding some details about the sources and methods by which American intelligence agencies learned of the North's plans so as to avoid compromising sensitive overseas operations in a country—North Korea—U.S. spymasters regard as one of the world's most difficult to penetrate."[7]

Notwithstanding the disclaimer, the story made waves. It appeared to disclose the existence of a confidential source (whether human or technical is not known) inside North Korea—a revelation that certainly set off alarm bells in Pyongyang. Fearing that consequence, and determined to deter further leaks on the subject, the Department of Justice (DoJ) began an extensive investigation into how Rosen came to have this classified information—information to which fewer than 100 people in government had access.

According to *The Washington Post*, in order to track the source of the leak, the DoJ reviewed Rosen's activities by tracking his visits to the Department of State (DoS), using phone traces, analyzing the timing of his calls, and reviewing his personal e-mails.[8] The evidence collected makes a powerful, albeit circumstantial, case that State Department contractor Stephen Jin-Woo Kim was Rosen's source.

Here's a summary of some of the most salient information—all taken from the affidavit of FBI agent Reginald Reyes:[9]

4

- On the day the story was published, Kim and Rosen apparently had a face-to-face meeting—at least, that is what the access logs to DoS headquarters at 2201 C St. NW suggest. A few hours before the story was published, "Mr. Kim departed DoS at or around 12:02 p.m. followed shortly thereafter by the reporter at or around 12:03 p.m." Then, "Mr. Kim returned to DoS at or around 12:26 p.m. followed shortly thereafter by the reporter at or around 12:30 p.m."

- Kim and Rosen had frequent contact by phone. Kim's phone records showed that seven calls lasting from 18 seconds to more than 11 minutes were placed between Kim's desk telephone and Rosen's cellphone and desk phone at the DoS. Over a two-month period, more than 36 calls were made from Kim's desk to Rosen. More to the point, at the very moment that Rosen and Kim were talking, computer records showed that Kim's user profile was logged in, viewing the classified report on which Rosen's report was based.

- Finally, Rosen and Kim appeared to take steps to conceal their contacts. In their e-mails, Rosen used the alias "Leo" to address Kim and called himself "Alex." Rosen instructed Kim to send him coded signals on his Google account: "One asterisk means to contact them (*i.e.*, Fox News) or that previously suggested plans for communication are to proceed as agreed; two asterisks means the opposite." In one email Rosen wrote: "What I am interested in, as you might expect, is breaking news ahead of my competitors," including "what intelligence is picking up. . . . I'd love to see some internal State Department analyses."

To collect this evidence, the government sought and received a warrant from a federal court, which found probable cause to believe that a crime had been committed. In the warrant application, the Justice Department labeled Rosen a "criminal co-conspirator" with Kim, the suspected source of the leaks. As is required by current regulations, Attorney General Eric Holder personally approved the search warrant for Rosen. Rosen did not know he was under surveillance or investigation until it was publicly disclosed by the press.

The collection of information about a reporter's contacts with a source has generated real controversy. To some, the Justice Department's aggressive investigative methods are a cause for concern because they might have a chilling effect on news organizations and degrade their ability to create transparency into government operations. As Fox News contributor and New Jersey Superior Court Judge Andrew Napolitano commented: "This is the first time that the federal government has moved to this level of taking ordinary, reasonable, traditional, lawful reporter skills and claiming they constitute criminal behavior."[10]

Balanced against this concern is the countervailing value of efficacy—efficacy of the government in keeping secrets and efficacy of the judicial system in enforcing the rule of law. One of the fundamental tenets of law is that those investigating a crime are entitled to every person's evidence. The exceptions to this general rule are few and far between (the most commonly known is the attorney-client privilege). Reporters often argue that they should be permitted to make a legally enforceable promise of confidentiality to their sources. But the Rosen case goes beyond that and suggests that some members of the press think that even the extrinsic physical evidence of their activities (where they go, for example) ought to be out of bounds, because it is essential to the performance of their jobs. Carving an exception like that into the general law for investigating criminal activity would be a significant and new departure from existing norms.

And so, this single case (emblematic of so many more) provides a host of interesting questions—questions both of policy and of law—and not all with satisfactory answers:

- Was Kim a whistleblower, or a traitor?
- What criminal laws did Kim violate?
- Who is a journalist? Rosen clearly is one, but is Julian Assange?
- Can Rosen be charged as a co-conspirator for violating the criminal laws?
- Can government investigations compel reporters to disclose the identity of their sources? Should federal law protect a reporter's privilege against disclosure?
- If there is a privilege, is it part of the First Amendment, or must it be created by statute?
- Can investigators look at physical evidence of reporters' activities to try to identify their sources?
- Are there alternatives to criminal prosecutions through civil enforcement?
- What if the leaked information was not appropriately classified in the first instance?
- How would classified information have been handled at Kim's trial (he has pled guilty, so there won't be one)?
- How would this case be handled in other countries?

One final observation about this case (and others like it) is a reflection on the changing norms of reporting on national security. As Fred Kaplan, the Edward R. Murrow fellow at the Council on Foreign Relations, wrote in 2013, opining on the Rosen/Kim matter: "It may seem odd for someone who has been reporting on national security matters for a few decades to say this, but just because the government is doing something in secret—and just because a leaker tells someone like me about it—that doesn't *necessarily* mean it should see the light of day. That is especially so if the secret activity in question doesn't break laws, expose deceit, kill people, violate basic decency, or . . . (feel free to add to this list)."[11] That traditional view of the role of the press—as overseers with responsibility for ferreting out wrongdoing—reflects the long-understood balance between secrecy and transparency.

6

But the times they are a-changing—and that balance may be shifting in favor of transparency. Consider, again, *The New York Times* article about NSA intrusions into Chinese computers. It met none of the criteria that Kaplan had articulated less than a year earlier. As Jack Goldsmith, a law professor at Harvard, noted:

> [T]his article shows how much publication norms have changed in recent years. . . . This is a story about the technical means and methods of surveillance against foreign countries, including our military adversaries, Russia and China. . . . I imagine that [reporters David] Sanger and [Thom] Shanker would say . . . [that] revelations about the NSA (including ones related to this story) are pouring out from scores of sources abroad, and that if they do not report this story someone else will. If these are the arguments, it is hard to see what NSA secrets the [*New York Times*] would not publish.[12]

And that, in a nutshell, captures the changing landscape.

* * *

In the pages that follow, we seek to provide an easily accessible introduction to the law and policy relating to national security, whistleblowers, and leaks to the media. There are ample numbers of legal texts—but no layman's guide. This volume aims to fill that niche.

This chapter and chapter 2 set the scene for the later chapters' outlines of the various laws related to whistleblowing and leaks. The chapters focus on recent controversies concerning leaks and the salience of the issue, from James Rosen of Fox News to the case of *New York Times* reporter James Risen, whose prosecution by the Justice Department for his stories on a secret NSA program involving spying on U.S. citizens, based on leaked information, has continued for years. The chapters also review the history of leaks and whistleblowers. The topic has been part of American history since its founding and has become even more prominent in the time since the 1970s and the growth of investigative journalism.

Chapters 3 and 4 review U.S. criminal and other relevant laws and efforts to change those laws. Criminal law has been applied to leakers at least since 1917. We examine the Espionage Act and trace its application in a variety of prosecutions. In addition, the chapters examine the perception that leak prosecutions have increased in recent years and that increasingly, the federal government is using more aggressive tactics to prevent reporters from accessing classified information. We survey the laws being used now and assess their historical provenance. We then look again at history, this time with a closer focus on efforts over time to stop leaks, draft leaks laws, or amend espionage laws. That history shows how difficult it is to craft the right language to protect secrets.

Leaks are "leaks" because they go to the press. If they go only to a foreign nation, they are espionage. But the press has certain First Amendment protections.

7

Chapter 5 surveys First Amendment arguments for news media protection. It also addresses why free speech as it applies to the press is not unlimited, and why there is no demonstrable constitutional basis for the open publication of properly classified information.

Chapter 6 reviews the panoply of laws that exist to protect whistleblowers in this country. Some are intended to protect those who go public in the media; others are intended to foster internal dissent within the government and protection from retribution.

Chapters 7 and 8 give the reader a primer on classification law, including how something gets classified and declassified and what the various classification levels mean, and a rundown of classification law. They also review how classified information is used (or, sometimes, not used) during criminal proceedings.

Chapter 9 is an examination of other countries' laws, looking at parallel legal systems for areas of congruence and divergence. And chapter 10 looks at the question from the law enforcement officer's perspective. What tools are available to the government to track down leakers and address breaches of security?

The issue of big data and leaks in the computer age get a thorough review in chapter 11. Among the issues: the post-9/11 change in emphasis from "need to know" to "need to share" among intelligence agencies. The conundrum for the press and leaks is exemplified by the remark of a federal investigator that never again would a subpoena need to be issued to a reporter for his or her testimony because the reporter's electronic trail would identify sources without the testimony. At the same time, big data allows for greater transparency when it is focused on government.

Readers of Chapter 11 should know that it was redacted late in the editing process at the request of the U.S. government. Because one of the authors of that chapter carries a security clearance, we accommodated the redaction at the author's request. The redaction serves, however, to highlight some of the overclassification and secrecy themes of this book since the material redacted referred to public reports by Dana Priest in her book *Top Secret America: The Rise of the New American Security State* that disclosed the still "classified" CIA secret rendition program. In the interest of transparency, we note that redaction here.

Chapter 12 reviews various ways leakers are or could be held accountable and offers thoughtful ideas on what might by a comprehensive U.S. approach to dealing with national security leaks.

Chapters 13 and 14 are styled as a "debate" and offer two views of the consequences of leaks—the loss of secrecy on one hand, and greater transparency on the other. Chapter 13 examines the origins and evolution of the government's right, including its constitutional basis, to protect information from public disclosure. Official secrecy and classification are well established in both statutory and case law. The chapter reviews the damage that leaks can cause to national security, particularly to intelligence sources and methods, and to military operations.

8

Foreign adversaries of the United States feed off press leaks, which some believe have become an even more important source of U.S. classified information to foreign adversary governments and non-state actors than foreign spying and espionage. In response, chapter 14 looks at leaks as an antidote to government secrecy and government power and examines the press's role as an external check and balance on government power.

Finally, we want to thank all of the authors who have written for us. They have given freely of their time and expertise and this volume would not exist without their efforts. We hasten to add, on their behalf (and especially for those of our authors who still work in government) that the views they express are their own and reflect neither the views of any institution where they work nor, for that matter, the opinions of the American Bar Association or the Medill School of Journalism, Media, Integrated Marketing Communications of Northwestern University. Leaks and the press are controversial topics—expect the views offered here to challenge you. Expect as well that this survey will shed light on an area of public discourse more frequently characterized by heat and passion.

In the realm of policy and law, we attempt, continually, to square the circle of transparency and secrecy, never succeeding and, quite possibly, never really expecting that we can succeed. Rather this unending tension calls for us to continually rebalance and reexamine fundamental values, trying our best to give effect to both as circumstances permit.

NOTES

1. VERNON WALTERS, SILENT MISSIONS (1978), *quoted in* CHARLES E. LATHROP, THE LITERARY SPY: THE ULTIMATE SOURCE FOR QUOTATIONS ON ESPIONAGE & INTELLIGENCE (2008).

2. THE FEDERALIST No. 70 (Alexander Hamilton).

3. David Sanger and Thom Shanker, "N.S.A. Devises Radio Pathway Into Computers," *New York Times*, January 14. 2014, http://www.nytimes.com/2014/01/15/us/nsa-effort-pries-open-computers-not-connected-to-internet.html?_r=0.

4. Letter to E. Carrington, May 27, 1788, *reprinted in* THE FOUNDERS' ALMANAC 157 (Matthew Spalding ed., 2002).

5. JOHN LOCKE, TWO TREATISES OF GOVERNMENT 305 (Peter Laslett ed., 1988).

6. James Rosen, "North Korea Intends to Match U.N. Resolution with Nuclear Test," *Fox News*, June 11, 2009, http://www.foxnews.com/politics/2009/06/11/north-korea-intends-match-resolution-new-nuclear-test/.

7. *Id.*

8. Ann Marimow, "A Rare Peek into a Justice Department Leak Probe," *Washington Post*, May 19, 2013, http://www.washingtonpost.com/local/a-rare-peek-into-a-justice-department-leak-probe/2013/05/19/0bc473de-be5e-11e2-97d4-a479289a31f9_story.html.

9. Affidavit in Support of Search Warrant, Mag. No. 10-291-M-01 (D.D.C. May 28, 2010), http://fas.org/sgp/jud/kim/warrant.pdf.

10. *"How Does Jay Carney Sleep at Night?,"* FOX NEWS INSIDER, May 21, 2013, http://foxnewsinsider.com/2013/05/21/judge-napolitano-government-has-never-gone-level-against-reporter.

11. Fred Kaplan, *Why James Rosen Is Not Blameless*, SLATE, May 29, 2013, http://www.slate.com /articles/news_and_politics/war_stories/2013/05/james_rosen_and_the_justice_department_leak _investigation_the_fox_news_reporter.html.

12. Jack Goldsmith, *Two Thoughts on the Sanger/Shanker Story*, LAWFARE, Jan. 15, 2013, http:// www.lawfareblog.com/2014/01/two-thoughts-on-the-sangershanker-story-on-nsa-infiltration-of -foreign-networks/#.UthBBbRDGV0.

Part I

Prosecuting Leaks

History of Leaks in the United States from the Pentagon Papers through WikiLeaks to Rosen

2

Gregg P. Leslie and Emily Grannis

The modern history of the prosecution of leaks to the news media and what that means to the public can best be understood through an examination of two cases—one of the first "modern" leaks controversies, and one of the most recent.

The first case involves Daniel Ellsberg's release of the Pentagon Papers in 1971.[1] Ellsberg, a researcher at the RAND Corporation, famously decided to share 43 volumes of a massive Pentagon study on the history of the war in Vietnam with *New York Times* reporter Neil Sheehan, holding back only the most recent four volumes, which he felt could affect peace talks of the then-ongoing war.

The newspaper's subsequent publication of articles starting on June 13, 1971, led to a "request" from the Department of Justice to stop publishing the reports. When that failed, the government sought an injunction from the federal district court in New York, forbidding the paper to continue to publish the revelations. The court declined, but the U.S. Court of Appeals for the Second Circuit imposed the restraint while sending the case back to the lower court for further consideration.[2] That order was overturned on June 30 of that year, when the U.S. Supreme Court struck it down as an unconstitutional prior restraint.

Ellsberg was subsequently charged with violations of the Espionage Act of 1917—the same statute that is today still being used to prosecute leakers of government information—but the charges were dismissed by a federal judge after it became clear that the White House had been gathering evidence against Ellsberg illegally.[3]

While the Pentagon Papers case is still held aloft by the news media as a standard for the proposition that the government cannot restrain the media from publishing even classified material, it nonetheless also stands as the first attempt by the government to prosecute the news media for reports of leaked national security information; no such prosecution had been brought before in the country's history.[4] In fact, Attorney General John Ashcroft, when asked by Congress in October 2002 if he felt that a British-style "official secrets" act was necessary, replied that current statutes, particularly the Espionage Act, "provide a legal basis to prosecute those who disclose classified information without authorization, if they can be identified."[5] Though no journalists have been prosecuted for espionage, the lesson the government has taken from the Pentagon Papers case is that while it cannot restrain publication beforehand, it can certainly prosecute disclosures after the fact.

The most recent important leaks case involves the prosecution of Stephen Jin-Woo Kim, who pleaded guilty on February 7, 2014, to one count of disclosing national defense information to an unauthorized person, namely, Fox News reporter James Rosen.[6] Kim, a State Department contractor, was charged on August 27, 2010, with the release of information about U.S. intelligence related to North Korea. The information allegedly was classified because it related to North Korea's military capacity and addressed U.S. intelligence sources and methods. Kim told Rosen that North Korea was planning to respond to a United Nations Security Council resolution by conducting a nuclear test.[7]

Kim argued through his lawyers that the statements he allegedly made contained "completely unremarkable observations about what a country would do if it was sanctioned for its poor behavior. These kinds of observations were well known to anyone paying attention to public sources and ought not be the basis for making someone a federal felon."[8]

Six months later, journalist Bob Woodward released his book *The Obama Wars*, which reported classified information obtained from Obama administration sources. At that point, Kim's lawyer argued in a letter to the U.S. Attorney's Office that prosecuting Kim for the comments he may have made to Fox News was not fair because the government was not prosecuting everyone who disclosed classified information to Woodward for his book. "How can it be in the U.S. government's interest to pursue Mr. Kim in the manner it has and allow this much more blatant event to go unaddressed?" Kim's attorney asked.[9]

Kim's case garnered greater attention after the May 2013 revelation that the Justice Department had told a judge that Rosen might be liable for conspiring to violate the Espionage Act. But the government did not truly intend to prosecute Rosen; the allegation that he was a conspirator was apparently just a technical step necessary to get Rosen's records, when the law was clear that the government should not have been able to do so.

Prosecutors had found themselves boxed into a corner. As they revealed in an affidavit in support of a search warrant,[10] they knew the Electronic Communications Privacy Act required them to get a search warrant from a court, rather than relying on a subpoena, before they could demand Rosen's Gmail records from Google. However, they also knew that the Privacy Protection Act of 1980 (PPA) barred the government from using search warrants to obtain journalistic work product, with the understanding that such material is better obtained through subpoenas, where the media would get an opportunity to contest the demand. Rather than let this legal roadblock stop their efforts, prosecutors then looked to the exception of the PPA that allows for search warrants when the journalist "has committed or is committing the criminal offense to which the materials relate."[11]

So prosecutors set about creating a scenario in which Rosen was "an aider and abettor and/or co-conspirator" of violations of section 793(d) of the Espionage Act.[12] Special Agent Reginald B. Reyes noted the exact times Kim examined a particular classified document; the exact times and durations of phone calls between Kim and Rosen on State Department desk phones; the exact times that their security badges were swiped to leave and re-enter the State Department building; and the number of other calls between Kim and "telephone numbers associated with the Reporter's news organization." He also revealed that a forensic analysis of Kim's office computer revealed deleted e-mail messages to and from Rosen. Reyes also noted that Rosen, unidentified in the affidavit, obtained information from Kim "by employing flattery and playing to Mr. Kim's vanity and ego." Reyes then concluded, "Based on the foregoing, there is probable cause to believe that the Reporter has committed a violation of 18 U.S.C. § 793 . . . at the very least, either as an aider, abettor and/ or co-conspirator of Mr. Kim."[13]

The affidavit makes clear two things: first, that the Federal Bureau of Investigation (FBI) has the ability to track an extensive amount of information about federal employees directly and about the reporters who interact with them, and second, even that information is not enough. The prosecution clearly had overwhelming evidence that Kim had released the information (he subsequently pled guilty and will serve 13 months in jail), but it wanted more; the affidavit was submitted to justify a search of the reporter's e-mail—*all* e-mail during the days of contacts between the two—on a clear fishing expedition to see what else could be discovered.

The affidavit in the Kim case only came to light after a much bigger sweep of journalists' phone records was revealed in an unrelated case involving an Associated Press (AP) story about a foiled bomb plot in Yemen that was based on information from an anonymous source. In hunting for the source, the FBI obtained records covering a two-month period of calls made from more than 20 telephone numbers from AP offices and its reporters' homes and cell phones.[14] Agents were able to use these records to find the source of the leaks, and months after the confiscation was revealed to AP, former FBI agent Donald Sachtleben pleaded guilty to providing the information to AP.[15]

The actions in the Kim and Sachtleben (his name would only be known to the public months later) cases prompted an outcry from the news media, and quickly led to a statement from Attorney General Eric Holder that his office does not plan to prosecute journalists as co-conspirators in leak cases.[16] In preparing a report to President Barack Obama on the two incidents, Holder also worked with news media representatives and other civil liberties groups to update the guidelines the Department of Justice is supposed to follow before demanding records and information from journalists. The new guidelines expand the applicability not just to direct evidence held by a reporter and telephone toll records held by phone companies, but to all newsgathering-related records. They also notably switch the presumption of openness in the efforts to obtain reporters' records from third parties; while the old policy allowed for disclosure to the news media only if it would not jeopardize the investigation, the new policy states that the news media will be notified before the records are obtained "in all but the most exceptional cases."[17]

But the lesson of the Sachtleben case is that even when the government violates its own policy on obtaining information from journalists, it will use that information to obtain convictions. In other words, journalists are left wondering about the point of improved guidelines from the Department of Justice if there is no disincentive to violate the policy.

While these leaks cases give a sense of what government policies on going after leakers mean to journalists and by extension to the public, the disclosures can look fairly minor when compared with the information disclosed by Private First Class Bradley (now Chelsea) Manning and former National Security Agency (NSA) contractor Edward Snowden.

Manning is the U.S. soldier convicted in 2013 for releasing classified documents to WikiLeaks. The government accused Manning of illegally downloading and disclosing tens of thousands of classified documents from the U.S. military and the State Department.[18]

Manning joined the Army in 2007 at age 19 and worked as an intelligence analyst. The Army sent Manning to Iraq despite concerns about unstable behavior. As he began to grow disillusioned with his work in Iraq, Manning started working with Julian Assange of WikiLeaks. Manning had done a lot of computer programming before joining the Army and favored public access to information. Around that time, Manning reached out to several prominent hackers, asking one of them, "[I]f you had free reign over classified networks for long periods of time . . . say, 8–9 months . . . and you saw incredible things, awful things . . . things that belonged in the public domain, and not on some server stored in a dark room in Washington DC . . . what would you do?"[19]

By 2011, Manning had been indicted on 26 charges ranging from disobeying an order to aiding the enemy. That final charge carried a possible death sentence. Manning was tried by a military judge in 2013. The judge found Manning guilty

The Attorney General Guidelines

Since 1970, the Department of Justice (DoJ) has followed a set of guidelines created by the U.S. attorney general for use by DoJ employees when they want to subpoena the news media. Formally titled *Policy Regarding Obtaining Information From, or Records of, Members of the News Media; and Regarding Questioning, Arresting, or Charging Members of the News Media*, and found at 28 C.F.R. § 50.10, they were amended in February 2014.

Key points:
- A statement of principles makes clear that the intent is "to provide protection to members of the news media from certain law enforcement tools, whether criminal or civil, that might unreasonably impair ordinary newsgathering activities."
- Subpoenas and search warrants directed at members of the news media are "extraordinary measures, not standard investigatory practices."
- A subpoena or search warrant must be approved by a U.S. Attorney or assistant attorney general (i.e., not just a prosecutor, but the appointed official he or she answers to), and must be authorized by the attorney general.
- In criminal cases, the information sought must be essential to a successful investigation or prosecution.
- In civil cases, the information sought must be essential to the success of the litigation, in a "case of substantial importance."
- Prosecutors must make "all reasonable attempts" to obtain the information from alternative, nonmedia sources.
- In all but the rarest cases, prosecutors should notify and negotiate with members of the news media before demanding their records from phone companies, e-mail providers, or other record holders.
- Proposed subpoenas should be limited to the verification of published information, be narrowly drawn, encompass a limited subject matter, cover a reasonably limited time period, and not be for a "large volume of material."
- In the limited cases where officials are allowed to serve search warrants on journalists or newsrooms (these are limited by the Privacy Protection Act of 1980, 42 U.S.C. § 2000aa), they should only be used where the journalist is a focus of an investigation unrelated to ordinary newsgathering activities.

of 17 of the 23 charges; Manning pleaded guilty to another three of them. Importantly, the judge found Manning not guilty of aiding the enemy, and also acquitted him of one Espionage Act charge. The convictions meant Manning faced up to 90 years in prison, but in July 2013, he was sentenced to 35 years.[20]

Snowden's leaks, delivered to journalists Glenn Greenwald and Bart Gell-man and published in, respectively, *The Guardian* and *The Washington Post*, have been even more newsworthy and shocking, and have prompted an extensive public debate about the breadth of efforts by the U.S. and U.K. governments to track not just terrorists, but everyone who uses a phone or the Internet.

Snowden was working for the NSA through defense contractor Booz Allen when he began leaking top-secret documents to media outlets in 2013.[21] Just weeks after he began the releases, Snowden was being called "one of America's most consequential leakers."[22] Snowden did not hide his identity; after beginning contact with the reporters, he fled from his home in Hawaii, first to Hong Kong and then to Russia, where he was granted temporary asylum in August 2013.[23]

Snowden had previously worked for the Central Intelligence Agency (CIA), during which time, he has said, he began to question U.S. government actions. He told the news media that after leaving the CIA for Booz Allen and seeing the level of surveillance the NSA was conducting, he decided the public needed to know what the government was doing. "The government has granted itself power it is not entitled to. There is no public oversight. The result is people like myself have the latitude to go further than they are allowed to," he told *The Guardian*.[24] Snowden is believed to have taken millions of classified documents and to have revealed only a fraction of them so far.[25]

The documents Snowden leaked have led to international anger and distrust of the U.S. government. Among other facts, Snowden revealed that the NSA had repeatedly exceeded its authority, tapped into major data centers around the world, and undermined Internet encryption systems. The documents he released also revealed that Director of National Intelligence James Clapper had misled Congress about the scope of the NSA programs and that the U.S. government spied on leaders of allied nations.[26]

Snowden was charged in June 2013 with theft of government property, unauthorized communication of national defense information, and willful communication of classified communications intelligence information to an unauthorized person.[27] In January 2014, *The New York Times* editorial board called Snowden a whistleblower and urged the U.S. government to offer him a plea bargain or clemency deal that would allow him to return to the United States. Many government officials, though, have labeled Snowden a traitor. Shortly after Snowden began releasing documents, House Speaker John Boehner said, "The disclosure of this information puts Americans at risk. It shows our adversaries what our capabilities are. And it's a giant violation of the law."[28] Two high-ranking Senate Democrats, Dianne Feinstein of California and Bill Nelson of Florida, agreed with Boehner's assessment of Snowden as a traitor.[29]

While the debate over how to treat Snowden continues, his leaks have led to major reconsiderations of government policies. Since Snowden began leaking documents, the Foreign Intelligence Surveillance Act Court (FISA Court), which oversees the NSA programs that Snowden has questioned, has criticized the NSA for misleading the court and violating the Fourth Amendment. "The Court is troubled that the government's revelations regarding NSA's acquisition of Internet transactions mark the third instance in less than three years in which the government had disclosed a substantial misrepresentation regarding the scope of a major collection program."[30] Following those revelations, two federal district courts split on the question of the constitutionality of the NSA surveillance programs, with one judge in Washington, D.C., holding them to be unconstitutional and another in New York City finding them legally sound.[31]

Obama also commissioned a review group to make recommendations for changes to government surveillance policies. The President's Review Group on Intelligence and Communications Technologies suggested amending surveillance laws to require higher standards of proof for orders requiring the disclosure of private information about individuals. It also recommended some sort of privacy advocate at the FISA Court and that the data the NSA collects be hosted on a nongovernment server so that the government would be forced to get a warrant or court order before accessing it.[32] In contrast to the review group, the Privacy and Civil Liberties Oversight Board (PCLOB), an independent agency charged with reviewing the country's anti-terrorism policies and flagging where those policies conflict with civil liberties, recommended in January 2014 that the government abandon the phone surveillance program. After raising serious questions about the surveillance program's constitutionality and compliance with federal law, PCLOB discussed at length the effect the program has had on public discourse and journalism. "Although we cannot quantify the full extent of the chilling effect, we believe that these results—among them greater hindrances to political activism and a less robust press—are real and will be detrimental to the nation," the report stated.[33]

Obama has proposed adopting several of the review group's recommendations, though he dismissed or failed to address many others. In a speech in January 2014, Obama indicated he would move toward storing phone record data on nongovernment servers, which would add one more step to the process if the government should choose to search the data. He also adopted the review group's recommendation that phone data collection may only track contacts within two steps of a suspected terrorist, instead of three. Finally, the president indicated the government will review FISA Court opinions annually to determine whether any may be declassified.[34]

Other leaks cases have revealed more about the legal standards that prosecutors must meet to prosecute the leakers and to compel disclosure of anonymous sources.

In 2004, as part of a plea deal on Espionage Act charges, Lawrence Franklin, an Iran analyst at the Pentagon, assisted the FBI with investigations of two individuals to whom he had provided information, lobbyists Steven J. Rosen and Keith Weissman, between 1999 and 2004.[35] Rosen was the director of foreign policy issues at the American Israeli Public Affairs Committee, or AIPAC, and

Weissman was the senior Middle East analyst in AIPAC's Foreign Policy Issues Department.[36] Rosen and Weissman were the first civilians who did not work for the government to be charged under the Espionage Act.[37]

Some of the information related to potential attacks on U.S. troops in Iraq, al-Qaeda, terrorism in central Asia, and U.S. policy on Iran. After receiving information from Franklin, the lobbyists would then convey the information to members of the media and to Israeli officials.

Franklin cooperated with the FBI, including by holding further meetings with the two lobbyists that were monitored by the government; he eventually was sentenced to 100 hours of community service and ten months in a halfway house.

Rosen and Weissman were accused in 2005 of conspiring to obtain classified information and disseminate it to the media and the Israeli government. When the two men were charged, the former director of legislative affairs at AIPAC said, "What Rosen and Weissman were doing is no different than what reporters, lobbyists, experts, Congress and half of the government is doing, which is to find out what the administration is up to. This can't be a crime in a free society."[38]

The federal judge in the case had to examine to what extent individuals could be charged under the Espionage Act when they were not government employees, but simply received information through conversations and shared it with others. Ultimately, U.S. District Judge T.S. Ellis III found that the prosecution would have to show that the information, if disclosed, was potentially harmful to the national security and that the defendants *knew* that the disclosure of the information would potentially be harmful. By May 2009, largely due to the higher standard of proof the prosecution would have to meet, the case against Rosen and Weissman had "collapsed," and the charges were withdrawn.[39]

Much of the logic in the Ellis findings came from an earlier case against a naval analyst named Samuel Morison. At the time of his conviction in 1985, Morison was the only government official ever convicted under the Espionage Act for giving classified information to the press.[40]

Morison was an analyst at the Naval Intelligence Support Center from 1974 until 1984 and held top-secret clearance. Morison also wrote for *Jane's Fighting Ships* and its sister publication, *Jane's Defence Weekly*, two British publications that cover international naval operations. Although the Navy had approved Morison's work for the magazines, Morison eventually wanted to move to working at *Jane's* full time.[41] At that point, Morison sent to *Jane's* reports about several explosions at a Soviet naval base. He also took, from the desk of another analyst, photos of a Soviet aircraft carrier. After he cut the edges off to remove the "secret" label and the warning that the photos involved "intelligence or source methods," he mailed them to the editor of *Jane's*. The magazine published the photos a few days later.

During a department investigation, Morison initially denied he had ever even seen the photos. In October 1984, when the FBI found Morison's fingerprint on a photo, he was arrested. Morison was eventually convicted of four counts of theft of government property and two counts of violating the Espionage Act. He was sentenced to two years in prison and lost an appeal to the U.S. Court of Appeals for the Fourth Circuit.[42]

The Fourth Circuit, in affirming Morison's conviction, said the laws at issue were clearly "intended to apply to disclosure simply to anyone 'not entitled to receive' national defense information and was specifically not restricted to disclosure to 'an agent . . . [of a] foreign government.'"[43] That decision made clear that release of classified information to the news media could be punished to the same degree as release of classified information to a foreign enemy government.

At the end of his presidency, President Bill Clinton pardoned Morison.

The case against CIA officer Jeffrey Sterling has raised issues concerning what the government needs to prove before it can compel a reporter to testify against an accused leaker whom it believes was the reporter's source.

Sterling worked for the CIA from 1993 until 2002. He was arrested in 2011 on charges of leaking classified information about U.S. attempts to disrupt Iran's nuclear program.[44]

The case involved a 2006 book by *New York Times* reporter James Risen in which Risen discussed a U.S. intelligence plan to sabotage Iran's nuclear program. The U.S. government had given faulty blueprints of nuclear components to a Russian nuclear scientist who had defected, and the scientist in turn passed the blueprints to the Iranian government. The book alleged the program failed when the scientist alerted the Iranians to the flaws in the blueprints. It wasn't clear whether the Iranians knew of the scientist's connection to the CIA before the publication of Risen's book.[45]

When the government indicted Sterling in 2011, it alleged that he had stolen classified documents when he left the CIA, mischaracterized the documents and misled members of Congress about the nature of the program, and deceived the CIA about his actions.[46] During the time Sterling was allegedly communicating with Risen, he was also in litigation with the CIA, having sued the agency for employment discrimination.

The investigation into Sterling, like the case against Kim, raised serious press freedom questions. The federal government, in trying to gather information about the source of the leak, twice subpoenaed Risen. A federal district judge ruled that Risen did not have to reveal his source, but that decision was overturned by the U.S. Court of Appeals for the Fourth Circuit, and Risen's request that the U.S. Supreme Court hear his appeal was rejected by the Court without comment.[47]

Other noteworthy prosecutions of leakers include those of three employees of the FBI, NSA, and CIA.

Shamai Kedem Leibowitz was a contract linguist with the FBI in 2009 when he passed along five classified documents to a blogger. The documents Leibowitz disclosed were transcripts of conversations that the FBI caught by wiretapping the Israeli Embassy in Washington. Leibowitz disclosed the information because he was concerned that Israel would strike nuclear facilities in Iran. Leibowitz pleaded guilty to violating the Espionage Act and was sentenced to 20 months in prison.[48]

Thomas Drake was a senior executive at the NSA when he allegedly took top-secret documents from his office and leaked them to a *Baltimore Sun* reporter. In April 2010, he was charged in a ten-count indictment with violating the Espionage Act. In May 2011, Drake told a reporter for the *New Yorker* that he was "facing prison for raising an alarm, period. I went to a reporter with a few key things: fraud, waste, and abuse, and the fact that there were legal alternatives to the Bush administration's 'dark side.'"[49]

Drake's concerns began just after the September 11, 2001, attacks. He had worked on a program to streamline NSA analysis of data, but the agency chose a different program to implement. The agency asked a private defense contractor to build the new system, but it was not ready by the fall of 2001. Believing the NSA improperly opted for a more expensive and unproven program that ultimately risked American lives, Drake began talking to congressional committees about what he saw as intelligence failures related to 9/11. Then in 2006 and 2007, he started giving information to a reporter.[50]

Drake maintained he never disclosed classified information, but prosecutors said some of the documents he did disclose *should* have been classified and that Drake should have known that. Prosecutors initially charged Drake with leaking classified documents and being part of a conspiracy to do so. When the Obama administration took over the investigation, the charges were reduced to unauthorized "willful retention" of five classified documents, which still could have led to 35 years in prison.

In June 2011, Drake pleaded guilty to misusing the NSA's computer system by giving "official NSA information" to an unauthorized person. The charge was a misdemeanor and Drake was not sentenced to any prison time or made to pay a fine. He was ultimately sentenced to 240 hours of community service and one year's probation.[51]

John Kiriakou was the first CIA officer sentenced to prison time for sharing classified information with journalists.[52] Kiriakou had been an analyst and counterterrorism officer with the CIA for 14 years until 2004. In 2007, Kiriakou began speaking out against waterboarding, saying it was torture. Around that same time, he disclosed the name of a former colleague to a journalist, despite the fact that the colleague was still working undercover for the agency.

Kiriakou was charged in 2012 with violating the Espionage Act. Those initial charges involved the 2007 disclosure of the undercover agent's name, as well as an accusation that Kiriakou was the source for a 2008 *New York Times* story that identified by name a CIA employee who played a role in interrogating a high-ranking member of al-Qaeda.[53] In January 2013, he pleaded guilty to violating the Intelligence Identities Protection Act, which criminalizes the intentional release of a covert agent's name or other identifying information. He was sentenced to two and a half years in prison, although the sentencing judge said she would have given him more prison time if the plea agreement had allowed for it.[54]

One of the more serious charges against any leaker involved the disclosure of the name of a CIA agent, in a case that centered as much around partisan politics as national security issues. I. Lewis "Scooter" Libby was chief of staff to Vice President Dick Cheney when Libby was accused of leaking the name of CIA operative Valerie Plame to reporters.

Libby joined the Bush administration in 2001 as Cheney's chief of staff. In his 2003 State of the Union address, President George W. Bush alleged that Iraq had recently tried to buy uranium from Niger.[55] Joseph Wilson, a diplomat who had investigated those allegations in Niger in 2002, claimed not to have found any evidence to support Bush's statements. When Wilson began to publicly question Bush's statement, Libby started meeting with journalists to discredit him.[56]

Robert Novak was the first journalist to report that Wilson's wife, Valerie Plame, was a CIA agent. His July 14, 2003, column in the *Chicago Sun-Times* identified her as a CIA "operative on weapons of mass destruction."[57] A story in *Time* magazine three days later by Matthew Cooper similarly alleged that Plame had been involved in sending Wilson to Niger.[58] The stories indicated that two White House staffers had contacted several journalists and told them about Plame and her involvement with the CIA's investigation.[59]

The Justice Department began an investigation into the leaks in the fall of 2003, and Special Counsel Patrick Fitzgerald convened a grand jury in December of that year. By the summer of 2004, the grand jury had issued subpoenas to Cooper and to Time, Inc., both of which fought to quash the subpoenas. Cooper eventually agreed to testify about his conversations with Libby after Libby gave him permission to do so. However, Cooper and *Time* were served with additional subpoenas for more information in September 2004 and were held in contempt when they refused to comply.[60]

In August 2004, the grand jury issued subpoenas to *New York Times* reporter Judith Miller for documents and testimony related to Miller's conversation with a particular government official regarding Wilson or Plame. Miller moved to quash the subpoena and lost. She was held in contempt.

Miller and Cooper filed a joint appeal, arguing that journalists had both a constitutional and an evidentiary right to refuse to disclose their confidential sources. The U.S. Court of Appeals for the District of Columbia, citing *Branzburg v. Hayes,*[61] found that the U.S. Supreme Court had already rejected the idea of a constitutional reporter-source privilege. On the common law privilege question, the circuit court split on the existence of such a privilege, but concluded that if it did exist, it was a qualified privilege and the government had met its burden to overcome it.

Cooper avoided testifying after an attorney for his source, presidential advisor Karl Rove, told *The Wall Street Journal* that Rove had not asked to be treated as a confidential source, "so if Matt Cooper is going to jail to protect a source, it's not Karl he's protecting."[62] *Time* had already decided that it was bound to comply after the appeal failed and turned over records stored on its computer system.

Libby had signed a blanket waiver to allow any reporters with whom he had talked to testify about their conversations with him, but Miller maintained she would not testify about her source without an individual waiver, and even then, only after ensuring the waiver had not been coerced. After spending 85 days in jail, Miller had a conversation with Libby in which he told her he was voluntarily giving her permission to testify.[63]

Libby was convicted in March 2007 of lying to the grand jury and to FBI agents when he claimed he had not talked with Miller and Cooper about Plame. He was sentenced to 30 months in prison.[64]

But in a final act that gives little comfort to the whistleblowers who stand up against government secrecy, Bush commuted Libby's sentence in July 2007. The lesson that whistleblowers learn is that, in the end, the public interest they serve may be less important than the political figures who support them.[65]

NOTES

1. N.Y. Times Co. v. United States, 403 U.S. 713 (1971). *See also* Hedrick Smith, *Mitchell Seeks to Halt Series on Vietnam, but* Times *Refuses*, N.Y. TIMES, June 15, 1971, http://nyti.ms/1e1cXxc; Fred P. Graham, *Court Here Refuses to Order Return of Documents Now*, N.Y. TIMES, June 16, 1971, http://nyti.ms/1bePKMU; R.W. Apple, *Lessons From the Pentagon Papers*, N.Y. TIMES, June 23, 1996, http://nyti.ms/1fb1obk.

2. United States v. N.Y. Times Co., 444 F.2d 544 (2d Cir. 1971).

3. Pentagon Papers Charges Are Dismissed; Judge Byrne Frees Ellsberg and Russo, Assails "Improper Government Conduct," N.Y. TIMES, May 11, 1973, at 1, http://nyti.ms/NXeOOE.

4. 403 U.S. at 715 (Black, concurring).

5. *Ashcroft: No Need for New Law to Punish Leakers*, REPORTERS COMM. FOR FREEDOM OF THE PRESS, Oct. 24, 2002, http://rcfp.org/x?Nvl9.

6. United States v. Kim, No. 1:10-cr-00225-CKK (D.D.C., indictment filed Aug. 19, 2010, plea agreement entered Feb. 10, 2014).

7. *A Rare Peek into a Justice Department Leak Probe*, WASH. POST, May 19, 2013, http://wapo.st /N1Qzh6. *See also* Letter of Abbe Lowell, Oct. 12, 2010, http://on-msn.com/1oF96OV; *Stephen Kim Pleads Guilty in Fox News Leak Case*, POLITICO, Feb. 7, 2014, http://politi.co/1dxLyTj.

8. Statement of Abbe D. Lowell, Aug. 27, 2010, http://on.wsj.com/NXivnm.

9. Josh Gerstein, *Under the Radar,* POLITICO, Oct. 19, 2010, http://politic.co/1kdT8g0.

10. E-Mail Account Redacted@Gmail.Com On Computer Servers Operated By Google, Inc., Headquartered At 1600 Amphitheatre Parkway, Mountain View, California, No. 1:10-mj-00291-AK (D.D.C.), Affidavit in Support of Application for Search Warrant, filed Nov. 7, 2011), at 6 (citing 42 U.S.C. § 2000aa(a)).

11. More specifically, the allowance of search warrants is a double-exception to that provision. Warrants are allowed if the journalist committed a crime, *except* if the crime is the possession or receipt of information; but that exception is overcome if the possession or receipt of information relates to the Espionage Act and other particular statutes.

12. 18 U.S.C. §§ 792–799.
13. See affidavit, *supra* note 10, at 26–27.
14. Mark Sherman, Gov't Obtains Wide AP Phone Records in Probe, AP, May 13, 2013, http:// bigstory.ap.org/article/govt-obtains-wide-ap-phone-records-probe.
15. Charlie Savage, *Former F.B.I. Agent to Plead Guilty in Press Leak*, N.Y. TIMES, Sept. 23, 2013, http://nyti.ms/1oJ38fV.
16. Josh Gerstein, *Holder Walks Fine Line on Prosecuting Journalists*, POLITICO, May 20, 2013, http://politi.co/1f9bM3n.
17. ATTORNEY GENERAL GUIDELINES ("Policy with regard to the issuance of subpoenas to members of the news media, subpoenas for telephone toll records of members of the news media, and the interrogation, indictment, or arrest of, members of the news media"), 28 C.F.R. § 50.10. *See also* DEP'T OF JUSTICE, REPORT ON REVIEW OF NEWS MEDIA POLICIES, July 12, 2013, http://www .justice.gov/ag/news-media.pdf. On February 21, 2014, the Guidelines were updated to reflect the policies announced in the July 12 report.
18. *Manning Faces New Charges, Possible Death Penalty*, NBC NEWS, Mar. 3, 2011, http:// nbcnews.to/1gSIZyG. *See also* Charge Sheet, Bradley E. Manning, http://wapo.st/1bWZDds.
19. Steve Fishman, *Bradley Manning's Army of One*, N.Y. MAG., July 3, 2011, http://nym.ag /1mndhAi; *see also Bradley Manning Is at the Center of the WikiLeaks Controversy: But Who Is He?*, Ellen Nakashima, WASH. POST, May 4, 2011, http://wapo.st/1bX0eMc.
20. Julie Tate & Ernesto Londoño, *Manning Found Not Guilty of Aiding the Enemy, Guilty of Espionage*, WASH. POST, July 30, 2013, http://wapo.st/1mndALF; Ernesto Londoño, Rebecca Rolfe & Julie Tate, *Verdict in Bradley Manning Case*, WASH. POST, July 30, 2013, http://wapo.st/1kN6f6i.
21. Glenn Greenwald, Ewen MacAskill & Laura Poitras, *Edward Snowden: The Whistleblower behind the NSA Surveillance Revelations*, GUARDIAN, June 9, 2013, http://www.theguardian.com /world/2013/jun/09/edward-snowden-nsa-whistleblower-surveillance.
22. *Id.*
23. Ashley Fantz, Phil Black & Michael Martinez, *Snowden out of Airport, Still in Moscow*, CNN, Aug. 1, 2013, http://cnn.it/1fsgAx8.
24. Greenwald et al., *supra* note 21.
25. *Id.*
26. Editorial, *Edward Snowden, Whistle-Blower*, N.Y. TIMES, Jan. 1, 2014, http://nyti.ms/1erpjRk; David E. Sanger & Alison Smale, *U.S.-Germany Intelligence Partnership Falters over Spying*, N.Y. TIMES, Dec. 16, 2013, http://nyti.ms/1f9eoOB.
27. Criminal Complaint, United States v. Snowden, No. 1:13 CR 265 (E.D. Va. June 14, 2013), http://s3.documentcloud.org/documents/716865/snowden-complaint.pdf.
28. Brett LoGiurato, *John Boehner: Edward Snowden Is a "Traitor,"* SFGATE.COM, June 11, 2013, http://www.sfgate.com/technology/businessinsider/article/JOHN-BOEHNER-Edward-Snowden-Is -A-Traitor-4593261.php.
29. *Id.*
30. *Judge's Opinion on N.S.A. Program*, N.Y. TIMES, Aug. 21, 2013, http://nyti.ms/1bDKGCq.
31. *See Federal Judge's Ruling on NSA Lawsuit*, N.Y. TIMES, Dec. 16, 2013, http://nyti.ms/1cxZfRR; Adam Liptak & Michael S. Schmidt, *Judge Upholds N.S.A.'s Bulk Collection of Data on Calls*, N.Y. TIMES, Dec. 27, 2013, http://nyti.ms/1btDLVw.
32. Liberty and Security in a Changing World: Report and Recommendations of the President's Review Group on Intelligence and Communications Technologies (Dec. 12, 2013), http://1.usa.gov /1cBct0k.
33. Privacy & Civil Liberties Oversight Bd., Report on the Telephone Records Program Conducted under Section 215 of the USA PATRIOT Act and on the Operations of the Foreign Intelligence Surveillance Court 164 (Jan. 23, 2014).
34. President Barack Obama, Remarks by the President on Review of Signals Intelligence, Jan. 17, 2014, http://1.usa.gov/1awEWY8.

35. David Johnston, *Pentagon Analyst Gets 12 Years for Disclosing Data*, N.Y. TIMES, Jan. 20, 2006, http://nyti.ms/1m1PXVa. The article provides a link to Franklin, Rosen, and Weissman's indictment.

36. United States v. Rosen, 557 F.3d 192 (4th Cir. 2009).

37. Nathan Guttman, *Once Labeled an AIPAC Spy, Larry Franklin Tells His Story*, JEWISH DAILY FORWARD, http://forward.com/articles/108778/once-labeled-an-aipac-spy-larry-franklin-tells-his/. *See also* Franklin indictment, http://www.globalsecurity.org/intell/library/reports/2005/franklin _indictment_04aug2005.htm; Jerry Markon, *Leak Investigation Ordered*, WASH. POST, Aug. 23, 2006, http://wapo.st/1e1fGXb.

38. Marc Perelman, *Leak Flap Seen Aiding Lobbyists' Case*, JEWISH DAILY FORWARD, April 14, 2006, (quoting Douglas Bloomfield), http://forward.com/articles/1224/leak-flap-seen-aiding-lobbyistse-case/.

39. Neil A. Lewis & David Johnston, *U.S. to Drop Spy Case Against Pro-Israel Lobbyists*, N.Y. TIMES, May 1, 2009, http://nyti.ms/1oIC1Sp.

40. Anthony Lewis, *Abroad at Home; The Pardons in Perspective*, N.Y. TIMES, Mar. 3, 2001, http://nyti.ms/1gNW3Xk.

41. United States v. Morison, 844 F.2d 1057, 1060–61 (4th Cir. 1988).

42. *Id.* at 1057; *see also* Michael Wright & Caroline Rand Herron, *Two Years for Morison*, N.Y. TIMES, Dec. 8, 1985, http://nyti.ms/1moYhC7.

43. 844 F.2d at 1065.

44. Pierre Thomas et al., *Ex-CIA Agent Jeffrey Sterling Arrested, Accused of Leaking to Reporter as Revenge*, ABC NEWS, Jan. 6, 2011, http://abcn.ws/1jKjz7f.

45. Charlie Savage, *U.S. Subpoenas Times Reporter over Book on C.I.A.*, N.Y. TIMES, Apr. 28, 2010, http://nyti.ms/1eJfsUX.

46. Sterling indictment, Dec. 22, 2010, http://cryptome.org/0003/sterling/sterling-001.pdf

47. *Judge Explains Decision to Quash Risen Subpoena*, REPORTERS COMM. FOR FREEDOM OF THE PRESS, Aug. 4, 2011, http://rcfp.org/x?TFTT.

48. Dep't of Justice, Office of Pub. Affairs, Former FBI Contract Linguist Pleads Guilty to Leaking Classified Information to Blogger, Dec. 17, 2009, http://www.justice.gov/opa/pr/2009/December /09-nsd-1361.html; *see also* Scott Shane, *Leak Offers Look at Efforts by U.S. to Spy on Israel*, N.Y. TIMES, Sept. 5, 2011, http://nyti.ms/1jLzUMW; Jesselyn Radack, *Government & MSM's Deliberate Obfuscation of the Difference Between "Leaking" & Whistleblowing*, DAILY KOS, June 27, 2012, http://bit.ly/1mUwW9s.

49. Jane Mayer, *The Secret Sharer: Is Thomas Drake an Enemy of the State?*, NEW YORKER, May 23, 2011, http://nyr.kr/1hoO1aR.

50. Scott Shane, *Ex-N.S.A. Aide Gains Plea Deal in Leak Case; Setback to U.S.*, N.Y. TIMES, June 9, 2011, http://nyti.ms/1gNXox9.

51. Scott Shane, *U.S. Pressing Its Crackdown against Leaks*, N.Y. TIMES, June 17, 2011, http://nyti .ms/Mt7lWx; *see also* Plea agreement, United States v. Drake, No. 10-181 (D. Md. June 9, 2011), http://static1.firedoglake.com/28/files/2011/06/110609-plea.pdf; Tricia Bishop, *NSA Employee Accused of Leaking Information Sentenced to Probation*, BALT. SUN, July 15, 2011, http://bit.ly/1cREVf5.

52. Michael S. Schmidt, *Ex-C.I.A. Officer Sentenced to 30 Months in Leak*, N.Y. TIMES, Jan. 25, 2013, http://nyti.ms/1m1SHSr.

53. Charlie Savage, *Ex-C.I.A. Officer Charged in Information Leak*, N.Y. TIMES, Jan. 23, 2012, http://nyti.ms/M6WrVA.

54. Ex-CIA Officer John Kiriakou Sentenced for Leaking Name on Agency's Use of Torture, CBS NEWS, Jan. 25, 2013, http://cbsn.ws/1gWD0c6.

55. *See Bush's State of the Union Speech*, CNN, Jan. 29, 2003, http://cnn.it/1gNYHfC.

56. Barton Gellman & Dafna Linzer, *A "Concerted Effort" to Discredit Bush Critic*, WASH. POST, Apr. 9, 2006, http://wapo.st/M6WIYF.

57. Robert Novak, *Mission to Niger*, WASH. POST, July 14, 2003, http://wapo.st/1iXGm4E.

58. Matthew Cooper, *A War on Wilson?*, TIME, July 17, 2003, http://content.time.com/time/nation /article/0,8599,465270,00.html.

59. *In re* Grand Jury Subpoena, Judith Miller, 438 F.3d 1141 (D.C. Cir. 2006).

60. *See Diverging Interests*, NEWS MEDIA & LAW 4 (Summer 2005), http://rcfp.org/x?1Jv1, & sidebar, *Double Super Secret Background: A Timeline*, http://rcfp.org/x?DP2f.

61. 408 U.S. 665 (1972).

62. Joe Hagan, *U.S. Prosecutor Says Reporters Deserve Jail*, WALL ST. J., July 6, 2005, http://online .wsj.com/news/articles/SB112058309596677473.

63. Carol D. Leonnig, *Lawyer Casts Blame on Reporter for Time in Jail*, WASH. POST, Oct. 4, 2005, http://wapo.st/1gcoiwM.

64. Neil A. Lewis, *Libby Guilty of Lying in C.I.A. Leak Case*, N.Y. TIMES, Mar. 6, 2007, http://nyti .ms/1cRGtFT.

65. Amy Goldstein, *Bush Commutes Libby's Prison Sentence*, WASH. POST, July 3, 2007, http:// wapo.st/1j5l2WI.

Prosecuting Leaks under U.S. Law

3

Stephen I. Vladeck

On February 6, 2014, Stephen Jin-Woo Kim, a former State Department contractor, pleaded guilty to leaking information from a highly classified report about North Korea to a Fox News reporter, in violation of 18 U.S.C. § 793(d)—part of the Espionage Act of 1917.[1] In the plea deal, Kim agreed to serve 13 months in prison in exchange for the government dropping additional charges and consenting to a relatively short prison term.[2] Kim was the seventh government official to be charged in a leak-related[3] prosecution brought by the Obama administration.[4] That figure is especially noteworthy given that, prior to 2009, there had been only three publicly disclosed cases in which the government had pursued criminal charges against a current or former employee for turning over national security secrets to an unauthorized third party—and only two convictions.[5]

Although politics has a lot to do with the historical paucity of national security leak prosecutions,[6] such cases have also been made more difficult by a dizzying array of overlapping, inconsistent, and vague criminal statutes—none of which is specifically addressed to national security leaking, as such.[7] Instead, as this chapter documents, the government has historically been forced to shoehorn national security "leaking" into criminal laws designed for far more egregious offenses (such as spying), or far more common offenses (such as conversion of government property). Because of the poor and antiquated fit of the relevant criminal statutes, and the related First Amendment questions that arise from such mismatches, the result has been a situation that Anthony

Lapham, then general counsel of the Central Intelligence Agency (CIA), described as the "worst of both worlds":

> On the one hand the laws stand idle and are not enforced at least in part because their meaning is so obscure, and on the other hand it is likely that the very obscurity of these laws serves to deter perfectly legitimate expression and debate by persons who must be as unsure of their liabilities as I am unsure of their obligations.[8]

Simply put, whether one is more sympathetic to, or skeptical of, national security leakers, the underlying legal regime leaves more than a little to be desired.

I. THE ESPIONAGE ACT

As the Kim case illustrates, the most common ground upon which current or former government employees have been prosecuted for unauthorized disclosures of national security information is the Espionage Act.[9] (See Table 1.) Enacted at President Woodrow Wilson's urging at the same time as the United States' entry into World War I, the statute's core provisions have been all but untouched since, and therefore predate not only technological advancements that render many of the statute's distinctions superfluous, but also the very concept of "classification" that undergirds national security information today.[10]

Table 1. U.S. Prosecutions of National Security Leakers (as of July 2014)

Lead Defendant	Subject of Leak	Year	Charges in Indictment	Disposition
Daniel Ellsberg	The Pentagon Papers	1973	18 U.S.C. §§ 371, 641, 793(c), (d), (e)	Case dropped by prosecutors.
Samuel Morison	Soviet aircraft carrier photos	1985	18 U.S.C. §§ 641, 793(d), (e)	Convicted; sentenced to two years in prison; pardoned in 2001.
Lawrence Franklin	U.S. policy toward Iran	2005	18 U.S.C. §§ 371, 793(d), (e), (g); 50 U.S.C. § 783	Pleaded guilty; sentenced to 12 years, reduced to ten months of community confinement.
Shamai Leibowitz	Classified information to a blogger	2009	18 U.S.C. § 798(a)	Pleaded guilty; sentenced to 20 months in prison.
Stephen Jin-Woo Kim	Information about North Korea to Fox News	2010	18 U.S.C. §§ 793(d), 1001(a)(2)	Pleaded guilty; sentenced to 13 months in prison.

Table 1. U.S. Prosecutions of National Security Leakers (as of July 2014), *continued*

Lead Defendant	Subject of Leak	Year	Charges in Indictment	Disposition
Thomas Drake	Details of NSA waste and mismanagement	2010	18 U.S.C. §§ 793(e), 1001(a), 1519	Pleaded guilty to misdemeanor in exchange for dropping of more serious charges; sentenced to one year of probation and community service.
Bradley (Chelsea) Manning	Massive cache of military and diplomatic files to WikiLeaks	2010	10 U.S.C. §§ 892, 904; 18 U.S.C. §§ 793(e), 1030(a)(1), 1030(a)(2)	Pleaded guilty to ten charges; convicted of 11 additional charges; sentenced to 35 years in prison.
Jeffrey Sterling	Efforts to sabotage Iranian nuclear research to *New York Times* reporter James Risen	2010	18 U.S.C. §§ 641, 793(d), (e), 1341, 1512(c)(1)	Case remains pending.
John Kiriakou	Identity of CIA officials involved in interrogation abuses	2012	18 U.S.C. §§ 793(d), 1001(a)(1); 50 U.S.C. § 421(a)*	Pleaded guilty to violating § 421(a); sentenced to 30 months in prison.
James Hitselberger	Classified materials concerning Bahrain to the Hoover Institution	2012	18 U.S.C. §§ 793(e), 2071(a)	Pleaded guilty to misdemeanor in exchange for dropping of more serious charges; sentenced to time already served and a $250 fine.

*This provision has since been moved to 50 U.S.C. § 3121.

As its informal title suggests, the Espionage Act was designed and intended to deal with classic acts of spying—what *Black's Law Dictionary* defines as "[t]he practice of using spies to collect information about what another government or company is doing or plans to do."[11] Because the statute was targeted at conventional espionage, the text of the Act fails to require a specific intent either to harm the national security of the United States or to benefit a foreign power. Instead, the Act requires only that the defendant know or have "reason to believe" that the wrongfully obtained or disclosed "national defense information" is to be used to the injury of the United States or to the advantage of any foreign nation.[12] In other words, even if the defendant did not mean to harm U.S. national security or benefit a foreign power—if, for example, his intent was only to expose abuse or illegality—the statute nevertheless encompasses conduct that a reasonable person would have expected to produce such an effect. And although separate provisions of the Act punish different variations on this same underlying theme (e.g., by distinguishing between the dissemination of such information by individuals who *are*,[13] and who are *not*,[14] authorized to possess it in the first place), no separate statute deals with the specific—and arguably distinct—offense of disclosing national defense information for more benign purposes.

Instead, in general terms, the provision of the Act most relevant to national security leaks makes it unlawful for any individual who

> lawfully having possession of, access to, control over, or being entrusted with any [of a range of tangible items], or information relating to the national defense which information the possessor has reason to believe could be used to the injury of the United States or to the advantage of any foreign nation, willfully communicates, delivers, transmits or [causes or attempts the same] to any person not entitled to receive it, or willfully retains the same and fails to deliver it on demand to the officer or employee of the United States entitled to receive it.[15]

To similar effect, § 793(f) also imposes liability upon those government officials who have lawful possession of such materials, only to have them removed by, or otherwise disclosed to, third parties unauthorized to receive them as a result of the officials' gross negligence or their omission to report their loss upon discovery of the theft.[16]

After World War II—and in response to the *Chicago Tribune*'s story shortly after the Battle of Midway that indirectly disclosed that the U.S. victory there was at least in part due to Americans' breaking of Japan's naval codes[17]—Congress amended the Espionage Act to add present-day 18 U.S.C. § 798. That provision also proscribes the unauthorized disclosure of information relating to "cryptographic" or "communication intelligence" activities of the United States or any foreign government.[18] Like § 793, however, § 798 brooks no distinction based upon the motives of the government employee who discloses such information.[19]

And a contemporaneous provision, codified as 50 U.S.C. § 783, even more categorically prohibits the communication of any classified information directly to a foreign government or individuals whom the leaker had reason to believe were agents thereof.[20]

Thus, the government has traditionally been forced to use these provisions of the Espionage Act to prosecute three distinct classes of offenses that raise three distinct sets of issues: classic espionage; leaking; and the retention or redistribution of national defense information by third parties. It is hard to imagine that the Congress that drafted the Espionage Act in the midst of World War I, or even the 1950 amendments thereto, meant for it to cover each of these three categories, let alone to cover each of them equally.

In addition, the Espionage Act does not focus solely on the initial party who wrongfully discloses national defense information, but also applies, via § 793(e), to anyone who knowingly disseminates, distributes, or even retains national defense information without immediately returning the material to the government officer authorized to possess it. In other words, the text of the Act draws no distinction between the leaker, the recipient of the leak, or the 100th person to redistribute, retransmit, or even retain the national defense information that, by that point, is already in the public domain. So long as the putative defendant knows or has reason to believe that the information in his possession relates to the national defense, and could be used to injure the United States or benefit a foreign power, he is violating the Act's plain language—regardless of his specific intent and notwithstanding the very real fact that, by that point, the proverbial cat is long since out of the bag. Thus, it is immaterial whether one is a leaker, a journalist, a blogger, a newspaper reader, or any other interested person—at least for purposes of the statute.[21]

This defect is part of why so much attention has been paid of late to the potential liability of the news media;[22] so far as the plain text of the Act is concerned, one is hard-pressed to see a significant distinction between the original leaker, subsequent disclosures by entities such as WikiLeaks, and the republication thereof by major media outlets. As noted below, the First Amendment may well require a *constitutional* distinction between leakers and leakees. But the statute itself is notoriously open-ended on this front, which goes a long way toward explaining why the government has historically been reluctant to push the Act to its textual limits even in leak prosecutions.

Indeed, in its 97-year history, the Espionage Act has been used to prosecute a third-party *recipient* of national defense information, as opposed to the government employee who disclosed it, exactly once—in the 2005 indictment of two lobbyists for AIPAC, the American Israel Public Affairs Committee, for facilitating a State Department employee's leaking of national security secrets to Israel. But that prosecution was ultimately abandoned after pretrial rulings by the U.S. district court, motivated largely by First Amendment concerns, imposed a far greater evidentiary burden upon the government.[23]

Finally, the Espionage Act does not deal in any way with the elephant in the room—situations where government employees disclose information that ought never to have been classified in the first place, including information about unlawful governmental programs and activities. Most significantly, every court to consider the issue has rejected the availability of an "improper classification" defense—a claim by the defendant that he cannot be prosecuted because the information he unlawfully disclosed was in fact improperly classified.[24]

In one sense, it is entirely understandable that the Espionage Act nowhere refers to "classification," since the United States' classification regime postdates the Act by more than 30 years. Nevertheless, given concerns with respect to overclassification, along with the perceived inadequacies of federal whistleblower laws, the absence of such a defense—or, more generally, of any specific reference to classification—is yet another reason why the Espionage Act's potential sweep is so unclear. Even where it is objectively clear that the disclosed information was erroneously classified in the first place, the individual who discloses the information (and perhaps the individual who receives the disclosure) would still contravene the plain language of the statute.

II. THE FEDERAL CONVERSION STATUTE

Perhaps because of the vagaries and complexities of the Espionage Act, the government has at times relied on a more property-oriented rationale for prosecuting unauthorized disclosures of classified materials—most notably the federal conversion statute, 18 U.S.C. § 641. That statute, which dates to 1875,[25] makes it a crime for anyone who "embezzles, steals, purloins, or knowingly converts to his use or the use of another, or without authority, sells, conveys or disposes of any record, voucher, money, or thing of value of the United States."[26]

Thus, in one of only three pre-2009 leak prosecutions, the government prosecuted Samuel Morison under both the Espionage Act and § 641 for transmitting classified photographs of a new Soviet aircraft carrier to *Jane's Defence Weekly*, an English publisher of defense information.[27] In affirming Morison's conviction, the Fourth Circuit U.S. Court of Appeals rejected efforts by both Morison and *The Washington Post*, as amicus curiae, to limit the scope of § 641. Both Morison and the *Post* argued that the offense was equivalent to the common law tort of conversion (which requires that the legitimate owner be deprived of possession, and would therefore not recognize theft of *copies* as conversion). As Circuit Judge Donald Russell explained, "The statute was not intended simply to cover 'larceny' and 'embezzlement' as those terms were understood at common law but was also to apply to 'acts which shade into those crimes but which, most strictly considered, might not be found to fit their fixed definitions.'"[28] Although *Morison* did not decide whether disclosures of wholly *intangible* information could violate § 641, the court of appeals had no trouble holding that Morison's disclosure—of "specific, identifiable tangible property," to wit, the photographs—fell within the statute's ambit.[29]

At the same time, such a broad reading of § 641 raises many of the same concerns as those identified above with respect to the Espionage Act—and without the same (modest) restrictions enshrined in the 1917 statute, which confines liability to "information relating to the national defense" the disclosure of which could reasonably be expected to harm the United States or aid a foreign power. As Judge Harrison Winter of the Fourth Circuit U.S. Court of Appeals explained in a more conventional "espionage" case (in which the government had also relied upon § 641),

> If § 641 were extended to penalize the unauthorized disclosure of [all] classified information, it would greatly alter this meticulously woven fabric of criminal sanctions. Unlike the espionage statutes, § 641 . . .

penalizes whomever "embezzles, steals, purloins, or knowingly converts." And, unlike § 798, § 641 would not penalize the disclosure of only a limited category of classified information. Rather, § 641 would outlaw the unauthorized disclosure of any "thing of value", that is, *any* classified information.[30]

Winter's concerns notwithstanding, *Morison* remains good law for the proposition that unauthorized disclosures of classified information can give rise to liability under § 641, at least in those cases in which the material that was disclosed has *some* tangible form.

III. OTHER PROHIBITIONS ON UNAUTHORIZED DISCLOSURE

As noted above, every leak prosecution to date has involved some combination of the Espionage Act and § 641. In addition to ordinary offenses arising out of leak *investigations* (e.g., obstruction of justice[31] and making false statements to investigators[32]), a handful of additional statutes could also provide the basis for criminal liability arising from an unauthorized disclosure of classified information.

For example, 18 U.S.C. § 952, which dates to 1933, makes it a crime for any government employee to "willfully publish[] or furnish[] to another" any diplomatic codes or "any matter prepared in any such code," without regard to the specific content of the communications, the employee's motive or intent, or whether the disclosed information in any way harms the United States or benefits a foreign power.[33] In other words, the statute makes it a crime for government employees to leak codes or materials prepared in code.

Another statute, 18 U.S.C. § 1030(a)(1), which prohibits the disclosure of protected national defense and foreign relations information retrieved through unauthorized access of a computer,[34] figured prominently in the court-martial proceedings of Private First Class Chelsea Manning, then known as Bradley Manning—and would also be relevant to future leak prosecutions in which the unauthorized disclosure originated in unauthorized access to a government computer.

A pair of more general statutes (with softer teeth) prohibit the disclosure of confidential information acquired in the course of employment "in any manner or to any extent not authorized by law,"[35] and the unauthorized removal and/or retention (without disclosure) of classified information—the offense to which former National Security Advisor Sandy Berger pleaded guilty in April 2005 after being charged for removing documents from the National Archives related to the 2000 "Millennium Plot" prior to his testimony before the 9/11 Commission.[36]

Finally, there are a range of specific disclosure prohibitions built into more thematically specific statutes—such as the Atomic Energy Act of 1954, two provisions of which prohibit the communication of "Restricted Data" relating to atomic energy, with intent or reason to believe such data would be used to injure the United States,[37] and the disclosure of any "Restricted Data" to unauthorized parties.[38]

To similar effect, the Intelligence Identities Protection Act of 1982 (IIPA) prohibits the *intentional* disclosure of any information that identifies covert intelligence officers, agents, informants, or sources by individuals with authorized access to classified information from which they learn such individuals' identity.[39] Although the IIPA's intent requirement has made this provision especially difficult to enforce as compared with the other statutes discussed herein,[40] it was the charge to which former CIA officer John Kiriakou pleaded guilty as part of a plea deal arising out of his prosecution for disclosing to a reporter classified information relating to various detainee abuses. And, to bring things full circle, Kiriakou only agreed to plead guilty after a pretrial ruling by the federal district court affirming that, on the more serious Espionage Act charges, the government needed to prove only that Kiriakou had reason to believe that the disclosed information could harm national security—not that he intended such harm to occur.[41]

IV. POTENTIAL FIRST AMENDMENT DEFENSES

As Winter's solo opinion in *Truong* noted (and as Judge J. Harvie Wilkinson III explained in his separate concurrence in the Fourth Circuit U.S. Court of Appeals' affirmance of the unauthorized disclosure conviction in *Morison*[42]), the potential breadth and open-endedness of these statutory prohibitions on unauthorized disclosures of classified information have raised a series of difficult First Amendment questions. After all, not only are the underlying disclosures of classified information *themselves* speech, but in leak cases, especially, the goal of such disclosures is often the dissemination of such information to the public—almost invariably through the press.

And along those lines, the Supreme Court's First Amendment jurisprudence has recognized both that in some cases the public's interest in receiving information from government employees can outweigh the government's interest in keeping secrets[43] and that media organizations may have a First Amendment right to retransmit secret information that they have lawfully come to possess.[44] Both lines of cases suggest that the First Amendment would impose at least *some* constraints on the government's ability to prosecute recipients of unauthorized disclosures in national security leak cases—constraints that may well explain the near total dearth of such prosecutions to date.

But the availability of First Amendment defenses to *leakers* going forward may have been somewhat curtailed by the Supreme Court's 2006 decision in *Garcetti v. Ceballos*,[45] a case having nothing at all to do with national security leaks. There, a 5–4 majority took a fairly skeptical view of the First Amendment rights of government employees, rejecting the use of so-called "*Pickering* balancing" (the Court's test for assessing the relative weight of the government's interest in confidentiality versus the public's interest in disclosure) to determine when government employee speech on matters of public concern should be constitutionally protected.

As Justice Anthony Kennedy wrote for the majority, "[W]hen public employees make statements pursuant to their official duties, the employees are not speaking as citizens for First Amendment purposes, and the Constitution does not insulate their communications from employer discipline."[46] If Kennedy had stopped there, *Ceballos* could have been viewed as recognizing a narrow exception to *Pickering* balancing in those cases where the speech at issue was performed by a public employee acting *as* a public employee.

But the *Ceballos* ruling went further, with the justices concluding that "[r]estricting speech that owes its existence to a public employee's professional responsibilities does not infringe any liberties the employee might have enjoyed as a private citizen."[47] In other words, the rule the Supreme Court enunciated "did not just apply to speech performed *as* a government employee, but to all speech that 'owes its existence to a public employee's professional responsibilities.'"[48] If read that broadly, such a per se rule that denies First Amendment protection to any speech by a public employee that could not have been undertaken "but for" his or her "professional responsibilities" would preclude First Amendment protections for any speech made by a government employee that could not have been undertaken if he were not a government employee.

As I've written elsewhere,

> Where classified national security information is concerned, the stopping point of this logic is immediately clear: National security secrets are, by definition, information to which the average private citizen does not have access. Speech related to national security secrets, then, would seem to fall squarely within the category of speech Justice Kennedy identified . . . as falling outside the First Amendment's umbrella. And whatever the merits of such a rule, its implications were readily understood by the dissenting Justices, each of whom wrote separately to emphasize the implications of the majority's categorical departure from *Pickering* balancing.[49]

Perhaps because of these alarming implications, the Court appeared to take a step back from such a reading of *Ceballos* in its most recent Term, when it held, in *Lane v. Franks*, that "the mere fact that a citizen's speech concerns information acquired by virtue of his public employment does not transform that speech into employee—rather than citizen—speech."[50] Instead, as Justice Sonia Sotomayor explained for a unanimous Court, "The critical question under [*Ceballos*] is whether the speech at issue is itself ordinarily within the scope of an employee's duties, not whether it merely concerns those duties."[51] Insofar as leaking and/or whistleblowing falls outside an employee's duties (which would presumably be in most cases), *Lane* suggests that the more protective First Amendment regime outlined in *Pickering* would apply.

At the same time, and for obvious reasons, it should follow that the Supreme Court would be that much *more* sympathetic to a broad reading of *Ceballos* in the national security sphere than, for example, in cases about public school teachers. At a minimum, it should be stressed that the scope of the First Amendment protections that might be available to a national security leaker today is hardly settled.

In all, then, as Columbia Law School Associate Professor David Pozen recently explained,

> Although there are many ambiguities in the statutes and the case law, it has been reasonably clear for at least the past few decades that (i) virtually any deliberate leak of classified information to an unauthorized recipient is likely to fall within the reach of one or more criminal statutes; and (ii) the government may prosecute most if not all employees, ex-employees, and contractors for such leaks so long as it can prove the information was not already in the public domain and the defendant knew or should have known her actions were unlawful.[52]

Indeed, these statutory and jurisprudential developments may have far more to say for the upsurge in national security leak prosecutions in recent years than any specific agenda on the part of the Obama administration, the intelligence community, or career prosecutors at the Justice Department. Especially after and in light of *Ceballos*, aggressive prosecutions of national security leaks will still prove controversial as a policy matter, but their precedential value for the legal liability of third parties may well be greatly diminished; not because the Supreme Court has *bolstered* the First Amendment rights of recipients of classified information, but because it has dramatically curtailed the rights of the government employee responsible for the disclosure.

* * *

In what may yet become the U.S. government's eleventh national security leak prosecution, federal prosecutors apparently obtained an indictment against Edward Snowden within five days of the first media stories reporting the details of secret surveillance programs that Snowden had leaked to the press.[53] Although the full indictment remains under seal as of this writing, the (ironically) leaked cover page indicates that the federal grand jury approved three principal charges— theft of government property in violation of 18 U.S.C. § 641, unauthorized disclosure of national defense information in violation of 18 U.S.C. § 793(d), and willful communication of classified communications intelligence activities to individuals unauthorized to receive such communication, in violation of 18 U.S.C. § 798(a)(3).[54] Notwithstanding its exceptional facts, then, the Snowden indictment appears fairly typical for national security leak prosecutions.

But inasmuch as the first two charges, at least, are based on statutes that never contemplated someone like Snowden—a U.S. government contractor responsible for the disclosure of massive amounts of classified information at least some of which touches on matters of significant public concern, who did so at least ostensibly for benign reasons—the Snowden revelations have renewed an age-old debate over whether the underlying statutory regime should be overhauled.

The problem, of course, is whether the solution might be worse than the disease. Thus, as Professors Hal Edgar and Benno Schmidt lamented more than four decades ago, "the longer we looked [at the Espionage Act], the less we saw."[55] Instead, they concluded, "we have lived since World War I in a state of benign indeterminacy about the rules of law governing defense secrets."[56] If anything, such indeterminacy has only become more pronounced in the 41 years since— and, if recent events are any indication, increasingly less benign.

NOTES

1. Act of June 15, 1917, ch. 30, 40 Stat. 217 (codified as amended at 18 U.S.C. §§ 793 *et seq.*).

2. *See, e.g.*, Ann Marimow, *Ex-State Dept. Adviser Pleads Guilty in Leak to Fox News*, WASH. POST, Feb. 8, 2014, at A4.

3. By "leak-related," I mean charges based on the *disclosure* of national security information to someone not entitled to receive it. This figure therefore does not include cases where the charges are based solely on unlawful *retention* and/or mishandling of classified information under 18 U.S.C. §§ 793(e) or 1924.

4. *See* Charlie Savage, *Ex-Contractor at State Dept. Pleads Guilty in Leak Case*, N.Y. TIMES, Feb. 8, 2014, at A10. Savage's count omits the case of James Hitselberger, indicted in 2012 for providing certain classified information about Bahrain to a Hoover Institution archive. *See* Indictment, United States v. Hitselberger, No. 12-231 (D.D.C. filed Feb. 28, 2013), http://www.fas.org/sgp/jud/hitsel /indict-sup.pdf.

5. *See* Scott Shane & Charlie Savage, *Administration Took Accidental Path to Setting Record for Leak Cases*, N.Y. TIMES, June 20, 2012, at A14; *see also* Charlie Savage, *Nine Leak-Related Cases*, N.Y. TIMES, June 20, 2012, at A14. The uptick in leak prosecutions may also reflect the increased sophistication of government surveillance capabilities, which almost certainly have made it far easier to detect the sources of national security leaks than has historically been the case.

6. *See generally* David E. Pozen, *The Leaky Leviathan: Why the Government Condemns and Condones Unlawful Disclosures of Information*, 127 HARV. L. REV. 512 (2013).

7. *See generally* Stephen I. Vladeck, *Inchoate Liability and the Espionage Act: The Statutory Framework and the Freedom of the Press*, 1 HARV. L. & POL'Y REV. 219 (2007).

8. *Espionage Laws and Leaks: Hearings before the Subcomm. on Legislation of the Permanent H. Select Comm. on Intelligence*, 96th Cong. 14 (1979) (statement of Anthony A. Lapham, Gen. Counsel, CIA).

9. Indeed, at least one charge for violating the Espionage Act has been included in the indictment in all nine leak prosecutions documented by *The New York Times*. *See* Savage, *supra* note 4.

10. The authoritative account of the history and scope of the Espionage Act remains Harold Edgar & Benno C. Schmidt, Jr., *The Espionage Statutes and Publication of Defense Information*, 73 COLUM. L. REV. 929 (1973).

11. BLACK'S LAW DICTIONARY (9th ed. 2009).

12. *See* 18 U.S.C. § 793; *see also* Gorin v. United States, 312 U.S. 19, 27–28 (1941).

13. *See* 18 U.S.C. § 793(d), (f).

14. *See id.* § 793(e).

15. *Id.* § 793(d).

16. *See id.* § 793(f).

17. *See* Jeffery A. Smith, *Prior Restraint: Original Intentions and Modern Interpretations*, 28 Wm. & Mary L. Rev. 439, 467 (1987).

18. 18 U.S.C. § 798.

19. The Espionage Act also includes more specific offenses that, likewise, do not require specific intent. Section 794, for example, is focused on the dissemination of information that leads to the death of a U.S. agent or the compromising of "major element[s] of defense strategy." 18 U.S.C. § 794(a).

20. 50 U.S.C. § 783. Both § 783 and 18 U.S.C. § 798 were added to the Espionage Act by the Subversive Activities Control Act of 1950, Title I of the Internal Security Act of 1950, Pub. L. No. 81-831, tit. I, §§ 4, 18, 64 Stat. 987, 991, 1003–05.

21. *See* Vladeck, *supra* note 7, at 222–24.

22. *See, e.g.*, Geoffrey R. Stone, First Amendment Ctr., Government Secrecy vs. Freedom of the Press (2006), http://www.firstamendmentcenter.org/madison/wp-content/uploads/2011/03/Govt.Secrecy.Stone_.pdf.

23. *See* United States v. Rosen, 445 F. Supp. 2d 602 (E.D. Va. 2006), *aff'd*, 557 F.3d 192 (4th Cir. 2009).

24. *See, e.g.*, United States v. Boyce, 594 F.2d 1246, 1251 (9th Cir. 1979).

25. *See* Act of Mar. 3, 1875, ch. 144, 18 Stat. 479 (codified as amended at 18 U.S.C. § 641).

26. 18 U.S.C. § 641.

27. *See* United States v. Morison, 844 F.2d 1057 (4th Cir. 1988).

28. *Id.* at 1077 (quoting Morissette v. United States, 342 U.S. 246, 269 n.28 (1952)).

29. *Id.*

30. United States v. Truong Dinh Hung, 629 F.2d 908, 924–25 (4th Cir. 1980) (Winter, J., concurring).

31. *See, e.g.*, 18 U.S.C. § 1510.

32. *See, e.g., id.* § 1001.

33. *See id.* § 952.

34. *See id.* § 1030(a)(1).

35. *See id.* § 1905.

36. *See id.* § 1924; *see also* Eric Lichtblau, *Ex-Clinton Aide to Admit Taking Classified Papers*, N.Y. Times, Apr. 1, 2005, at A1.

37. 42 U.S.C. § 2274.

38. *See id.* § 2277.

39. *See* 50 U.S.C. § 3121.

40. *See, e.g.*, Adam Liptak, *Little-Tested Law Is Used against Journalists in Leak*, N.Y. Times, Oct. 10, 2004, at A33.

41. *See* Charlie Savage, *Former CIA Operative Pleads Guilty in Leak of Colleague's Name*, N.Y. Times, Oct. 24, 2012, at A16.

42. *See* United States v. Morison, 844 F.2d 1057, 1083–84 (4th Cir. 1987) (Wilkinson, J., concurring).

43. Such a balancing approach derives from the Court's decision in *Pickering v. Board of Education*, 391 U.S. 563 (1968), which looked to balance the government employee's interests as a citizen in commenting upon "matters of public concern" and the state's interests as an employer in fostering efficient public services. *See id.* at 568; *see also, e.g.*, City of San Diego v. Roe, 543 U.S. 77 (2004) (per curiam); Connick v. Myers, 461 U.S. 138 (1983).

44. *See, e.g.*, Bartnicki v. Vopper, 532 U.S. 514 (2001); Fla. Star v. B.J.F., 491 U.S. 524 (1989); Smith v. Daily Mail Publ'g Co., 443 U.S. 97 (1979).

45. 547 U.S. 410 (2006).

46. *Id.* at 421.
47. *Id.* at 421–22.
48. Stephen I. Vladeck, *The Espionage Act and National Security Whistleblowing after* Garcetti, 57 AM. U. L. REV. 1531, 1540 (2008).
49. *Id.* at 1540–41 (footnotes omitted).
50. Lane v. Franks, 1234 S. Ct. 2369, 2379 (2014).
51. *Id.*; *see also* Steve Vladeck, Lane v. Franks *and the First Amendment Rights of National Security Leakers*, Just Security, June 19, 2014, 3:25 p.m., http://justsecurity.org/11949/first-amendment-leakers/.
52. Pozen, *supra* note 6, at 524–25 (footnotes omitted).
53. *See* Scott Shane, *Ex-Contractor is Charged in Leaks on N.S.A. Surveillance*, N.Y. TIMES, June 22, 2013, at A1.
54. *See* Criminal Complaint, United States v. Snowden, No. 1:13-CR-265 (E.D. Va. June 14, 2013), https://s3.amazonaws.com/s3.documentcloud.org/documents/716888/u-s-vs-edward-j-snowden-criminal-complaint.pdf.
55. Edgar & Schmidt, *supra* note 10, at 930.
56. *Id.* at 936.

RESOURCES

SUSAN BUCKLEY, REPORTING ON THE WAR ON TERROR: THE ESPIONAGE ACT AND OTHER SCARY STATUTES (2d ed. 2006).

Harold Edgar & Benno C. Schmidt, Jr., *The Espionage Statutes and Publication of Defense Information*, 73 COLUM. L. REV. 929 (1973).

Harold Edgar & Benno C. Schmidt, Jr., Commentary, Curtiss-Wright *Comes Home: Executive Power and National Security Secrecy*, 21 HARV. C.R.-C.L. L. REV. 349 (1986).

Heidi Kitrosser, *Free Speech Aboard the Leaky Ship of State: Calibrating First Amendment Protections for Leakers of Classified Information*, 6 J. NAT'L SEC. L. & POL'Y 409 (2013).

Melville B. Nimmer, *National Security Secrets v. Free Speech: The Issues Left Undecided in the Ellsberg Case*, 26 STAN. L. REV. 311 (1974).

David E. Pozen, *The Leaky Leviathan: Why the Government Condemns and Condones Unlawful Disclosures of Information*, 127 HARV. L. REV. 512 (2013).

Jamie Sasser, Comment, *Silenced Citizens: The Post-*Garcetti *Landscape for Public Sector Employees Working in National Security*, 41 U. RICH. L. REV. 759 (2007).

Paul M. Secunda, Garcetti*'s Impact on the First Amendment Speech Rights of Federal Employees*, 7 FIRST AMEND. L. REV. 117 (2008).

GEOFFREY R. STONE, FIRST AMENDMENT CTR., GOVERNMENT SECRECY VS. FREEDOM OF THE PRESS (2006), http://www.firstamendmentcenter.org/madison /wp-content/uploads/2011/03/Govt.Secrecy.Stone_.pdf.

Stephen I. Vladeck, *Inchoate Liability and the Espionage Act: The Statutory Framework and the Freedom of the Press*, 1 HARV. L. & POL'Y REV. 219 (2007).

Stephen I. Vladeck, *The Espionage Act and National Security Whistleblowing after* Garcetti, 57 AM. U. L. REV. 1531 (2008).

U.S. Efforts to Change Leak Laws 4

Edward R. McNicholas*

Leaks, so it would seem, are an inevitable part of our Republic's balance of the executive's desire for secret power and the First Amendment's service as a bulwark for civil liberties. Alexander Hamilton and his followers have frequently seen secrecy as a necessary support for an energetic executive branch.[1] Nonetheless, the front pages of *The New York Times*, *The Washington Post*, and *The Wall Street Journal*—not to mention *The Guardian*—make clear that the current patchwork of laws regarding leaks has not proved entirely effective in protecting such secrets. Leaks remain part of our landscape despite multiple efforts to amend or create laws to curtail them.

No major piece of legislation addressing leaks of classified information has become law in nearly 30 years; the last "new" law addressed computer espionage, and tracked its language from the Espionage Act of 1917.[2] The vast social changes and technological advances in the interim have led one federal court to observe that "the time is ripe for Congress to engage in a thorough review and revision of these provisions to ensure that they reflect both these changes, and contemporary views about the appropriate balance between our nation's security and our citizens' ability to engage in public debate about the United States' conduct in the society of nations."[3] U.S. District Judge T.S. Ellis's call is but one

*The author wishes to acknowledge with gratitude the material assistance of his colleagues Yasir Latifi and Vivek Mohan in preparing this chapter. The views expressed herein, however, are those of the author and do not necessarily reflect the views of his colleagues, law firm partners, or clients.

of the voices raised to suggest a need to revise the laws that govern unauthorized disclosures.

This chapter chronicles past efforts to reform leak laws in light of the constitutional considerations and security problems they have attempted to address, including the seminal Willard Report, President Bill Clinton's veto of one such effort based on constitutional concerns, the Bush administration's Ashcroft Report and L'Affaire Plame, and the Obama administration's efforts to overcome the practical and legal hurdles to restricting leaks.

I. DEFINING THE PROBLEM

The nature of the legislative challenge tends to depend on one's perspective. Are leaks a healthy flow of information to the press that supports a democratic discourse or a source of potentially grave harm to the collective security? One's answer to the question tends to determine the definition of the problem with leaks and one's views on the need for reforms in the laws dealing with them.

Regardless of one's perspective, what is clear is that the United States has no Official Secrets Act;[4] no one federal law comprehensively addresses all unauthorized disclosures of classified materials, much less directly covers all unauthorized disclosures to the media. Although chapter 3 more fully discusses these laws, it bears repeating that unauthorized disclosures may violate three different types of federal laws:

1. Laws that prohibit the general theft of government property or information;[5]
2. Laws that prohibit specific kinds of unauthorized disclosures, for example, nuclear weapons secrets, diplomatic codes, secret patent applications, or identities of covert agents;[6]
3. Laws that prohibit espionage, that is, revealing information to advantage a foreign nation or revealing information in order to harm the United States.[7]

These laws protect classified and sensitive information in a somewhat convoluted way. Some laws do not weigh whether the disclosed information is classified—for example, if the information simply relates to "the national defense"—thereby punishing leakers broadly.[8] Other laws, however, cut more narrowly because they require a specific intent or knowledge of harm for unauthorized disclosures. Consequently, observers have concluded:

> As a result, persons who leak [classified] information to further public debate may do so with impunity, as long as the information they disclose is not protected by one of the more narrowly directed statutes. . . . [And] Congress has ignored large categories of information that should not be

disclosed with impunity. In summary, Congress has not constructed a principled and consistent scheme of criminal sanctions to punish the disclosure of vital government secrets.[9]

These conflicting visions of the utility of leaks have repeatedly undermined attempts to amend or create laws that restrict the unauthorized disclosure of classified information to the media, and such laws have often otherwise proven frequently futile for a variety of practical and constitutional reasons. On the practical side, it has proven more feasible to suggest and enforce internal regulatory and procedural reforms against would-be leakers than to prosecute possibly high-profile individuals after a leak occurs—with the attendant risk of further disclosures during public prosecutions. Intelligence directives[10] and other internal regulations indeed tend to delineate the actual consequences of leaks at least as much as any of the relevant statutes.

In addition, the post-September 11, 2001, increase in the volume and extent of classified documents and security clearances has further impeded the government's efforts to thwart leaks with the limited investigative and prosecutorial resources available. At the end of 2012, nearly 5 million people had some kind of security clearance with the federal government. Almost 1.5 million of these people had "top secret" clearance.[11] Related to the number of clearances given, moreover, is the massive amount of classified documents that exist in the federal government. In 2011 alone, some 92 million decisions to classify information were made, many of which some consider unnecessary.[12]

More profoundly, what some of have seen as Washington's "culture of leaking" has hardly changed since the federal government's first major report on unauthorized disclosures in 1982. Some commentators have even suggested that this culture plays such a significant, albeit counterintuitive, function in *advancing* the presidential policy agenda by allowing disavowed communications with the press, populace, and foreign powers that "[i]t can be seen as a strategic response facilitated by Presidents and their appointees."[13]

Constitutional tensions arise when considering legislation targeted at unauthorized disclosures to the media. On one hand, the executive branch is charged with safeguarding the secrets of the country. The intelligence community certainly accepts the so-called "Lunev Axiom" when describing the importance of this responsibility: media disclosure of classified intelligence is as effective as foreign espionage.[14] On the other hand, the First Amendment guards the news media's ability to pursue and publish sensitive stories for the public good. For instance, the chilling effect certain laws may have on free speech is a major reason why Clinton vetoed proposed legislation intended to rein unauthorized disclosures, and why similar bills have failed in Congress in recent years.

The end result is a disparate set of federal laws that some have considered inadequate and are determined to amend, while others have warned of a potentially draconian U.S. Official Secrets Act stifling informed debate.

II. THE WILLARD REPORT

A 1982 report by Deputy Assistant Attorney General Richard Willard (the Willard Report) stands as the seminal Cold War–era report on the reform of leak laws. A chorus of officials at the White House and in the intelligence community, led by Deputy Secretary of State William Clark, led to the establishment of an interagency task force on unauthorized disclosures. Clark sought the Justice Department's help with leak reforms, and Attorney General William French Smith appointed Willard to lead an interagency group that would explore unauthorized disclosures.[15] Willard's team reached its pragmatic conclusions after examining what it saw as the faulty policies and procedures that existed within the federal government to stop leaks.

Willard's approach was uncompromising in identifying the problem of the "culture of leaking":

[O]fficials may seek to advance their personal policy objectives by leaks of classified information, on the assumption that there will be no serious harm to national security. Because leaks are so prevalent and leakers rarely caught, some officials may believe there is nothing wrong with leaking classified information and that everyone does it.

Similarly, many journalists appear to believe they have a duty to divulge virtually any newsworthy secret information that can be acquired by whatever means they choose to employ. To their way of thinking, leaks are part of a game in which the government tries to keep information secret and the media tries to find it out. . . .

Under these circumstances, only a fundamental change in prevailing attitudes will alleviate the problem of unauthorized disclosures. We must seek to develop a sense of discipline and self-restraint by those who work with or obtain classified information.[16]

Willard's comment highlights one of the most basic dynamics of a leak: It is a mutually beneficial exchange that benefits the journalist who wants the story as well as the government employee who wishes to expose information—for whatever higher calling, public interest, petty politics, or personal aggrandizement he or she seeks. No matter how pure or tainted their motive, neither party has an incentive to expose the source of the information. Although Willard viewed journalists as subject to both law enforcement and national security statutes— 18 U.S.C. § 798 (the signals intelligence statute) and 50 U.S.C. § 421 (the Intelligence Identities Protection Act)—he knew full well the practical constraints on investigation. As Willard emphasized, "Leak investigations do not focus on the receiving journalist for a variety of reasons," including the observation that "journalists are unlikely to divulge their sources in response to a subpoena for documents or testimony before a grand jury, and contempt sanctions against journalists in other types of cases have not been effective."[17] Willard, however, recommended thorough investigation of governmental leaks and strong administrative punishments. He took particular aim at "some high ranking officials" who engaged in unauthorized "'friendly' leaks" to journalists (sometimes called "plants"[18]), which he viewed as "just as unlawful as any other unauthorized disclosure of classified information."[19]

The Willard Report pointed to a further litany of practical issues with the approach to leak investigations, focusing on the challenges of criminally prosecuting leakers. In Willard's view, frequent disputes between the Department of Justice and agencies that suffered leaks had led to an "approach to leak investigations [that] has been almost totally unsuccessful and frustrating. . . . This ineffectual system has led to the belief that nothing can be done to stop leaks of classified information."[20]

A key concern was that agencies that discover their classified information has leaked must report violations to the Criminal Division of the Department of Justice. From there, the wronged agency has limited authority to conduct a preliminary investigation. The Criminal Division thus serves as the gatekeeper for agency leak reports, forwarding only the most damaging leaks to the Federal Bureau of Investigation (FBI) for investigation and fully investigating only a fraction of these referrals in light of competing priorities.[21] For Willard, the difficulties of prosecution were such that he concluded that "the threat of criminal prosecution is so illusory as to constitute no real deterrent to the prospective leaker. A more promising approach involves better efforts to identify leakers and the resolve to impose administrative sanctions."[22]

Willard's proposed solution to these issues involved a multipronged approach. First, he advocated for criminal penalties for almost all intentional unauthorized disclosures of classified information; that is, he championed a U.S. version of the U.K. Official Secrets Act. Second, having deemed the criminal law inadequate, he called for enhanced civil enforcement via signed secrecy agreements. Third, he emphasized the need for robust internal leak detection policies and practices, and, perhaps out of a particular enthusiasm for the then-advanced technology, he advocated for the enhanced use of polygraph devices in order to detect and deter future leaks as well as the thorough review of future publications by cleared personnel.[23]

Later congressional reports and hearings continued to reflect much of the Willard Report's findings, including a 1996 report by the National Counterintelligence Policy Board, which found essentially the same problems of a lack of political will to address leaks and their use as a policy tool.[24] Likewise, a 2005 report that evaluated the intelligence failures after the Iraq War cited the Willard Report and reached very similar conclusions: that leaks persist because of the use of leaks to influence policy, a lack of political will to address the issue firmly, and the difficulty in identifying the leaker.[25] In particular, the 2005 report emphasized the lack of a "single indictment or prosecution" resulting from "hundreds" of leaks reported to the Department of Justice. As these later studies demonstrate, the analysis in the Willard Report remains timely in understanding why unauthorized disclosures continue.[26]

III. PRESIDENT CLINTON'S CONSTITUTIONAL CONCERNS

The calls of the Willard Report and other reports based on its findings for a broad restriction on the disclosure of classified information echoed into the administration of President Bill Clinton, and led to a significant confrontation with the First Amendment's foundational protections in 2000. That year, Clinton vetoed one of the most significant efforts to enhance the federal government's statutory ability to suppress unauthorized disclosures to the media. The circumstances surrounding the veto present a useful case study into the constitutional problems that hound any such new legislation.

In the fall of 2000, Congress adopted the Intelligence Authorization Act for Fiscal Year 2001, which included a provision known as the Shelby Amendment (after its sponsor, Senator Richard Shelby of Alabama). This amendment would have added a section on "unauthorized disclosure of classified information" to Title 18 of the U.S. Code. It read as follows:

> Whoever, being an officer or employee of the United States, a former or retired officer or employee of the United States, any other person with authorized access to classified information, or any other person formerly with authorized access to classified information, knowingly and willfully discloses, or attempts to disclose, any classified information acquired as a result of such person's authorized access to classified information to a person (other than an officer or employee of the United States) who is not authorized access to such classified information, knowing that the person is not authorized access to such classified information, shall be fined under this title, imprisoned not more than 3 years, or both.[27]

Unlike some federal laws, the proposed amendment ignored the *kind* of disclosure at issue. Rather, *any* disclosure of classified information fell under the statute with only narrow exceptions for disclosures to Article III courts, to certain congressional committees, and for authorized disclosures to persons acting on behalf of a foreign power. Also, while specific intent was needed ("knowingly or willfully discloses, or attempts to disclose"), the provision removed the requirement found in other espionage statutes about harming the country or aiding a foreign nation. The bill also placed no time limit on these restrictions; former or retired employees would be subject to this rule for the rest of their lives.

Prior to its passage, Attorney General Janet Reno voiced her view that the bill was unnecessary and could punish individuals who commit "inadvertent disclosures." She also stated that the bill should exempt disclosures made during "authorized diplomatic and intelligence activities."[28] Several free-speech groups and news organizations also rallied against the bill and urged the president to veto the measure, arguing that the Shelby Amendment would function like an Official Secrets Act, akin to that adopted by the United Kingdom.[29] Other congressional members were similarly distressed, believing the act might deter whistleblowers as well as leakers.[30]

On November 4, 2000, Clinton vetoed the bill. In his veto message, the president invoked the Pentagon Papers case to underscore the need to insulate government secrets while balancing the need to inform a citizenry:

> [I]t is my obligation to protect not only our Government's vital information from improper disclosure, but also to protect the rights of citizens to receive the information necessary for democracy to work. Furthering these two goals requires a careful balancing, which must be assessed in light of our system of classifying information over a range of categories.[31]

In declaring the bill "badly flawed," Clinton concluded that it would "unnecessarily chill legitimate activities that are at the heart of a democracy."[32] In explaining the "undue chilling effect" the bill would have on current and former government employees, the president highlighted several practical matters. For instance, employees may have had to avoid participation in public debates, press briefings, and the like, and former employees might well have avoided future teaching or writing opportunities. For Clinton, "[i]ncurring such risks is unnecessary and inappropriate in a society built on freedom of expression and the consent of the governed and is particularly inadvisable in a context in which the range of classified materials is so extensive."[33] Although the law would have undoubtedly filled a gap in federal laws on unauthorized disclosures, the First Amendment infirmities with the amendment trumped executive authority concerns, resulting in Clinton's veto.

His veto, however, did not end efforts to enact the law.

The 107th Congress considered an identical provision, but declined to include it in the overall Intelligence Authorization Act for Fiscal Year 2002,[34] and the same language was introduced again late in the 109th Congress, but it never left committee, despite the intervening attacks of September 11.[35] The Shelby Amendment language has not been introduced in Congress since then.

IV. THE ASHCROFT REPORT

Concerns about the ability to pursue the global war on terrorism no doubt fueled a resurgent interest in efforts to have robust tools to prosecute leakers. Claims that a 1998 leak of the government's ability to track Osama bin Laden through his satellite phone limited the ability to gather intelligence on his activities were widespread (although now debated) after a White House press statement related to National Security Agency (NSA) information was issued:

> In 1998, for example, as a result of an inappropriate leak of NSA information, it was revealed about NSA being able to listen to Osama bin Laden on his satellite phone. As a result of the disclosure, he stopped using it. As a result of the public disclosure, the United States was denied the opportunity to monitor and gain information that could have been very valuable for protecting our country.[36]

49

In this environment, Attorney General John Ashcroft completed a report in 2002 (the Ashcroft Report) that emphasized the need to strengthen internal procedures throughout the federal government.[37]

Although the attorney general acknowledged that no single statute criminalized all intentional disclosure of classified information, he expressed confidence that "current statutes provide a legal basis to prosecute those who engage in unauthorized disclosures, if they can be identified."[38] To his mind, the need then was for "rigorous investigation" and "vigorous enforcement," not necessarily new legislation.[39]

A key practical problem Ashcroft saw was the significant number of individuals with clearances and the broad use of classification. Related to the number of clearances given, moreover, was the massive number of classified documents that existed in the federal government. Logically, an increased likelihood of unauthorized disclosures followed from more people with greater access to a growing number of classified documents. Indeed, the attorney general's 2002 report could not have foreseen how significant this concern would become today, after more than a decade of intense covert operations under the leadership of Presidents George W. Bush and Barack Obama.

Technology was a potential solution for Ashcroft, however, giving him hope that a "reinvigorated information security regime may be able to substantially improve the management and control of classified information."[40] In particular, he emphasized the potential for dynamic digital rights management technologies to track information and documents and suggested significant study of this new technology. In retrospect, of course, technological advancements have both helped and hindered leak investigations. Better storage and tracking of electronic documents are possible with faster internal databases and digital rights management technologies. But new technologies allow for more sophisticated threat vectors to emerge that may permit rogue employees to grab massive amounts of data quickly. Edward Snowden, for one, used social engineering and technical exploits in conjunction to steal hundreds of thousands of documents from the NSA.[41]

As in the Willard Report, the Ashcroft Report recommended strong administrative sanctions for employees who were found to have leaked classified information.[42] Beyond immediate termination, however, other more punitive measures found little traction because of the questions about the deterrent value of sanctions.

V. THE PLAME HEARINGS

The rigorous enforcement called for in the Ashcroft Report was soon tested in the Valerie Plame incident, resulting in further congressional attention to the Intelligence Identities Protection Act (IIPA).[43] The IIPA was enacted in 1947 to prohibit the intentional, unauthorized disclosure of covert agent identities, but it has been only used twice to prosecute leakers: Sharon Scranage in 1985, a Central Intelligence Agency (CIA) clerk who provided classified information about the CIA's operations in Ghana to a Ghanaian agent; and John Kiriakou in 2012, a CIA analyst who disclosed the name of a covert CIA officer when giving classified documents to a journalist about detainees at the Guantanamo Bay detention facility.[44]

Paradoxically, the prosecution related to the disclosure of the identity of Plame, a former CIA officer, never used the IIPA to charge the two officials who disclosed Plame's name to reporters Robert Novak and Matthew Cooper—reportedly Deputy Secretary of State Richard Armitage and White House Senior Advisor Karl Rove.[45] Instead, I. Lewis "Scooter" Libby, chief of staff to Vice President Dick Cheney, was convicted only of perjury, making false statements to federal investigators, and obstruction of justice in the Plame investigation (only to have his sentence commuted).[46] And a related civil case seeking compensation involving Plame was dismissed by the U.S. District Court and reportedly settled on appeal.[47]

A 2007 congressional hearing about the political saga highlighted two important obstacles to using the IIPA for criminal prosecutions. First, the Act defines "covert agent" more narrowly than how CIA officials use the term, calling into question whether Plame was truly "covert" under the IIPA. Second, the Act imposes a specific intent requirement on would-be leakers, targeting only those whom the government can prove knew both that the agent was "covert" under the definition of the Act and that the United States was actively securing that agent's identity at the time of the disclosure.[48] It was not clear from the evidence that the Bush administration officials acted with this high level of intent, and Congress chose not to amend the IIPA to clarify the issue for future cases.

VI. PRESIDENT OBAMA'S RESPONSE TO LEAKS

The problems delineated in the Willard Report, the Ashcroft Report, and other episodes continue to this day and are frequently raised in congressional hearings about media leaks.[49] In response to these concerns, the Obama administration has traced leaks more actively than other administrations—with the president himself declaring a "zero tolerance" policy against government leakers.[50] At the same time, *internal* whistleblowing protections and mechanisms have been bolstered. Nonetheless, the Obama administration has continued to face political opposition on many of these fronts, and it remains to be seen whether the new policies actually establish an effective zero tolerance policy for leaks by future administrations.

The efforts to foster a culture of internal whistleblowing merit special attention. As a U.S. senator, Obama urged greater whistleblower protections in his 2008 presidential campaign.[51] To that end, as President, Obama has strengthened the Office of Special Counsel, an independent federal investigative agency that facilitates whistleblower-related complaints and investigates incidents of employees who may have been terminated in retaliation for blowing the whistle on agency misconduct.[52] The administration also supported the passage of the Whistleblower Protection Enhancement Act of 2012,[53] which augmented existing whistleblower aid for employees who complain about wrongdoing internally to their agencies. The bill would allow wrongfully terminated whistleblowers to recover compensatory damages, and require all inspector general offices to house an internal whistleblower-protection ombudsman. A Presidential Policy Directive extended the same whistleblower assurances to employees in the intelligence community for the first time ever.[54]

While facilitating disclosure through internal channels, the Obama administration has also moved to curb leaks to the media. To date, the administration has prosecuted eight people for unauthorized disclosures to the media under the Espionage Act of 1917, a number greater than all previous administrations combined: Thomas Drake, Shamei Leibowitz, Chelsea (formerly Bradley) Manning, Stephen Kim, Jeffrey Sterling, John Kiriakou, James Hitselberger, and Edward Snowden.[55] Perhaps most aggressively, the government (somewhat unsuccessfully) tried Private Manning for "aiding the enemy" in violation of the Uniform Code of Military Justice (a crime punishable by death) for Manning's role in providing classified documents to WikiLeaks.[56]

The president also issued an Executive Order in 2011 that created an "Insider Threat Program" that provides minimum standards for monitoring employees' access to classified information in order to prevent unauthorized disclosures.[57] The program gives agencies full authority to formulate these internal monitoring programs and to even probe disclosures of nonclassified information. The program, however, has been criticized as a heavy-handed maneuver to quash leaks.[58]

Most recently, a 2014 Intelligence Community Directive requires that all intelligence community employees "obtain authorization for contacts with the media" with respect to essentially all intelligence-related matters and that they report "unplanned or unintentional contact with the media on covered matters."[59] This Directive again reflects a focus on internal regulation in order to punish governmental leakers, thereby creating further tensions between the intelligence community and journalists, while attempting "to mitigate risks of unauthorized disclosures of intelligence-related matters that may result from such contacts."

Meanwhile, the Obama administration and the Department of Justice (DoJ) have revised their practices regarding investigation of the media for receipt of unauthorized disclosures. The administration has supported passage of a federal media shield law, which would shield reporters from penalties for refusing to reveal confidential sources and permit reporters to stop subpoenas of their phone records.[60] And the DoJ has issued new guidelines about investigations involving media members, limiting earlier investigative authorities.[61] Under the new rules, for example, DoJ will, in nearly all cases, provide notice to a media outlet when it seeks records of the outlet's employees. Moreover, it will not name a reporter as a "criminal co-conspirator" in a leak investigation if the reporter's actions were solely related to his or her newsgathering activities. Finally, the guidelines require DoJ to review whether the leaked information at issue was properly classified in the first place and track DoJ requests for reporters' records.

VII. OBAMA-ERA CONGRESSIONAL EFFORTS

Recent congressional attempts at reform have focused on the use of the Espionage Act of 1917 and related laws when prosecuting media leakers.[62] As has been mentioned, because the Act does not expressly focus on media leaks, a debate continues about whether the government should investigate and try members of the press under the Act for publishing classified material.

In both 2010 and 2011, for instance, the SHIELD Act[63] was proposed as an amendment to the Espionage Act. The SHIELD Act would retain the Espionage Act's specific intent requirements (intent to aid a foreign nation or harm the United States) but add a prohibition on communicating or publishing classified material that concerned any "human intelligence activities of the United States or any foreign government" or concerned the identity of intelligence community individuals. A 2010 congressional hearing discussed these issues in relation to the Espionage Act,[64] and a separate congressional hearing considered how the Act might be used or amended to charge WikiLeaks after its release of classified documents.[65] Some were concerned that the DoJ had been reluctant to prosecute WikiLeaks out of concern that the Act could be used against more established media organizations like *The New York Times* whenever they, too, published classified material.[66] Critics have bemoaned the burden serious journalistic endeavors would face under the SHIELD Act,[67] and the bill has died in committee both times.

More recently, the Senate Select Committee on Intelligence was forced to drop unauthorized disclosure proposals from the Intelligence Authorization Act (IAA) bills for fiscal years 2011 and 2013, primarily because of objections from one of its members, Senator Ron Wyden of Oregon. The 2011 bill proposed that the Director of National Intelligence or another appropriate intelligence official could determine the disciplinary actions for an intelligence employee who committed an unauthorized disclosure, including the removal of a former or retired employee's pension benefits.[68] Wyden expressed skepticism about entrusting such singular responsibility to intelligence heads without any further guidance regarding how to adjudicate disciplinary actions.[69] Such vast power, in Wyden's view, could precipitate retaliatory actions against employees and muzzle would-be whistleblowers from exposing agency abuses. He also questioned the due process problems that might arise from denying one's pension benefits without requiring a formal hearing.[70]

Wyden also criticized the committee's 2013 IAA proposal. In the summer of 2012, the Senate intelligence committee added 12 new provisions about unauthorized disclosures to the IAA,[71] including the same measure stripping pension benefits for employees that Wyden had criticized in 2011. Two other provisions also troubled Wyden.[72] One banned people with top-secret security clearances from "entering into any contract or other binding agreement" with "the media" to provide "analysis or commentary" regarding intelligence activities for a full year after that employee left the government. A second provision prohibited nearly all intelligence agency employees from providing briefings to the press, unless those employees gave their names and provided the briefing on the record.

In Wyden's view, those measures severely limited public discourse and encroached on the freedom of the press. Further, he believed the restrictions would lead to a "less-informed debate on national security issues," to the detriment of the public at large.[73] In the end, only one of the 12 leak provisions survived the bill's final passage—a requirement that the Director of National Intelligence inform Congress when an authorized disclosure about intelligence information will be made to the public.[74]

As of the writing of this chapter, the Intelligence Authorization Act for Fiscal Year 2014 also included language that concentrates on unauthorized disclosures. At that point, however, the Senate intelligence committee had not proposed any new restrictions on would-be leakers and focused, instead, on improving the security clearance process across intelligence agencies and protecting whistleblowers in the intelligence community.[75]

VIII.   CONCLUSION

Over the last three decades, efforts to stop leaks and to change U.S. leak laws have continued to hit the same practical, cultural, and legal stumbling blocks. While little progress has been made designing new legislation that passes constitutional muster, the Obama administration has been using the Espionage Act to battle leakers and, in some cases, the journalists who publish their classified information. The Obama administration's approach is contentious for the same reasons that wholesale changes to leak laws have remained elusive in the past: frustration with changing the culture of leaking in Washington; questions about the strength of internal safeguards against unauthorized disclosures; limits to internal resources for wide-ranging leak investigations and prosecutions; and First Amendment and due process–related unease about restricting press freedoms, public conversation, and employee freedoms. And in an age of new media and an ever-growing amount of secret documents and clearances, these concerns show no sign of waning anytime soon.

NOTES

1. THE FEDERALIST No. 70 (Alexander Hamilton) ("That unity is conducive to energy will not be disputed. Decision, activity, secrecy, and dispatch will generally characterize the proceedings of one man in a much more eminent degree than the proceedings of any greater number; and in proportion as the number is increased, these qualities will be diminished.").

2. *See* Act of Oct. 12, 1984, Pub. L. No. 98-473, §§ 2102(a), 98 Stat. 2190 (codified as amended at 18 U.S.C. §§ 1030 (2012)).

3. United States v. Rosen, 445 F. Supp. 2d 602, 646 (E.D. Va. 2006).

4. *See, e.g.,* Official Secrets Act, 1989, c. 6 (U.K.).

5. *See* 18 U.S.C. § 641 (punishing individuals who steal and sell government property or information); *id.* § 1924 (punishing individuals who improperly remove classified material).

6. *See* 18 U.S.C. § 952 (prohibiting improper sharing of diplomatic codes); 35 U.S.C. §§ 181–188 (prohibiting disclosure of patent applications the government has deemed secret); 42 U.S.C. § 2277 (prohibiting unauthorized disclosure of nuclear weapons secrets); 50 U.S.C. §§ 421–426 (prohibiting unauthorized disclosure of a covert agent).

7. *See* 18 U.S.C. §§ 792–799 (codifying the Espionage Act of 1917); 18 U.S.C. § 1030 (dealing with computer espionage); 50 U.S.C. § 783 (prohibiting individuals from sharing a classified document with a foreign government or its agent).

8. *See* JENNIFER K. ELSEA, CONG. RESEARCH SERV., PROTECTION OF NATIONAL SECURITY INFORMATION (2006), http://www.fas.org/sgp/crs/secrecy/RL33502.pdf.

9. Eric E. Ballou & Kyle E. McSlarrow, Note, *Plugging the Leak: The Case for a Legislative Resolution of the Conflict between the Demands of Secrecy and the Need for Open Government,* 71 VA. L. REV. 801, 815 (1985).

10. *See, e.g.,* Intelligence Community Directive 119: Media Contacts, Mar. 20, 2014.

11. *See* Leigh Munsil, *Leak Risk: So Many Security Clearances,* POLITICO (Jun. 11, 2013, 5:44 p.m.), http://www.politico.com/story/2013/06/snowden-leak-risk-security-clearance-92606.html.

12. *See* LEONARD DOWNIE JR., COMM. TO PROTECT JOURNALISTS, THE OBAMA ADMINISTRATION AND THE PRESS: LEAK INVESTIGATIONS AND SURVEILLANCE IN POST-9/11 AMERICA 6 (2013), http://cpj.org/reports/us2013-english.pdf.

13. *See* David Pozen, *The Leaky Leviathan: Why the Government Condemns and Condones Unlawful Disclosures of Information,* 127 HARV. L. REV. 512, 634 (2013).

14. *See, e.g.,* James B. Bruce, *The Consequences of Permissive Neglect: Laws and Leaks of Classified Intelligence, in* INSIDE CIA: LESSONS IN INTELLIGENCE 300 (Sharad S. Chauhan ed., 2004) ("I was amazed—and Moscow was very appreciative—at how many times I found very sensitive information in American newspapers. In my view, Americans tend to care more about scooping their competition than about national security, which made my job easier" (quoting Stanislav Lunev, THROUGH THE EYES OF THE ENEMY 135 (1998)), https://www.cia.gov/library/center-for-the-study-of-intelligence/csi-publications/csi-studies/studies/vol47no1/article04.html.

15. *See* ANGUS MACKENZIE, SECRETS: THE CIA'S WAR AT HOME 93, 96 (Univ. of Cal. Press New ed. 1999).

16. *Report of the Interdepartmental Group on Unauthorized Disclosures of Classified Information, in Presidential Directive on the Use of Polygraphs and Prepublication Review: Hearings before the Subcomm. on Civil and Constitutional Rights of the H. Comm. on the Judiciary,* 98th Cong. 170 (1983) [hereinafter Willard Report], https://www.ncjrs.gov/pdffiles1/Digitization/101326NCJRS.pdf.

17. *Id.* at 168.

18. *See* ELIE ABEL, LEAKING: WHO DOES IT? WHO BENEFITS? AT WHAT COST? 2 (1987).

19. Willard Report, *supra* note 16, at 167.

20. *Id.* at 168.

21. *See* Pozen, *supra* note 13, at 537–38 (suggesting that 15 percent of reported leak cases are investigated, while fewer still are prosecuted).

22. Willard Report, *supra* note 16, at 178–79.

23. *See id.* at 169.

24. *See* NAT'L COUNTERINTELLIGENCE POLICY BD., REPORT TO THE NSC ON UNAUTHORIZED MEDIA LEAK DISCLOSURES (1996).

25. *See* COMM'N ON THE INTELLIGENCE CAPABILITIES OF THE UNITED STATES REGARDING WEAPONS OF MASS DESTRUCTION, REPORT TO THE PRESIDENT OF THE UNITED STATES 381–83 (2005). The 2005 report cites to the 1996 report as well as to the Willard Report.

26. *See, e.g.*, JAMES B. BRUCE & W. GEORGE JAMESON, FIXING LEAKS: ASSESSING THE DEPARTMENT OF DEFENSE'S APPROACH TO PREVENTING AND DETERRING UNAUTHORIZED DISCLOSURES, at xi (RAND 2013) (citing the "longstanding Organizational culture in DoD that treats leaking classified information to the media as nearly risk-free, which suggests to some that the behavior is acceptable").

27. Intelligence Authorization Act for Fiscal Year 2001, 106th Cong. § 303 (2000), http://www.gpo .gov/fdsys/pkg/BILLS-106hr4392eas/pdf/BILLS-106hr4392eas.pdf.

28. Statement of Janet Reno, Att'y Gen., U.S. Dep't of Justice, before the Senate Select Comm. on Intelligence, Concerning Unauthorized Disclosure of Classified Information (Jun. 14, 2000), http:// www.fas.org/sgp/othergov/renoleaks.pdf.

29. The U.K. law is discussed in chapter 9.

30. *See* David G. Savage, *Clinton Vetoes Bill on Leaking of U.S. Secrets*, L.A. TIMES, Nov. 5, 2000, http://articles.latimes.com/2000/nov/05/news/mn-47358.

31. 146 CONG. REC. 26,022 (2000) (Veto Message from the President of the United States), http:// www.gpo.gov/fdsys/pkg/CRECB-2000-pt18/pdf/CRECB-2000-pt18-Pg26022-3.pdf.

32. *Id.*

33. *Id.*

34. *See* Classified Information Protection Act of 2001, H.R. 2943, 107th Cong. (2001); *see also* Intelligence Authorization Act for Fiscal Year 2002, Pub. L. No. 107-108, § 310 (2001) (authorizing the attorney general to review existing policies about unauthorized disclosures).

35. *See* S. 3774, 109th Cong. (2006).

36. Bruce, *supra* note 14, at 301 (quoting White House press statement from June 20, 2002); *see also* David Rosenbaum, *Bush Account of a Leak's Impact Has Support*, N.Y. TIMES, Dec. 20, 2005, http:// www.nytimes.com/2005/12/20/politics/20fact.html?_r=0. *But see* Glenn Kessler, *File the Bin Laden Phone Leak under Urban Myths*, WASH. POST, Dec. 22, 2005, http://www.washingtonpost.com/wp-dyn /content/article/2005/12/21/AR2005122101994.html; Jack Shafer, *Don't Blame the* Washington Times *for the Osama Bin Laden Satellite Phone "Leak,"* SLATE (Dec. 21, 2005, 7:03 p.m.), http://www.slate .com/articles/news_and_politics/press_box/2005/12/dont_blame_the_washington_times.html.

37. *See* Letter from John Ashcroft, Att'y Gen. of the United States, to the Honorable J. Dennis Hastert, Speaker of the House of Representatives (Oct. 15, 2002), http://www.fas.org/sgp/othergov /dojleaks.pdf.

38. *Id.* at 3.

39. *Id.* at 9.

40. *Id.* at 4.

41. *See* Shaun Waterman, *NSA Leaker Ed Snowden Used Banned Thumb-Drive, Exceeded Access*, WASH. TIMES, Jun. 14, 2013, http://www.washingtontimes.com/news/2013/jun/14/nsa-leaker-ed -snowden-used-banned-thumb-drive-exce/?page=all.

42. *See* Letter from John Ashcroft, *supra* note 37, at 5.

43. 50 U.S.C. §§ 421–426 (2012).

44. *See* JENNIFER K. ELSEA, CONG. RESEARCH SERV., INTELLIGENCE IDENTITIES PROTECTION ACT 6–7 (2013).

45. *See* Dan Froomkin, *The Second Source*, WASH. POST (Jul. 15, 2005, 1:00 p.m.), http://www .washingtonpost.com/wp-dyn/content/blog/2005/07/15/BL2005071500978_pf.html (noting Rove

Notes

as a source); Michael Isikoff, *The Man Who Said Too Much*, Newsweek (Sept. 3, 2006, 8:00 p.m.), http://www.newsweek.com/man-who-said-too-much-109351 (revealing Armitage as a source). Novak used both sources while Cooper only used Rove.

46. *See* Michael J. Sniffen & Matt Apuzzo, *Libby Found Guilty in CIA Leak Trial*, USA Today, Mar. 6, 2006, http://usatoday30.usatoday.com/news/washington/2007-03-06-715324468_x.htm.

47. *See* Wilson v. Libby, Civ. No. 06-1258-JDB (D.D.C. 2007).

48. *See White House Procedures for Safeguarding Classified Information: Hearing before the H. Comm. on Oversight and Government Reform*, 110th Cong. 87–98 (2007) (exchange between members of committee and attorneys Mark Zaid and Victoria Toensing).

49. *See, e.g., National Security Leaks and the Law: Hearing before the Subcomm. on Crime, Terrorism, and Homeland Security of the H. Comm. on the Judiciary*, 112th Cong. 10–14 (2012) (testimony of Kenneth L. Wainstein), http://www.gpo.gov/fdsys/pkg/CHRG-112hhrg74977/pdf /CHRG-112hhrg74977.pdf.

50. Christi Parsons, *Obama: "Zero Tolerance" for Leaking Classified Information*, L.A. Times, Jun. 8, 2012, http://articles.latimes.com/2012/jun/08/news/la-pn-obama-news-conference-leaks -20120608.

51. Press Release, Obama for America, The Change We Need in Washington 7 (Sept. 22, 2008), http://www.govexec.com/pdfs/092208ts1.pdf.

52. *See* Lilly Maier, *Better Protection for Most, but Not the Intelligence Community*, Politifact .com, Nov. 21, 2013, http://www.politifact.com/truth-o-meter/promises/obameter/promise/426/increase -protections-for-whistleblowers/.

53. Pub. L. No. 112-199, 126 Stat. 1465 (2012).

54. *See* Presidential Policy Directive 19, Protecting Whistleblowers with Access to Classified Information (Oct. 10, 2012), https://www.fas.org/irp/offdocs/ppd/ppd-19.pdf.

55. *See* Kevin Goztola, *Snowden Becomes Eighth Person to Be Charged with Violating the Espionage Act under Obama*, Firedoglake (Jun. 21, 2013, 8:26 p.m.), http://dissenter.firedoglake .com/2013/06/21/snowden-becomes-eighth-person-to-be-indicted-for-espionage-by-the-obama -justice-department/.

56. Charlie Savage, *Manning Found Not Guilty of Aiding the Enemy*, N.Y. Times, Jul. 31, 2013, at A1, http://www.nytimes.com/2013/07/31/us/bradley-manning-verdict.html?_r=0.

57. *See* Exec. Order 13,587, 76 Fed. Reg. 63,811 (Oct. 7, 2011), http://www.gpo.gov/fdsys/pkg /FR-2011-10-13/pdf/2011-26729.pdf; Press Release, Office of the Press Sec'y, Presidential Memorandum—National Insider Threat Policy and Minimum Standards for Executive Branch Insider Threat Programs (Nov. 21, 2012), http://www.whitehouse.gov/the-press-office/2012/11/21 /presidential-memorandum-national-insider-threat-policy-and-minimum-stand#storylink=relast.

58. *See* Marisa Taylor & Jonathan S. Landay, *Obama's Crackdown Views Leaks as Aiding Enemies of U.S.*, McClatchy, Jun. 20, 2013, http://www.mcclatchydc.com/2013/06/20/194513/obamas -crackdown-views-leaks-as.html.

59. *See* Intelligence Community Directive 119: Media Contacts, Mar. 20, 2014.

60. *See* Free Flow of Information Act of 2013, S. 987, 113th Cong. (2013), https://www.govtrack .us/congress/bills/113/s987/text.

61. *See* Zeke J. Miller, *Five Changes to Justice Department Guidelines Designed to Protect Reporters*, Time, July 12, 2013, http://swampland.time.com/2013/07/12/five-changes-to-justice -department-guidelines-designed-to-protect-reporters/.

62. *See* 18 U.S.C. §§ 792–799 (2012) (codifying the Espionage Act of 1917); *id.* § 1030 (dealing with computer espionage); 50 U.S.C. § 783 (2012) (prohibiting individuals from sharing a classified document to a foreign government or its agent).

63. *See* S. 315, 112th Cong. (2011), http://www.gpo.gov/fdsys/pkg/BILLS-112s315is/pdf/BILLS -112s315is.pdf; H.R. 6506, 111th Cong. (2010), http://www.gpo.gov/fdsys/pkg/BILLS-111hr6506ih /pdf/BILLS-111hr6506ih.pdf.

64. *See generally The Espionage Statutes: A Look Back and a Look Forward: Hearing before the Subcomm. on Terrorism and Homeland Security of the S. Comm. on the Judiciary*, 111th Cong. (2010) (discussing the scope of the Espionage Act and other espionage laws).

65. *See Espionage Act and the Legal and Constitutional Issues Raised by WikiLeaks: Hearing before the H. Comm. on the Judiciary*, 111th Cong. 3–4 (2010) (statement of Louis B. Gohmert, Jr., Ranking Member, H. Comm. on the Judiciary).

66. *See* Sari Horwitz, *Julian Assange Unlikely to Face U.S. Charges over Publishing Classified Documents*, WASH. POST, Nov. 25, 2013, http://www.washingtonpost.com/world/national-security /julian-assange-unlikely-to-face-us-charges-over-publishing-classified-documents/2013/11/25 /dd27decc-55f1-11e3-8304-caf30787c0a9_story.html.

67. *See, e.g.*, Benjamin Wittes, *Espionage Act Amendments*, LAWFARE (Dec. 6, 2010, 11:40 a.m.), http://www.lawfareblog.com/2010/12/espionage-act-amendments/.

68. *See* S. 719, 112th Cong. § 403 (2011), http://www.gpo.gov/fdsys/pkg/BILLS-112s719pcs/pdf /BILLS-112s719pcs.pdf.

69. *See* S. REP. NO. 112-12, at 10–12 (2011) (Conf. Rep.) (Minority Views of Sen. Wyden), http://www.intelligence.senate.gov/pdfs112th/11212.pdf.

70. *See* 158 CONG. REC. S6793, 6794 (daily ed. Nov. 14, 2012) (statement of Sen. Ronald L. Wyden), http://www.gpo.gov/fdsys/pkg/CREC-2012-11-14/pdf/CREC-2012-11-14-pt1-PgS6793-3.pdf.

71. *See* S. 3454, 112th Cong. §§ 501–512 (2012) (as reported by S. Select Comm. on Intelligence, Jul. 26, 2012), http://www.fas.org/irp/congress/2012_cr/ssci-leaks.pdf.

72. *See* 158 CONG. REC. at 6794.

73. *Id.*

74. *See* Intelligence Authorization Act for Fiscal Year 2013, Pub. L. No. 112-277, 125 Stat. 2468; Josh Gerstein, *Senate Panel Nixes Anti-Leak Measures*, POLITICO (Dec. 22, 2012, 10:24 a.m.), http:// www.politico.com/blogs/under-the-radar/2012/12/senate-panel-nixes-antileak-measures-152684 .html.

75. *See* S. 1681, 113th Cong. §§ 501–505, 601–604 (2013), https://www.govtrack.us/congress /bills/113/s1681/text.

RESOURCES

The Willard Report: http://www.fas.org/sgp/library/willard.pdf.

The Ashcroft Report: http://www.fas.org/sgp/othergov/dojleaks.pdf.

Veto Message from the President of the United States, 146 CONG. REC. 26,022 (2000), http://www.gpo.gov/fdsys/pkg/CRECB-2000-pt18/pdf/CRECB-2000 -pt18-Pg26022-3.pdf.

Eric E. Ballou & Kyle E. McSlarrow, Note, *Plugging the Leak: The Case for a Legislative Resolution of the Conflict between the Demands of Secrecy and the Need for Open Government*, 71 VA. L. REV. 801 (1985).

James B. Bruce, *The Consequences of Permissive Neglect: Laws and Leaks of Classified Intelligence, in* INSIDE CIA: LESSONS IN INTELLIGENCE (Sharad S. Chauhan ed., 2004).

LEONARD DOWNIE JR., COMM. TO PROTECT JOURNALISTS, THE OBAMA ADMINISTRATION AND THE PRESS: LEAK INVESTIGATIONS AND SURVEILLANCE IN POST-9/11 AMERICA 6 (2013), http://cpj.org/reports/us2013-english.pdf.

Harold Edgar & Benno C. Schmidt, *The Espionage Statutes and the Publication of Defense Information*, 73 COLUM. L. REV. 929 (1973).

JENNIFER K. ELSEA, CONG. RESEARCH SERV., PROTECTION OF NATIONAL SECURITY INFORMATION (2006), http://www.fas.org/sgp/crs/secrecy/RL33502.pdf.

David Pozen, *The Leaky Leviathan: Why the Government Condemns and Condones Unlawful Disclosures of Information*, 127 HARV. L. REV. 512 (2013).

Part II

The Constitution and Other Applicable Laws

First Amendment Considerations on National Security Issues: From Zenger to Snowden

5

Gene Policinski

A free press is where Americans turn to find the inside details of what happened yesterday, the unfettered, breaking news of what is happening now, and the best information available about what's likely to happen tomorrow—be that the weather, politics and policy, financial information, or our national security.

The nation's founders believed an unrestrained press to be one of the basic freedoms needed for a new, democratic society—protected and preserved by a Bill of Rights that included a First Amendment rooted in the idea that government cannot legally control the free flow of information to its citizens.

Many scholars trace the first expressions of the concept of a free press to John Milton's *Aeropagitica* tract, written in 1644, which attempted to persuade the English Parliament to repeal a licensing law enacted a year earlier. Milton argued that the benefits of a vigorous public debate far outweighed the dangers to society of unregulated public discourse.[1]

In the American provision for a free press, Milton's concept was expressed by others as the "marketplace of ideas" in which the truth would naturally assert itself over untruth if facts and opinion were not censored or otherwise limited by authority.

Yet that conception of a free press sometimes conflicts with the goal of national security. Two years before the Bill of Rights was ratified in 1791, Congress and the people approved the Constitution with a federal government that had responsibility for the "common defense." Some argue now as then that protecting our national security is the primary role of the federal government.

When it comes to reconciling the First Amendment's protection of a free press with the necessity to keep secrets in the name of national security, the legal and political issues raised today are much as they have been throughout the nation's history: unsettled and, at times, unsettling.

President Barack Obama—speaking in May 2013 in response to two controversial moves to gain information from journalists about national security "leaks"—defined the core conflicts and challenges:

> As Commander-in-chief, I believe we must keep information secret that protects our operations and our people in the field. To do so, we must enforce consequences for those who break the law and breach their commitment to protect classified information.
>
> But a free press is also essential for our democracy. That's who we are, and I'm troubled by the possibility that leak investigations may chill the investigative journalism that holds government accountable. Journalists should not be at legal risk for doing their jobs. Our focus must be on those who break the law.[2]

The time-honored common law precept is that "the public has a right to every man's evidence," except for those persons protected by a constitutional, common law, or statutory privilege.[3]

Recent events make quite evident the tension between national security and free press that the president spoke of. In 2010, the Department of Justice, in seeking a warrant, described Fox News Washington correspondent James Rosen as an "aider, abettor and/or co-conspirator" in the leak of classified information from a State Department source about a pending North Korean missile launch.[4]

And Justice Department officials in 2012 seized two months of telephone records from the Associated Press (AP) offices and some employees' personal lines, in what AP President Gary Pruitt called a "massive and unprecedented intrusion" into newsgathering activities.[5]

Such conflicts echo issues faced by the writers of the Constitution. This chapter addresses three main questions with regard to a free press and unauthorized national security disclosures:

1. Will the government ever charge a reporter under the Espionage Act of 1917 with endangering national security for disclosing classified information?
2. Why does leaking secret national security information to a reporter trigger a "free press" defense when providing that same information to the agent of a foreign power would likely justify a charge of treason?
3. Where does a proposed national "shield law" stand—and will it settle the issue of protection of confidential sources for prosecutors, courts and journalists?

I. SETTING THE STAGE: A BIT OF HISTORY

Supreme Court Justice Potter Stewart's observations while speaking in 1974 at Yale Law School set out the circumstances today as well as any can: "So far as the Constitution goes . . . [t]he press is free to do battle against secrecy and deception in government. But the press cannot expect from the Constitution any guarantee that it will succeed. There is no constitutional right to have access to particular government information, or to require openness from the bureaucracy. . . . The Constitution, in other words, establishes the contest, not its resolution."[6]

To properly parse the state of the law surrounding the free press versus national security debate—and the passion on all sides of the issue—one must consider that the conflict dates to colonial days, and has been an evolutionary process. As noted by Justice Clarence Thomas, in concurring with the majority in 1995 in *McIntyre v. Ohio Elections Commission*:

> The earliest and most famous American experience with freedom of the press, the 1735 Zenger trial, centered on anonymous political pamphlets. . . . Although the case set the Colonies afire for its example of a jury refusing to convict a defendant of seditious libel against Crown authorities, it also signified at an early moment the extent to which anonymity and the freedom of the press were intertwined in the early American mind.[7]

Thomas's opinion and other scholars cite additional early examples of the concern among the nation's Founders about the connection between anonymity and a free press. These include an example from 1779 in which the Continental Congress attempted to discover the identity of a writer and critic identified only as "Leonidas."[8] After warnings the effort would intrude on press liberty, delegates were reported to have "sat mute" on a motion to haul a suspect and his printer before Congress.[9]

In 1791, the states ratified the Bill of Rights—the first ten amendments to the new U.S. Constitution—led off by the First Amendment. But just seven years later, Congress enacted the Sedition Act, providing for the prosecution and jailing of editors critical of the president, House, or Senate.[10] Under the Act, there were 25 arrests, 15 indictments, and ten convictions.[11]

From the time the Sedition Act was allowed to expire on March 3, 1801, through the start of U.S. involvement in World War I, there was virtually no direct federal legislation dealing with seditious expression, nor legal prohibitions on publishing information harmful to the nation's national defense interests.[12]

But that doesn't mean there was no collision between a rapidly growing press and the increased activity and national presence of a growing federal government. "The focus of American journalism . . . began to center on the new capital, Washington D.C., in 1810 [and on] objective reports of congressional debates and other governmental events to the public's attention. . . . Newspapers, which could now be produced rapidly and more cheaply, were becoming the catalyst to social change by bringing information on many national issues to the masses."[13]

In 1812, an editor for *The Alexandria Herald* refused to identify the sources of a news story and was cited for contempt.[14] Further, in 1848, the "first reported case in American courts in which a journalist sought to shield the identity of his source" occurred when a federal judge ruled that the courts had no power to intervene when a correspondent for the *New York Herald*, John Nugent, refused to reveal the source of a copy of a draft of a treaty ending the Mexican-American War.[15] Nugent later was jailed for contempt of the Senate when he would say only that the information had not come from a senator or staffer.[16]

During the Civil War, President Abraham Lincoln essentially ignored legal conflicts over identifying sources of confidential information about or reports critical of Union motives or military actions: He simply jailed some editors and publishers and threatened prosecution of others in the North who vigorously opposed the Union side.[17]

First Amendment law regarding speech and the press came into sharp collision with national security as a result of World War I and rising concern over socialism and communism. Congress and the Supreme Court began to set out the mix of policy and law against which today's conflict between the news media and national security concerns plays out.

- The Espionage Act of 1917 was upheld in *Schenck v. United States*, 249 U.S. 47 (1919), where Justice Oliver Wendell Holmes created the "clear and present danger" concept. "The most stringent protection of free speech would not protect a man in falsely shouting fire in a theatre and causing a panic." Likening that example to the situation facing a nation at war, Holmes said, "The question in every case is whether the words are used in such circumstances and are of such a nature as to create a clear and present danger that they will bring about the substantive evils that Congress has a right to prevent." *Advantage: government.*
- In *Near v. Minnesota*, 283 U.S. 697 (1931), the Supreme Court set out a definition of freedom of the press and prohibited the government from restraining a publication prior to distribution without a showing of a "clear and present danger" to society. *Advantage: free press.*
- In *New York Times Co. v. Sullivan*, 376 U.S. 254 (1964), while setting a new libel standard of "actual malice," the Supreme Court repudiated the idea that mere criticism of government—the target of the Sedition Act almost two centuries earlier—was sufficient to justify criminal charges. Justice William Brennan wrote, "The maintenance of the opportunity for free political discussion to the end that government may be responsive to the will of the people and that changes may be obtained by lawful means, an opportunity essential to the security of the Republic, is a fundamental

principle of our constitutional system. . . . Although the Sedition Act was never tested in this Court, the attack upon its validity has carried the day in the court of history." *Advantage: free press.*

- The Pentagon Papers case (*New York Times Co. v. United States*, 403 U.S. 713 (1971), involving a confidential report of how the United States became involved in and conducted the Vietnam War, was another victory over prior restraint. The court said the government had failed to show the necessary degree of danger to national security—"direct, immediate and irreparable to the nation or its people"—relying in part on the view expressed in *Near*.

  However, Justice Byron White noted in a dissent that news media might be held criminally liable after publication for disclosure of sensitive national secrets. *Advantage: In national security matters, a tie.* Except in the most extraordinary circumstances, publication cannot be prevented—but prosecution and punishment face a lower hurdle to overcome.

- One year after the news media euphoria over the Pentagon Papers ruling, the press was on the losing side in the seminal Supreme Court decision on journalist's privilege, the right—either statutory or constitutional—of reporters to protection from being forced to reveal information about or the identity of a confidential source. The consolidated cases were known as *Branzburg v. Hayes*, 408 U.S. 655 (1972).

  Justice White wrote there was no constitutional right for journalists testifying in federal court to refuse to identify confidential sources. He said journalists were asking the court to set out "a testimonial privilege that other citizens did not have; and that while not being able to protect a source's identity might crimp the news gathering process, "from the beginning of the country the press has operated without constitutional protection for press informants, and the press has flourished." *Advantage: Clearly government, but the press gets a foothold on "privilege."*

Branzburg—in the manner of decisions that characterize national security and press issues—need not be considered an absolute defeat for the press. In a dissent, Justice Potter Stewart set out the now widely accepted proposition that in seeking a subpoena compelling a journalist to testify, the government must "convincingly show a substantial relation between the information sought and a subject of overriding and compelling state interest."[18]

Still, the letter of the law—not motive—governed 16 years later. In *United States v. Morison*, Samuel L. Morison, a staffer at the Naval Intelligence Support Center and part-time writer for *Jane's Defence Weekly*, was convicted under the Espionage Act of providing *Jane's* with a classified photo of a Soviet aircraft carrier.[19] The conviction noted he had given the classified information to "one not entitled to receive it" and that *Jane's* was "not entitled" to get the photos. But *Jane's*, a highly respected publication on the military, never faced charges.[20]

Morison's defense presented the claim that he had not engaged "in classic spying and espionage activity" by persons who, in the course of that activity, had transmitted "national security secrets to agents of foreign governments with intent to injure the United States"—and therefore should not be convicted under the Espionage Act.

The Fourth Circuit Court of Appeals, however, disagreed that the Espionage Act, in total, was limited to "classic spying" and upheld Morison's conviction. But in a discussion about First Amendment concerns, the decision noted:

> The First Amendment interest in informed popular debate does not simply vanish at the invocation of the words "national security." . . .
>
> Public security can . . . be compromised in two ways: by attempts to choke off the information needed for democracy to function, and by leaks that imperil the environment of physical security which a functioning democracy requires. The tension between these two interests is not going to abate, and the question is how a responsible balance may be achieved. . . .
>
> . . . Where matters of exquisite sensitivity are in question, we cannot invariably install, as the ultimate arbiter of disclosure, even the conscience of the well-meaning employee.[21]

In *Morison*, the government got a conviction and the press got support in dicta for its protection of the nation. But the big losers were government officials and whistleblowers who, like National Security Agency (NSA) analyst-turned-leaker Edward Snowden, would hope to use public benefit to defend against criminal charges stemming from leaking secret documents to the press. In 2001, the Supreme Court said in *Bartnicki v. Vopper*[22] that it was unconstitutional to convict journalists for publishing information they were given, even if the source gathered it illegally—as long as the journalists were not involved in that act. But that case involved an intercepted cell phone conversation, not classified information and national security, where courts may see things differently.

II. YES, NO, OR MAYBE: PURSUING AND PROSECUTING JOURNALISTS FOR NATIONAL SECURITY LEAKS

Including charges filed against Snowden in June 2013, the Obama administration has filed charges in eight cases under the Espionage Act. Only three cases resulting in indictments had been filed in all the years before Obama took office, all against government officials or employees for leaks—not the news media reporters they communicated with.[23]

Thus, to date, in American history, no journalist ever has been prosecuted under the Espionage Act of 1917,[24] the basis for a variety of statutes and regulations intended to prevent and punish the unauthorized communication of national security information.[25]

But "not yet" is not "never will."

A brush with criminalizing a journalist's work in obtaining confidential material on matters of national security was revealed last year, in the details of a 2011 Federal Bureau of Investigation (FBI) warrant request regarding Fox News' Rosen, sparking outcry from First Amendment advocates and news media leaders.

Officials successfully obtained a warrant to collect copies of Rosen's e-mails and phone records, in part by noting that "from the beginning of their relationship, the Reporter [Rosen] asked, solicited and encouraged" State Department contractor Stephen Jin-Woo Kim "to disclose sensitive United States internal documents and intelligence information."[26]

The seizure from a third party of bulk telephone records involving AP kicked up an even bigger fuss. The news agency reported that the Justice Department secretly obtained two months of personal and work telephone records for several reporters and editors, as well as general AP office numbers in New York, Washington, and Hartford, Connecticut, and for the main number for the AP in the House of Representatives press gallery.[27]

A bit of 21st-century spice also has been added to the treason versus journalism mix: Traditional news media now are joined by decidedly untraditional blogs, social media, and an instant, global audience. The government has the ultimate power in this perpetual face-off, from subpoena power to prosecutorial initiatives that include fines, loss of jobs and pension benefits, imprisonment for government "leakers," and the aforementioned Espionage Act.

With the executive and legislative branches armed with the statutory government "sword," it was the judiciary that removed the premise of a common law "shield" for journalists at the federal level. In 1972, the Supreme Court denied a journalist "privilege" to avoid compulsory grand jury testimony, in *Branzburg*, mentioned above.

The court found that reporters had no more right than any other citizen, that is, none, to refuse to disclose confidential information to grand jurors or government authorities.

The Supreme Court could have brought more resolution to the issue by choosing to hear arguments in an appeal by *New York Times* reporter James Risen, who has been fighting since 2008 the government's efforts to force him to name a confidential source. But it did not.

In 2010, CIA officer Jeffrey Sterling was charged with leaking information about the spy agency's efforts against Iran's nuclear program. In the most prominent battle over national security disclosures and journalists' privilege, Risen was ordered in May 2011 to testify at Sterling's trial. Prosecutors believe that Sterling provided classified information to Risen for Risen's 2006 book *State of War*.[28]

Risen had been fighting the subpoena with some limited success, but in July 2013, the Fourth Circuit Court of Appeals declared that no reporter's privilege exists that could allow him not to testify. The language used in the appellate decision echoed the government's position:

> Risen is the only eyewitness to the crime. He is inextricably involved in it. Without him, the alleged crime would not have occurred, since he was the recipient of illegally-disclosed, classified information. And it was through the publication of his book, *State of War*, that the classified information made its way into the public domain. He is the only witness who can specify the classified information that he received, and the source or sources from whom he received it.[29]

In January, Risen asked the Supreme Court to hear his appeal. In a supporting petition filed March 26, 2014, a group of major news operations noted, circuit by circuit, the multiple divisions at the federal appellate court level over whether a privilege for journalists exists at all in law, and whether it should apply to both civil and criminal cases.

The petition said that "the lack of uniformity across the federal courts—in and of itself—has an inhibiting effect on the gathering and reporting of news about matters of public concern precisely because neither sources nor reporters and editors can safely predict what law will apply in a manner that allows them to make informed decisions about what legal protection, if any, will be available to them."[30]

The groups argued that, "Simply put, whether rooted in the First Amendment or in the common law, our national commitment to a free press and to the democratic values it serves dictates that those interests must, at a minimum, be weighed in every case. Because the Fourth Circuit determined that *Branzburg* precluded it from undertaking any such balancing, under either the First Amendment or at common law, its decision is inconsistent with our historical conception of freedom of the press."[31]

Notwithstanding these arguments, in June 2014 the Supreme Court declined to review Risen's case, without explanation, leaving the Fourth Circuit decision undisturbed.

The Risen case, against the backdrop of WikiLeaks "data dumps," the conviction of Manning, and ongoing Snowden disclosures, could have served as the "right case at the right time" for the court to define the next big issue: treason or journalism.

In the most recent examples of the potential risk for journalists involved in the disclosure of national security data, White House and congressional officials are raising the idea that reporters are "selling" access to NSA documents leaked by Snowden, and they could risk facing criminal charges as "accomplices" or "fences."

In late January 2014, Director of National Intelligence James Clapper told the Senate Select Committee on Intelligence that "Snowden and his accomplices"—journalists who have published articles based on documents he provided—should return the remaining materials to avoid the "profound damage that his disclosures have caused and continued to cause."[32]

And, on February 4, 2014, FBI Director James Comey, responding to a question from Representative Mike Rogers of Michigan, chairman of the House Permanent Select Committee on Intelligence, said, "It's an issue that can be complicated if it involves newsgathering, a news promulgation function, but in general, fencing or selling stolen property is a crime."[33]

Another exchange: (Rogers) "If I'm a newspaper reporter for, fill-in-the-blank, and I sell stolen material, is that legal because I'm a newspaper reporter?" (Comey) "If you're a newspaper reporter and you're hocking stolen jewelry, it's still a crime."[34]

But the government has cited the purported $1 million-plus value of Risen's book, and freelance writing contracts by former *Guardian* newspaper reporter Glenn Greenwald, whose articles are at the heart of the Snowden disclosures, as showing a sale for personal gain of the access to classified material.

"For personal gain, he's now selling his access to information. . . . A thief selling stolen material is a thief," Rogers said prior to the hearing.[35]

Journalism advocates responded by saying that while sale of secret documents without any news purpose would not raise First Amendment defenses, publishing stories based on Snowden-like "leaks" is in the public interest, and that Clapper and Rogers were attempting to intimidate journalists from working with government whistleblowers and sources.

III.   WHY IS IT "JOURNALISM" IN THIS CASE, "TREASON" IN THAT ONE?

While not directly implicating journalists, the concept that a successful prosecution under the Espionage Act of nongovernment persons turns on the issue of harm to the United States was a significant factor in the failed prosecution in 2005 of two lobbyists for the American Israel Public Affairs Committee.

The case is the sole prosecution by the government under the Espionage Act of a person other than the individual, that is, the government employee, responsible for taking or leaking classified information.

Steven J. Rosen and Keith Weissman were charged under the Act with disclosing confidential information to colleagues, journalists, and Israeli officials, information which had been obtained from high-ranking U.S. officials. U.S. District Judge T. S. Ellis III, later upheld by a federal appeals court, said that prosecutors could prove their case only if they introduced evidence that Rosen and Weissman knew that relaying the information to others would harm U.S. national security.[36]

Such a legal posture brings us to the concept that the press—if not warranting a distinct class for legal purposes—carries a unique constitutional role worthy of legal recognition because of its role in how our nation governs itself.

In 1980, in a concurring opinion in *Richmond Newspapers, Inc. v. Virginia*, Justice William Brennan set out a strong defense of the role of a free press as more than just being a conduit for information: "The First Amendment embodies more than a commitment to free expression and communicative interchange for their own sakes; it has a *structural* role to play in securing and fostering our republican system of self-government."[37]

Still government officials press the concept—if not the actual practice—of prosecuting journalists in connection with national security leaks.

On May 21, 2006, on ABC's *This Week* news program, Attorney General Alberto R. Gonzales raised the possibility that journalists (he was likely alluding to *New York Times* journalists Risen and Eric Lichtbau) could be prosecuted for publishing classified information about the NSA's surveillance of terrorist-related calls between the United States and abroad:

> There are some statutes on the book which, if you read the language carefully, would seem to indicate that that is a possibility. . . . I understand very much the role that the press plays in our society, the protection under the First Amendment we want to promote and respect. . . . [B]ut it can't be the case that that right trumps over the right that Americans would like to see, the ability of the federal government to go after criminal activity.[38]

Matthew W. Friedrich, principal Deputy Assistant Attorney General, in testimony before the Senate Judiciary Committee about Gonzales's remarks, said Gonzales was referring to the 1917 Espionage Act. Friedrich also noted that "several statutes prohibit the unauthorized disclosure of certain categories of classified information, the broadest of which is Section 793 of Title 18, which prohibits the disclosure of information 'relating to national defense.' Also, Section 798 of Title 18 prohibits the unauthorized disclosure of information relating to communications intelligence activities."[39] But in 1973, just two years after the Pentagon Papers case, law professors Harold Edgar and Benno C. Schmidt Jr. argued that Congress only intended the Espionage Act to punish those who had intent to injure the United States.[40]

Similarly, Seventh Circuit Court of Appeals Judge Richard A. Posner argued in his 2006 book *Not a Suicide Pact* that because the Espionage Act of 1917 requires that an individual have reason to believe information being passed on could be used to injure the United States or advantage a foreign nation, it could not be used to punish the press for disseminating classified information. In addition, Posner concluded that no other statutes explicitly authorize punishing journalists.[41]

There are those who see potential vulnerability for the press to be prosecuted for merely "possessing" national security documents or data provided by a "leaker," sliding neatly around the intent question raised by publication, that is, communication of the documents or data.

Derigan A. Silver, assistant professor in the Department of Mass Communications and Journalism Studies at the University of Denver, examined the law around "possession" of such leaked information in a 2008 report, *National Security and the Press*.[42] The report concluded that until Congress amended existing law, "there are some statutes that can be read to allow for the prosecution of journalists for possessing or publishing national security information."[43] Silver's final lines note that "while no mainstream journalist has yet been prosecuted under any of the statutes identified by this research, there remains a chill in the air."[44]

IV.   THE FREE FLOW OF INFORMATION ACT: A SHIELD FOR SOME, NOT FOR ALL?

Forty states and the District of Columbia provide journalists with a "reporter's privilege," protecting them if a state government seeks to compel the disclosure of confidential information, including the identity of a source. Nine other states provide the protection through case law.[45]

But state courts and journalists reporting on state-level issues rarely, if ever, deal in matters of national security—and therein is the difference and barrier between the evolution of shield laws in the states and a federal version.

According to a history assembled by the Reporters Committee for Freedom of the Press, the push for federal protection against forced disclosure of confidential sources began within months of the *Branzburg* decision, in 1972. Half a dozen bills were introduced in Congress, none successful. The American Bar Association, in 1974, voted against enactment of any form of shield law for journalists, saying the news media was attempting to put itself "above the law."

Regular attempts to gain congressional approval of a shield law through the 1980s fell short, in part because of a lack of a news media consensus around who would be covered and concerns that any law effectively would permit the government to determine who is a journalist—questions that persist today.

In renewed pushes since 2004 for a shield law, advocates have gotten close to passage. In 2010, the House passed a proposal that was ready for a final vote in the Senate when WikiLeaks made headlines in disclosing confidential information about the U.S. government and military action in Iraq and Afghanistan—and the measure stalled.

In 2014, Congress could act on Senate Bill 987, the latest iteration of the Free Flow of Information Act.[46]

The proposal would provide the first federal shield law, still the subject of intense debate in legal and journalistic circles. The bill does not attempt to specifically define who is a journalist by allowing judges to apply the protection to any person who, in the interest of justice, should be considered a practicing journalist.

Earlier versions of the bill drew criticism from journalism and First Amendment advocates because it provided protection only for those who regularly reported news or who could show a certain level of income from journalism or who could show evidence of having worked for or being employed by news operations. Critics said such definitional language would exclude bloggers, students, freelancers, and the self-published—all of whom have increased presence and reach in the digital era.

In a September 2013 panel discussion at the Newseum, organized by the John S. and James L. Knight Foundation, the Newseum Institute, and the Robert R. McCormick Foundation, concerns were raised that the proposed law provided little to no protection for sources or journalists in national security matters. Scott Armstrong, director of a government accountability project called the Information Trust,[47] warned against defining a journalist and establishing national security exemptions because it could be "beginning to paint ourselves into a corner."[48]

Armstrong, a veteran investigative journalist, told the group that national security reporters opposed the proposed shield law "because it won't protect us. We're going to get exempted out of it one way or another."

Another complication today is that views of the "press" as a monolithic institution are in conflict with a variety of new groups, often based online, that assert a free-press identity while also espousing opposition—if not anarchistic—intentions toward the operation of organized governments.

The question of whether WikiLeaks and others who claim journalist credentials would be protected by a federal shield law divides traditional news media.

The Washington Post's editorial board said "no" in mid-2013 to WikiLeaks as journalism:

As a newspaper, The Post thrives on revelatory journalism and often benefits from leaks, sometimes inspired by dissent and other times by spin. . . . WikiLeaks . . . differs from journalism in methods if not goals. The Post and many others in print and broadcast journalism sift and check information and take care not to reveal sources and methods or to endanger lives in bringing secrets to light. WikiLeaks . . . spilled classified government data into the open, in some cases endangering individuals who were identified in diplomatic cables.[49]

But James Goodale, who was general counsel for *The New York Times* during the Pentagon Papers case and the architect of the paper's legal defense, argues that WikiLeaks and founder Julian Assange can claim the journalist's mantle. In a May 17, 2013, luncheon at the offices of the Committee to Protect Journalists, Goodale noted disclosures of classified information from Manning and said, "If you're angry at Assange for publishing the information, you should be mad at *The New York Times*, too. Assange is [reporter] Neil Sheehan and *The New York Times*" in the Pentagon Papers case. He added, "Assange is the publisher so there shouldn't be any question we are dealing with a First Amendment issue. If we don't recognize that in the digital age, we are in a lot of trouble."[50]

National intelligence expert Gary Ross, in his 2011 book *Who Watches the Watchmen*, may well have set out the best course for both press and prosecutors, one that the Obama administration would seem to be test-driving with vigor: Absent true danger to the nation, Ross recommends keeping the focus on the leaker—and, to a very high degree, on the potential leaker—as the most effective means of preventing and punishing illegal disclosure of classified information: loss of employment, security clearances, and pensions combined with an internal system of early detection (including staffers spying on each other).[51]

Not all agree with taking the prosecutorial bull's-eye off journalists.

"Every day in newspapers across country there is classified information being reported," Kenneth L. Wainstein, former assistant attorney general for national security and homeland security advisor, said at a "Sources and Secrets" conference presented in conjunction with the George Polk Awards and hosted by *The New York Times*, in March 2014. "That is against the Espionage Act and could be prosecuted. The DOJ doesn't do that. It goes after cases that are particularly egregious."

"The reason there weren't subpoenas of journalists for fifty or sixty years after the Espionage Act [of 1917] is because the press had a cozier relationship with the government, and they didn't report things," Robert Litt, general counsel for the Office of the Director of National Intelligence, told the same conference. "That changed with Vietnam and Watergate, and the press institutionalized a more adversarial approach. I happen to think that's a good thing, but it goes two ways. It's the job of the press to find out things government doesn't want it to. It's the job of the government to stop the press from finding out those things."[52]

In the latest salvo in the Obama administration's war on leaks, a March 2014 directive from James Clapper, director of national intelligence, barred officials at 17 agencies from speaking to journalists about unclassified intelligence-related topics without permission, and required employees to report any unplanned contact with journalists.[53] And, in April, the director barred the agency's current and former personnel from citing a source "that comes from known leaks, or unauthorized disclosures of sensitive information" to avoid the appearance of validating the leaked information.[54]

Ultimately, Americans will need to ask themselves how far in the direction of press protection or vigorous prosecution they want the government to go in national security matters. The country may decide—as has been the case for more than two centuries—that "unsettled" is just fine, to be adjusted as circumstances require.

In 1971, U.S. District Judge Murray I. Gurfein, in an early Pentagon Papers ruling that ultimately was upheld, spoke to that indeterminate value: "The security of the Nation is not at the ramparts alone. Security also lies in the value of our free institutions. A cantankerous press, an obstinate press, an ubiquitous press must be suffered by those in authority in order to preserve the even greater values of freedom of expression and the right of the people to know."[55]

NOTES

1. JOHN MILTON, AEROPAGITICA: A SPEECH FOR THE LIBERTY OF UNLICENSED PRINTING TO THE PARLIAMENT OF ENGLAND, Project Gutenberg E-Book, http://www.gutenberg.org/files/608/608-h /608-h.htm.

2. President Barack Obama, Remarks at the National Defense University (May 23, 2013), http:// www.whitehouse.gov/the-press-office/2013/05/23/remarks-president-national-defense-university.

3. United States v. Nixon, 418 U.S. 683, 709 (1974) (citing United States v. Bryan, 339 U.S. 323, 331 (1949)).

4. *DOJ Targets Fox News*, FOXNEWS.COM, May 20, 2013, http://nation.foxnews.com/james-rosen /2013/05/20/report-doj-investigated-fox-news-reporter-2009-leak-probe.

5. Charlie Savage & Leslie Kaufman, *Phone Records of Journalists Seized by U.S.*, N.Y. TIMES, May 13, 2013, http://www.nytimes.com/2013/05/14/us/phone-records-of-journalists-of-the-associated -press-seized-by-us.html.

6. Potter Stewart, *Or of the Press*, 26 HASTINGS L.J. 631 (1975).

7. McIntyre v. Ohio Elections Comm'n, 514 U.S. 334, 361–62 (1995).

8. Leonidas, who actually was Dr. Benjamin Rush, had attacked the members of Congress for causing inflation throughout the states and for engaging in embezzlement and fraud. *See* 13 LETTERS OF DELEGATES TO CONGRESS 1774–1789, at 141 n.1 (G. Gawalt & R. Gephart eds., 1986).

9. "Elbridge Gerry, a delegate from Massachusetts, moved to bring Rush and the Packet's printer before Congress. Virginia delegate Meriwether Smith opposed the motion, noting that "[w]hen the liberty of the Press shall be restrained . . . the liberties of the People will be at an end." Henry Laurens, *Notes of Debates*, July 3, 1779, in *id.*, at 139–41.

10. The Sedition Act, July 6, 1798; Fifth Congress; Enrolled Acts and Resolutions; General Records of the United States Government; Record Group 11; National Archives.

11. ENCYCLOPEDIA OF THE FIRST AMENDMENT, 976. (John R. Vile, David L. Hudson Jr. & David Schultz eds., 2009).

12. Stephen J.I. Vladeck, *Inchoate Liability and the Espionage Act: The Statutory Framework and Freedom of the Press*, 1 HARV. L. & POL'Y REV. 221 (2007).

13. Ill. First Amendment Ctr., First Amendment Research Information, http://www.illinoisfirst amendmentcenter.com/freedom_press_history.php.

14. Media Law Res. Ctr. Inst., The Reporter's Privilege: A Historical Overview, http://www.gsspa.org /conferences/fall/10051964_1%20-%20Historical%20Overiview%20of%20the%20Reporter_s%20 Privilege.PDF.

15. *Id.*

16. *Ex parte* Nugent, 18 F. Cas. 471 (C.C.D.C. 1848).

17. Constitutional Rights Found., Lincoln and the Writ of Liberty (2014), http://www.crf-usa.org /america-responds-to-terrorism/lincoln-and-the-writ-of-liberty.html.

18. David Hudson, Remembering Potter Stewart, FIRST AMENDMENT CTR., Feb. 27, 2012, http:// www.firstamendmentcenter.org/remembering-justice-potter-stewart.

19. 44 F.2d 1057, 1072 (4th Cir. 1988).

20. NATIONAL SECURITY LAW IN THE NEWS (Paul Rosenzweig, Timothy J. McNulty & Ellen Shearer eds., 2012).

21. United States v. Morison, 844 F.2d 1057, 1081–83 (4th Cir. 1988).

22. 532 U.S. 514 (2001).

23. Cora Currier, *Charting Obama's Crackdown on National Security Leaks*, PROPUBLICA, July 30, 2013, http://www.propublica.org/special/sealing-loose-lips-charting-obamas-crackdown-on-national -security-leaks.

24. Ch. 30, tit. I § 3, 40 Stat. 217, 219.

25. Emily Peterson, *WikiLeaks and the Espionage Act of 1917*, REPORTERS COMM. FOR FREEDOM OF THE PRESS (2011), http://www.rcfp.org/browse-media-law-resources/news-media-law/wikileaks -and-espionage-act-1917.

26. *See* Application for Search Warrant, Case No. 1:10-mj-00291-AK (D.D.C. filed Nov. 07, 2011), WASH. POST, May 20, 2013, http://apps.washingtonpost.com/g/page/local/affidavit-for -searchwarrant/162/.

27. Charlie Savage & Leslie Kaufman, *Phone Records of Journalists Seized by U.S.*, N.Y. TIMES, May 13, 2013, http://www.nytimes.com/2013/05/14/us/phone-records-of-journalists-of-the-associated -press-seized-by-us.html.

28. Currier, *supra* note 23.

29. United States v. Sterling, No. 11-5028 (4th Cir. July 19, 2013).

30. Petition for Writ of Certiorari, Risen v. United States, No. 13-1009 (4th Cir. Mar. 26, 2014).

31. *Id.*

32. Spencer Ackerman, *James Clapper Calls for Snowden and "Accomplices" to Return NSA Documents*, GUARDIAN.COM, Jan. 29, 2014, http://www.theguardian.com/world/2014/jan/29/james -clapper-condemns-snowden-senate-testimony.

33. Catherine Herridge, *Criminal Charges Possible if Journalists Sold Access to Snowden Documents*, FOXNEWS.COM, Feb. 5, 2014, http://www.foxnews.com/politics/2014/02/05/criminal-charges-possible -if-journalists-sold-access-to-snowden-documents/.

34. *Id.*

35. Spencer Ackerman, *Senior U.S. Congressman Mike Rogers: Glenn Greenwald is a 'Thief,'* Guardian.com, June 30, 2014, http://www.theguardian.com/world/2014/feb/04/us-congressman -mike-rogers-glenn-greenwald-thief-snowden-nsa.

36. Neil A. Lewis & David Johnston, *U.S. to Drop Spy Case Against Pro-Israel Lobbyists*, N.Y. TIMES, May 1, 2009, http://www.nytimes.com/2009/05/02/us/politics/02aipac.html.

37. Richmond Newspapers, Inc. v. Virginia, 448 U.S. 555, 587–88 (1980).

38. Walter Pincus, *Prosecution of Journalists Possible in NSA Leaks*, WASH. POST, May 22, 2006, at A-4.

39. *See Examining the DOJ's Investigation of Journalists Who Publish Classified Information: Lessons from the Jack Anderson Case: Hearing before the S. Comm. on the Judiciary*, 109th Cong. (2006) (statement of Matthew Friedrich, Principal Deputy Assistant Att'y Gen.).

40. Harold Edgar & Benno C. Schmidt Jr., *The Espionage Statutes and Publication of Defense Information*, 73 COLUM. L. REV. (1973).

41. RICHARD A. POSNER, NOT A SUICIDE PACT: THE CONSTITUTION IN A TIME OF NATIONAL EMERGENCY (2006).

42. Derigan A. Silver, *National Security and the Press: The Government's Ability to Prosecute Journalists for the Possession or Publication of National Security Information*, 13 COMM. L. & POL'Y 447 (2008), https://www.law.upenn.edu/institutes/cerl/conferences/ethicsofsecrecy/papers /reading/Silver.pdf.

43. *Id.* at 483. These statutes include section 641 of Title 18 of the U.S. Code, which punishes the theft of government property; section 793 of the Espionage Act, which prohibits the communication or retention of national defense information; sections 795 and 797 of the Espionage Act, which punish the unauthorized publication of photographs or sketches of vital defense installations; section 798 of the Espionage Act, which punishes the disclosure of classified "communication intelligence"; the Atomic Energy Protection Act, which prevents the disclosure of data concerning atomic weapons; and the Intelligence Identities Protection Act, which protect the identities of covert agents.

44. *Id.* at 483.

45. *Number of States with Shield Law Climbs to 40*, REPORTERS COMM. FOR FREEDOM OF THE PRESS (2014), http://www.rcfp.org/browse-media-law-resources/news-media-law/news-media -law-summer-2011/number-states-shield-law-climbs.

46. Eric Newton, *Paying Attention to Shield Law's Critics*, COLUM. JOURNALISM REV., Sept. 24, 2013, http://cjr.org/behind_the_news/paying_more_attention_to_the_s.php.

47. http://www.informationtrust.org.

48. Wash. Post Editorial Bd., *Don't Charge WikiLeaks*, WASH. POST, Dec. 11, 2010, http://www .washingtonpost.com/wp-dyn/content/article/2010/12/11/AR2010121102564.html.

49. Sara Rafsky, *Goodale: Pentagon Papers Have Lessons for AP Case*, COMM. TO PROTECT JOURNALISTS, May 17, 2003, http://www.cpj.org/blog/2013/05/goodale-pentagon-papers-have-lessons -for-ap-case.php.

50. GARY ROSS, WHO WATCHES THE WATCHMEN: THE CONFLICT BETWEEN NATIONAL SECURITY AND FREEDOM OF THE PRESS (2011).

51. Ben Adler, *Sources and Secrets*, COLUM. JOURNALISM REV., Mar. 21, 2014, http://cjr.org/behind _the_news/sources_and_secrets.php?page-all.

52. *New York Times Company v. United States—The Government Moves to Stop the Leak*, AM. L. & LEGAL INFO. (2014), http://law.jrank.org/pages/23258/New-York-Times-Company-v-United-States -Government-Moves-Stop-Leak/.

53. Charlie Savage, *Intelligence Chief Issues Limits on Press Contacts*, N.Y. TIMES, Apr. 21, 2014, http://www.nytimes.com/2014/04/22/us/politics/intelligence-chief-issues-limits-on-press-contacts.html.

54. Charlie Savage, *Memo Revisits Policy on Citing Leaked Material, to Some Confusion*, N.Y. TIMES, May 9, 2014, http://www.nytimes.com/2014/05/10/us/politics/memo -revisits-policy-on-citing-leaked-material-to-some-confusion.html.

55. United States v. N.Y. Times Co., 328 F. Supp. 324, 331 (S.D.N.Y. 1971).

EXPERTS

Lucy A. Dalglish, Professor and Dean, Philip Merrill College of Journalism, University of Maryland; (301) 405-8806; dalglish@umd.edu.

Lee Levine, Partner, Levine Sullivan Koch & Shultz, LLP, Washington, D.C.; (202) 508-1110; llevine@lskslaw.com.

Gary Ross, author, *Who Watches the Watchmen*; (703) 498-7008; Gary.Ross@ ymail.com.

Gabriel Schoenfeld, Senior Fellow, Hudson Institute; author, *Necessary Secrets*; (646) 410-2476; schoenfeld.g@gmail.com.

RESOURCES

FLOYD ABRAMS, SPEAKING FREELY—TRIALS OF THE FIRST AMENDMENT (2005).

JAMES BAKER, IN THE COMMON DEFENSE—NATIONAL SECURITY LAW FOR PERILOUS TIMES. CAMBRIDGE UNIVERSITY PRESS (2007).

Harold Edgar & Benno C. Schmidt Jr., *The Espionage Statutes and Publication of Defense Information*, 73 COLUM. L. REV. (1973).

ENCYCLOPEDIA OF THE FIRST AMENDMENT (John R. Vile, David L. Hudson Jr. & David Schultz eds., 2009).

THE FIRST AMENDMENT: FREEDOM OF THE PRESS IN CONSTITUTIONAL HISTORY AND THE CONTEMPORARY DEBATE (Garrett Epps ed., 2008).

NATIONAL SECURITY LAW IN THE NEWS (Paul Rosenzweig, Timothy J. McNulty & Ellen Shearer eds., 2012).

RICHARD A. POSNER: NOT A SUICIDE PACT. THE CONSTITUTION IN A TIME OF NATIONAL EMERGENCY (2006).

GARY ROSS, WHO WATCHES THE WATCHMEN: THE CONFLICT BETWEEN NATIONAL SECURITY AND FREEDOM OF THE PRESS (2011).

GABRIEL SCHOENFELD, NECESSARY SECRETS: NATIONAL SECURITY, THE MEDIA AND THE RULE OF LAW (2010).

Derigan A. Silver, *National Security and The Press: The Government's Ability to Prosecute Journalists for the Possession or Publication of National Security Information*, 13 COMM. L. & POL'Y 447 (2008), https://www.law.upenn.edu /institutes/cerl/conferences/ethicsofsecrecy/papers/reading/Silver.pdf.

The National Security Whistleblower's Tightrope: Legal Rights of Government Employees and Contractors

6

Thomas M. Devine and Steven L. Katz

I. SETTING THE STAGE: A CHANGING GOVERNMENT IN THE CHANGING WORLD

The phrase "government whistleblower" in a newspaper or a TV newscast easily strikes an emotional chord with the public, journalists, and government officials, and can also trigger legal ramifications for all directly involved. Since September 11, 2001, the term "national security whistleblower" has taken on even greater currency and concern because such cases set off a series of conflicting alarms. First, they signal possible weaknesses or problems inside the national security establishment. Second, the inherently secret nature of the agencies raises questions about whether such information should reach the public. Third, the impact on the national security whistleblower creates suspicions that First Amendment or due process rights are being suspended.

Particularly important is that such cases are receiving increased media attention, but that scrutiny and understanding is often focused on the specifics of each case, resulting in repeated "first drafts of history." Often individual whistleblowers, attorneys, and the media would all benefit by examining the history, context, culture, and legal frameworks of whistleblowing—and grasp what is changing and what is not.

A. *Characteristics and Examples of Post-9/11 National Security Whistleblowers*

Historically, many individuals who become whistleblowers do so primarily out of loyalty to their institution's role in sustaining our nation's prosperity, freedoms, and national defense. Usually they have encountered acute breakdowns or misconduct that they believe are in conflict with the Constitution, statutes, regulations, government ethics, or mission of their agency.

However, as in all contexts it is important to note that the range of motives is limited only by the scope of human values and emotions. Some also may be motivated in part due to frustration with lack of attention to their complaints, being passed over for advancement or other personal issues that, while not negating the validity of their disclosures, cannot be ignored. And some use whistleblowing as a cover to embarrass their agency about issues that do not violate the law or ethics.

Several qualities tend to characterize national security and other whistleblowers, particularly at a time of significant change within government. Often these individuals:

- Are in the midst of careers that may include having held positions in the government, the military, or the intelligence community;
- Are surprised to discover something wrong, and are reporting it to ensure the integrity and legality of the government program and action;
- Did not set out to be a whistleblower;
- Lack experience or knowledge to navigate the whistleblower and investigative framework or procedures;
- Discover that there is a legal tightrope that they must walk to protect their name, reputation, and job;
- Believe they are merely honoring professional standards that were non-controversial or even expected in other contexts.

Yet the post-9/11 era gave rise to numerous cases of individuals who thought that they were doing their duty to strengthen defenses, to stop terrorism, or to strengthen management or accountability by reporting through channels the problems they had identified. The adage that "whistleblowers are our first line of defense against waste, fraud, and abuse"[1] does not serve as a shield for federal employees.

Table 1 lists some examples of post-9/11 whistleblowing by federal law enforcement agents and intelligence officials.

The federal government's reaction to those raising these issues too often appeared to reflect cultures, particularly in law enforcement and intelligence agencies, that don't always honor laws designed to enhance government accountability and protect whistleblowers. Retaliation, suspension, reassignment, psychological evaluation, raids on offices and homes, and criminal prosecution under the Espionage Act are examples.[2] Stronger national security whistleblower protections may be needed.

82

Table 1. Examples of Whistleblowing by Federal Employees

Agency	Issue
Federal Aviation Administration (FAA)	Reports to FAA and Congress of weaknesses in airport security.[a]
Federal Bureau of Investigation (FBI)	Agent reports to FBI and Congress of FBI ignorance of al-Qaida and violent Islamist extremism in 2005; the struggle to correct illegal collection of thousands of phone records of Americans between 2003 and 2006; need to fill top counterterrorism vacancies.[b]
Federal Bureau of Investigation (FBI)	Agent reports to FBI superiors and officials regarding violations of federal wiretap law and regulations in counterterrorism investigations.[c]
National Security Agency (NSA)	Employee reports to the NSA and Congress of illegal domestic surveillance, as well as wasteful and potentially fraudulent contracts for grossly expensive surveillance systems performance for intelligence purposes compared with existing technological capabilities.[d]
U.S. Marshals Service	Exposure and prevention of orders to abandon all marshal coverage during a confirmed more ambitious rerun of the 9/11 hijacking; leadership disagreement over official dress code policy that increased risk to the anonymous identity of federal air marshals.[e]

[a] Letter from Office of Special Counsel to President Barack Obama (May 8, 2012), http://mspbwatch.files.wordpress.com/2012/05/osc-letter-to-president-re-faa.pdf; *FAA May Have Highest Whistle-Blower Count in Government*, ABC NEWS, May 8, 2012, http://abcnews.go.com/blogs/politics/2012/05/faa-may-have-highest-whistle-blower -count-in-government/.

[b] *FBI Whistleblower Trial Highlights Bureau's Post-9/11 Transformation*, WASH. POST, Sept. 28, 2010, http://www.washingtonpost.com/wp-dyn/content/article/2010/09/28 /AR2010092807213.html.

[c] *Report Finds Cover Up in an FBI Terror Case*, N.Y. TIMES, Dec. 4, 2005, http://www .nytimes.com/2005/12/04/politics/04fbi.html?pagewanted=print&_r=0; MICHAEL GERMAN, THROUGH THE EYES OF A TERRORIST: INSIGHTS OF A FORMER FBI AGENT (2007).

[d] *Prosecution of Thomas Drake Was Ill Considered, Former Agency Spokesman Says*, WASH. POST, Mar. 12, 2012, http://www.washingtonpost.com/blogs/checkpoint-washington /post/prosecution-of-ex-nsa-official-thomas-drake-was-ill-considered-former-agency -spokesman-acknowledges/2012/03/12/gIQAXE6L7R_blog.html.

[e] *Supreme Court to Decide Whether Air Marshal Should Be Protected as Whistle-blower*, WASH. POST, May 19, 2014.

B. From Micro to Macro: Seismic Shifts in Government Structure and Function, and the Status of Whistleblower Rights

Scant attention has been paid to whether the statutory framework and process that shape whistleblower rights are needed. Since 9/11, the federal government, particularly the national and homeland security community, have added responsibilities that include:

1. Significant expansion and immediate implementation of new national security laws, authorities, and expanded agency and programmatic authorization and spending for defense, intelligence, law enforcement, and diplomacy;[3]
2. Increased vulnerabilities to fraud, waste, and abuse common with fast-track and classified military and intelligence spending; and
3. The perpetuation of weak legal and due process mechanisms and protections for national security whistleblowers.[4]

As chairman of the U.S. Senate Committee on Governmental Affairs, then-Senator John Glenn authored and helped promulgate the laws establishing most of today's government accountability infrastructure, including the Inspector General Act, the Whistleblower Protection Act, the Chief Financial Officers Act, and others from procurement reform to government downsizing. Yet even he acknowledged the lack of public interest in accountability laws.

He often mentioned at hearings and on the Senate floor: "I know sometimes it is about as interesting as watching paint dry or mud dry. These issues involve peculiarities of law and one-word interpretations in the courts and things like that. But these are the things of which this legislation is made."[5]

Later, in the Clinton administration, shifts in government began to bear directly on everything that has happened since.

This included laws and policies that have had the following impacts:

1. Redefined the size, structure, and national security mission of the federal government;[6]
2. Significantly increased federal spending in support of the wars in Iraq and Afghanistan to more than $1.2 trillion;[7]
3. Increased the number of security clearances issued to federal employees (by 48 percent) and contractors (by 25 percent) between 1995 and 2012;[8]
4. Increased the risks and pressures on federal managers, employees, and contractors related to readiness and results in a crisis-driven environment—across national security, intelligence, and defense agencies, and the implementation of new laws and U.S. concerns on a global basis;

5. Raised the expectation of interagency collaboration and information-sharing among those unaccustomed and unaligned to do so;
6. Amplified already strong cultural influences in national security and intelligence agencies that have historically opposed strong internal or independent government accountability, whistleblower protections, and disclosure mechanisms;
7. Magnified the lack of government accountability, whistleblower disclosure and protection mechanisms, or other available channels for reporting fraud, waste, abuse, or other concerns; and
8. Reinforced the historical pattern in Congress to sidestep creating parallel government accountability and whistleblower protection against retaliation in national security and intelligence agencies despite the risks created by a significant post-9/11 surge in the size and complexity of budgets, workforces, and responsibilities.

Unfortunately, the core and underlying problems set in place 20 years ago and augmented post-9/11 have grown in intensity. This is explored in depth in the May 2014 report *Embracing Change: CHCO's Rising to the Challenge of an Altered Landscape.*[9]

C. Important Whistleblower Reforms

More than two decades have passed since the 1994 law caused the downsizing of departments. New offices and agencies, notably the Department of Homeland Security (DHS), the National Counter Terrorism Center, and the Office of the Director of National Intelligence (ODNI), have been created. Congress addressed government accountability challenges in the new agencies, in particular by establishing presidentially appointed inspectors general in DHS and ODNI. Lawmakers also provided for accountability for the billions of dollars spent in Iraq and Afghanistan through creation of special inspectors general for Iraq reconstruction in 2004,[10] and for Afghanistan in 2008.[11]

At the same time, Congress passed laws requiring greater awareness of and education about employee rights against discrimination and whistleblower retaliation. Yet Congress continued to stop short of substantial reforms in whistleblower law.[12]

Expectations rose for increased whistleblower protections after the election of President Barack Obama, but instead there has been a chilling effect, according to journalists and some inside the government, stemming from an unprecedented use of criminal prosecutions that many perceive has overwhelmed gains from administration-led new job-related rights. Since 2009, investigations and prosecutions by the U.S. government against both whistleblowers and journalists have been the most numerous in recent history.[13]

In 2011, the U.S. Merit Systems Protection Board, the federal agency that adjudicates cases brought under the Whistleblower Protection Act, including by the Office of Special Counsel, issued a report based on a 2010[14] employee survey that found federal whistleblowers were nine times more likely to be fired in 2010 than in 1992.

During this same period, Congress was working to improve the Whistleblower Protection Act in significant ways[15] for the first time since its enactment in 1989. Congress was well aware of the need to include protections for national security and intelligence community whistleblowers. The Senate report on its bill issued in April 2012 reflected this view:

Additionally, the lack of remedies under current law for most whistleblowers in the intelligence community and for whistleblowers who face retaliation in the form of withdrawal of the employee's security clearance leaves unprotected those who are in a position to disclose wrongdoing that directly affects our national security.[16]

However, as the Whistleblower Protection Enhancement Act of 2012[17] passed the House and Senate and headed for enactment on November 27, 2012, Obama took an unusual step to address the needs of whistleblowers with access to security classified information, including across the intelligence community. It was unusual for two reasons. First, Congress and Obama had refused to include coverage of such employees with the same whistleblower rights as in civilian agencies that were being amended under the Whistleblower Protection Enhancement Act. Second, because Obama's chosen means of executing these changes was through a National Security Council directive.

On October 10, 2012, Obama issued a presidential national security directive[18]—Presidential Policy Directive 19, Protecting Whistleblowers with Access to Classified Information—that states:

This Presidential Policy Directive ensures that employees (1) serving in the Intelligence Community or (2) who are eligible for access to classified information can effectively report waste, fraud, and abuse while protecting classified national security information. It prohibits retaliation against employees for reporting waste, fraud, and abuse.[19]

Pursuant to that directive, the Office of the Director for National Intelligence formed a special group within the inspector general community to establish related whistleblower disclosure, reporting, and protection procedures and programs. Doing so requires special attention to the culture and climate within the intelligence and national security communities in government.[20] On March 20, 2014, guidelines were issued for consistent agency implementation by June.[21] As this latest development takes shape, national security whistleblowers must determine the legal and procedural path toward making disclosures, whether they have protections and rights, and if so, under which of the numerous laws and regulations.

II. WHEN DOES WHISTLEBLOWING BEGIN?

While former National Security Administration contractor Edward Snowden may or may not define or characterize other whistleblowers, his disclosures have caused a spike in awareness of national security whistleblowing and leaks among the media and the public. This is particularly important for attorneys in the media and for reporters in interacting with individuals making disclosures, whether the individuals are handing over documents or simply stating what they observed, know, or heard. Some will be skeptical that the individual is a whistleblower and a legitimate source until some or all of the following occur:

- Publication or broadcast of a story using the information;
- The whistleblower is publicly identified;
- Retaliation occurs for the disclosure (most commonly by raising issues and reporting wrongdoing internally);
- A lawsuit or investigation begins; or
- The whistleblower becomes the subject of a government investigation or prosecution.

However, whether or not a media outlet decides to air or publish information based on the whistleblower's account or documents provided, whistleblowing begins when a government or corporate employee communicates relevant information to a third party.

That is the moment at which a national security employee or contractor who makes a disclosure must consider the legal tightrope and procedures to be navigated. It is also the moment when reporters may wonder what purpose they are serving for the whistleblower. Before trying to gain public attention through the media, whistleblowers first must have pursued their concerns through internal legal and investigative channels. They may even have gone to Congress independent of these venues. Yet either before or after following the procedures, they may have concluded that the legal process was too difficult or slow to produce meaningful results, involved costs for legal representation that they lacked, that their career and reputation had been placed at risk, or that the problem was too big to be ignored by the media and public.

III. WHISTLEBLOWER LAWS AND REGULATIONS

A. *Walking the Legal Tightrope*

Attorneys, reporters, and government officials in general are surprised to learn that whistleblowers may not know they have rights under laws or regulations. Further, whistleblowers may expect those whom they are consulting with or disclosing information to—from reporters to congressional staff—to serve as informal counsel who will shield them from retaliation. While publicity that generates public solidarity often is a prerequisite for survival, reporters cannot ethically advocate for anyone involved in their stories. The laws, steps, procedures, and investigative offices established to enforce whistleblower laws and programs were established precisely to remove or minimize the risk to whistleblowers and increase their formal options for disclosure and protection. In theory, even national security whistleblowers who are not covered by these laws due almost solely to political demands by the U.S. House Intelligence Committee[22] would be well served by consulting these offices or resources.

In theory this would include consulting the whistleblower ombudsmen in their respective Offices of Inspector General (OIGs), offices that were created by the Whistleblower Protection Enhancement Act of 2012. The purpose and limitations of such offices are described as: "To educate employees about prohibitions on retaliation for protected disclosures; and their rights and remedies against retaliation for protected disclosures. . . . The law does not permit the Whistleblower Protection Ombudsman to act as a legal representative, agent, or advocate for employees."[23] Whistleblowers should be wary when seeking this help, however. There are no standards or dedicated funding for implementation, and many OIGs have appointed the general counsel or another official with an institutional conflict of interest to handle this duty. Reporters and media attorneys should consult a menu of legal rights and options for whistleblowers so they are aware of when they or the whistleblower are veering outside of those protections. They also should direct the whistleblowers to the menu of rights, and direct them to attorneys or legal support organizations to teach them the boundaries of their legal rights and provide expert navigation.[24]

The legal landscape has been changing rapidly through enactment of the Whistleblower Protection Enhancement Act of 2012 (WPEA),[25] implementation and potential codification of Presidential Policy Directive 19,[26] and establishment of whistleblower protection procedures in the intelligence community. Running parallel to the makeover of federal employee rights in the WPEA, there has been a legal revolution strengthening whistleblower rights on the corporate level, including for government contractors.[27] But the reforms are piecemeal, no two have identical boundaries, and all recent statutory breakthroughs have included an exception for intelligence community employees. Currently, the Constitution and 16 laws could be helpful for federal employees and contractors.

B. The Constitutional and Statutory Framework

The First Amendment. This is the cornerstone for all free speech rights. Since the 1968 decision in *Pickering v. Board of Education*,[28] in which a public school teacher had written a letter to the editor of her local newspaper criticizing weaknesses in local schools, the First Amendment has protected public employees who communicate a matter of public concern that does not outweigh corresponding disruption of legitimate management functions. However, since the 2006 decision in *Garcetti v. Ceballos*,[29] the First Amendment does not apply to duty speech that is part of job responsibilities. In *Garcetti*, a government attorney faced retaliation because he challenged possible illegality that he discovered while conducting fact-finding for a case he was prosecuting. Besides their duty as officers of the court, prosecutors have to maintain a clean record or risk defeat and public scandal, as occurred in the prosecution of Senator Ted Stevens, where his conviction was voided before sentencing due to evidentiary cheating.[30] But in a 5–4 decision, the Supreme Court rejected the "officer of the court" protection, holding that "duty speech" is not protected by the First Amendment.

State and municipal employees can enforce their First Amendment rights through jury trials in U.S. district court.[31] Federal workers are limited to administrative hearings where indirect enforcement is available for First Amendment rights as a merit system principle.[32]

The Whistleblower Protection Act (WPA).[33] First passed as part of the Civil Service Reform Act of 1978 and then separated into its own law in 1989, this act applies the *Pickering* balancing test to provide absolute protection for disclosures of information that an employee reasonably believes is evidence of illegality, gross waste, abuse of authority, gross mismanagement, or a substantial and specific danger to public health or safety.[34] Reflecting its significant impact on government abuses of power, the law has had a phoenix-like history of death and rebirth—endlessly attacked, gutted, and revived. The WPA is invaluable for congressional oversight. As a result, Congress unanimously reaffirmed and strengthened its original mandate three times—the latest through the Whistleblower Protection Enhancement Act of 2012 after a 13-year campaign.[35] The WPEA restored the Act's original free speech mandate by systematically canceling 13 years of hostile precedents from the Court of Appeals for the Federal Circuit, expanded coverage, strengthened protections against gag orders generally and scientific censorship in particular, and temporarily restored normal appellate review in all circuit courts of appeal during a four-year study on full access to the courts.

All alleged violations of whistleblower rights can be enforced through investigations by the Office of Special Counsel (OSC), with subsequent opportunity for an administrative Individual Right of Action due process hearing at the U.S. Merit Systems Protection Board if the OSC has not obtained requested relief for the employee within 120 days.[36] For cases that involve severe consequences to the employee, such as suspension of greater than two weeks or termination, the employee can assert the whistleblower defense through an appeal straight to the board.[37] However, statutory rights in WPA do not apply to employees with national security intelligence jobs.[38]

Government Contractors. In the annual National Defense Authorization Act in 2012, a law funding the Department of Defense, all defense contractor whistleblowers except those in the intelligence community gained whistleblower rights, including access to U.S. district court jury trials if they do not get expeditious relief from investigations by relevant agency OIGs.[39]

Beginning on July 1, 2013, government contractor and subcontractor whistleblowers obtained substantial additional rights and protections based on the provisions enacted on January 2, 2013, in the National Defense Authorization Act for Fiscal Year 2013. In light of these enhancements, government contractors and subcontractors should consider taking proactive measures to address employee concerns and prevent and detect retaliation. In addition, these contractors enjoy protection against retaliation whether the disclosure was made to an inspector general, the Government Accountability Office, or the Department of Justice. In a pilot test through September 30, 2016, all government contractors will have that same right.[40] For now, access to jury trials gives all government contractor whistleblowers stronger due process rights than available for civil service employees.

The False Claims Act and Major Fraud Act.[41] These laws provide anti-retaliation rights for government contractor employees who challenge fraud in government contracts, grants or Medicare payments. Unlike the Major Fraud Act, which enforces criminal liability, the False Claims Act is a private attorney general statute that lets the whistleblower file a qui tam (in which a plaintiff files a claim on behalf of the government) in a lawsuit that can award treble fraud damages and give the whistleblower 15 percent to 30 percent of recovered funds. It also includes anti-retaliation rights in federal court[42], but they are not available for federal employees.

Anti-Gag Statute.[43] This annual appropriations rider, included in spending bills from fiscal year 1988 through 2013, prevents the government from spending funds to implement or enforce nondisclosure policies, forms, or agreements against any government employee or contractor that contradict free speech rights in whistleblower laws or the right to communicate with Congress, as well as action against disclosures of any information alleged to be classified but without specific designations providing notice of its secret status.

Federal Banking Agencies.[44] This statute allows employees of the Federal Reserve Board, Federal Deposit Insurance Corporation, and other federal banking agencies to file claims in U.S. district court for a jury trial, with a two-year statute of limitations and compensatory damages. It does not include preliminary administrative remedies or burdens of proof.

Foreign Service Act.[45] This law mirrors the WPA, but its anti-retaliation rights are enforced through a Foreign Service Board appointed by the secretary of state rather than the OSC and Merit Systems Protection Board.

Intelligence Community Rights. The Intelligence Community Whistleblower Protection Act of 1998 (ICWPA)[46] was established to create a forum for disclosures by intelligence agency employees, but its own regulations specifically state that it does not exist to protect government intelligence employees or contractors against reprisal. Instead it serves primarily as a classified conduit for specific types of "urgent actions" to be referred to by OIGs of the various intelligence agencies or to the intelligence committees in Congress.[47] Section 702 of the Act defines "urgent concerns" to include false statement to Congress, whistleblower retaliation, or a "flagrant problem, abuse, violation of law or Executive order, or deficiency relating to the funding, administration, or operation of an intelligence activity involving classified information, but does not include differences of opinions concerning public policy matters."

These rights are vague and weak on their face. A whistleblower must guess whether misconduct is sufficiently "flagrant" or "deficient," and only can complain about retaliation rather than formally seek its legally ordered reversal. It hasn't been used often. An October 19, 2009, report from the ODNI to the chairman of the House Permanent Select Committee on Intelligence stated that in the ten years since the law's enactment only four intelligence community inspector generals had received a total of ten ICWPA complaints.[48]

As mentioned earlier, in October 2012, the president issued Presidential Policy Directive 19, a substitute for intelligence community protections that the House Permanent Select Committee on Intelligence removed from the Whistleblower Protection Enhancement Act. It protects against retaliatory actions to deny or remove a security clearance. The directive shields the same whistleblowing disclosures as the WPA, but only for in-house communications within institutional channels or to the relevant inspector general. Also, the rights are enforced through internal hearings by the agency whose actions the employee challenges as retaliatory. With normal independent due process, this agency would be the adversarial party, rather than institutional judge of its own actions. Further, the only appeal is to a board of intelligence community inspectors general who are not trained as appellate judges, often actually conduct the retaliatory investigations of whistleblowers, and only have the authority to remand rather than reverse an agency action.

FBI Rights.[49] This system provides what by law must be equivalent rights as those available for civil service workers. However, neither the FBI nor the presidential policy directive system protects any public freedom of expression for any dissent, even for information that is unclassified and unrestricted by any other authority. The FBI hearings are conducted by the Department of Justice Office of Attorney Management and Recruitment, compared with the independent due process at the U.S. Merit Systems Protection Board.

Military Whistleblower Protection Act.[50] This law has been in effect since 1988, but not until December 2013 did amendments to the annual Defense Department authorization include the right to a guaranteed due process hearing for enforcement. While possible, there never had been an administrative hearing granted, and the OIG provided relief for barely more than 1 percent of complainants. After an extensive overhaul, military service members now have the legal right to disclose the same misconduct as civil service employees, but only within their chain of command, to their OIG, or to Congress. They also are entitled to an administrative hearing at the Board of Correction of Military Records for their service.

Inspector General Act.[51] Section 7 of the Inspector General Act provides Offices of Inspectors General with the authority to investigate retaliation against whistleblowers and recommend corrective actions. But as previously noted, these offices have institutional conflicts of interest; and some have been accused of conducting retaliatory investigations of whistleblowers for agency managers. At best, OIGs seldom make reprisal investigations a priority due to backlogs on direct misconduct, and the decision-makers for any supportive recommendations are agency political appointees who may be threatened by a whistleblower's dissent. However, section 117 of the WPEA adds a potentially significant new role for inspectors general by requiring that each agency's inspector general designate a whistleblower protection ombudsman—with the exception of intelligence community agencies, or units whose principal function is foreign intelligence or counterintelligence. The ombudsman's role is to educate agency employees about prohibitions on retaliation for protected disclosures and their rights and remedies if they have been retaliated against for making protected disclosures.

Nonappropriated Fund Employees at Military Services.[52] This law, an untitled amendment to the 2013 National Defense Authorization Act, covers civilian employees at military services who provide support services, such as employees of the Army and Air Force Exchange Service or the Defense Finance and Accounting Service. It provides rights equivalent to those in the WPA, but they are enforced under the Military Whistleblower Protection Act through regulations issued by the secretary of defense.

Dodd-Frank Wall Street Reform and Consumer Protection Act.[53] The "bounty" provision of Dodd-Frank does not offer money for federal workers who blow the whistle, but the anti-retaliation provision covers any federal employee who discloses a violation of laws enforced by the Securities and Exchange Commission. The rights include a six-year statute of limitations, the longest in the U.S. code for whistleblowers. The law also provides for bench (judge) trials in U.S. district court. It does not specify legal burdens of proof, have any preliminary administrative remedy, include access for jury trials, or provide compensatory damages.

Energy Reorganization Act.[54] This law offers rights to employees of the nuclear power and weapons industries and government workers at the Nuclear Regulatory Commission and Department of Energy who act as whistleblowers. It provides for an initial Department of Labor investigation and administrative hearing if the whistleblower alleges retaliation by supervisors for his disclosures. If there is no ruling within 365 days, the whistleblower can file for a de novo jury trial in U.S. district court. Reinstatement and compensatory damages are available in either forum.

American Recovery and Reinvestment Act.[55] This law provided best practice whistleblower rights for contractor employees who challenged misspending under the stimulus law, including an initial OIG investigation and, if there was no ruling within 210 days, a subsequent jury trial in court starting de novo, or from a blank slate.

Lloyd Lafollette Act.[56] This 1912 law created an unrestricted free speech right for government employees to communicate freely with Congress. It does not have a direct remedy, but federal employees can enforce it as a merit system right under the Civil Service Reform Act of 1978.

C. Discussion and Examples: Application of the Civil Service Reform Act of 1978

In addition to rights directly protecting free speech, the Civil Service Reform Act of 1978 (CSRA) has ancillary provisions that can be relevant. Besides reorganizing civil service duties to eliminate conflicts of interest, the CSRA created a series of merit system principles to maintain a nonpolitical, professional federal workforce and associated rights enforced as prohibited personnel practices, of which whistleblower protection is one.[57] This law was at the heart of the modern whistleblower protections in government, and the establishment of the U.S. Merit Systems Protection Board and the OSC. It also provides specific protections such as the provision that protects those who refuse to violate the law.[58] Another protects federal workers from retaliation for membership in outside organizations or other off-duty conduct that does not undermine their performance on the job.[59]

These rights, however, do not provide reliable or even credible protection in terms of formal results. None is relevant against criminal prosecutions. Even in the personnel context, only four employees prevailed during the first decade after enactment of the Civil Service Reform Act of 1978.[60] Five years after the Act's passage, among some 500,000 federal workers who witnessed illegality or misspending involving a half million dollars or more, would-be whistleblowers' fear of retaliation doubled from 19 percent to 37 percent as the reason they remained silent observers.[61] During that era, leadership at the U.S. OSC taught courses for federal managers on how to fire whistleblowers without getting caught by its own investigators.[62]

After 1994 amendments to the WPA made it the strongest free speech law in history on paper, various federal appellate courts ruled against whistleblowers in 231 out of 234 decisions on the merits prior to passage of the Whistleblower

Protection Enhancement Act of 2012.[63] Whistleblower protection groups were so alarmed that they advised employees not to exercise their anti-retaliation rights.

The John White Case. In the late 1980s the Air Force was trying to train its professionals in new computer technologies. Specialist John White noticed duplicative, expensive training programs run by unqualified ex-officers and buddies of the Las Vegas base commander that contradicted courses run by acknowledged experts at universities. His subsequent whistleblowing was so well taken that a management review backed White's charges, and after a site visit the secretary of the Air Force canceled the program. But in 1992 the base commander stripped White of his duties and reassigned him to work at new, temporary quarters in the desert. White exercised his whistleblower rights, but despite three administrative victories the case dragged out due to repeated government appeals. In 1999 a federal appeals court canceled the administrative victories on grounds that White did not have a "reasonable belief" he was disclosing mismanagement, despite the secretary's agreement and agency cancellation of the program. The court reasoned that in order to have a reasonable belief that information discloses evidence of misconduct, a whistleblower must first overcome a presumption that the government operates "lawfully, correctly and in good faith" by "irrefragable proof."[64] "Irrefragable," whose roots were King George's authority over the colonies before the American Revolution, means "undeniable, incontrovertible, or incapable of being overthrown."[65] After further administrative proceedings, White finally lost irrevocably in 2003, 11 years after he began asserting his rights.[66]

These laws are ongoing works in progress. Before 1978 there were no statutory free speech rights for government employees. Pioneer rights such as those in the WPA now are in their fourth generation as painful lessons learned. Congress has held firm by repeatedly, unanimously reenacting its original 1978 free speech mandate and legislatively overturning hostile rulings that gutted it, and the OSC has regained confidence due to effective leadership from Special Counsel Carolyn Lerner.[67] Previously untouchable agencies, such as the Central Intelligence Agency and National Security Agency, now have comparatively weak rights where previously there were none. It appears there is momentum to shield whistleblowers who challenge illegal or unethical abuses of power.

Even the weaker laws can be valuable resources to shield whistleblowers because they force the government to earn its retaliation through prolonged, draining proceedings. Further, the process of pretrial discovery, such as document demands and depositions of government witnesses, can be an opportunity both for journalists and whistleblowers to investigate the government agency conducting retaliation. Often the formal outcome of who wins is not even the most significant factor, because agencies cannot withstand public exposure of the issues or actions under scrutiny or actions against the employees who are whistleblowers.

IV. NAVIGATING THE WHISTLEBLOWER LEGAL FRAMEWORK FROM INSIDE GOVERNMENT

Taking steps as a federal whistleblower begins either as a result of (1) utilizing disclosure channels to seek an investigation of perceived wrongdoing or (2) in the course of exercising due process rights against retaliation, discussed below.

The two are not mutually exclusive. Evidence of associated government misconduct also is disclosed through other official venues such as occurs when filing a complaint with an agency Office of Civil Rights or in relation to a complaint filed with the Equal Opportunity Commission.

There no longer are any arbitrary limits of time, context, formality, or audience on whistleblowing rights for federal employees outside intelligence agencies and positions.[68] Someone can also become a whistleblower and trigger the appropriate legal rights because of carrying out a job duty or discussing concerns with a supervisor or higher up the managerial chain of command.[69] Others, such as legendary Pentagon whistleblower Ernest Fitzgerald, who exposed Air Force lies about a $2.3 billion cost overrun for the C-5 cargo aircraft, bear witness through congressional testimony.[70] Pioneer domestic surveillance whistleblower Thomas Drake contacted both the National Security Agency and Pentagon OIGs.[71] Many stories do not involve retaliation, and whistleblowers often play a significant and constructive but covert role in congressional oversight and media investigations.

A. The U.S. Office of Special Counsel

The U.S. OSC[72] and each agency's Office of Inspector General[73] are the primary venues for executive branch accountability. Federal employees can make a disclosure to the OSC requesting an investigation, after which the OSC can order an investigation by a relevant agency head, who normally assigns the investigation to the agency OIG. However, certain categories of employees do not have rights in law before the OSC,[74] including those not covered by the WPA such as the Central Intelligence Agency (CIA), Federal Bureau of Investigation (FBI), Government Accountability Office, and U.S. Postal Regulatory Commission.

Disclosures and requests for investigation are filed with these government offices specifically established to stop fraud, waste, and abuse; to facilitate anonymous or confidential reports of problems; and to provide legally safe disclosure and investigative channels for whistleblowers. Significantly, the OSC is an *independent* agency within the federal government. The investigative report has to follow strict guidelines for full disclosure of investigative methodology and results. At the end of the process the whistleblower has the last word, commenting on the report that has been delivered to the OSC by the agency head and inspector general who produced it. Then the OSC gives a final pass or fail report card before forwarding the whole package to the president, leaders of the House and Senate, and the public through the OSC website.[75]

B. Offices of Inspectors General

OIGs are autonomous components within individual agencies as enumerated in the Inspector General Act of 1978,[76] as amended, the purpose of which is "to create independent and objective units" with the following responsibilities:

- Conduct independent and objective audits, investigations and inspections,
- Prevent and detect waste, fraud, and abuse,
- Promote economy, effectiveness, and efficiency,
- Review pending legislation and regulation,
- Keep the agency head and Congress fully informed, and point out the necessity for and progress of corrective action.

C. Issues of OIG Independence

OIGs are viewed as autonomous, with dual reporting requirements to Congress and the agency head[77] described by the Council on Inspector General Integrity and Efficiency as: "While by law, IGs are under the general supervision of the agency head or deputy, neither the agency head nor the deputy can prevent or prohibit an IG from conducting an audit or investigation."[78]

Historically this has led to certain concerns involving conflicts of interest where an agency head has review authority and control over IG staff bonus, performance review, and related budgetary decisions.[79] The Inspector General Reform Act of 2008[80] addressed the subject of bonuses by barring inspector general bonuses for those who were appointed by the president, or by agency heads in Designated Federal Entities, and also extended specifically to presidentially appointed IGs in the Office of the Director for National Security and the CIA. Under the IG Act, the National Security Agency is a Designated Federal Entity.[81]

IGs do not receive performance appraisals from agency heads, though IG staff do receive performance appraisals by the inspector general, and IGs must be vigilant in their efforts to remain structurally and functionally independent of the agency head and the agency itself. They are supported in this endeavor through application of the *Silver Book: Quality and Standards of Federal Inspectors General*, prepared and published by the Council on Inspector General Integrity and Efficiency.[82]

D. National Security Exceptions to Audit and Investigative Scope

Most significant for purposes of understanding the legal framework governing national security whistleblowers who turn to their agency inspector general is the statutory exception granting the secretary of defense authority to prohibit an inspector general's audit and investigative authority in the intelligence community. The provision also requires notice to Congress and relevant committees of jurisdiction.[83]

V. WHAT IS A FEDERAL EMPLOYEE TO DO?

It may be helpful to stand in the shoes of a national security whistleblower to better understand the procedural challenges involved. Assume that you are a whistleblower considering a disclosure about a sensitive matter. The first stop is usually the OSC, which offers a specific disclosure channel for whistleblowers. Federal employees can click to the OSC disclosure channel on their computer. An example is shown in the box.

For civil service workers, structurally this is a superior option compared with filing a complaint with the agency Office of Inspector General. In addition to institutional independence, the WPA has unique controls and provisions enfranchising OSC whistleblowers in the process to follow through on their disclosures:

1. The OSC only refers cases for investigation, review and corrective actions commitments to the agency chief, who must sign to vouch for their resolution.[84] While he or she frequently assigns the inspector general to investigate, the buck for corrective action must stop with the agency head, who has the authority to act on a probe's findings and recommendations.

2. The special counsel only requires an agency investigation after finding that there is a "substantial likelihood" the whistleblower's concerns are correct.[85] This sharply changes the dynamic. Normally agencies act on accusations by an isolated whistleblower who often can be easily discredited. By contrast, the OSC "substantial likelihood finding" is like a bureaucratic Good Housekeeping Seal of Approval, substituting for the lone dissident's accusations about the same suspect activity. Investigations ordered by the OSC have led to cancellation of or significant repairs at nuclear power plants under construction; prevented the Department of Agriculture from replacing federal inspection of government-approved meat and poultry with corporate honor systems; sparked creation of a national testing program for illegal animal drugs

97

OSC Whistleblower Disclosure Channel

The OSC Disclosure Unit serves as a secure channel that can be used to disclose:

- a violation of law, rule or regulation;
- gross mismanagement;
- gross waste of funds;
- abuse of authority;
- substantial and specific danger to public health or safety.

OSC does **not** have authority to investigate the disclosures that it receives. The law provides that OSC will (a) refer protected disclosures that establish a substantial likelihood of wrongdoing to the appropriate agency head, and (b) require the agency to conduct an investigation, and submit a written report on the findings of the investigation to the Special Counsel. . . .

The Disclosure Unit has jurisdiction over federal employees, former federal employees, and applicants for federal employment. It is important to note that a disclosure must be related to an event that occurred in connection with the performance of an employee's duties and responsibilities. The Disclosure Unit has **no jurisdiction** over disclosures filed by employees of the:

- U.S. Postal Service and the Postal Rate Commission
- members of the armed forces of the United States (i.e., noncivilian military employees)
- state employees operating under federal grants
- employees of federal contractors.

Source: Information About Filling a Whistleblower Disclosure With the Office of Special Counsel, Form OSC-12, http://www.osc.gov/documents/forms/osc12.htm.

in commercial milk; prevented the planned trillion-dollar next generation of the Star Wars anti-ballistic missile system; and even forced an overhaul of military burial policies. All ensuing nonclassified resulting reports are sent to the president, congressional leaders, and maintained in a public file that can be accessed through the OSC website.[86]

3. The contents and timing of the agency investigative report are controlled by statute. Agencies do not have the option to let an investigation gather dust and then issue a short "no misconduct" conclusion after the scandal has died down. The WPA requires them to submit a response within 60 days that includes a summary of the whistleblower's evidence, the investigative methodology, summary of evidence obtained during the probe, findings on relevant legal violations, and corrective action commitments.[87]

4. When the agency report arrives, the whistleblower has an opportunity to comment on its adequacy as a resolution.[88]
5. OSC can reject an agency report as incomplete or unreasonable and either require further review until satisfied or flunk the effort.[89]
6. When the case is closed OSC sends the agency report, the whistleblower's evaluation, and its own assessment to the president and relevant congressional offices, as well as placing the package in a public file, currently available on its website.[90]

VI.   WHAT IS A FEDERAL CONTRACTOR TO DO?

Federal contractors may work side by side with civil service employees, but when blowing the whistle they face a far different reality. Nonnational security contractor whistleblowers have stronger rights against retaliation, but national security contract employees have virtually none that are enforceable. Without access to the OSC, for them the primary designated audience within the executive branch is the OIG.

While there is a single special counsel, there are 73 statutory inspectors general[91] plus several more in the military, and not all have the autonomy of the IG Act. Those not enumerated and included in the IG Act work directly for the managers often targeted by a whistleblower's disclosure. In some OIG offices, specific attention is paid to contractors. As an example, the Department of Defense Office of Inspector General has separate whistleblower disclosure programs for employees and contractors, and each must meet specific criteria. But the programs are uneven, perceived as "hit or miss," and can even backfire. A common complaint by whistleblowers is that the OIG investigated them instead of their allegations of government or contractor misconduct.

The Case of Marines Science Advisor Franz Gayl. Marines Science Advisor Franz Gayl successfully blew the whistle on failure to deliver MRAPs, or Mine-Resistant Ambush Protected vehicles, with ensuing delays responsible for some one-third of American casualties in Iraq before they finally arrived. After prevailing in a retaliation case, at his request Gayl's initial settlement had him work with OIG auditors and report on ways to prevent those fatal mistakes from recurring. But hostile Marine supervisors had the Naval Criminal Investigative Service and OIG place Gayl under criminal investigation for his work on the report, on petty charges of security breaches preparing it that could not withstand scrutiny. The probe led to loss of his security clearance to see classified documents necessary for his work, and would have led to his removal absent 2011 intervention by the OSC. Gayl still has his job and the clearance was restored, but the Marines will not let him enter rooms where classified information is kept.[92]

The Case of NSA Whistleblower Thomas Drake. Thomas Drake and his colleagues followed all the rules, spending hundreds of hours with OIG investigators and House Permanent Select Committee on Intelligence staff. But the OIG referred them to the FBI as suspects for criminal classified leaks to *The New York Times* that in reality were made by Thomas Tamm, a Justice Department whistleblower. Drake and his whistleblowing partners all faced FBI raids at gunpoint in which their homes were ransacked, property seized, and families terrorized. Although he eventually prevailed, Drake faced a 30-year prison sentence for violating the Espionage Act, went bankrupt and lost his home and his wife, and now works in an Apple computer store as a salesman—all for working within the system as an OIG witness, the way posters in every government agency remind employees is their duty.[93] Intelligence community employees and contractors face another fundamental challenge when blowing the whistle: none of their whistleblower laws or regulations protects public freedom of expression. Free speech rights only exist in-house or as OIG witnesses. This is particularly significant for journalists working with intelligence community employees: There are no whistleblower protections for transmission of any information to the public, whether or not classified.

VII. CONCLUSION

The legal tightrope that whistleblowers must walk is uniquely challenging. Despite some attention to the needs to enhance and strengthen whistleblower protection rights and processes, it remains to be seen whether Congress, the administration, and the agencies can develop and implement something needed for government employees and contractors expected to be the front line against fraud, waste, and abuse. As repeatedly confirmed by global studies, whistleblowers are more effective at exposing crimes like fraud than auditors, internal investigations, and law enforcement combined.[94] Corporations are much further in the lead in this regard in both affording their employees independent hotlines and other confidential procedures and mechanisms for reporting concerns and wrongdoing than does government.

Of course, not all disclosures of information from government are "leaks," nor do these necessarily constitute whistleblowing. However, sometimes the only realistic hope whistleblowers have comes from reporting such concerns to Congress and the press.

Despite the patchwork quilt nature of federal employee, and to a lesser degree contractor whistleblower, rights—attorneys and reporters in the media may find such work and reporting on it constitutes an essential exercise of the First Amendment from multiple perspectives. This is freedom of speech when it counts the most—both in preventing serious consequences of holding accountable those whose abuses of power pose the most severe threats to society, and in maintaining the social fabric of institutional checks and balances necessary for government agencies, and society, to be functional. The more attorneys in the media and journalists understand the legal framework involved in being a whistleblower, the better able they will be able to make editorial decisions and when and how best to report on government misconduct. There is no more powerful challenge to fraud, waste, and abuse than the partnership between whistleblowers and journalists.

NOTES

1. U.S. Senator Claire McCaskill, press release announcing introduction of whistleblower legislation (Oct. 1, 2009), http://www.mccaskill.senate.gov/?p=press_release&id=1557.

2. *Blurred Line Between Espionage and Truth*, N.Y. TIMES, Feb. 2, 2012.

3. *E.g.* Patriot Act, establishment of Department of Homeland Security, Office of the Director for National Intelligence (ODNI). *See also* DEPARTMENT OF HOMELAND SECURITY: PROGRESS MADE AND WORK REMAINING IN IMPLEMENTING HOMELAND SECURITY MISSIONS 10 YEARS AFTER 9/11, GAO-11-181 (Sept. 2011), http://www.gao.gov/assets/330/322889.pdf.

4. *See National Security Whistleblowers Deserve More Protection*, WASH. POST, July 2, 2010.

5. *In Regulatory Overhaul Bill, Every Word Counts*, N.Y. TIMES, July 19, 1995.

6. *See* Top Secret America, *Washington Post* series of articles from July 2010, at http://projects.washingtonpost.com/top-secret-america/.

7. AMY BELASCO, CONG. RES. SERV., THE COST OF IRAQ, AFGHANISTAN, AND OTHER GLOBAL WAR ON TERROR OPERATIONS SINCE 9/11 (Mar. 29, 2011), https://www.fas.org/sgp/crs/natsec/RL33110.pdf.

8. The 2012 Annual Report on Security Clearance Determinations issued in January 2013 by the Office of the Director for National Security is the most recent report. *See* http://www.dni.gov/index.php/newsroom/reports-and-publications/193-reports-publications-2013/841-2012-report-on-security-clearance-determinations?tmpl=component&format=pdf. *See also Hearing before the Permanent Subcomm. on Investigations, Senate Governmental Affairs Comm., Improvements Needed in the Government's Personnel Security Clearance Program*, Apr. 16, 1985, http://www.fas.org/sgp/gao/041685.pdf (statement of Bill W. Thurman, Deputy Director, National Security and International Affairs Division); GOV'T ACCOUNTABILITY OFFICE, GAO/NSAID-95-101, BACKGROUND INVESTIGATIONS, http://www.fas.org/sgp/gao/nsiad-95-101.pdf. Note: The Intelligence Authorization Act for the Fiscal Year 2010 established a requirement for the president to submit an annual report to Congress on the security clearance process, to include the total number of security clearances across government and in-depth metrics on the timeliness of security clearance determinations in the Intelligence Community (IC).

9. http://ourpublicservice.org/OPS/publications/viewcontentdetails.php?id=244.

10. The Office of the Special Inspector General for Iraq Reconstruction (SIGIR) was created in October 2004 as the successor to the Coalition Provisional Authority Office of Inspector General (CPA-IG), overseeing more than $50 billion in U.S. reconstruction funds. It concluded its work in October 2013. *See* http://cybercemetery.unt.edu/archive/sigir/20130930184730/http://www.sigir.mil/.

11. National Defense Authorization Act for FY 2008, Pub. L. No. 110-181 (Jan. 28, 2008).

12. The Notification and Federal Employee Antidiscrimination and Retaliation Act of 2002, Pub. L. No. 107-174 (2002)—known as the No FEAR Act—has several features, including the requirement that "an agency must provide annual notice to its employees, former employees, and applicants for Federal employment concerning the rights and remedies applicable to them under the employment discrimination and whistleblower protection laws."

13. *Looking for Balance in Handling Leakers*, WASH. POST. Aug. 5, 2013, http://www.washington post.com/world/national-security/looking-for-balance-in-handling-leakers/2013/08/05/8e6e587c -fc4d-11e2-8752-b41d7ed1f685_story.html.

14. U.S. MERIT SYS. PROT. BD., REPORT TO THE PRESIDENT AND CONGRESS (Nov. 2011), http:// www.usda.gov/oig/webdocs/Blowing_The_Whistle.pdf.

15. For a useful summary of the change in law, see Jason Zuckerman, *Congress Strengthens Whistleblower Protections for Federal Employees*, ABA SEC. LABOR & EMPL. L. NEWSL., Nov.–Dec. 2012, http://www.americanbar.org/content/newsletter/groups/labor_law/ll_flash/1212_abalel_flash /lel_flash12_2012spec.html.

16. S. REP. NO. 112-155, Whistleblower Protection Enhancement Act of 2012, S. 743, Apr. 10, 2012.

17. Pub. L. No. 112-199 (Nov. 27, 2012).

18. HAROLD RELYEA, CONG. RES. SERV., PRESIDENTIAL DIRECTIVES: BACKGROUND AND OVER-VIEW (Aug. 9, 2007), http://assets.opencrs.com/rpts/98-611_20070809.pdf.

19. Presidential Policy Directive 19, Oct. 10, 2012, http://www.fas.org/irp/offdocs/ppd/ppd-19.pdf.

20. Steven L. Katz, *How to Design Whistleblower Protection for the Intel Community*, FED. TIMES, Dec. 12, 2012, http://www.federaltimes.com/article/20121209/ADOP06/312090004/How-design -whistle-blower-protection-intel-community.

21. Office of the Dir. of Nat'l Intelligence, Intelligence Community Directive 120: Intelligence Community Whistleblower Protection (Mar. 20, 2014).

22. *BI Whistleblower Trial Highlights Bureau's Post-9/11 Transformation*, WASH. POST, Sept. 28, 2010.

23. Whistleblower Protection Enhancement Act of 2012 § 117, http://www.gpo.gov/fdsys/pkg/BILLS -112s743enr/pdf/BILLS-112s743enr.pdf.

24. Even if unable to take a case, nonprofit support organizations such as the Government Account-ability Project (GAP), http://www.whistleblower.org, and Public Employees for Environmental Responsibility (PEER), http://www.peer.org, have extensive attorney referral networks. Membership lists and local chapters for the American Civil Liberties Union (ACLU) or the National Employment Lawyers Association (NELA) also are helpful resources.

25. Pub. L. No. 112-19, 126 Stat. 1465.

26. Presidential Policy Directive 19, Protecting Whistleblowers with Access to Classified Informa-tion (Oct. 10, 2012), https://www.fas.org/irp/offdocs/ppd/ppd-19.pdf.

27. DEVINE & MAASSARANI, THE CORPORATE WHISTLEBLOWER'S SURVIVAL GUIDE: A HANDBOOK FOR COMMITTING THE TRUTH (2011).

28. 391 U.S. 563 (1968).

29. 547 U.S. 410 (2006).

30. *Prosecution of Former Senator Ted Stevens, Hearings before the Subcomm. on Crime, Terrorism and Homeland Security of the U.S. House Judiciary Comm.*, 112th Cong., 2d Sess. (Apr. 19, 2012), http://www.gpo.gov/fdsys/pkg/CHRG-112hhrg73861/html/CHRG-112hhrg73861.htm.

31. 42 U.S.C. § 1983.

32. 5 U.S.C. § 2302(b)(11).

33. The Act's operative free speech right is in 5 U.S.C. § 2302(b)(8).

34. *Id.*

35. Pub. L. No. 112-199, 126 Stat. 1465, 112th Cong., 2d Sess. (Nov. 27, 2012). The WPEA sys-tematically closed judicially created loopholes, expanded the scope of coverage, removed due pro-cess barriers, banned contradictory agency gag orders, strengthened the OSC's authority, and began a pilot test of normal access to appeal courts. For a detailed list of changes, see http://www.whistle blower.org/blog/42-2012/2380-president-signs-whistleblower-protection-enhancement-act-wpea-.

36. 5 U.S.C. § 1221.

37. *Id.* § 7701.

38. At press time, House and Senate negotiators were moving toward agreement to upgrade Presi-dent Obama's PPD 19 protections into permanent statutory rights.

39. 10 U.S.C. § 2409.
40. 41 U.S.C. § 4712.
41. 31 U.S.C. § 3730; 18 U.S.C. § 1031(h).
42. 31 U.S.C. § 3730(h).
43. Section 713, Omnibus Appropriations Act of 2012, 112th Cong. 2d Sess.
44. 31 U.S.C. § 5328.
45. 22 U.S.C. § 3905.
46. Title VII, Pub. L. No. 105-272, 105th Cong., 2d Sess. (1998).
47. http://www.dni.gov/index.php/about-this-site/no-fear-act/whistleblower-protection-laws.
48. http://www.fas.org/irp/dni/icig/icwpa-use.pdf; *see also* http://www.fas.org/sgp/news /secrecy/2014/03/032714.html.
49. 5 U.S.C. § 2303; PPD 19.
50. 10 U.S.C. § 1034.
51. 5 U.S.C. app.; *see also* http://www.treasury.gov/about/organizational-structure/ig/Pages/igdesk book.aspx.
52. 10 U.S.C. § 1587.
53. 15 U.S.C. § 78u-6(h).
54. 42 U.S.C. § 5851.
55. Pub. L. No. 111-5 § 1553 (stimulus law).
56. 5 U.S.C. § 7211.
57. *Id.* §§ 2301, 2302.
58. *Id.* § 2302(b)(9)(D).
59. *Id.* § 2302(b)(10).
60. Devine, *The Whistleblower Protection Act of 1989: Foundation for the Modern Law of Employment Dissent*, 51 ADMIN. L. REV. 534 (Spring 1999).
61. U.S. MERIT SYS. PROTECTION BD., OFFICE OF MERIT SYS. REVIEW AND STUDIES, BLOWING THE WHISTLE IN THE FEDERAL GOVERNMENT: A COMPARATIVE ANALYSIS OF 1980 AND 1983 SURVEY FINDINGS 31, 34 (1984).
62. Devine & Aplin, *Abuse of Authority: The Office of the Special Counsel and Whistleblower Protection*, 4 ANTIOCH L.J. 27–28 (Summer 1986).
63. DEVINE, GOV'T ACCOUNTABILITY PROJECT, MEMORANDUM ON FEDERAL CIRCUIT WHISTLEBLOWER DECISIONS SINCE PASSAGE OF 1994 AMENDMENTS (Aug. 16, 2013).
64. White v. Lachance, 174 F.3d 1378, 1381 (Fed. Cir. 1999), *cert. denied*, 528 U.S. 1153 (2000).
65. WEBSTER'S NEW WORLD COLLEGIATE DICTIONARY (4th ed. 1999).
66. White v. Dep't Air Force, 95 M.S.P.R. 1, 7–8 (2003).
67. http://www.washingtonpost.com/politics/under-carolyn-lerner-special-counsel-office-is-doing -its-job-now-observers-say/2012/06/28/gJQApX229V_story.html.
68. The Whistleblower Protection Act literally covers "any" credible disclosure of significant misconduct, with specified exceptions for public release of information that is classified or specifically restricted by statute. 5 U.S.C. § 2302(b)(8).
69. *Another FBI Employee Blows Whistle on Agency*, N.Y. TIMES, Aug. 2, 2004, http://www.nytimes .com/2004/08/02/politics/02whistleblower.html.
70. http://en.wikipedia.org/wiki/A._Ernest_Fitzgerald.
71. David Wise, *Leaks and the Law: The Story of Thomas Drake*, SMITHSONIAN MAG., July-Aug. 2011, http://www.smithsonianmag.com/history-archaeology/Leaks-and-the-Law-The-Story-of-Thomas -Drake.html.
72. An independent U.S. government agency established in 1979 pursuant to the Civil Service Reform Act, the OSC has authority to investigate and litigate against violations of merit principles, including whistleblower retaliation, and as a secure channel for disclosures of violations of law, rule or regulation; gross mismanagement; gross waste of funds, abuse of authority; and substantial and specific danger to public health and safety. 5 U.S.C. §§ 1211–2012.

73. The Inspector General Act of 1978, 5 U.S.C. app., established independent offices within federal agencies to conduct audits, investigations, and inspections. The Council on Inspector General Integrity and Efficiency (CIGIE) is a useful guide and directory to the laws, responsibilities and offices of inspectors general. *See* https://www.ignet.gov/igs/faq1.html.

74. http://www.osc.gov/documents/pubs/oscrole.pdf. The following are not covered employees with rights before the OSC: The Central Intelligence Agency, Defense Intelligence Agency, National Security Agency, and certain other intelligence agencies excluded by the president; the Government Accountability Office; U.S. Postal Regulatory Commission; and the Federal Bureau of Investigation. Government corporations unless listed at 31 U.S.C. § 9101 are covered by statutory whistleblower protections.

75. 5 U.S.C. § 1213.

76. Pub. L. No. 95-452, §§ 1–2, Oct. 12, 1978, 92 Stat. 1101, http://www.ignet.gov/pande/leg/igact asof1010.pdf.

77. *Id.* §§ 2(3), 4(a)(5), 5(b); THE SILVER BOOK: QUALITY STANDARDS FOR OFFICES OF FEDERAL INSPECTORS GENERAL, http://www.ignet.gov/pande/standards/Silver%20Book%20Revision%20-%208 -20-12r.pdf.

78. *See* http://www.ignet.gov/igs/faq1.html.

79. Gov't Accountability Office, GAO-07-1089T, Inspectors General: Opportunities to Enhance Independence and Accountability.

80. Pub. L. No. 110-409, §§ 3(f), 4(a)(3), For a valuable compendium of IG laws and accountability community background, standards, and authorities, see 1–4 THE INSPECTOR GENERAL DESKBOOK (2011), compiled by the Inspector General for the Department of the Treasury, http://www.treasury .gov/about/organizational-structure/ig/Pages/igdeskbook.aspx.

81. Applicability of certain pay provisions to other inspectors general. Act Oct. 14, 2008, Pub. L. No. 110-409, § 4(a)(3), 122 Stat. 4303; Oct. 7, 2010, Pub. L. No. 111-259, tit. IV, Subtitle A, § 405(b), 124 Stat. 2719, provides:
(A) In general. Notwithstanding any other provision of law, the annual rate of basic pay of the Inspector General of the Intelligence Community, the Inspector General of the Central Intelligence Agency, the Special Inspector General for Iraq Reconstruction, and the Special Inspector General for Afghanistan Reconstruction shall be that of an Inspector General as defined under section 12(3) of the Inspector General Act of 1978 (5 U.S.C. App.) (as amended by section 7(a) of this Act).
(B) Prohibition of cash bonus or awards. Section 3(f) of the Inspector General Act of 1978 (5 U.S.C. App.) (as amended by section 5 of this Act) shall apply to the Inspectors General described under subparagraph (A).
Inspectors General of designated federal entities; savings provisions. IG Reform Act Oct. 14, 2008, Pub. L. No. 110-409.

82. http://www.ignet.gov/pande/standards/Silver%20Book%20Revision%20-%208-20-12r.pdf.

83. Inspector General Act of 1978, as amended, § 8(2)(A)–(D). As stated § 8G 2(A)–(D) of the Inspector General Act, as amended:
The Secretary of Defense, in consultation with the Director of National Intelligence, may prohibit the inspector general of an element of the intelligence community specified in subparagraph (D) from initiating, carrying out, or completing any audit or investigation if the Secretary determines that the prohibition is necessary to protect vital national security interests of the United States.
The elements of the intelligence community specified in this subparagraph are as follows:
(i) The Defense Intelligence Agency.
(ii) The National Geospatial-Intelligence Agency.
(iii) The National Reconnaissance Office.
(iv) The National Security Agency.

84. 5 U.S.C. § 1213(c)(1).

85. *Id.* § 1213(b).

86. *Id.* § 1213(f). For detailed descriptions of these and other examples, see the OSC website, http://www.osc.gov/PublicFile1213AgencyRpt.htm; DEVINE & MAASSARANI, *supra* note 27, at ch. 1.

87. 5 U.S.C. § 1213(c)(1)(B), (d).

88. *Id.* § 1213(e)(1).

89. *Id.* § 1213(e)(2).

90. *Id.* § 1213(e)(3), 1219; http://www.osc.gov/PublicFile1213AgencyRpt.htm.

91. https://www.ignet.gov/.

92. Special Counsel *ex rel.* Gayl v. Navy, MSPB No. CB-1208-12-000 1-U-1 (Oct. 13, 2011); Jeff Stein, *Whistleblower Punches a Hole in Gates Memoir*, NEWSWEEK (Feb. 27, 2014), http://mag .newsweek.com/2014/02/28/whistle-blower-punches-hole-memoir-robert-gates.html.

93. DEVINE & DEVINE, GOV'T ACCOUNTABILITY PROJECT, WHISTLEBLOWER WITCH HUNTS: THE SMOKESCREEN SYNDROME 13–18 (2010), http://www.whistleblower.org/storage/documents/WWH final.pdf (researched summaries of Drake and Gayl, and a series of analogous retaliatory investigations of whistleblowers by those whose job is to protect them).

94. PRICEWATERHOUSECOOPERS & MARTIN LUTHER UNIV. ECON. & CRIME RESEARCH CTR., ECONOMIC CRIME: PEOPLE, CULTURE AND CONTROLS 10 (4th Biennial Global Economic Crime Survey 2007), http://www.pwc.com/en_GX/gx/economic-crime-survey/pdf/pwc_2007gecs.pdf; SOC'Y OF CERTIFIED FRAUD EXAMINERS, 2008 REPORT TO THE NATION ON OCCUPATIONAL FRAUD AND ABUSE 4, 30 (2008).

Regulating Classified and Controlled Unclassified Information

7

Andrew D. Fausett and Steven G. Stransky

I. INTRODUCTION

At the core of the debate regarding leaks and whistleblowers is the fact that an individual or organization discloses (or at least attempts to disclose) to the general public certain national security-related or otherwise sensitive information that the federal government has sought to keep within its custody or control. Generally speaking, in order to prevent the widespread disclosure of such information, the executive branch "classifies" the information, which itself is a term defined by law to refer to information that requires "protection against unauthorized disclosure" and has been specifically marked to indicate its classified status.[1] Executive Order 13,526, "Classified National Security Information,"[2] is the current executive order prescribing the system and the procedures by which executive branch departments and agencies classify, declassify, downgrade, and safeguard information and intelligence related to national security. Additionally, the president has created a framework regulating "controlled but unclassified information" and, in doing so, created procedures and policies that prohibit the disclosure of certain unclassified information to the general public.

This chapter discusses the legal authority under which the executive branch may classify or otherwise control the access to national security or other sensitive information; the procedures and policies governing how executive branch departments and agencies classify, downgrade, declassify, and safeguard such information; and the legal and policy framework for the safeguarding of, and access to, information that is unclassified, but still sensitive in nature.

II. THE LEGAL AUTHORITY TO CLASSIFY AND REGULATE ACCESS TO INFORMATION

The president's authority to classify national security-related information and regulate the access to and disclosure of sensitive but unclassified information derives from both the president's inherent authority under the Constitution and from relevant laws passed by Congress. Executive Order 13,526 itself explicitly acknowledges that the president's ability to develop the classification system is based upon both "the authority vested in . . . [the] [p]resident by the Constitution and laws of the United States."[3]

Regarding the former, Article II of the Constitution provides that "[t]he executive Power shall be vested in a President of the United States of America,"[4] and that the President "shall take care that the Laws be faithfully executed."[5] It also provides that "[t]he President shall be Commander in Chief of the Army and Navy of the United States, and of the Militia of the several States, when called into the actual Service of the United States."[6] Based on Article II authorities, the president is recognized as "the sole organ of the nation in its external relations, and its sole representative with foreign nations."[7]

The Supreme Court has relied upon these provisions and characterizations to make broad proclamations regarding the president's ability to classify or withhold information from public disclosure. For instance, in 1948 in *Chicago & Southern Air Lines, Inc. v. Waterman Steamship Corp.*,[8] the court noted that "[t]he President, both as Commander-in-Chief and as the Nation's organ for foreign affairs, has available intelligence services whose reports are not and ought not to be published to the world."[9] Similarly, in *United States v. Curtiss-Wright Export Corp.*, the court opined that the president "has his confidential sources of information. He has his agents in the form of diplomatic, consular and other officials. Secrecy in respect of information gathered by them may be highly necessary, and the premature disclosure of it productive of harmful results."[10] In his concurring opinion in 1971 in *New York Times Co. v. United States*,[11] Justice Potter Stewart provided his interpretation with regard to presidential authority in this area:

[I]t is the constitutional duty of the Executive—as a matter of sovereign prerogative and not as a matter of law as the courts know law—through the promulgation and enforcement of executive regulations, to protect the confidentiality necessary to carry out its responsibilities in the fields of international relations and national defense.[12]

One of the more often cited cases supporting the proposition that the president has broad inherent authority to restrict the disclosure of information held within the executive branch is *Department of the Navy v. Egan*.[13] Justice Harry Blackmun, writing on behalf of the Supreme Court, stated, "The President, after all, is the 'Commander in Chief of the Army and Navy of the United States.' His authority to classify and control access to information bearing on national security . . . flows primarily from this constitutional investment of power in the President and exists quite apart from any explicit congressional grant."[14] Blackmun reiterated the fact that the Supreme Court has previously "recognized the Government's 'compelling interest' in withholding national security information from unauthorized persons in the course of executive business. . . . The authority to protect such information falls on the President as head of the Executive Branch and as Commander in Chief."[15] The executive branch itself has broadly interpreted the president's authority in this realm, and the Department of Justice stated that "the President's roles as Commander in Chief, head of the Executive Branch, and sole organ of the Nation in its external relations require that he have ultimate and unimpeded authority over the collection, retention and dissemination of intelligence and other national security information in the Executive Branch."[16]

Although the president has inherent authority to classify and otherwise regulate the access to national security information, Congress has played a significant role in this area, and the Supreme Court has even suggested that "Congress could certainly [provide] that the Executive Branch adopt new [classification procedures] or [establish] its own procedures—subject only to whatever limitations the Executive Privilege may be held to impose on such congressional ordering."[17] Generally speaking, Congress has regulated how the executive branch protects, grants access to, and discloses national security-related information by passing laws that either directly establish information-handling procedures or that mandate executive branch officials develop and implement their own policies for classifying and protecting certain types of information.

For example, in the Atomic Energy Act of 1954, as amended,[18] Congress created an in-depth framework for how the executive branch uses, protects, and communicates nuclear-related "Restricted Data,"[19] including procedures related to the classification and declassification of Restricted Data, who may access Restricted Data, and the dissemination of such data to both executive and non-executive branch personnel.[20] Additionally, Congress has passed laws that prohibit individuals from gathering, transmitting, or disseminating certain national security-related information,[21] prohibit the unauthorized transmittal of information concerning code, cipher, or cryptographic systems or other communication intelligence activities,[22] and prohibit the unauthorized disclosure of the identities of undercover intelligence officers, informants, or sources.[23] Congress has even regulated the manner in which the president may share "intelligence information" with the United Nations.[24]

Congress has also mandated that the president and other executive branch officials create their own procedures and policies related to classified information and other discrete types of national security information, respectively. In the National Security Act of 1947, as amended,[25] Congress provided that "the President shall, by Executive order or regulation, establish procedures to govern access to classified information which shall be binding upon all departments, agencies, and offices of the executive branch of Government."[26] Through the Freedom of Information Act (FOIA),[27] Congress explicitly exempted from public disclosure information held within the executive branch that, by way of executive order, must be "kept secret in the interest of national defense or foreign policy" and is "in fact properly classified pursuant to such Executive order."[28] According to the Department of Justice, "[t]he Supreme Court has recognized that Congress intended for the President to bear immediate responsibility for protecting national security, which includes the development of policy that establishes what information must be classified to prevent harm to national security," and by including this exemption within FOIA, Congress "afford[ed] protection" to "properly classified information."[29]

Congress has also mandated that certain other executive branch officials develop their own procedures for regulating access to discrete types of national security-related information. For example, Congress mandated that the director for national intelligence "protect intelligence sources and methods from unauthorized disclosure"[30] and that the head of the Transportation Security Administration "prescribe regulations prohibiting the disclosure" of transportation-related information under certain circumstances.[31] Similar to how it addressed classified information in FOIA, Congress explicitly exempted from public disclosure (in the context of FOIA) information held within the executive branch that has been "specifically exempted from disclosure by statute," such as information related to intelligence sources and methods,[32] certain transportation security-related information,[33] and, as noted above, nuclear-related material information[34] and information concerning communication intelligence activities.[35]

Ultimately, there is a broad range of authority that permits the executive branch to classify and prohibit the disclosure of national security-related information. As noted, the president relies upon both inherent authority in Article II of the Constitution and the laws passed by Congress to classify and regulate access to such information.

III.   CLASSIFYING INFORMATION: THE PROCESS

Although the government has sought to protect sensitive information and intelligence from public disclosure since the time of its founding,[36] it was not until World War I that the first classification framework based on the relative sensitivity of information was implemented by the executive branch,[37] and not until World War II that such a system was formalized through an executive order.[38]

The most recent such presidential directive, Executive Order 13,526, was issued by President Barack Obama in December 2009.[39] It continued the executive branch policy of delineating three levels of classification—Top Secret, Secret, and Confidential—based upon the degree of harm to the national security that could result from the unauthorized disclosure of such information.[40] Specifically, the designations of Top Secret, Secret, and Confidential apply to the types of information whose unauthorized disclosure "could be expected to cause," respectively, "exceptionally grave damage," "serious damage," or "damage" to "the national security" of the United States.[41] See Table 1.

Table 1. Classification Designations

Classification	Definition	Marking
Top Secret	Information, the unauthorized disclosure of which reasonably could be expected to cause exceptionally grave damage to the national security that the original classification authority is able to identify or describe	TS
Secret	Information, the unauthorized disclosure of which reasonably could be expected to cause serious damage to the national security that the original classification authority is able to identify or describe	S
Confidential	Information, the unauthorized disclosure of which reasonably could be expected to cause damage to the national security that the original classification authority is able to identify or describe	C

The executive order, in turn, defines "damage to the national security" to mean "harm to the national defense or foreign relations of the United States from the unauthorized disclosure of information, taking into consideration such aspects of the information as the sensitivity, value, utility, and provenance of that information."[42]

Information may be originally classified at the Top Secret, Secret, or Confidential level only if four conditions are satisfied:

- The government official classifying the information is designated an "original classification authority";
- The information in question is owned by, produced by or for, or under the control of the federal government;
- The information falls within one or more classification categories; and
- The individual that classifies the information determines (as discussed above) that the unauthorized disclosure of the information reasonably could be expected to result in damage to the national security, and can identify or describe such damage.[43]

Regarding the first condition, Executive Order 13,526 grants the president and officials designated by the president, vice president, or heads of executive branch agencies (such as cabinet-level secretaries) the authority to "classify information originally."[44] The presidential "order" that was issued in accordance with Executive Order 13,526 identified more than 20 officials and offices as having original classification authority for the Top Secret level, and several other officials who have such authority for the Secret level.[45] It should be noted that government officials who are authorized to classify information at a specified level are also authorized to classify information at a lower classification level.[46] The executive order provides that the heads of agencies may delegate original classification authority to subordinate officials, subject to certain requirements, such as ensuring that such designated subordinates "have a demonstrable and continuing need to exercise" the original classification authority, requiring any delegation of authority to be in writing, and mandating training for officials with original classification authority.[47]

The practice of how the heads of executive branch agencies delegate their original classification authority varies by agency. For example, the secretary of defense has delegated Top Secret original classification authority to well over 100 Defense Department officials, ranging from senior level military, policy, intelligence, and legal personnel to the president of the National Defense University.[48] On the other hand, the secretary for homeland security has delegated Top Secret original classification authority to only 18 officials.[49] According to a government report, in fiscal year 2012, there were 2,326 government officials with original classification authority.[50]

Although there are a limited number of officials that possess original classification authority, all government officials that reproduce, extract, or summarize classified information exercise "derivate classification authority."[51] Derivate classification refers to incorporating, paraphrasing, or generating in a new document or instrument, information that is already classified.[52] Information may be derivatively classified in two ways: (1) through the use of a source document generated by an original classification authority; or (2) through the use of a security classification guide.[53] According to the government, there were more than 95 million derivative classification actions taken in fiscal year 2012.[54]

Regarding the "classification categories" noted above, Executive Order 13,526 provides that information cannot be classified unless it pertains to one or more of the following categories:

- Military plans, weapons systems, or operations;
- Foreign government information;
- Intelligence activities (including covert action), intelligence sources or methods, or cryptology;
- Foreign relations or foreign activities of the United States, including confidential sources;

- Scientific, technological, or economic matters relating to the national security;
- Government programs for safeguarding nuclear materials or facilities;
- Vulnerabilities or capabilities of systems, installations, infrastructures, projects, plans, or protection services relating to the national security; or
- The development, production, or use of weapons of mass destruction.[55]

The order also provides guidelines regarding how classified information must be identified or "marked."[56] Specifically, it mandates that, at the time of the original classification, the classified information itself must identify:

(1) the level of classification [i.e., Top Secret (TS), Secret (S), or Confidential (C)];

(2) the identity of the original classification authority;

(3) the agency from which the information originated;

(4) declassification instructions, including when the document shall be declassified; and,

(5) the reason for the classification, including a citation to the applicable classification category described above.[57]

Agencies that originate classified information are responsible for clearly marking which portions of the information are classified and unclassified.[58] The order delegates to the director of the Information Security Oversight Office (ISOO) within the National Archives and Record Administration (NARA) the authority to develop and issue directives implementing Executive Order 13,526.[59] In response, the ISOO promulgated 32 C.F.R. Parts 2001 and 2003 to provide guidance to agencies and departments on original and derivative classification, downgrading and declassifying information, and on the safeguarding of classified national security information.[60]

To further assist officials that possess, retain, or disseminate classified information, ISOO issued a booklet, *Marking National Security Information*,[61] with examples of classification markings for a wide range of scenarios. Appendix I at the end of this chapter is one such example.[62]

IV. CLASSIFICATION RELATED TO INTELLIGENCE ACTIVITIES AND CONTROLLED ACCESS PROGRAMS

The director of national intelligence—the DNI—was given the discretion to issue directives that implement Executive Order 13,526 with respect to the protection of intelligence sources, methods, and activities.[63] In accordance with this authority, the DNI issued Intelligence Community Directive 710,[64] and, through the Controlled Access Program Coordination Office (an office overseen by the DNI), published the *Intelligence Community Authorized Classification and Control Markings Register and Manual*.[65] These documents, inter alia, created a marking system for controlled access programs, such as Sensitive Compartmented Information (SCI)[66] and special access programs, and identify other authorized classification and control markings used to communicate classification levels, compartmentalization, dissemination controls, disclosure or release authorizations, and other warnings.[67] The Office of the Director of National Intelligence published a training manual[68] that provides helpful examples of markings used to identify classification, SCI, and other dissemination controls,[69] and Appendix II at the end of this chapter is an official government document that has been recently declassified and contains similar classification, SCI, and control markings.[70]

Separately, Executive Order 13,526 authorizes the DNI, the attorney general, and the secretaries of the Departments of State, Defense, Energy, and Homeland Security (or their principal deputies) to create special access programs (SAPs).[71] A SAP is not a classification level, but rather is a "program established for a specific class of classified information that imposes safeguarding and access requirements that exceed those normally required for information at the same classification level."[72] A SAP may only be created to protect highly sensitive policies, initiatives, or programs, and only when (1) authorized by statute or (2) upon a specific finding that there is an "exceptional" vulnerability of, or threat to, specific information, and the normal criteria for granting access to information at the same classification level is not "deemed sufficient" to protect the information subject to a SAP from unauthorized disclosure.[73] All SAPs have identifiers that represent the program's assigned nickname, code word, or abbreviation. As part of its training manual, the Office of the Director of National Intelligence provided examples of what a marking would look like to identify information within a special access program.[74]

Executive Order 13,526 specifically dictates that government officials must "keep the number of [special access programs] at an absolute minimum."[75] According to some commenters, however, the Defense Department's "list of code names for [special access programs] runs 300 pages," and "[t]he intelligence community has hundreds more."[76] DNI James R. Clapper noted a few years ago that "[t]here's only one entity in the entire universe that has visibility on all SAPs—that's God."[77]

V. DECLASSIFYING AND DOWNGRADING INFORMATION

Executive Order 13,526 requires that classified information be "declassified as soon as it no longer meets the standards for classification" under the order.[78] To ensure that information is declassified or downgraded in a timely manner, both the order and its implementing regulations permit government officials to challenge the classification status of information and established declassification processes within the executive branch.[79] These processes permit government employees (and contractors) as well as members of the public to challenge the classification of a document.

Regarding the ability of government officials to challenge the classification status of information, the law provides that "[a]uthorized holders of information who, in good faith, believe its classification status is improper are encouraged and expected to challenge the classification status of [that] information."[80] An "authorized holder" refers to "any individual who has been granted access to specific classified information,"[81] in accordance with Executive Order 13,526; that is, a person who has been determined by an agency head (or the agency head's designee) to be eligible for access to classified information, has signed an approved nondisclosure agreement, and has a need to know the information.[82]

Authorized holders of classified information who seek to challenge the classification of a document must first present the challenge "to an original classification authority with jurisdiction over the information."[83] Each agency is responsible for establishing its own procedures for processing, tracking, and recording such challenges.[84] If the challenge is denied or if the agency fails to respond within 120 days of the challenge (or fails to respond to an internal appeal within 90 days of the appeal), the challenger may forward the challenge to the Interagency Security Classification Appeals Panel (ISCAP) located at the National Archives and Records Administration.[85] According to a report issued by the ISOO last year, in fiscal year 2012, government officials undertook 402 "formal challenges" to the classification status of information;[86] of the 402 challenges, 266 were "fully affirmed" at their classification level, 126 were "overturned either in whole or in part," and ten classification challenges were not concluded by the time the report was issued.[87]

There are four declassification processes within the executive branch:

1. *Automatic declassification* removes the classification of information at the close of every calendar year when that information reaches the 25-year threshold.
2. *Systematic declassification review* is required for records of permanent historical value that are exempted from automatic declassification.
3. *Discretionary declassification review* is conducted when the public interest in disclosure outweighs the need for continued classification, or when the agency feels the information no longer requires protection and can be declassified earlier.
4. *Mandatory declassification review* provides direct, specific review for declassification of information when requested by the public.[88]

As an initial matter, Executive Order 13,526 generally provides that classified records be *automatically* declassified if they (1) are more than 25 years old and (2) have "permanent historical value" as a matter of federal law.[89] Agency heads may, however, exempt from this requirement information that, if released, would:

- Reveal the identity of a confidential human source, a human intelligence source, a relationship with an intelligence or security service of a foreign entity, or a nonhuman intelligence source; or impair the effectiveness of an intelligence method currently in use, available for use, or under development;
- Reveal information that would assist in the development, production, or use of weapons of mass destruction;
- Impair U.S. cryptologic systems or activities or "state-of-the-art technology within a U.S. weapon system";
- Expose "named or numbered" U.S. war plans still in effect (or operational or tactical elements of prior plans contained within the current plans);
- Seriously harm the relations of the United States with another country;
- Impair the protection of the president, vice president, and other individuals who receive protective services in the interests of national security;
- Disrupt national security emergency preparedness plans or identify the current vulnerabilities of systems, installations, or infrastructures relating to national security; or
- Violate a statute, treaty, or international agreement prohibiting declassification of the information at 25 years.[90]

According to the Department of Justice, "The objective of automatic declassification is to declassify information without compromising national security. The presumption is that 25 year old information is declassified unless it clearly falls under one or more of the 9 exemptions."[91] Under the automatic declassification review process, in fiscal year 2012, agencies and departments reviewed approximately 40 million pages of classified information and declassified approximately 17.7 million pages.[92]

Each federal department and agency that has originated classified information must "establish and conduct a program for *systematic* declassification review for records of permanent historical value exempted from automatic declassification."[93] In addition, the U.S. Archivist is responsible for conducting a systematic declassification review program for certain classified information.[94] In fiscal year 2012, departments and agencies reviewed 4.17 million pages of classified information under a systematic declassification review process and declassified approximately 2 million pages.[95]

Executive Order 13,526 and its implementing regulations also provide a *discretionary* declassification process. "It is presumed," according to the order, "that information that continues to meet the classification requirements under [the] order requires continued protection."[96] It states, however, that "[i]n some exceptional cases . . . the need to protect such information may be outweighed by the public interest in disclosure of the information, and in these cases the information should be declassified."[97] Agencies may establish a discretionary declassification program separate from their automatic, systematic, and mandatory review programs.[98] According to Professor Jennifer E. Sims, "Discretionary declassification provides policymakers a means of aligning classification determinations with contemporary events and superseding the abstract deadlines associated with time-based declassification. To a greater extent, declassification of contemporary information freed from the constraints of arbitrary declassification dates empowers democratic discourse and enables more transparent and informed decision making."[99] Sims cited President Obama's decision in 2010 to release the size of the U.S. nuclear stockpile as an example of the value of the discretionary declassification process, but also noted that this process "is seldom used" by government officials.[100] In fiscal year 2012, the government reviewed approximately 846,000 classified pages under a discretionary review process and declassified approximately 180,000 pages.[101]

Finally, any member of the general public may initiate the *mandatory* declassification review process by requesting a declassification review from an agency, which the agency head must provide so long as (1) "the request for a review describes the document or material containing the information with sufficient specificity to enable the agency to locate it with a reasonable amount of effort"; (2) the document or material is not contained within an "operational file" exempted from search, review, and disclosure under FOIA;[102] and (3) "the information is not the subject of pending litigation."[103]

According to the ISOO, mandatory declassification review is "popular with some researchers" because it is viewed "as a less litigious alternative to requests under the [FOIA]," and "[i]t is also used to seek the declassification of [p]residential papers or records not subject to FOIA."[104] As with challenges filed by "authorized holders" of classified information, agencies are generally required to develop and implement their own procedures for performing mandatory declassification reviews;[105] however, the secretary of defense is charged with developing special procedures applying to mandatory declassification review requests for cryptologic information,[106] and the DNI is required to develop such procedures for requests "pertaining to intelligence sources, methods, and activities."[107] Agencies are required to make their decisions regarding requests for mandatory declassification within one year from the date of receipt of the request and must provide the requester with the right to administratively appeal a partial or complete denial of the request.[108]

Like denied classification challenges by authorized holders, denials of requests for mandatory declassification reviews may be appealed to the ISCAP,[109] but only if the requester has received a final agency decision denying the request or has not received an initial decision from the agency within one year of filing the request or has not received a final decision of an agency appeal within 180 days of the filing of the appeal.[110]

The ISCAP review process is similar for both classification challenges by authorized holders and requests for mandatory declassification review. In both cases, the executive secretary for ISCAP will perform an initial review of the appeal to determine whether ISCAP may assert jurisdiction.[111] That review determines whether, among other things, the appeal meets the basic requirements for consideration of the underlying challenge or request set forth in Executive Order 13,526,[112] whether the appeal has been filed within 60 days of the agency denial or expiration of the time period provided to the agency to respond,[113] and whether the appeal contains enough information for the executive secretary to obtain all of the pertinent documents about the challenge or request from the affected agency.[114]

Assuming the appeal is not rejected on jurisdictional grounds, the executive secretary will prepare and present an appeal file to ISCAP for its review prior to a vote on the appeal.[115] ISCAP is empowered to affirm the agency's decision, reverse its decision in whole or in part, or remand the matter to the agency for further consideration,[116] but "[a] decision to reverse an agency's decision requires the affirmative vote of at least a majority of the members present."[117]

Ultimately, though, the president retains final authority over the declassification or downgrading of classified information. If ISCAP reverses an agency decision, "the agency head may petition the President through the National Security Advisor to overrule the [ISCAP's] decision."[118] Further, "[t]he information at issue remains classified until the President has issued a decision."[119]

VI. CONTROLLED UNCLASSIFIED INFORMATION

In contrast to the well-regulated framework for identifying, marking, handling, and reviewing classified information, information that does not implicate the national security of the United States through its unauthorized disclosure, yet still is considered sensitive by a particular agency for some other reason, remains subject to processes and procedures that are developed at the agency level. This information, sometimes referred to as "Sensitive But Unclassified," "For Official Use Only," or "Limited Distribution," has in recent years been captured under the umbrella designation of "Controlled Unclassified Information." While governance of CUI at the interagency level remains nascent, the government has taken some initial steps toward codifying CUI and its various subcategories, most notably through the issuance of Executive Order 13,556 on November 4, 2010.[120]

The order sets forth a basic framework for the governance and regulation of CUI. It requires that CUI categories and subcategories "serve as exclusive designations for identifying unclassified information throughout the executive branch"[121] and designates NARA as the executive agent for implementation of the order.[122] In that capacity, NARA is directed to "approve categories and subcategories of CUI and associated markings to be applied uniformly throughout the executive branch"[123] once they are published in a public CUI registry "reflecting authorized CUI categories and subcategories, associated markings, and applicable safeguarding, dissemination, and decontrol procedures."[124]

NARA is further empowered to "develop and issue such directives as are necessary to implement" the order, including "policies and procedures concerning marking, safeguarding, dissemination, and decontrol of CUI."[125] These policies and procedures are intended to remain consistent across the executive branch "to the extent practicable and permitted by law, regulation, and Government-wide policies."[126] NARA published the first iteration of the CUI public registry on November 4, 2011.[127] Originally, the registry contained 16 approved categories and 74 associated subcategories for CUI based on 398 unique restrictions.[128] Since then, the number of approved categories and subcategories has ballooned to 22 and 102, respectively.[129] As of this date, however, the NARA has not released to the public any government-wide policies or procedures for safeguarding, disseminating, decontrolling, or marking CUI.[130]

Executive Order 13,556 and its implementation through the CUI registry represent important steps in the development of a robust governance framework for executive branch information that, while sensitive, does not meet the standards for classification set forth in the order. These steps are, however, subject to problems of their own. As at least one commenter has noted, the CUI categories and subcategories are "prone to proliferation," which "may call into question the accuracy of information categorized under a particular category or subcategory."[131]

Even more worrisome, the definition of CUI provided in the order may not be broad enough to encompass all types of sensitive (but unclassified) data.

The order defines CUI as unclassified "information that requires safeguarding or dissemination controls pursuant to and consistent with law, regulations, and [g]overnment-wide policies."[132] But not all types of unclassified sensitive data arise from "law, regulations, [or] [g]overnment-wide policies." For example, Law Enforcement Sensitive (LES) data has historically been viewed as protected by a common-law privilege rather than by statute or regulation.[133] To address this potential gap in the applicability of CUI framework, the government has issued guidance that permits "provisional approval" of proposed CUI categories that provide the protection afforded to information marked as CUI, but, like the LES marking, are not recognized anywhere in statute, regulation, or government-wide policy.[134] In other words, this guidance permits executive branch departments and agencies to submit proposed CUI categories that do not have a statutory, regulatory, or government-wide policy foundation for its issuance by using the same process as other categories or subcategories, subject to certain procedural restrictions.[135]

Thus, an agency that supports including LES as a category in CUI could now submit that category for inclusion in the CUI registry *provided* that, within the following 12 months, that agency either (1) exercised preexisting authority or was granted new authority to issue a government-wide policy recognizing LES data as a type of information subject to special protections *or* (2) commenced a rulemaking process to identify LES data in this way.

NOTES

1. Exec. Order No. 13,526, § 6.1(i), Classified National Security Information, 75 Fed. Reg. 1013 (Dec. 29, 2009); *see also* 50 U.S.C. § 3126(1) (2012) (formerly 50 U.S.C. § 426).
2. Exec. Order No. 13,526, 75 Fed. Reg. 1013 (Dec. 29, 2009).
3. *Id.* pmbl.
4. U.S. CONST. art. II, § 1, cl. 1.
5. *Id.* art. II, § 3.
6. *Id.* art. II, § 2, cl. 1.
7. United States v. Curtiss-Wright Exp. Corp., 299 U.S. 304, 319 (1936) (quoting John Marshal, *Annals*, 6th Cong., col. 613 (Mar. 7, 1800)).
8. 333 U.S. 103 (1948).
9. *Id.* at 111.
10. *Curtiss-Wright Exp. Corp.*, 299 U.S. at 320.
11. 403 U.S. 713 (1971).
12. *Id.* at 729–30 (Stewart, J., concurring).
13. 484 U.S. 518 (1988).
14. *Id.* at 527 (quoting U.S. CONST. art. II, § 2, cl. 1) (citing Cafeteria Workers v. McElroy, 367 U.S. 886, 890 (1961)).
15. *Id.* (internal citation and quotation marks omitted).
16. Brief for the Appellees, Am. Foreign Serv. Ass'n v. Garfinkel, 488 U.S. 923 (1988) (No. 87-2127), at 42. *See* Christopher H. Schroeder, Acting Assistant Att'y Gen., Dep't of Justice, the Office of Legal Counsel, Memorandum Opinion for the General Counsel, Cent. Intelligence Agency, Access to Classified Information, at 2 (Nov. 26, 1998).
17. Envtl. Prot. Agency v. Mink, 410 U.S. 73, 83 (1973).
18. 42 U.S.C. § 2011.
19. The term "Restricted Data" is defined as "all data concerning (1) design, manufacture, or utilization of atomic weapons; (2) the production of special nuclear material; or (3) the use of special nuclear material in the production of energy, but shall not include data declassified or removed from the Restricted Data category pursuant to section 2162 of this title." *Id.* § 2014(y).
20. *Id.* §§ 2162–2168.
21. 18 U.S.C. §§ 793–794.
22. *Id.* § 798.
23. 50 U.S.C. § 3121 (formerly cited as 50 U.S.C. § 421).
24. *Id.* § 3047 (formerly cited as 50 U.S.C. § 404g).
25. *Id.* § 3002 (formerly cited as 50 U.S.C. § 401).
26. *Id.* § 3161 (formerly cited as 50 U.S.C. § 435). Congress promulgated limited requirements that must be included in the procedures established by the president, such as the requirement that individuals with access to classified information successfully complete a background check. *Id.*
27. 5 U.S.C. § 552.
28. *Id.* § 552(b)(1).
29. DEP'T OF JUSTICE, GUIDE TO THE FREEDOM OF INFORMATION ACT 141 (2013).
30. 50 U.S.C. § 3507 (formerly cited as 50 U.S.C. § 403g).
31. 49 U.S.C. § 114(r)(1).
32. *See* Cent. Intelligence Agency v. Sims, 471 U.S. 159, 167–68 (1985).
33. *See* Elec. Privacy Info. Ctr. v. U.S. Dep't of Homeland Sec., 928 F. Supp. 2d 139, 145–46 (D.D.C. 2013); Skurow v. U.S. Dep't of Homeland Sec., 892 F. Supp. 2d 319, 331–33 (D.D.C. 2012); Tooley v. Bush, No. 06-306, 2006 WL 3783142 (D.D.C., Dec. 21, 2006), *rev'd in part on other grounds sub nom.* Tooley v. Napolitano, 556 F.3d 836 (D.C. Cir. 2009).

Notes

34. *See* Meeropol v. Smith, No. 75-1121, slip op. at 53–55 (D.D.C. 1984), *aff'd in relevant part & remanded in part on other grounds sub nom.* Meeropol v. Meese, 790 F.2d 942 (D.C. Cir. 1986).

35. *See* Larson v. Dep't of State, 565 F.3d 857, 868–69 (D.C. Cir. 2009).

36. Louis Henkin, *The Right to Know and the Duty to Withhold: The Case of the Pentagon Papers*, 120 U. Pa. L. Rev. 271, 273 (1971).

37. Dep't of the Navy v. Egan, 484 U.S. 518, 527 (1988) (citing Note, *Developments in the Law: The National Security Interest and Civil Liberties*, 85 Harv. L. Rev. 1130, 1193–94 (1972)).

38. *Id.* at 527–28. *See* Exec. Order No. 8381, Defining Certain Vital Military and Naval Installations and Equipment, 5 Fed. Reg. 1147 (Mar. 26, 1940).

39. Exec. Order No. 13,526, 75 Fed. Reg. 1013 (Dec. 29, 2009); *see also* 32 C.F.R. pts. 2001 & 2003, Classified National Security Information (June 25, 2010).

40. Exec. Order No. 13,526, § 1.2 (a)–(b).

41. *Id.* § 1.2 (a).

42. *Id.* § 6.1(l).

43. *Id.* § 1.1(a). It should be noted that Executive Order No. 13,526 specifically prohibits information from being classified in order to "conceal violations of law, inefficiency, or administrative error; prevent embarrassment to a person, organization, or agency; restrain competition; or prevent or delay the release of information that does not require protection in the interest of the national security." *Id.* § 1.7(a).

44. *Id.* § 1.3(a).

45. President Barack H. Obama, Original Classification Authority, Dec. 29, 2009, 75 Fed. Reg. 735 (Jan. 5, 2010).

46. Exec. Order No. 13,526, § 1.3(b).

47. *Id.* § 1.3(a)(3), (c)–(d).

48. U.S. Dep't of Def., Internal Memorandum, Delegation of Top Secret Original Classification Authority (May 5, 2011) (on file with the author).

49. U.S. Dep't of Homeland Sec., Delegation No. 8100, Delegation of Original Classification Authority (June 4, 2010) (on file with the author).

50. Info. Sec. Oversight Office, Report to the President for Fiscal Year (FY) 2012, at 2 (June 20, 2013), http://www.archives.gov/isoo/reports/2012-annual-report.pdf [hereinafter ISOO Report].

51. *See* Exec. Order No. 13,526, § 2.1(a)–(b); 32 C.F.R. § 2001.22(a).

52. Exec. Order No. 13,526, § 2.1(a)–(b).

53. 32 C.F.R. § 2001.22(a). A security classification guide is a set of instructions promulgated by an original classification authority that identifies elements of information on a specific subject matter that must be classified and establishes the level and duration of classification for each such element. *See* Exec. Order No. 13,526, § 2.2; ISOO Report, *supra* note 50, at 7.

54. ISOO Report, *supra* note 50, at 7.

55. Exec. Order No. 13,526, § 1.4.

56. *Id.* § 1.6.

57. *Id.* § 1.6(a).

58. *Id.* § 1.6(c).

59. *Id.* § 5.1(a). The director of the ISOO performs this function under the direction of the Archivist and in consultation with the National Security Advisor. *Id.*

60. 32 C.F.R. pts. 2001 & 2003.

61. Info. Sec. Oversight Office, Marking National Security Information (Dec. 2010) (rev. 2, Jan. 2014), http://www.archives.gov/isoo/training/marking-booklet.pdf.

62. *Id.*

63. Exec. Order No. 13,526, § 5.1(c).

64. Office of the Dir. of Nat'l Intelligence, Intelligence Community Directive 710: Classification and Control Markings System (June 21, 2013) [hereinafter ICD 710], http://www.dni.gov/files /documents /ICD/ICD_710.pdf.

65. *See* OFFICE OF THE DIR. OF NAT'L INTELLIGENCE, OFFICE OF THE NAT'L COUNTERINTELLI-GENCE EXECUTIVE, INTELLIGENCE COMMUNITY CLASSIFICATION AND CONTROL MARKINGS IMPLE-MENTATION MANUAL (May 31, 2011) [hereinafter CAPCO MANUAL], http://fas.org/sgp/othergov /intel/capco_imp.pdf.

66. Sensitive Compartmented Information, or SCI, refers to intelligence or information related to or derived from intelligence sources, methods, or analytical processes, and requires special handling procedures within a formal access control system established by the DNI. *Id.* at 43.

67. *See* ICD 710, *supra* note 64; CAPCO MANUAL, *supra* note 65.

68. Office of the Dir. of Nat'l Intelligence, Classification Management and the IC Markings System Course (Feb. 2012), http://www.ncix.gov/training/WBT/docs/CM_AltText_021312.pdf [hereinafter IC Marking System].

69. The Office of the Director of National Intelligence provided the following example of classification markings related to an SCI program: SECRET//TK//NOFORN [abbreviated as (S//TK//NF)] This classification marking refers to information that is classified at the Secret (S)-level, contains information from the TALENT KEYHOLE (TK) SCI control system, and cannot be disseminated to foreign nationals (NOFORN (NF)). *Id.* at 93. The term "Talent Keyhole" or "TK" is the SCI control system for information or activities related to the space-based collection of imagery or signals intelligence, or reconnaissance satellites. CAPCO Manual, *supra* note 65, at 65. *Id.* at 94. The term "Talent Keyhole" or "TK" is the SCI control system for information or activities related to the space-based collection of imagery or signals intelligence, or reconnaissance satellites. CAPCO MANUAL, *supra* note 65, at 65. The term "Special Intelligence" or "SI" is the SCI control system for "technical and intelligence information derived from the monitoring of foreign communications signals by other than the intended recipients." *Id.* at 58. GAMMA is a compartment of SI. *Id.* at 62–63. The term "Originator Control" or "ORCON" is marked for information in which one can ready identify "intelligence sources or methods that are particularly susceptible to countermeasures that would nullify or measurably reduce their effectiveness." *Id.* at 100. Information that is marked as "ORCON" generally cannot be further disseminated (except under certain defined circumstances) without advanced permission from the originator. *Id.*

70. Appendix II is identified as a "February 25, 2009 [National Security Agency] notification memorandum to the House Permanent Select Committee on Intelligence (HPSCI) of compliance incidents identified during an on-going NSA-initiated End-to-End review of its collection of bulk telephony metadata pursuant to Section 215 authorities." The Office of the Director of National Intelligence, "IC on the Record," http://icontherecord.tumblr.com/post/65365104024/dni-clapper -declassifies-additional-intelligence.

71. Exec. Order No. 13,526, § 4.3(a).

72. *Id.* § 6.1(oo).

73. *Id.* § 4.3(a).

74. The example: TOP SECRET//SAR-BP//NOFORN [abbreviated as (TS//SAR-BP//NF)] identifies information that is classified at the Top Secret (TS)-level, contains information from a SAP that is code-named BUTTERED POPCORN (or BP), and is not releasable to foreign nationals (NOFORN (NF)). IC MARKING SYSTEM, *supra* note 68, at 94. The acronym SAR stands for "Special Access Required" and is used to identify that the subsequent letters in a classification marking relate to a SAP. *Id.* at 90.

75. Exec. Order No. 13,526, § 4.3(a).

76. Dana Priest & William M. Arkin, *Top Secret America: The Rise of the New American Security State*, WASH. POST (July 20, 2010).

77. *Id.*

78. Exec. Order No. 13,526, § 3.1(a).
79. ISOO Report, *supra* note 50, at 9.
80. Exec. Order No. 13,525, § 1.8(a).
81. 32 C.F.R. § 2001.14(a).
82. Exec. Order No. 13,526, § 4.1(a).
83. 32 C.F.R. § 2001.14(a).
84. Exec. Order No. 13,526, § 1.8(b); *see also* 32 C.F.R. § 2001.14(b). These procedures must ensure that individuals are not subject to retribution for bringing a challenge, that challenges are reviewed by an impartial officer or panel, and that challengers are informed of their right to appeal the agency decision. Exec. Order No. 13,526, § 1.8(b)(1)–(3).
85. 32 C.F.R. § 2001.14(b)(3). The Interagency Security Classification Appeals Panels is composed of officials from the Departments of State, Defense, and Justice, the National Archives, the Office of the Director of National Intelligence, and the National Security Advisor and, in certain circumstances, the Central Intelligence Agency. Exec. Order No. 13,526, § 5.3.
86. ISOO Report, *supra* note 50, at 8.
87. *Id.*
88. *Id.*
89. Exec. Order No. 13,526, § 3.3(a).
90. *Id.* § 3.3(b).
91. U.S. Dep't of Justice, Declassification: Frequently Asked Questions, http://www.justice.gov /open/ declassification-faq.html.
92. ISOO Report, *supra* note 50, at 10.
93. Exec. Order No. 13,526, § 3.4(a) (emphasis added).
94. *Id.* § 3.4(b).
95. ISOO Report, *supra* note 50, at 10.
96. Exec. Order No. 13,526, § 3.1(d).
97. *Id.*
98. 32 C.F.R. § 2001.35(b).
99. Jennifer Sims, *Discretionary Declassification and Release of Contemporary National Security Information*, Nat'l Archives Blog (Mar. 29, 2011), http://blogs.archives.gov/transformingclassific ation/?p=116.
100. *Id.*
101. ISOO Report, *supra* note 50, at 10.
102. *See* 50 U.S.C. § 3141 (authorizing the director of the Central Intelligence Agency (CIA) to exempt "operational files" from FOIA); *id.* § 3142 (authorizing the same for the director of the National Geospatial Agency (NGA)); *id.* § 3143 (authorizing the same for the director of the National Reconnaissance Office (NRO)); *id.* § 3144 (authorizing the same for the director of the National Security Agency (NSA)). While properly classified information is generally exempt from *disclosure* under FOIA pursuant to 5 U.S.C. § 552(b)(1), most agencies are still required to compile, review, and, to the greatest extent possible, redact for release such information if it is responsive to a FOIA request. Agencies with operational files exemptions, on the other hand, are completely exempt from the requirements of the statute insofar as their operational files are concerned, alleviating the administrative and logistical burdens inherent in responding to FOIA requests. *See* 50 U.S.C. § 3141 (permitting the director of the CIA, in conjunction with the DNI, to "exempt operational files" of the CIA "from the provisions of [FOIA] which require publication or disclosure, or search or review in connection therewith"); *id.* § 3142 (providing the same with respect to the director of the NGA); *id.* § 3143 (providing the same with respect to the director of the NRO); *id.* § 3144 (providing the same with respect to the director of the NSA).
103. Exec. Order No. 13,526, § 3.5(a). Information originated by the incumbent president, incumbent vice president, their staff, committees, commissions, or boards appointed by the incumbent president, or "other entities within the Executive Office of the President that solely advise and assist

the incumbent President" is exempt from mandatory declassification review, *id.* § 3.5(b), as are "[d]ocuments required to be submitted for prepublication review or other administrative process pursuant to an approved nondisclosure agreement," *id.* § 3.5(g). In addition, "[r]equests for mandatory declassification review made to an element of the Intelligence Community by anyone other than a citizen of the United States or an alien lawfully admitted for permanent residence[] may be denied by the receiving Intelligence Community element." 32 C.F.R. § 2001.33(i).

104. ISOO REPORT, *supra* note 50, at 14.

105. Exec. Order No. 13,526, § 3.5(e).

106. 32 C.F.R. § 2001.33(c). These procedures must be jointly developed by the Secretary of Defense and the Director of National Intelligence insofar as they pertain to situations where "cryptologic information pertains to intelligence activities." *Id.*

107. *Id.* § 2001.33(d).

108. *Id.* § 2001.33(a)(2)(ii). Administrative appeals must be filed within 60 days of the agency denial. *Id.*

109. *See id.* § 2001.33(a)(2)(iv) (providing for appeals of agency decisions in accordance with "rules and procedures" to be published by the ISCAP "for bringing mandatory declassification appeals before it").

110. *Id.* § 2003.13(a)(3).

111. *See id.* § 2003.11(d) (establishing this initial review in the context of classification challenges by authorized holders of classified information); *id.* § 2003.13(d) (establishing the same review in the context of requests for mandatory declassification reviews).

112. *See id.* § 2003.11(a) (setting forth the jurisdictional requirements for ISCAP review of classification challenges by authorized holders of classified information); *id.* § 2003.13(a) (setting forth the jurisdictional requirements for ISCAP review of denials of requests for mandatory declassification review).

113. *See id.* § 2003.11(c) (establishing this requirement in the context of classification challenges by authorized holders of classified information); *id.* § 2003.13(c) (establishing the same requirement in the context of requests for mandatory declassification reviews). For both denials of classification challenges by authorized holders of classified information and denials of requests for mandatory declassification review, appeals should be sent via e-mail to ISCAP@nara.gov or by mail to Executive Secretary, Interagency Security Classification Appeals Panel; c/o Information Security Oversight Office; National Archives and Records Administration; 700 Pennsylvania Avenue NW, Room 503; Washington, DC 20408. *Id.* §§ 2003.11(b), 2003.13(b). The submission should specify whether it is directed to "Classification Challenge Appeals" or "Mandatory Declassification Review Appeals" in the attention line of the mailing. *Id.*

114. *See id.* § 2003.11(b)(2) (setting forth this requirement in the context of classification challenges by authorized holders of classified information); *id.* § 2003.13(b)(2) (setting forth this requirement in the context of requests for mandatory declassification review).

115. *Id.* § 2003.11(e); *see also id.* § 2003.13(e) (same).

116. *Id.* § 2003.11(f); *see also id.* § 2003.13(g) (same).

117. *Id.* § 2003.11(f); *see also id.* § 2003.13(g) (same).

118. *Id.* § 2003.11(h); *see also id.* § 2003.13(i) (same).

119. *Id.* § 2003.11(h); *see also id.* § 2003.13(j) ("Information that is subject to an appeal from an agency decision denying declassification under the mandatory review provisions of [Executive Order No. 13,526] remains classified unless and until a final decision is made to declassify it.").

120. *See generally* Exec. Order No. 13,556, Controlled Unclassified Information, 75 Fed. Reg. 68,675 (Nov. 4, 2010).

121. *Id.* § 2(a).

122. *Id.* § 2(c).

123. *Id.* § 4(a).

124. *Id.* § 4(d).

125. *Id.* § 4(b).

126. *Id.*

127. Nat'l Archives & Records Admin., 2012 Report to the President 2 (Nov. 20, 2012), http://www.archives.gov/cui/reports/report-2012.pdf.

128. *Id.*

129. *See* Nat'l Archives, Controlled Unclassified Information (CUI), CUI Registry, http://www.archives.gov/cui/registry/category-list.html#categories (listing the current categories and subcategories of CUI).

130. In its latest report to the president, the NARA indicated that "policy consolidation and finalization," including formal comment and rulemaking, was planned for February of 2013. 2012 Report to the President, *supra* note 127, 4–5.

131. Keir X. Bancroft, *Regulating Information Security in the Government Contracting Industry: Will the Rising Tide Lift All Boats?*, 62 Am. U. L. Rev. 1145, 1179 (June 2013).

132. Exec. Order No. 13,556, § 1.

133. *See, e.g.*, Friedman v. Bache Halsey Stuart Shields, Inc., 738 F.2d 1336, 1341 (D.C. Cir. 1984) ("There surely is such a thing as a qualified common-law privilege . . . for law enforcement investigatory files."); *see also* Commonwealth of Puerto Rico v. United States, 490 F.3d 50, 64 (1st Cir. 2007) (recognizing this privilege based upon "persuasive authority from other circuits, the law enforcement exception set forth in the FOIA, and 'the public interest in effective law enforcement'" (quoting Roviaro v. United States, 353 U.S. 53, 59 (1957))); *In re* Dep't of Homeland Sec., 459 F.3d 565, 569 n.1 (5th Cir. 2006) (collecting cases recognizing the privilege); United States v. Myerson (*In re* Dep't of Investigation of City of N.Y.), 856 F.2d 481, 483–84 (2d Cir. 1988) (noting that "the law enforcement privilege . . . has been recognized in the absence of a statutory foundation").

134. Info. Sec. Oversight Office, Nat'l Archives & Records Admin., Controlled Unclassified Information (CUI) Notice 2013-01: Provisional Approval of Proposed CUI Categories and Subcategories 1 (May 22, 2013), http://www.archives.gov/cui/documents/2013-cuio-notice-2013-01-provisional-category-approval.pdf.

135. *Id.*

Appendix I
ISOO Classification Example

SECRET

 Department of Good Works
Washington, D.C. 20006

June 27, 2010

MEMORANDUM FOR THE DIRECTOR

From: John E. Doe, Chief Division 5

Subject: (U) Examples

1. (U) Paragraph 1 contains "Unclassified" information. Therefore, this portion will be marked with the designation "U" in parentheses preceding the portion.

2. (S) Paragraph 2 contains "Secret" information. Therefore, this portion will be marked with the designation "S" in parentheses preceding the portion.

3. (C) Paragraph 3 contains "Confidential" information. Therefore, this portion will be marked with the designation "C" in parentheses preceding the portion.

Classified By: John E. Doe, Chief Division 5
Reason: 1.4(c)
Declassify on: 20150701

SECRET

128

Appendix II
Example of Classification, SCI, and Control Markings

~~TOP SECRET//COMINT//NOFORN~~
NATIONAL SECURITY AGENCY
FORT GEORGE G. MEADE, MARYLAND 20755-6000

Serial: GC/009/09
25 February 2009

MEMORANDUM FOR STAFF DIRECTOR, HOUSE PERMANENT SELECT COMMITTEE ON INTELLIGENCE

SUBJECT: (U) Congressional Notification - Incidents of Noncompliance - INFORMATION MEMORANDUM

(U) The purpose of this correspondence is to notify the Committee of compliance matters that are currently under review by the Foreign Intelligence Surveillance Court and which relate to subjects of prior testimony to the Congress.

(TS//SI//NF) Under two separate sets of orders issued by the Court pursuant to Sections 1841 and 1861 of the Foreign Intelligence Surveillance Act of 1978, as amended ("FISA"), the National Security Agency ("NSA" or "Agency") receives telephony and electronic communications metadata in order to produce foreign intelligence related to the activities of ▮▮▮▮▮▮ the ▮▮▮▮▮▮▮▮▮▮▮▮▮▮▮▮▮▮▮▮▮▮▮▮▮▮ On 15 January 2009, the Department of Justice ("DoJ") notified the Court that an automated alert process NSA used to compare the telephony metadata against a list of telephone identifiers that were of foreign intelligence interest to NSA's counterterrorism personnel did not operate in conformity with the Court's orders. The Government also advised the Court that NSA had incorrectly described the alert process in prior reports to the Court. As part of a comprehensive review ordered by the Director of NSA, the Agency identified another automated process used to query the telephony metadata that also did not operate in conformity with the Court's orders. The review also identified some manually entered queries that were noncompliant with the Court's orders. None of the compliance incidents resulted in the dissemination of any reporting from NSA to any other department or agency. Upon discovery of these compliance incidents, NSA immediately made changes to its processes to ensure that the Agency is handling and querying the telephony metadata in accordance with the Court's orders. The corrective measures include implementation of controls that prevent any automated process from querying the telephony metadata NSA receives pursuant to the Court's orders and which also guard against manual querying errors.

Derived From: NSA/CSSM 1-52
Dated: 20070108
Declassify On: ~~20320108~~
~~TOP SECRET//COMINT//NOFORN~~

(TS//SI//NF) In response to the Government's compliance notice, on 28 January 2009, the Court directed the Government to file a brief and supporting documentation describing how the compliance and misreporting incidents occurred so the Court can determine what remedial action, if any, is warranted. Since the Court was aware that there are similarities between NSA's processing of telephony metadata and electronic communications metadata under separate orders, the Court also directed the Government to determine whether NSA has been processing the electronic communications metadata in accordance with the terms of the Court's orders for this category of material. As part of this review, the Government concluded that NSA was processing the electronic communications metadata in accordance with the terms of the Court's orders, with one exception. The review identified one particular process that the Government concluded was not in conformity with the Court's order. NSA had employed the process in a small number of cases to approve queries against the electronic communications metadata. Although the Agency had previously reported the process to the Court █ ███ this process, too, has been discontinued.

(S) NSA and DoJ have already identified a number of steps designed to improve the Agency's ability to comply with the relevant orders and implementation of these changes has begun. Also, in addition to notifying the Court, the Government has notified a number of senior Executive Branch officials about these compliance matters. Officials who have received such notification include the President's Intelligence Oversight Board, the Director of National Intelligence, NSA's Inspector General, and the Under Secretary of Defense for Intelligence. My office is also prepared to brief the Committee on these matters at the Committee's convenience.

(U) Should you have any questions, please contact Jonathan E. Miller, Associate Director of Legislative Affairs, at ████████

VITO T. POTENZA
General Counsel

Copy Furnished:
  Minority Staff Director, House Permanent
  Select Committee on Intelligence

The Classified Information Procedures Act 8

S. Elisa Poteat

I. INTRODUCTION

When leaks happen, the leakers often get prosecuted.[1] A recurring question facing trial judges is how to deal with classified information in leak trials. That information might be used to prove the leaker is guilty, or a defendant might want to use that information in his own defense. Before 1980, there was no legal framework for the use of classified information in criminal cases. No law said that classified information could be disclosed to the defense attorneys, nor under what conditions if it was. There was no guidance on how to handle or store classified information in courthouses or courtrooms. No statute explained whether jurors could be permitted to see classified information to assist them in determining the guilt or innocence of a leaker. As a result, many leakers—maybe most leakers—were not punished through the criminal justice system.

The Classified Information Procedures Act[2] (CIPA) was enacted in 1980 to respond to this issue. In what may seem remarkable given today's legislative stagnation, CIPA passed with bipartisan support in both houses of Congress and the backing of the civil rights and intelligence communities. CIPA set up a framework for judges, prosecutors, and defense attorneys to use when dealing with classified information in court. CIPA's guidance covered criminal procedures from the moment charges are

133

filed through the appeal of a case after conviction. To understand CIPA is to begin to understand how a leak case might unfold before the parties are in trial, during trial, and through appeal. To learn CIPA's history is to learn how courts have struggled with classified or secret documents since the birth of the nation more than 200 years ago.

It is important to set forth some basic principles reflected in CIPA's text to have an accurate understanding of how classified information is used or excluded in criminal cases. These principles will apply regardless of who leaked the information and who received it.

First, classified information will only be provided to the defense in discovery when it is deemed both relevant and helpful to the defense.[3] Discovery is nothing more than the material—documents, recordings, statements, reports, e-mails, or physical things—that are relevant to a case.[4] Even if the information is turned over in discovery, it may not be admissible in court. When deciding whether classified evidence is admissible, courts will apply the Federal Rules of Evidence. What is journalistically interesting or noteworthy may be very different from what is relevant in legal terms.

Second, a defendant who expects or desires to use classified information as part of his defense must provide notice of that fact in writing to the court.[5] If he does not, he will be unable to use that evidence at trial.

Third, hearings under CIPA will take place mostly ex parte and in camera, meaning without the defendant or his counsel present and in the judge's chambers.[6] Journalists should anticipate that these hearings will not be open to the public or the press, and attorneys will not be permitted to speak about them to anyone other than persons permitted by the trial judge to be told.

Fourth, national security information has enjoyed a more than 200-year history of protection, through wars and conflicts, and, like the Republic itself, will continue to be a part of America's defenses.

This chapter explores the history of classified information in criminal cases before and after CIPA was enacted. Then it explores how CIPA functions in criminal cases.

II. HISTORY OF PROTECTING CLASSIFIED INFORMATION IN CRIMINAL CASES

A. National Security and Criminal Cases in a Fragile New Republic

The framers of the U.S. Constitution understood that the national security depended on the ability to keep secrets from America's enemies. They even believed secrecy could protect Congress and help it to function:

Each House shall keep a Journal of its Proceedings, and from time to time publish the same, *excepting such Parts as may in their Judgment require Secrecy*; and the Yeas and Nays of the Members of either House on any question shall, at the Desire of one fifth of those Present, be entered on the Journal.[7]

In his first State of the Union address, President George Washington requested that Congress fund an intelligence service, the Contingent Fund of Foreign Intercourse, to protect the national security interests of the country.

The interests of the United States require, that our intercourse with other nations should be facilitated by such provisions as will enable me to fulfill my duty, in that respect, in the manner which circumstances may render most conducive to the publick good: And to this end, that the compensations to be made to the persons who may be employed, should according to the nature of their appointments, be defined by law; and a competent fund designated for defraying the expenses incident to the conduct of our foreign affairs.[8]

Washington's own military secrets were passed to the British by his trusted advisor, Dr. Benjamin Church.[9] Washington then moved to create an intelligence agency to prevent it from occurring again.

When Thomas Jefferson became president for a second term, on March 4, 1805, America's sovereignty was already facing challenges. Jefferson wrote, "I like a little rebellion now and then. It is like a storm in the atmosphere."[10] Yet he also created a cipher to conceal his communications with explorer Meriwether Lewis for strategic purposes. The cipher allowed Jefferson and Lewis to use the word "artichoke" where the two meant "antipode."[11]

The first time the executive branch sought to withhold its national security information from a defendant was in the case against Aaron Burr. In 1806, just 30 years after the Declaration of Independence was penned, more than a thousand "Spanish troops ha[d] crossed the Sabine River" on the Louisiana-Texas border.[12] Burr, Jefferson's former vice president, had fled to avoid prosecution for treason. While on the run, Burr was suspected of planning a coup d'état.[13] After learning that Burr was likely hiding in Louisiana, Jefferson sent Louisiana Governor John Graham to spy on Burr and report his findings.[14] When Burr was arrested and charged with treason, he requested the government provide him with an encoded letter sent from General John Wilkinson to Jefferson. Burr claimed that the letter would support his defense.[15] Prosecutor George Hay agreed to turn over the letter in response to a writ, but he reserved the right to withhold any confidential information in the letter, thereby invoking a somewhat vague executive privilege.[16] In denying the writ, Supreme Court Justice John Marshall acknowledged the existence of an executive privilege protecting "secret" information from unauthorized disclosure during court proceedings.[17] Presaging later cases that directly addressed a defendant's right to have privileged information for his defense, Marshall expressed concern about withholding relevant but privileged information from criminal defendants.[18]

[In] Criminal cases . . . courts will always apply the rules of evidence to criminal prosecutions so as to treat the defense with as much liberality and tenderness as the case will admit. . . .

[I]t is a very serious thing, if such a letter should contain any information material to the defense, to withhold it from the accused the power of making use of it. It is a very serious thing to proceed to trial under such circumstances. I cannot precisely lay down any general rule for such a case. Perhaps the court ought to consider the reasons which would induce the president to refuse to exhibit such a letter as conclusive on it, unless such a letter could be shown to be absolutely necessary in his defense. The president may himself state the particular reasons which may have induced him to withhold a paper, and the court would unquestionably allow their full force to those reasons. At the same time, the court could not refuse to pay proper attention to the affidavit of the accused.[19]

In the end, however, Marshall declined to suggest specific procedures courts should follow when dealing with privileged information, such as classified presidential communications. Congress did not enact such procedures for almost 200 years after the Burr case. Yet there were random cases over those decades that reflect the continued valuation of classified information and courts' efforts to find a fair way to handle it in court.

In 1875, for example, the Supreme Court also discussed the protection of information related to national security in *Totten v. United States*.[20] In *Totten*, the widow of a spy who was operating behind Confederate lines sued to collect monies owed by the government for spy services. The court acknowledged the authority of the president as commander in chief to "employ secret agents to enter the rebel lines and obtain information respecting the strength, resources, and movements of the enemy," but said the contract was secret and could not be the subject of a civil lawsuit. As a consequence the suit was dismissed without any adjudication of the merits of the widow's claim.

B. The Secret Agreement Not to Prosecute Cases and Its Demise

The procedures for the use of military and state secrets information in civil cases emerged with clarity in 1953 in *United States v. Reynolds*.[21] These procedures would differ significantly from those later included in CIPA. In *Reynolds*, the Supreme Court determined that, when the state secrets privilege was properly "invoked," it would completely block the discovery of the information.[22] However, the *Reynolds* case did not extend to criminal cases by its own terms. As the

Supreme Court noted, a prosecutor cannot bring a case against a defendant and then withhold classified information that would support his defense. So where were the criminal cases that should have been prosecuted during the Cold War?

They were cloaked in secrecy by an internal executive agreement. Within a year of the *Reynolds* decision, the Central Intelligence Agency (CIA) and Department of Justice (DoJ) entered a clandestine agreement that allowed the CIA to not report internal violations of the law to DoJ.[23] This agreement limited the development of law on the subject of a classified information privilege for at least two and a half decades during the height of the Cold War. According to those familiar with the agreement, its terms ensured that no espionage cases would be initiated by DoJ.[24] The agreement only came to public light when it was exposed by the Rockefeller Commission in 1975.[25] Commenting on the reasons for this secret agreement to *The Washington Post*, then-Attorney General Griffin Bell stated, "[T]he intelligence community had come to believe that every time you prosecuted a spy you would lose the secret, and that it was better public policy—the best of two evils—to let the spy go and keep the secret. But I had the idea that you could prosecute these cases without losing the secret."[26]

C. CIPA Sprang in Part from the Leak Cases of the 1970s

Immediately following the revocation of this agreement and before CIPA's enactment, several espionage cases were prosecuted. In one case, popularly known as "The Falcon and the Snowman case," and later memorialized in a book by Robert Lindsey, the judge used procedures that looked very similar to those later outlined in CIPA.[27]

Leak cases finally drove Congress to act. Those concerned about intelligence leaks formed alliances with those outraged by the actions of the CIA. In the 1970s, following the publication of the Rockefeller Commission Report and the Church Committee hearings,[28] Congress needed to respond to the public's concern that leakers and bad intelligence actors could get away with crimes by threatening to expose classified information in the course of their defense. The Church Commission hearings dealing with misconduct on the part of the CIA concluded at the end of 1975 by finding that the CIA had been involved in plots to overthrow foreign governments, assassinate leaders, and engage in unlawful activities targeting U.S. citizens in the United States.[29]

Then-Assistant Attorney General Phillip Heyman, disgusted by his inability to prosecute cases involving classified information, implored Congress to act to create[30] clear procedures for handling such sensitive discovery and evidence:

> In recent years there have been a number of highly publicized criminal cases in which the disclosure of sensitive classified information has been an issue. Such cases include but are not limited to traditional espionage trials as well as cases involving alleged wrongdoing by government officials. In the past, the government has foregone the prosecution of some

cases in order to avoid compromising national security information. [The dismissal of such cases] foster[s] the perception that government officials and private persons with access to military or technical secrets have a broad *de facto* immunity from prosecution.[31]

Vice President Joe Biden, then a senator, introduced CIPA:

Mr. President, I am pleased to support the Classified Information Procedures Act. This bill is the product of over three years of effort in the Intelligence and Judiciary Committees to resolve the quote "graymail" problem. Graymail is the tactic used by defendants in national security cases to force the Department of Justice to drop criminal cases by threatening to disclose classified information.

In a report issued by the Subcommittee on Secrecy and Disclosure in 1978, the Senate Intelligence Committee listed a number of cases where this tactic was a factor:

First, the perjury prosecution of former CIA Director Richard Helms [who was suspected of lying to Congress about CIA activities];
Second, a number of recent serious espionage cases;
Third, leak cases;
Fourth, bribery cases, including the TCIA investigation [likely *K*CIA, an investigation into allegations of illegal transactions between U.S. government officials the Korean government];
Fifth, narcotics trafficking cases [allegedly by CIA operatives in Asia];
Sixth, the Nha Trang murder investigation during the Vietnam War [the alleged murder of a Vietnamese person working for U.S. Special Forces after he was suspected of acting as a double agent, questioned and killed by Special Forces allegedly acting at the behest of the CIA]; and
Seventh, part of the Watergate case.[32]

When it finally issued its joint report on CIPA on July 11, 1979, Congress specifically referred to how privileges would need to be conditional in criminal cases, meaning that information relevant and helpful to a defendant charged with a crime had to be given over in discovery even if it was classified, though not necessarily in its classified form:

The disclose-or-dismiss dilemma can never be eliminated entirely. Inherent in every espionage trial for example is the principle set out in innumerable court decisions [] that when the government chooses to prosecute an individual for a crime, it cannot deny him the right to meet the case against him by introducing relevant documents, even those otherwise privileged.[33]

CIPA was "intended to create[] uniform procedures allowing a court in criminal cases to rule on the admissibility of classified information before its introduction in court."[34] It was intended to allow the government to determine "whether it should proceed with a prosecution knowing the risks to national security posed by the disclosure of relevant classified information at trial."[35] In what may seem remarkable in light of today's political climate, CIPA moved forward with bipartisan support within Congress, and support from intelligence agencies, like the CIA, and civil rights groups, like the American Civil Liberties Union. Once CIPA was law, prosecutions began.

III.   CIPA'S PROCEDURES: A REVIEW OF CIPA'S COMPREHENSIVE SCOPE FROM FILING TO APPEAL

Imagine a case charging a leaker whose identity is a composite of people charged and convicted in espionage cases throughout history (see box).

Journalists covering Leaker's trial should understand that no decision would be made immediately or in public regarding the classified information. Because CIPA was intended to "permit the government to ascertain the potential damage to national security of proceeding with a given prosecution before trial,"[36] CIPA allowed courts to make "an individualized determination about each piece of [classified] evidence."[37]

CIPA will surely be used in the case because it is about a leak of classified information. According to CIPA § 1, its procedures apply to

> any information or material that has been determined by the United States Government pursuant to an Executive order, statute, or regulation to require protection against unauthorized disclosure for reasons of national security and any restricted data, as defined by paragraph r. of the section 11 of the Atomic Energy Act of 1954 (42 U.S.C. [§] 2012(y)).[38]

Top Secret material is classified pursuant to an executive order, in this case Executive Order 13,526.

The government will file a motion alerting the court that classified information is involved in the case. The motion will not identify the specific information at issue. CIPA § 2 allows either party to move for a pretrial conference to consider matters related to classified information "that may arise in connection with the prosecution." In most cases, this allows the trial judge to plan dates for hearings and get ready to receive classified information. Often a judge will have to acquire suitable storage for classified information and obtain proper security clearances for courtroom staff. Any hearing on this motion will take place out of the view of the public in the judge's chambers, and it is highly unlikely that the defendant or his counsel will be present. Even if the motion under CIPA § 2 is not sealed, it will make only oblique references to the classified information.

Neither will the specific classified information discussed at the CIPA § 2 conference be disclosed in open court or filings, and the court will order the defendant and his attorneys not to disclose the information to anyone outside of the defense

A Leaker, a Journalist, and CIPA

Leaker is a former CIA official, now working in the National Security Council (NSC). Leaker is under pressure from administration officials to create an unclassified narrative justifying the president's plan to conduct a naval blockade of the main port of the island nation known as the Republic of Banking, or ROB.

The administration has accused ROB of allowing its robust banking sector to launder money that is being used to finance the development of a nuclear arsenal for Enemy State. Enemy has been under economic sanctions by the United States and the United Nations for more than 35 years. The American president is a member of the Republican Party. Congress is controlled by the Democratic Party. The House of Representatives has recently held a number of committee hearings that have raised questions about the veracity of the administration's claim that the ROB was a knowing actor in the financing of Enemy's nuclear arsenal.

Leaker has access to a large volume of Top Secret data that would tend to suggest that the ROB was a knowing actor in the finance scheme. Using his NSC computer, Leaker has attempted to segregate and download only the Top Secret documents that would support the administration's claims about the ROB. Each morning Leaker receives approximately 400 intelligence cables at all classification levels on various subjects. His staff is expected to review these cables for him so that he is not overwhelmed, and present to him only those cables that fall within his area of responsibility. The overwhelming majority of the cables given to Leaker are classified at the Secret level.

After a few drinks one night, Leaker approaches Paul, who is one of several "at large" bloggers for Politics in a Nanosecond (Nanosecond). Unknown to Leaker, Paul's main source of income does not come from his blog, but from his chief foreign sponsor, the economic rival of the Republic of Banking, the Kingdom of Digital Coin (Kingdom). Paul writes speeches for the prime minister of Kingdom and advises him on the U.S. media's role in influencing Congress.

Over drinks, Leaker and Paul agree that Leaker will download certain Top Secret data proving the administration's claims onto a thumb drive. The two men will then meet at a Caribbean island where Paul can view the data. Paul understands that Leaker has a political agenda, but he hopes that Nanosecond will be able to monetize the publication of the Top Secret data, expand into a dominant news source, and promote him to editor in chief. If Nanosecond decides not to publish the data, Paul might sell some of it to the Kingdom if he can figure out which of the data will not harm the United States. Paul feels sure that despite having never served in any national security job in the government, he will be able to tell which of the classified information from Leaker will harm the United States and which will not.

In his excitement over the story, Paul failed to read the executive order explaining the definition of Top Secret information.

(continued)

The following day, Leaker is stopped by FBI special agents at Dulles Airport. They seize the thumb drive and arrest him. Leaker is advised that his security clearance was revoked the previous day and he has been locked out of his office. Paul oversleeps after having too many drinks and misses his flight. Within days Leaker is charged with a number of offenses. Paul never gets the thumb drive, but the story of Paul's meeting and the contents of the thumb drive flies through Washington's competitive journalistic circles. Paul begins to speculate that he might have told his colleagues about Leaker's revelations while he was drunk. Worse, Paul begins to think that Leaker may have told other journalists the same thing.

Paul is never prosecuted, and he breaks off all contact with the prime minister of the Kingdom. He stops drinking and decides to move to Oxford, England, and takes a stable, quiet, well-paying job unrelated to politics or international affairs.

The *August Washington Press*, whose online edition has recently eclipsed Nanosecond's, publishes a series of stories that appear to reflect the information that Paul was told by Leaker. No one from *August* is prosecuted either.

team. The court may order the defense attorneys not to disclose the classified information to their own client. CIPA § 3 requires the court to issue a protective order to "protect against the disclosure of any classified information disclosed by the United States to any defendant."

Any motions pertaining to the classified information will likely be filed under seal through the court information security officer, who is responsible for protecting classified information during the court process. These motions will not be available to journalists nor through the PACER (the Public Access to Court Electronic Records) system. Instead the material will be provided to the court in a classified setting, using media authorized to hold classified material. Although many opinions discussing the media's access to discovery and court filings include a First Amendment analysis, no court has ever ruled that a journalist has a need to know classified information.

The prosecutor will probably file a classified motion under of CIPA § 4 requesting permission to withhold certain classified information from discovery in the case, or summarize certain discovery to avoid revealing intelligence sources and methods. Like the CIPA § 2 motion, the CIPA § 4 motion will likely be filed ex parte, meaning it will be filed with the judge and not served on Leaker or his counsel. Section 4 motions sometimes have both an unclassified portion and a classified version. The unclassified version may explain in broad terms why the information should be withheld or summarized, but these will be general references to the harm to national security that may result from disclosure of the classified information. In some cases, possibly in the case against Leaker, the classified information may be declassified, though that is less likely in the case of Top Secret information because its disclosure is presumed to harm national security under the applicable executive order. If the judge agrees with the government, the prosecution may give the defense the relevant classified information in a summary format that strips it of the sources and methods while communicating the simple facts.

CIPA § 4 allows the trial court to assist in navigating the government's discovery obligations. Section 4 authorizes the government to (1) withhold from discovery—meaning not turn over to the defense—classified information;[39] (2) produce to the defendant a substitution for the actual classified information;[40] or (3) produce to the defendant a summary in lieu of the classified information. Even if a summary or substitution of classified information is given to the defense team, it may still be classified at a lower classification level, such as Secret. Material classified Secret cannot be made public. If it is given to defense counsel, its dissemination and handling will be restricted by the judge through a protective order similar to the one normally issued under CIPA § 3. The defense attorneys will have to acquire a security clearance that is as high as the highest level of classification of the information they receive in discovery. In some cases, the protective order issued by the judge will prevent a defendant's attorney from showing the classified material to their client, who will likely not have a security clearance.

In some cases classified information may be highly relevant, but that will depend on the charges brought against the defendant and the elements of the offenses charged, each of which will have to be proved to a standard of beyond a reasonable doubt. Classified information may be used to prove the defendant's guilt. However, the government can withhold it from discovery if it is not helpful to the defense. When the classified information is not relevant and helpful to the defense, the government will not use that information at trial because to do so may compromise sensitive sources and methods. This may happen where the government has learned from a foreign intelligence agency that it has information proving a defendant's guilt, for example. While that information might be relevant, and might help the government, if it is only helpful to the prosecution and not to Leaker, the government can withhold it from discovery. Discussions between the prosecutors and the judge about the relevance and helpfulness of the classified information will take place under CIPA § 4.

The practice of holding CIPA § 4 hearings ex parte and in camera has repeatedly been held to be constitutional because the practice is intended to prevent the disclosure of classified information unless and until it is deemed discoverable.[41] Courts have noted that disclosure of classified information to defense counsel with security clearances can still cause damage to the national security.[42]

Just the fact that Leaker once held a Top Secret security clearance is no guarantee that he will be able to see every bit of classified information that the trial judge might review. I. Lewis "Scooter" Libby, Vice President Dick Cheney's former chief of staff, was accused of leaking the identity of then-covert CIA agent Valerie Plame to *New York Times* reporter Judith Miller. Libby asked that the CIPA § 4 hearing take place in his presence since he had already seen the information that was to be discussed in the hearing.[43] The trial judge ruled that Libby's former access to the information and the security clearances held by members of the defense team did not entitle them to view the classified documents because they had not established that they had a "need to know," which was (and remains) a requirement under an executive order setting forth classification standards.[44]

In Leaker's case the judge may find that only the level of classification of the material in question—Top Secret—is relevant to the charges. The judge may further decide that the contents of each intelligence cable Leaker downloaded has no relevance to his charges and is not discoverable. The judge could find that only certain portions of the attached e-mails are relevant and helpful and order that only redacted versions of the e-mails be provided in discovery.[45]

A journalist may feel that the classification level of the documents is insignificant compared with what the documents reveal about the administration's plans for the blockade and Congress's posturing, but the legal standard for discovery of the documents is very different.

If the government charges Leaker with an offense that would require the prosecution to prove he acted with the intent of harming the United States or benefiting its enemies, the content of the classified documents may be deemed relevant in some small measure. All discussion with the judge about the relevance of the Top Secret documents will take place in a closed hearing out of the view of journalists. Leaker and his attorney will likely not be permitted to participate in these discussions unless the court rules that some of the classified information is both relevant and helpful to the defense, and further finds that the defendant has a need to know the information. Sometimes experienced defense attorneys will provide the judge with information about their planned defense ex parte to help the judge make an accurate determination about the relevance and helpfulness of the classified information to the planned defense.

As part of his defense, Leaker claims in an ex parte motion that he needs to reveal the facts contained in a Top Secret e-mail and several Top Secret documents. Leaker claims that these documents will demonstrate that he was given authorization to by the president to give the cables to Paul. In order to present this defense, Leaker says that he will have to expose this classified information in open court. The government counters that Leaker is just attempting to graymail the government into dropping the case.

CIPA § 5(a) requires a defendant to notify the court in writing if he would expose classified information in the course of his defense. Leaker's filing of a motion might provide sufficient notice. If a defendant fails to file this notice, he can anticipate being barred from admitting classified information is his defense, according to CIPA § 5(b). This obligation is a continuing one that does not end with a single filing. Indeed, section 5 also states:

> Whenever a defendant learns of additional classified information he reasonably expects to disclose at any such proceeding, he shall notify the attorney for the United States as soon as possible thereafter and shall include a brief description of the classified information.[46]

143

This requirement under CIPA § 5 does not mean that a defendant's privilege against self-incrimination is violated by forcing him to reveal classified aspects of his own potential trial testimony.[47] Nor does CIPA guarantee that a defendant can use classified information at trial that would not be admissible if it were unclassified information.

Courts have barred defendants from revealing classified information where it would not be relevant to their defense or would be inadmissible for reasons other than its classification level. In the case of *United States v. Wilson*, the defendant gave notice under CIPA § 5 that he was going to have to disclose classified information in his case to establish that his actions were done with the consent and authority of a U.S. intelligence agency. The trial court ruled that the classified evidence should be excluded, not because it was classified, but because it would confuse the jury, waste time, and was otherwise cumulative under Federal Rule of Evidence 403.[48] In other words, the judge would not have allowed admission of the evidence even if it were unclassified.

Former CIA agent Edwin Wilson left the CIA in the 1970s, started his own firm, and began negotiating for the sale of weapons to the Libyans. After he was prosecuted, Wilson said he was just acting to gain bona fides with the Libyans so he could get intelligence on Libya for the CIA. By contrast, the prosecution theory was that Wilson was simply trying to enrich himself with a lucrative arms deal. Wilson had not obtained a license from the Department of the Treasury to do business with the Libyans, which was required by law. The evidence at trial showed that Wilson's employees purchased several weapons, including machine guns, then shipped them to Libyans in a number of different countries.

As required by CIPA § 5, Wilson gave written notice that he would expose classified information. He also attempted to subpoena 17 people, including high-ranking government officials, and requested the prosecution turn over a wide range of documents through subpoena duces tecum from several government agencies.

The trial judge held ex parte and in camera hearings and concluded that none of the classified information Wilson sought was relevant or material to the issues in the case. Wilson was permitted to provide the jury with evidence of the fact that he had met twice with government officials in Europe when he was negotiating with the Libyans. The jury also heard that Wilson was given a list of Russian military equipment from a CIA agent during the same time period, and that he attempted to properly store and secure a piece of Soviet equipment and to penetrate the operation of an international arms distributor. Wilson was permitted to present his defense that he was working for the United States in an undercover capacity in Libya, and to call witnesses to corroborate this claim, "so long as none of the classified information determined to be irrelevant would be disclosed thereby." Wilson never called any of the high-ranking witnesses, all of whom were made available to testify, and ended up presenting evidence on "only two of the ten areas discussed in his pretrial submission—the transmission of 'atomic bomb' plans and the receipt of a Russian equipment list . . ." However, the jury did not believe that Wilson was still working for the government, or that he had ever been authorized by government officials to export firearms illegally and they found him guilty.[49]

The appellate court determined that Wilson was not deprived of the "opportunity to mount his defense."[50]

Likewise in 1990, in *United States v. Badia*, the Court of Appeals for the Eleventh Circuit ruled that a defendant charged with hijacking a plane could present evidence of his relationship to the CIA in support of his defense that he acted at the behest of the CIA.[51]

More recently, "Scooter" Libby also filed a CIPA § 5 notice wherein he provided a list of 412 classified documents he claimed would support one of his defenses: that he saw so much information, including classified information, that he had a faulty memory and lacked the intent to lie to the grand jury or expose Plame's covert status.[52]

In Leaker's case, in a classified hearing in chambers under CIPA §§ 4 and 5, the trial judge reviews the single e-mail that Leaker said would support his defense that the president authorized him to disclose the information to Paul. The e-mail reads, "Paul, too bad we can't just call Wally over at the August and show him how flagrantly ROB acted in allowing its banks to be used for this terrible purpose. It would sure make dealing with those folks on the Hill a lot easier. Fondly, POTUS."

Attached to the e-mail are several Top Secret documents, only one of which mentions ROB. The judge might rule that the e-mail in question is relevant and helpful to Leaker along with all of the attachments. The government may then file a classified motion asked the court to deny the motion to admit the attachments under CIPA § 6. Alternatively, the government might agree that the e-mail itself can be summarized in such a way that it can be declassified. If the government disagrees with the judge's ruling, it might file a motion to admit only a summary of the information contained in the single potentially relevant e-mail. The trial court may agree to allow this summary, or it may order disclosure of the e-mail itself.

CIPA also provides for an elaborate process under section 6 whereby the government may challenge the defendant's plan to use or reveal classified information. Under CIPA § 6 the government may also challenge a court's ruling on information it seeks to withhold from discovery under section 4 is indeed discoverable and/or admissible. The government may seek a hearing on the use, relevance, and admissibility of the information. As to each item of classified information, the court must set forth in writing the basis for its determination. The government then may move under section 6, that, in lieu of the disclosure of classified information, the court order a substitution for such information of either (1) a statement admitting facts that the information would tend to prove or (2) a summary of the specific information.

CIPA § 6(f) also requires reciprocity of discovery so that a defendant who provides notice of the classified information he may disclose at trial prompts the government to respond with whatever classified information it may use in rebuttal of that evidence.

If the federal district judge denies the government's motion to prevent the defense from using the e-mail attachments in trial, the government may decide to appeal the judge's ruling right away and before trial. CIPA § 7 allows for an interlocutory appeal to be taken from the U.S. district court's ruling on any item of classified evidence. That means that the appeal can take place after the court's ruling, and before the case in concluded. Section 8 allows for the admission of classified evidence at trial, and for a court order restricting further dissemination of that classified material.

Eventually, if the appeals court rules that only the e-mail (but not the attachments) can be used by Leaker, the case will be remanded and only the "POTUS" e-mail will be provided. The reasons for the court's ruling will never be public. However, the appeals court may file an unclassified opinion that concludes that the e-mail attachments are not relevant and helpful to the defense. The district court may then enter a protective order barring the parties from disclosing anything about the e-mail attachments.

The values of secrecy and the right to put on a defense are sometimes in irreconcilable conflict. Indeed the attorney general can use the authority given him under CIPA to withhold even relevant documents where the disclosure of those documents would result in damage to the national security under CIPA § 6. However, the trial judge is vested with concomitant authority to impose sanctions (to include dismissal) on the government when the attorney general refuses to turn over classified material that the trial court has determined is both relevant and helpful to the defense.

IV. CONCLUSION

CIPA has proven to be a durable procedural tool that had endured the test of time. Perhaps CIPA's success is due in part to the fact that it was a product of more than 200 years of American jurisprudence, congressional hard work, and wide support from disparate groups.

In a time of rapid changes in the concepts of journalism and leaks, CIPA provides clear guidance on how classified evidence will be handled by courts in criminal cases even when much of what happens is out of the public's view.

NOTES

1. Because this chapter involves criminal prosecution, the source of the disclosed classified information will be referred to as the source of a "leak."
2. Classified Information Procedures Act, 18 U.S.C. app. III, §§ 1–16 (1980).
3. United States v. Yunis, 867 F.2d 617, 621 (D.C. Cir. 1989); CIPA § 4.
4. Fed. R. Crim. P. 16.
5. CIPA § 5.
6. CIPA § 4.
7. U.S. Const. art. I, § 5 (emphasis added).
8. President George Washington, First State of the Union Address, Jan. 8, 1790; *see also* The Evolution of the U.S. Intelligence Community—An Historical Overview 1, http://www.gpo.gov /fdsys/pkg/GPO-INTELLIGENCE/html/int022.html.
9. G.J.A. O'Toole, Honorable Treachery: A History of U.S. Intelligence, Espionage, and Covert Action from the American Revolution to the CIA 15 (1991).
10. Erin Allen, *A Birthday Fit for a President*, Library of Cong. Blog (Apr. 12, 2013), http:// blogs.loc.gov/loc/2013/04/a-birthday-fit-for-a-president/.
11. *Id.*
12. Nancy Isenberg, Fallen Founder: The Life of Aaron Burr 304–06 (2007).
13. *See id.* at 308, 311.
14. *See id.* at 311.
15. *See id.* at 312, 342; 2 Mary-Jo Kline, Political Correspondence and Public Papers of Aaron Burr (1983).
16. *See* Isenberg, *supra* note 12, at 345.
17. United States v. Burr, 25 F. Cas. 187, 192 (C.C.D. Va. 1807).
18. *Id.* at 192.
19. *Id.* at 191–92.
20. 92 U.S. 105, 106 (1875). Totten was followed by the Second Circuit in *Doe v. CIA*, 576 F.3d 95 (2d Cir. 2009). *See also* Dep't of the Navy v. Egan, 484 U.S. 518, 525 (1988).
21. *See generally* United States v. Reynolds, 345 U.S. 1 (1953).
22. In *Reynolds*, widows of men killed in a military plane crash sued the government, but when they requested discovery, the Secretary of the Navy advised the trial court that the disclosure of that information would damage the national security. *See id.* at 2, 5–6.
23. For the findings on the impact of the clandestine agreement, see Cent. Int. Agency, Report of Investigation: Allegations of Connections Between CIA and the Contras in Cocaine Trafficking to the United States (96-0143-IC), vol. II: The Contra Story, Findings (1998), https://www.cia.gov/library/reports/general-reports-1/cocaine/contra-story/findings.html [hereinafter CIA Report].
24. Griffin B. Bell, Taking Care of Law 100 (1982); Thomas B. Allen & Norman Polmar, Merchants of Treason 154 (1988). *See* Exec. Order No. 11,905, 41 Fed. Reg. 7703 (Feb. 18, 1976); Comm'n on CIA Activities within the United States, Report to the President 48–57 (1975) [hereinafter Rockefeller Comm'n Report]. P.E. Tyler, *Record Year Puts Spy-Catchers in Spotlight*, Wash. Post, Nov. 30, 1985, at A24. Telephone interview with Robert Keuch (Oct. 2012 & Nov. 2012). Telephone interview with George Jameson (Apr. 2013).
25. *Justice Dep't Treatment of Criminal Cases Involving CIA Personnel and Claims of National Security, Hearings before a Subcomm. of the Comm. on Gov't Op.*, 94th Cong. 401–29 (1975).
26. The Rockefeller Commission was established by Exec. Order No. 11,828, 40 Fed. Reg. 1219 (Jan. 4, 1975), and issued its report in July 1975. *See* Rockefeller Comm'n Report, *supra* note 24. For the findings on the impact of the clandestine agreement, see CIA Report, *supra* note 23.

27. *See generally, e.g.*, United States v. Boyce, 594 F.2d 1246 (9th Cir. 1979).

28. S. REP. NO. 94-755 (1976). Senate Select Committee to Study Governmental Operations with Respect to Intelligence Activities ("The Church Committee Report") Book II: Intelligence Activities and the Rights of Americans, S. REP. NO. 95-755, 290 (1976).

29. H.R. S. 1482, at H10, 315–16 (Remarks by Representative Romano L. Mazzoli; Classified Information Procedures Act) (1980); Proceedings and Debates of the 96th Congress, H.R. 4736, Classified Information Procedures Act, Oct. 1, 1980, at S14,078–79 (Remarks of Senator Joseph Biden); H. REP. NO. 96-931, pt. 1, at 7 (1979).

30. Telephone interview with Philip Heyman (Sept. 2012).

31. H.R. REP. NO. 96-831, pt. 2, at 2, 7 (1979) (quoting the testimony of former Deputy Attorney General Phillip Heyman and citing *Reynolds*).

32. http://www.intelligence.senate.gov/pdfs/78secrecy.pdf, Hearing Before the Subcommittee on Secrecy and Disclosure of the Select Committee on Intelligence of the United States Senate, 95th Congress, Second Session, March 1,2,6, 1978, 95–995.

33. H.R. REP. NO. 96-831, pt. 2, at 3 nn.8–9 (1979) (citing United States v. Andoschek, 142 F.2d 503 (2d Cir. 1944); United States v. Coplon, 185 F.2d 629, 638 (2d Cir. 1950)). "The government must decide whether the public prejudice of allowing the crime to go unpunished is greater than the disclosure of those states secrets which might be relevant to the defense." *Id.* at 3. Likewise there are other bits of legislative history that suggest Congress presupposed a privilege, such as when Representative Edwards of California addressed the prejudice to the government that would ensue if it could not use "relevant documents, *even those otherwise privileged.*" *Id.* (statement of Representative Marvin Edwards) (emphasis added).

34. United States v. Wilson, 721 F.2d 967, 970 (4th Cir. 1983) (citing S. REP. NO. 96-823, *reprinted in* 1980 U.S.C.C.A.N. 4294).

35. *Id.*

36. S. REP. NO. 96-823, at 1 (1980).

37. United States v. Hitselberger, 2013 WL 5933655 (D.D.C. 2013) (citing CIPA § 6(a) ("As to each item of classified information, the court shall make an individualized determination about each piece of evidence.")).

38. CIPA §§ 1–3.

39. Case law and the legislative history indicate that the only information that must be turned over in discovery is information that is "relevant *and* helpful" to the defense. United States v. Yunis, 867 F.2d 617, 622 (D.C. Cir. 1989) (quoting United States v. Roviaro, 353 U.S. 453, at 60–61 (1957)); *see* S. REP. NO. 96-832, at 25 (1980) (indicating that the informant's privilege standard of relevant and helpful should apply under CIPA).

40. *See* United States v. Sedaghaty, 728 F.3d 885, 898–91 (9th Cir. 2013) (finding that government can use substitutions of classified information but that the substitution in that case was not adequate).

41. United States v. Klimavisius-Viloria, 144 F.2d 1249, 1261 (9th Cir. 1998). This is also consistent with the legislative history of CIPA. "[Because] the government is seeking to withhold classified information from the defendant [through CIPA's processes] an adversary hearing with defense knowledge would defeat the very purpose of the discovery rules." H.R. REP. NO. 96-831, at 27 n.22 (1980). This is similar to Federal Rule of Criminal Procedure 17(d), which allowed the court to hold ex parte hearings to inspect evidence. United States v. Campa, 529 F.3d 980, 995 (11th Cir. 2008); Aref v. United States, 533 F.3d 72, 81 (2d Cir. 2009) (rejecting argument that the district court improperly conducted ex parte hearing).

At the time of CIPA's passage, Mort Halperin testified before Congress on behalf of the American Civil Liberties Union (ACLU). Halperin explained that he did not want CIPA to allow the government to "submit an explanation for the basis of the classification [of the particular information at issue]" to be reviewed in camera. Halperin was concerned that courts would be unduly influenced by the reasons for classification. Interview with Halperin, Senior Advisor of the Open Society Institute and former director of the ACLU in Washington (Sept. 19, 2012). At the time they testified before Congress about CIPA, Halperin, Michael Sheininger, and Prof. William Greenhalgh believed that judges would "be unduly influenced by the government's explanation and as a result would treat the information in question differently simply because it is classified." S. REP. NO 96-823, at 7 (1980).

42. United States v. Libby, 429 F. Supp. 2d 46, 48 (D.D.C. 2006).

43. 429 F. Supp. 2d 18, 18–23 (D.D.C. 2006).

44. *Id. See* Exec. Order No. 15,356, § 4.1(2)(3); Exec. Order No. 12,958, § 4.2(a)(3), 60 Fed. Reg. 19,825 (Apr. 17, 1995), as amended by Exec. Order No. 13,292, 68 Fed. Reg. 15,315 (Mar. 25, 2003) ("A person may have access to classified information provided that . . . the person has a need-to-know the information.").

45. *See* United States v. Kim, 2013 WL 3866540 (D.D.C. 2013) (granting a defendant's motion to compel discovery of redacted e-mails where the redacted materials were referenced elsewhere, e-mails were relevant and helpful to the defense and e-mails supported defendant's belief about potential harm to national security).

46. CIPA § 5.

47. *See* United States v. Hitselberger, 2013 WL 5933655 (D.D.C. 2013) (denying defendant's motion to declare CIPA § 5 unconstitutional). CIPA § 5 "requires merely a general disclosure as to what classified information the defense expects to use at trial, regardless of the witness or the document through which that information is to be revealed." United States v. Poindexter, 75 F. Supp. 13, 33 (D.D.C. 1989); *see also* United States v. Drake, 818 F. Supp. 2d 909, 914 (D. Md. 2011); United States v. Hashmi, 621 F. Supp. 2d 76, 81 (S.D.N.Y. 2008) ("The potential of precluding the disclosure [of classified information under CIPA] does not amount to a penalty for the defendant's exercising of his right to remain silent."); United States v. Lee, 90 F. Supp. 2d 1324, 1327 (D.N.M. 2000) (finding that CIPA does not require a defendant to specify whether he will testify).

48. United States v. Wilson, 750 F.2d 7, 8–9 (2d Cir. 1984); *accord* United States v. Pringle, 751 F.2d 419, 427–28 (1st Cir. 1984) (holding that trial court properly excluded classified information that was not relevant *and* helpful to the defense).

49. United States v. Wilson, 721 F.2d 967, 975 (4th Cir. 1983).

50. *Id.*

51. United States v. Badia, 827 F.2d 1458 (11th Cir. 1987).

52. United States v. Libby, 467 F. Supp. 2d 1, 7–9 (D.D.C. 2006). Libby also claimed that he leaked Plame's identity without intent because he really intended to simply respond to Ambassador Joseph Wilson's editorial stating that the Bush administration's statements about the proof that Iraq was purchasing "yellow cake" were without merit. *Id.* Libby also defended himself with claims that Plame's identity was really an "open secret" among the Washington press corps. United States v. Libby, 475 F. Supp. 2d 73, 74–77 (D.D.C. 2007); United States v. Libby, 453 F. Supp. 2d 35, 37–44 (D.D.C. 2006).

Part III

A Changing World of Leak Investigations

International Perspectives on National Security, Leaks, and Whistleblowers

9

Judith K. Boyd

Protecting national security, providing public access to government-held information, and addressing leaks of classified information are not issues limited to the United States. To the contrary, many countries in the world grapple with these issues. To illustrate, consider what happened to Brazilian citizen David Miranda on Sunday, August 18, 2013. He boarded a plane in Berlin, Germany, to return to his home in Rio de Janeiro, Brazil. The journey was uneventful until the stopover at London's Heathrow Airport, during which Miranda was detained by the Metropolitan Police and questioned for nine hours. According to his lawyer, Miranda was held in a room and questioned by six agents about his "entire life." They confiscated his laptop, an additional hard drive, two memory sticks, a mobile phone, a smart watch, and a video games console, and he was required to divulge the passwords to all his devices.[1]

Miranda is the partner of Glenn Greenwald, the journalist who published several articles on the activities of the United States and United Kingdom intelligence agencies based on classified material provided by Edward Snowden, a U.S. citizen and former contractor who worked at the National Security Agency. Miranda was traveling on flights paid for by the *Guardian* newspaper but, according to the newspaper, was not an employee. Rather he "often assists" with Greenwald's work.[2] Miranda is challenging the legality of his detention and, according to his lawyer, Matthew Ryder, trying to determine whether it was "permissible for government to use powers to be able to get material

153

from journalists" without enabling them "to argue their case before a court as to why they shouldn't have to answer questions or give up that material."

At the time, the U.K. government did not officially release details about the legal basis for detention other than a statement by Home Secretary Theresa May asserting it was justified under Schedule 7 of the Terrorism Act of 2000 and that the police must act if someone has "highly sensitive stolen information."[3] Was the detention and seizure of documents of a "journalistic nature" based on a legitimate national security interest? Or, as asserted by Greenwald, did it amount to "bullying" by the United Kingdom as part of an attempt to intimidate journalists from writing on the topic of United States and United Kingdom intelligence activities?[4] Were the actions of the United Kingdom consistent with international and European laws related to human rights, right to information, and whistleblower protection?

To provide greater insight into non-United States models of governance and oversight, this chapter will explore international and European trends and standards related to the right to access information, classification of information, and whistleblowing. This will be followed by an in-depth country study of the laws of the United Kingdom and conclude with an examination of trends for the future.

I. INTERNATIONAL TRENDS AND STANDARDS

A. The Right to Information

In 1989, only 13 countries had access to information laws.[5] Since the fall of the Berlin Wall, more than 80 countries governing 3 billion people have adopted laws regarding access to information, including Brazil, China, India, Indonesia, and Russia.[6] All of these countries recognize a public right of access to government-held information, but the disclosure obligations vary from country to country.[7] There is also a growing movement outside of the United States by numerous international bodies to consider the right to information as a fundamental human right, including the United Nations, regional human rights bodies, and the Organization of American States, the Council of Europe, and the African Union.[8]

United Nations. The concept of "freedom of information" (without reference to government-held information) was introduced by the United Nations during its first session in Resolution 59(1), which stated: "Freedom of information is a fundamental human right and . . . the touchstone of all the freedoms to which the UN is consecrated."[9] This concept was further amplified by Article 19 of the Universal Declaration of Human Rights, adopted by the UN General Council in 1948 and considered binding customary international law:

> Everyone has the right to freedom of opinion and expression; this right includes freedom to hold opinions without interference and to seek,

receive and impart information and ideas through any media and regard-less of frontiers.[10]

The International Covenant on Civil and Political Rights contains a similar provision guaranteeing the right to freedom of opinion and expression, also at Article 19.[11] The treaty was adopted by the UN General Assembly in 1966 and as of July 2007 had been ratified by 160 states (but notably not the United States or United Kingdom).[12]

At the time these international statements were adopted, the right to informa-tion was not generally understood to include the right to access information held by public bodies. Since 1998, the United Nations has asserted that the right to freedom of expression includes the right to access information held by the state.[13] However, this right is not viewed as absolute, with governments often implement-ing restrictions on this right to information and freedom of speech "where neces-sary to protect a legitimate national security interest or the individual's legitimate right to privacy."[14] Because the terms and definitions of these terms vary widely, it is difficult to identify a universal definition of national security as an exception to government disclosure obligations. However, it is clear there is a presumption in many countries that when there is doubt about whether disclosure of informa-tion would harm national security, the law does not favor disclosure.[15] The United Nations has noted an increasingly common use of "national security as a justi-fication for restricting access to information held by Governmental entities" and cautions that "national security should never be used as an excuse to prevent or limit the clarification of human rights violations."[16]

European Views. Many of the allies of the United States are members of the European Union, an economic and political framework for cooperation among 28 member states. When the Treaty of Lisbon entered into force on Decem-ber 1, 2009, the EU Charter of Fundamental Rights became legally binding on the EU institutions and on the national governments of member states. The char-ter serves as the foundation document for information access and whistleblower protection, covering the right to liberty and personal security (Art. 6), right to privacy (Art. 7), right to respect for private and family life (Art. 8), right to free-dom of expression (Art. 11), and prohibition of discrimination (Art. 14).[17] When EU countries implement EU law, they must also respect the fundamental rights enshrined in the charter. The charter does not replace national constitutions and courts; rather, it is places responsibility upon the national courts to enforce these fundamental rights.

Many U.S. allies also are members of the Council of Europe (COE), the lead-ing human rights organization on the European continent with 47 members, 28 of which are members of the EU.[18] The foundational document for the COE is the European Convention for the Protection of Human Rights and Fundamental Free-doms, which guarantees freedom of expression and information as a fundamental human right in Article 10.[19] All Council of Europe members have signed the Euro-pean Convention on Human Rights and the European Union is preparing to sign as well. The European Court of Human Rights oversees the implementation of the European Convention in member states.

The Council of Europe recently promulgated the first binding international legal instrument to recognize a general right to access official documents held by public authorities by publishing the Council of Europe Convention on Access to Official Documents on June 18, 2009.[20] It establishes a right to access official documents that may only be limited in order to protect interests related to national security, defense, or privacy.[21] The convention also provides minimum standards to be applied by governments when processing requests for access to official documents and review procedures. Since its issuance, ten countries have signed and six have ratified the treaty.[22] Ten states must ratify the treaty for it to take effect and thus far, the United Kingdom is not one of them.

B. Unauthorized Disclosure and Whistleblowers

Related to the right to access information is the responsibility to protect information from unauthorized disclosure and to establish whistleblower protections. Most countries have publicly available rules that describe the process for classification of information at varying levels, such as Top Secret, Secret, Confidential, and Restricted.[23] One notable exception is the United Kingdom, which has no such formal system of classification and instead relies on an informal information system to highlight how information must be handled within the government.[24] Punishments for unauthorized disclosure of classified national security information varies worldwide, but most countries examined by scholars thus far indicate criminal penalties are proscribed.[25] Where there has been no espionage, treason or disclosure to a foreign state, the penalties are far less than in the United States and prosecutions are rare.[26] For example, the maximum punishment is up to two years' imprisonment in Great Britain, four years in Spain and Sweden, five years in Germany and Poland, and seven years in France.[27]

There is a small body of international law relating to whistleblowers, the most significant being the Convention against Corruption, adopted by the UN in 2003.[28] Articles 32 and 33 obligate countries to provide protection for individuals reporting facts in good faith to competent authorities and giving testimony concerning offenses. The convention has been signed by 140 countries and formally ratified by 137 countries and organizations, including the United States, United Kingdom, and the EU. There are also four international conventions that provide guidance and best practices for nations to consider when developing their domestic laws.[29]

There is no common definition of "whistleblower" within the EU, and many countries lack any kind of whistleblower protection. Some countries, such as the Netherlands and Hungary, take into consideration the public's interest in disclosure of information when trying to decide whether to impose criminal penalties or it may be raised as a defense.[30] Other countries, such as Italy and Germany, require a showing by the prosecutor that there has been either actual or probable harm resulting from the disclosure in order for a penalty to be imposed.[31] The lack of harm of disclosure as well as having attempted to use internal reporting procedures prior to public disclosure may also be raised as valid defenses.[32]

In countries that may have no whistleblower protection laws, a whistleblower is often forced to rely on a creative attorney to develop a defense based on a piecemeal application of treaties, regulations, and statutes. Currently 20 of the 28 European Union countries have laws that partially protect government and/or private sector whistleblowers from retaliation.[33] However, only six EU countries have stand-alone whistleblower laws with comprehensive protection that cover public and private sector workers, including contractors and consultants and provide a process for reporting, investigation, and appeal: the United Kingdom, Norway, Netherlands, Hungary, Romania, and Switzerland.[34] Whistleblower cases in Europe brought before the European Court of Human Rights tend to focus on Article 10, asserting that their employer interfered with their freedom of information.[35] This approach has been particularly successful for whistleblowers in countries that do not have relevant national laws that provide comprehensive whistleblower protection.[36]

The lack of any EU standards for whistleblower protection, other than those described in EU Staff Regulations for EU employees,[37] is in large part attributed to the fact that EU member states have not conferred competence on these issues to the EU to act, such as through a harmonizing resolution or directive that would bind all 28 member states.[38] Another reason may be attributed to the fact that many European companies and banks are listed on the New York Stock Exchange and thus already subject to U.S. security laws and the whistleblower provisions of the Sarbanes-Oxley Act of 2002[39] and the Dodd-Frank Act of 2012.[40]

II. IN-DEPTH COUNTRY STUDY: THE UNITED KINGDOM

As the United Kingdom is one of the United States' most powerful allies, it is useful to be familiar with its laws as well as relevant international and European trends and standards related to national security, leaks, and whistleblowers. A comparison of the two legal systems is also instructive. While the two countries are both pluralistic democracies with legislative systems, there are differences in the regulatory schemes related to the right to information, information disclosure practices, and whistleblower protections.

A. The Right to Information in the United Kingdom

The primary right to information legislation in the United Kingdom is the Freedom of Information Act (FOIA) and the Data Protection Act. The FOIA was passed in 2000 but did not come into full force until 2005. Similar to the U.S. Freedom of

Information Act, there is an assumption within the language of the statute in the favor of disclosure of information.[41] Also similar to the U.S. FOIA, this provision is subject to a number of exemptions provided for in sections 21–44 of the Act. Section 2(2)(b) states that where an exemption is qualified, information will only be exempt if the public interest in maintaining the exemption outweighs the public interest in disclosing it.

The U.K. Data Protection Act was passed in 1998 and was intended to bring the United Kingdom into compliance with the EU Data Protection Directive of 1995.[42] The Data Protection Act is similar to the U.S. Privacy Act in that the primary purpose of the legislation is to outline procedures for how data about individuals will be handled by the government. It differs significantly from the U.S. Privacy Act in that it contains extensive provisions describing the data protection principles that the government must follow. Section 28 of the Data Protection Act provides an exemption from disclosure for national security reasons.

The normal process for information disclosure pursuant to these laws begins with an individual submitting a request to a public authority of the U.K. government. If the request is for recorded data held by the agency, it is submitted pursuant to the Freedom of Information Act. If the request is for personal data the agency holds about the requester, it is submitted pursuant to the Data Protection Act.[43] If an exemption applies, the request is denied and the individual may file a complaint with the U.K. Information Commissioner. The commissioner will investigate the complaint and provide a decision notice to the individual. Depending on the outcome, either the individual or the public official may appeal to the First-Tier Tribunal (Information Rights). Further appeals are possible to the U.K. Court of Appeal and eventually to the U.K. Supreme Court. Since its implementation there have been very few cases appealed to the appeals courts. Most matters of interpretation and application of the law have been handled by the Information Commissioner and the Tribunal for Information Rights.[44]

Two U.K. FOIA provisions are focused specifically on national security—sections 23 and 24. Section 23 of FOIA provides an exemption for information that was provided by, or relates to, a security body (the term "relates to" is interpreted broadly).[45] Section 24 of FOIA provides that information is exempt from disclosure if required for the purposes of safeguarding national security.[46] There is no specific definition of "national security" within the U.K. FOIA but there is a statutory list of what it includes in the Security Service Act of 1989: "protection against threats from espionage, terrorism and sabotage, from the activities of agents of foreign powers and from actions intended to overthrow or undermine parliamentary democracy by political, industrial or violent means."[47]

While the two FOIA provisions are related and are intended to work together, there are some important distinctions between the two. Section 23 applies only to information supplied by or relating to certain listed bodies and not *all* national security information. It is also applies absolutely to *all* information provided by or relating to any of these bodies listed in the section and requires no analysis of

The U.K.'s Most Famous FOIA case: Cabinet Office v. IC[1]

A FOIA request was submitted requesting disclosure of the March 2003 Cabinet meeting minutes where it was decided to commit U.K. armed forces to military action in Iraq. At the time of the request, the Government was accused of misleading Parliament and the public on the basis for the war. There were also questions about the legality of the war under international law. The Tribunal decided by a two-to-one majority that the minutes of the two Cabinet meetings should be disclosed, despite the long-standing extremely strong presumption that such minutes remain strictly confidential. The majority of the Tribunal thought that the strong public interest in the confidentiality of Cabinet minutes did not, in this instance, outweigh the public interest in disclosure. For unknown reasons the Tribunal did not analyze the case under sections 23 or 24, but rather section 25 (formation of Government policy). Despite the decision of the Tribunal, the minutes were never released. Section 53 of the FOIA allows for a ministerial override, whereby a minister may lawfully refuse to give effect to a decision notice or to a tribunal decision where "on reasonable grounds" he has formed the opinion that it is appropriate to do so. To invoke section 53 the minister presents the ministerial certificate to the Information Commissioner and Parliament. The Lord Chancellor and Secretary of State for Justice, Jack Straw, presented the first ever sec. 53 ministerial veto to Parliament on February 24, 2009. His actions have led some to question whether a ministerial veto should exist at all within a FOIA regime.

---

1. EA/2008/0024 and EA/2008/0029.

---

the content of the information nor an assessment of the likely effect of disclosure. There is no requirement for a public interest test in disclosure for any records under 30 years old but there is for historical records.[48] Furthermore, a government official may rely on section 23 to neither "confirm nor deny" whether it holds information.[49]

Section 24 does not provide an absolute exemption and instead outlines the process for the release of information to be subject to a public interest test.[50] According to the U.K. Information Commissioner, it is not sufficient that the information be related to national security for the exemption to apply. Rather, the focus of section 24 is on whether disclosure of information serves the public interest, and whether disclosure would cause an actual harm to national security (e.g., consider the security of the citizens of the United Kingdom, implications for another country's security, and whether disclosure may discourage cooperation with other countries).[51]

Unique to the U.K. FOIA process is the concept of a ministerial certificate signed by a Minister of the Crown (specified in section 25(3) of the act as a member of the Cabinet, the attorney general, or the advocate general for Scotland or for Northern Ireland). It is not required before the exemption may be relied upon, but if a ministerial certificate is obtained under section 23, it is considered conclusive evidence that the information is covered by the exemption and no further steps need be taken by the government agency to demonstrate that the information can be withheld.[52] If a ministerial certificate is obtained under section 24 it, too, is considered conclusive evidence that the information is covered by the exemption. However, the information is still subject to the public interest test.[53] The Information Commissioner will still make his own decision on where the public interest lies.

In addition to providing a mechanism for requesting information, there is a very limited statutory obligation for the government to publish information related to national security consistent with the publishing scheme it develops consistent with section 19 of FOIA.[54] This has been implemented primarily through the publication of annual reports to the oversight bodies for the Secret and Security Services, namely, the Intelligence and Security Committee and the Commissioners for Interception of Communications and for the Security Service.[55]

B. The Official Secrets Act of 1989

Immediately after his detention on August 19, 2013, David Miranda filed an appeal with the Court of Appeal (the United Kingdom's second highest appeals court below the Supreme Court) challenging his detention and requesting an injunction to prevent the government from reviewing the material seized. After considering the arguments of Miranda's attorney and statements submitted by Britain's deputy national security advisor, the court authorized the police to investigate whether possession of the material by Miranda constituted a crime under the Terrorism Act as well as a violation of section 1 of the Official Secrets Act.[56]

The Official Secrets Act of 1989 is the primary legislation governing disclosure of information by current and former government employees, government contractors, and members of the public who have, or have had, official information in their possession. The 1989 Act replaced the Official Secrets Acts of 1920 and 1939. It creates six categories of official information that are subject to criminal penalties if disclosed: security and intelligence; defense; international relations; foreign confidences; information that might lead to the commission of crime; and the special investigation powers under the Interception of Communications Act 1985 and the Security Service Act 1989.[57]

The act further sets out specific harm tests for the six categories, each of which generally requires some particular damage to the national interest. However, there is *no* damage test applied if the disclosure is made by (1) present or former members of the security and intelligence services; (2) individuals who have been notified in writing that they are subject to section 1(1) of the 1989 Act; or (3) individuals whose work is connected with the security and intelligence services. The fact of disclosure by any of those individuals is considered an absolute offense.

The 1989 Official Secrets Act also provides for criminal sanctions for secondary disclosures of covered information. Section 5 provides that it is an offense for anyone to make a damaging disclosure of information relating to security or intelligence, defense, or international relations communicated in confidence to another state or an international organization and came into that person's possession without the authority of that state or organization.[58]

Prosecutions under the Official Secrets Act are only undertaken with the permission of the attorney general and are quite rare. Table 1 summarizes the cases filed since 1997.

Table 1. Official Secrets Act Cases Since 1997

Year	Charges	Outcome
1997	Richard Tomlinson, a former MI6 officer, was charged after he gave a four-page synopsis of a proposed book detailing his career to an Australian publisher.	Tomlinson pleaded guilty, was sentenced to 12 months in prison, and released after six months for good behavior. He was charged again on the basis that he intended to make damaging disclosures. Tomlinson fled the United Kingdom to a series of countries, fighting extradition and injunctions in each country. In 2001, he published a book about his career through a publisher in Moscow. The British government initially obtained an order to confiscate all proceeds. In September 2008, MI6 ended its legal objections and admitted that the previous legal actions had been disproportionate to the offense. However, Tomlinson was not compensated for loss of proceeds or his pension.
1997	David Shayler was charged with passing to a newspaper protected information that related to potentially serious allegations against the Secret Service.	Shayler initially fled to France, which refused to comply with a British extradition request. Eventually Shayler returned to the United Kingdom to face trial. He was convicted and sentenced to six months' confinement. He actually served seven months under a home detention curfew arrangement. Discussion of the case within the House of Lords indicated that it might be possible to use a "defence of necessity by duress of circumstances," but the defense has never been used.

(continued)

Table 1. Official Secrets Act Cases Since 1997 (*continued*)

Year	Charges	Outcome
1998	Tony Geraghty's home was searched after a book he wrote on intelligence operations in Northern Ireland was published; he was charged with taking possession of protected documents and making damaging disclosures.	No protected documents cited in the book were found in his home, and the charges were dropped.
1998	The home of Nigel Wylde was also searched for protected documents cited in the book written by Geraghty. Wylde was a former government contractor.	Evidence indicated that five confidential documents were passed to Geraghty, but charges were dropped when it became evident that the book contained no information that was not already publicly available.
1998	Steven Hayden, a chief petty officer in the Royal Navy, was charged with selling protected information to a newspaper about an alleged plot by Saddam Hussein to launch anthrax attacks in the United Kingdom.	Hayden pleaded guilty and was imprisoned for 12 months.
2003	Katharine Gunn, a translator for Government Communications Headquarters (GCHQ), was accused of leaking an e-mail from the U.S. National Security Agency requesting the United Kingdom's assistance in bugging the offices of six UN Security Council members considered swing votes on the issue of approving the invasion of Iraq.	Charges dropped after the court asked for any advice rendered related to the legality of the war and the government chose not to produce any responsive documents. Gunn was fired from her job by GCHQ.
2005	Neil Garrett of ITV News was arrested after publishing internal police information about a man shot dead by the London police. The deceased was misidentified by the police as a suspect in failed bombing attempts on July 21, 2005.	Charges were dropped after it was discovered the police had misled the public about the deceased's actions before he was shot.
2006	Derek Paquill, a Foreign Office civil servant, was charged with leaking to the media documents related to U.S. engagement in extraordinary rendition and U.K. government policy toward Muslim groups.	Charges were dropped after internal governmental discussion about the leak started a constructive debate about the lack of actual harm caused to national security and international relations by the disclosure. Paquill was dismissed from his job for gross misconduct.

Year	Charges	Outcome
2007	Thomas Lund-Lack, a Scotland Yard employee, was charged for leaking secret information about a planned al-Qaeda attack to a newspaper.	Lund-Lack pleaded guilty to wilful misconduct in a public office and denied the charge of breaching the Official Secrets Act. He was sentenced to eight months' imprisonment for wilful misconduct.
2007	David Keogh, a civil servant with the Ministry of Defence, and Leo O'Conner, a Minister of Parliament researcher, were charged with disclosing a memo about a meeting on the situation in Iraq between President George Bush and Prime Minister Tony Blair at the White House in April 2004.	The defense argued that the disclosure was not damaging, but the government argued that it was damaging to international affairs. Keogh was convicted and sentenced to six months in jail and fined £5,000 toward the costs of prosecution. O'Conner was in jail for three months.
2008	Nicholas Thompson, a senior government detective, was accused of leaking sensitive information and naming the maker of a confidential phone call.	The detective was found not guilty. However, he had been forced to resign from the police when charged and did not get his job back.
2008	Richard Jackson, a senior civil servant with the Ministry of Defence, was charged with disclosing protected information when he accidentally left the documents on a train, and they were found by members of the public.	Jackson pleaded guilty and was fined £2,500.

Sources: Lucinda Maer & Oonagh Gay, U.K. House of Commons Library, Official Secrecy 6 (Dec. 30, 2008), http://www.fas.org/irp/world/uk/secrecy.pdf; Sandra Coliver, Open Soc'y Justice Initiative, The United Kingdom's Official Secrets Act 1989 (Dec. 2013) (on file with author); Chris Summers, *When Should a Secret Not Be a Secret,* BBC News, May 20, 2007, http://news.bbc.co.uk/2/hi/uk_news/6639947.stm.

C. *Whistleblower Protection in the United Kingdom*

The United Kingdom was one of the first European states to implement legislation providing for whistleblower protection.[59] The Public Interest Disclosure Act (PIDA) was introduced in the late 1990s to protect whistleblowers from victimization and dismissal where they raised genuine concerns about a range of criminal offenses, risks to health and safety, miscarriages of justice, and environmental damage. The PIDA adds to and amends the Employment Rights Act of 1996. It applies to almost all workers and employees, including contract workers and trainees who ordinarily work in Great Britain.

There is no direct definition of "whistleblower" within the PIDA. Instead there are provisions directed at protecting qualifying "disclosures" by "workers" and protections and remedies for such disclosures. A "qualifying disclosure" includes information regarding criminal offenses, failure to comply with legal obligations, a miscarriage of justice, and the health or safety of individuals.[60] Under PIDA, whistleblowers in the United Kingdom will be protected when they follow one prong of a three-pronged approach and reasonably believe that their disclosure is in the public interest.[61] First, the whistleblower must use internal mechanisms within the organization in order to give a company a chance to address the problem. Second, in the absence of any internal mechanisms or if they fail to work, the individual must raise concerns with prescribed persons such as the Health and Safety Executive, the Inland Revenue, the Audit Commission, and utility regulators. Third, other means, such as the media, may be used in the event of a serious matter where there is fear of reprisal or cover-up or the matter was reported internally or to a prescribed person but has not been dealt with properly.[62]

Furthermore, confidentiality clauses such as those found in employment contracts and severance agreements that conflict with the PIDA will not be considered legally binding.[63]

Whistleblowers in the United Kingdom may bring a retaliation claim directly to the United Kingdom Employment Tribunal, and the tribunal's decision is reviewable by the higher United Kingdom courts.[64] Whistleblower cases in the United Kingdom have increased exponentially since the law was implemented in 1999, with 70 percent of the claims settled or withdrawn without a hearing and about 22 percent won with compensation awarded in the range of £113,000 to £9.5 million.[65]

Tables 2 and 3 summarize characteristics of United States and United Kingdom whistleblowing legislation[66] and penalties for unauthorized disclosure.[67]

Key distinctions to note are that the U.S. legislation protects disclosures made by federal employees *irrespective of the method of disclosure*, to include disclosures to the media. There is also no express requirement for the individual to report to an internal point of contact. The United Kingdom model has a less protective scheme and instead uses the three-pronged approach toward disclosures and protection for those who make them. The wide scope of the U.K. act for both public and private sector employees, as well as for a wide range of information types, is seen by experts in this area as one of its key strengths. The act also encourages reporting internally as a first step and thus provides an incentive for employers to put internal reporting procedures in place.[68] However, the law does not have any statutory protection if the disclosure itself would constitute a criminal offense, such as violating the Official Secrets Act.

Table 2. Whistleblowing Legislation

Primary Legislation	Who Is Protected	Information Protected	Disclosure Routes Protected	Motive for Disclosure
United States: Whistleblower Protection Act	Federal workers. The act excludes employees of the intelligence agencies and FBI as well as congressional and judicial staff.	Any information that the employee reasonably believes violates law, rule, or regulation, a gross waste of funds, gross mismanagement, abuse of authority, or a significant and specific danger to public health and safety.	Internal and external disclosure channels. Any disclosure channel is protected, including making allegations to the press. The U.S. Office of Special Counsel operates a confidential disclosure channel.	Good faith/ reasonable belief.
United Kingdom: Public Interest Disclosure Act	Public and private sector employees. An amendment made it applicable to the police. It does not apply to members of the armed forces (see section 192 of the Employment Rights Act). It also does not apply to employees of the Security Service, Security Intelligence Service and GCHQ (see section 193 of the Employment Rights Act).	A qualifying disclosure constitutes (1) a criminal offense; (2) a failure to comply with any legal obligation; (3) a miscarriage of justice; (4) danger to the health and safety of any individual; (5) damage to the environment; (6) deliberate concealment of information relating to any of the above has been, is being, or is likely to be committed.	Prescribed disclosure channels: (1) internal; (2) prescribed routes; (3) media.	In the public interest.

Table 3. Unauthorized Disclosure Penalties

	Maximum Penalty for Unauthorized Possession	Maximum Penalty for Unauthorized Disclosure	Limited Offenses or Decreased Penalties	Heightened Offenses or Penalties	Definitions
United Kingdom	Up to 51 weeks imprisonment for possession, with different provisions available for public servants and private persons. (Official Secrets Act, Secs. 8,10)	Up to two years for unauthorized disclosure by public servants, and other persons who have accessed information through unauthorized disclosures. (Official Secrets Act, Sec. 8(1)) In the case of private persons and public servants not in the security or intelligence services, offense requires disclosure to be "damaging." (Official Secrets Act, Sec. 5(3))	Specific provisions reserved for public servants with authorized access to information, and different defense and heightened standards available for private persons.	Up to 14 years for spying.	"Spying": "for any purpose prejudicial to the safety or interests of the state . . . (c) publishes, or communicates to any other person any secret official code word, or pass word, or any sketch, plan, model, article, or note, or other document which is calculated to be or might be or is intended to be directly or indirectly useful to an enemy." (Official Secrets Act, Sec. 1(c))
U.S.	Ten years for possession of national defense information. (18 U.S.C. § 793(e)(f))	Ten years for disclosure of national defense information, with particular provisions for public servants. Offense requires the disclosure to be prejudicial to the safety or interests of the United States or to the benefit of any foreign government and to the detriment of the United States. (18 U.S.C. § 793(d),(f)) With possible offense of conspiracy. (18 U.S.C. § 793(g))	Public servants and private persons may be penalized for unauthorized disclosure of information relating to national defense, but only public servants and others with authorized access are subject to penalties for certain other unauthorized disclosures, e.g., diplomatic material or classified materials. (See, e.g., 18 U.S.C. § 952, 18 U.S.C. § 1924; 50 U.S.C.S. § 783)	Up to life imprisonment, or death penalty (for particular offenses), for espionage.	"Espionage: Whoever with intent or reason to believe that it is to be used to the injury of the United States or to the advantage of a foreign nation, communicates, delivers, or transmits, or attempts to communicate, deliver, or transmit, to any foreign government, or to any faction or party or military or naval force within a foreign country, whether recognized or unrecognized by the United States, or to any representative, officer, agent, employee, subject, or citizen thereof, either directly or indirectly, any . . . information relating to the national defense." (18 U.S.C. § 794 (a)) With possible offense of conspiracy. (18 U.S.C. § 794(c)) Military also subject to Uniform Code of Military Justice, with similar definition but lower standard for imposition of the death penalty. (Uniform Code of Military Justice, 10 U.S.C. § 906a(l))

III. CONCLUSION: TRENDS FOR THE FUTURE

In February 2014 a three-judge panel within the United Kingdom's lower court (similar to U.S. district court) dismissed Miranda's challenge that his nine-hour detention and seizure of computer materials was unlawful, ruling it was lawful under Schedule 7 of the Terrorism Act of 2000 and did not breach European human rights protections of freedom of information.[69] While it acknowledged that the seizure of computer materials was "an indirect interference with press freedom," the court determined that there was not only compelling but "very pressing" evidence of a risk to national security. Based on the testimony of Oliver Robbins, the deputy national security advisor at the Cabinet Office, the judges determined that the release of 58,000 highly classified Government Communications Headquarters (CGHQ) files would be very likely to cause great damage to security and possible loss of life.[70] Going further, the judges refused to recognize that the seized files were "journalistic material" and insisted that they included stolen raw data that did not warrant any freedom of expression safeguards.[71]

Critics of the decision argued that the Terrorism Act of 2000 was never meant to apply to journalists and were concerned that this unprecedented application of the law will have a chilling effect on whistleblowers and embolden security agencies to take a very broad view of who may be considered a "terrorist."[72] Miranda was expected to exercise his right to written appeal to the court of appeals for review, though he has not done so as of July 2014. Other judicial review options for Miranda include the United Kingdom's Supreme Court and the European Court of Human Rights.

While the British judicial system reviews the detention and seizure for legality under U.K. law, the reader should assess these governmental actions and the corresponding debate with an eye toward assessing whether we are seeing the beginning of a process of developing customary international law. This type of review is underway by several nongovernmental organizations. According to country studies conducted by the Open Society Justice Initiative, nearly all of the existing right to information laws authorize government officials to withhold information from the public on the grounds of national security and/or internal security.[73] However, few of these laws define national security for the purpose of information withholding. Furthermore, as noted in recent testimony of a leading expert in the field, few of these laws set forth clear standards or procedures for:

- Classifying or otherwise withholding information on security grounds;
- Encouraging the proactive disclosure of information of high public interest;
- Making clear the categories of information that should be available to independent oversight bodies and the courts tasked with overseeing the handling of national security information;
- Protecting whistleblowers; and
- Punishing unauthorized disclosures.[74]

To respond to this gap in existing laws, as well as to promote best practices for identifying and safeguarding information that should be kept from public scrutiny, the Open Society Justice Initiative developed the draft Global Principles on National Security and the Right to Information (the Tshwane Principles) in close consultation with officials from the UN, regional organizational entities, nongovernmental organizations, and some 400 experts from 73 countries. The Tshwane Principles are based on international and national law, standards, and best practices identified by experts and intended to influence the development and reform of laws.[75]

Other nongovernmental organizations, such as Transparency International, have focused on advocating for whistleblower protection and rights as well as establishing responsible reporting processes. In 2009, in conjunction with experts and practitioners around the world, Transparency International developed recommended draft principles for whistleblowing legislation. These draft principles include defining whistleblowing, guiding principles, disclosure procedures, protections for the whistleblower, enforcement mechanisms, and a suggested legislative structure.[76]

A final trend worth watching is the impact the recent and ongoing financial crisis in many countries has had on prompting a greater debate on public and corporate accountability. The Open Government Partnership, an international multistakeholder initiative founded by the presidents of the United States and Brazil, focuses on promoting fiscal transparency, access to information, and citizen engagement. It currently has 63 participating states and is unique with its financial support coming from direct contributions from member nations and private companies and foundations.[77]

NOTES

1. *David Miranda Heathrow Detention: No 10 "Kept Abreast of Operation,"* BBC NEWS, Aug. 20, 2013, http://www.bbc.co.uk/news/uk-23769324.

2. *Id.*

3. Nicholas Watt, *Theresa May Rejects Claim Miranda Was Detained with No Legal Basis,* GUARDIAN, Aug. 21, 2013, http://www.theguardian.com/politics/2013/aug/21/theresa-may-david -miranda-legal-basis.

4. *US Given "Heads Up" on David Miranda Detention,* BBC NEWS, Aug. 19, 2013, http://www .bbc.co.uk/news/uk-23761918, 19 Aug. 2013.

5. Open Soc'y Founds., Understanding the Tshwane Principles, http://www.opensocietyfoundations .org/briefing-papers/understanding-tshwane-principles.

6. Testimony of Sandra Coliver to the Legal Affairs & Human Rights Comm. of the Parliamentary Assembly of the Council of Europe, National Security and the Right to Information, Dec. 11, 2012, Paris, http://www.opensocietyfoundations.org/sites/default/files/coliver-nsp-pace-20121220.pdf.

7. Amanda Jacobsen, *National Security and the Right to Information in Europe,* RIGHT2INFO .ORG, http://www.right2info.org/resources/publications/national-security-page/national-security -expert-papers/jacobsen_nat-sec-and-rti-in-europe, 11; Testimony of Sandra Coliver, *supra* note 6.

8. TOBY MENDEL: FREEDOM OF INFORMATION: A COMPARATIVE LEGAL SURVEY 7, (2d ed., 2008), http://unesdoc.unesco.org/images/0015/001584/158450e.pdf.

9. United Nations, Resolution 59(1), adopted Dec. 14, 1946, http://www.ilsa.org/jessup/jessup08 /basicmats/ga59191.pdf.

10. For judicial opinions on human rights guarantees in customary international law, see, for example, *Barcelona Traction, Light and Power Co. Ltd. Case (Belgium v. Spain) (Second Phase)*, 1970 I.C.J. 3; *Namibia Opinion*, 1971 I.C.J. 16, Separate Opinion, Judge Ammoun; and *Filartiga v. Pena-Irala*, 630 F.2d 876 (2d Cir. 1980).

11. Full text, http://www.ohchr.org/en/professionalinterest/pages/ccpr.aspx.

12. United Nations, General Assembly Resolution 2200 A (XXI), adopted Dec. 16, 1966, entered into force Mar. 23, 1976.

13. Report of the Special Rapporteur on the Promotion and Protection of the Right to Freedom of Opinion and Expression Frank LaRue, UN Doc. E/CN.4/1998/40, Jan. 28, 1998, para. 14, *cited in* MENDEL, *supra* note 8, at 8–9.

14. Organization of American States, Lima Principles, art. 8, approved on Nov. 16, 2000, drafted by the United Nations Special Rapporteur on Freedom of Opinion and Expression, the Westminster Foundation for Democracy (United Kingdom) and Human Rights Watch, among others, http://www .oas.org/en/iachr/expression/showarticle.asp?artID=158&lID=1.

15. Jacobsen, *supra* note 7, at 9.

16. Statement by the Special Rapporteur on the Promotion and Protection of the Right to Freedom of Opinion and Expression Frank LaRue to the 68th session of the United Nations General Assembly, Oct. 25, 2013. http://papersmart.unmeetings.org/media2/703368/statement-by-frank-la-rue-item -69b.pdf.

17. Full text of the Charter of Fundamental Rights of the European Union may be found at http:// eur-lex.europa.eu/LexUriServ/LexUriServ.do?uri=OJ:C:2010:083:0389:0403:en:PDF.

18. The Council of Europe in Brief (2013), http://www.coe.int/aboutCOe/index.asp.

19. The full text of the Convention may be found at http://conventions.coe.int/Treaty/en/Treaties /Html/005.htm.

20. The full text of the Convention may be found at http://conventions.coe.int/Treaty/EN/Treaties /Html/205.htm.

21. Overview of the Council of Europe Convention on Access to Official Documents, Council of Europe, http://conventions.coe.int/Treaty/EN/Summaries/Html/205.htm.

22. The status of the Convention may be found at http://conventions.coe.int/Treaty/Commun /ChercheSig.asp?NT=205&CM=1&DF=&CL=ENG.

23. Jacobsen, *supra* note 7, at 20–21.

24. *Id.*

25. Open Soc'y Justice Initiative, Understanding the Tshwane Principles 6 (June 12, 2013), http:// www.opensocietyfoundations.org/sites/default/files/briefing-understanding-tshwane-06122013%20 %2Bsc.pdf.

26. *Id.*

27. *Id.*

28. Full text, http://www.whistleblowers.org/storage/whistleblowers/documents/international homepage/un%20convention%20against%20corruption.pdf.

29. These include the Inter-American Convention Against Corruption (arts. III & XVI), adopted in 1996 by the Organization of American States; the African Union Convention of Preventing and Combating Corruption (arts. 5, 6, and 17); the ADB OECD Anti-Corruption Initiative for Asia-Pacific (Pillars 1, 2, & 3); the Southern African Development Community—Protocol Against Corruption (arts. 4 & 8); and the OECD Convention on Combating on Bribery of Foreign Public Officials in International Business Transactions (arts. 3 & 9).

30. Jacobsen, *supra* note 7, at 48–49.

31. *Id.* at 49.

32. *Id.* at 50.

33. THAD M. GUYER & NIKOLAS F. PETERSON, GOV'T ACCOUNTABILITY PROJECT, THE CURRENT STATE OF WHISTLEBLOWER LAW IN EUROPE 7, http://www.europarl.europa.eu/meetdocs/2009_2014 /documents/libe/dv/gap_whistleblowerlawineu_/gap_whistleblowerlawineu_en.pdf.

34. *Id.*

35. *Id.* at 9.

36. *See* Heinisch v. Germany, App. No. 28274/08, Eur. Ct. H.R. (July 21, 2001), http://hudoc.echr .coe.int/sites/eng/pages/search.aspx?i=001-105777.

37. European Comm'n, Staff Regulations of Officials of the European Communities, arts. 22a & 22b, http://ec.europa.eu/civil_service/docs/toc100_en.pdf.

38. Transparency Int'l, Draft Avenues for Transparency International to Advocate for Whistle Blower Protection at EU-Level 21, http://www.right2info.org/resources/publications /publications/10_04_27%20ti-EU%20advocacy%20for%20WB%20protection.pdf.

39. 18 U.S.C. § 1514.

40. 12 U.S.C. § 5333. *See* GUYER & PETERSON, *supra* note 33, at 8.

41. Information Commissioner's Office, http://ico.org.uk/foikb/PolicyLines/FOIPolicyPresumption infavourofdisclosure.htm.

42. European Union Directive 95/46/EC, as amended, http://eur-lex.europa.eu/LexUriServ/Lex UriServ.do?uri=CELEX:31995L0046:en:HTML.

43. Info. Comm'r's Office, How to Make a Freedom of Information (FOI) Request, https://www .gov.uk/make-a-freedom-of-information-request/the-freedom-of-information-act.

44. Adam Tomkin, National Security and Access to Information in the United Kingdom 3 (Winter 2010) (on file with author).

45. Info. Comm'r's Office, Security Bodies (Section 23) Freedom of Information Act, http://ico .org.uk/~/media/documents/library/Freedom_of_Information/Detailed_specialist_guides/security _bodies_section_23_foi.ashx. The term "security body" is defined in section 3 and includes among others the Security Service, the Secret Intelligence Service, the Government Communications Head-quarters, the special forces, the National Criminal Intelligence Service, and the Serious Organised Crime Agency.

46. Info. Comm'r's Office, Safeguarding National Security (Section 24) Freedom of Information Act, http://ico.org.uk/for_organisations/guidance_index/~/media/documents/library/Freedom_of _Information/Detailed_specialist_guides/safeguarding_national_security_section_24_foi.ashx.

47. Security Service Act of 1989, full text, http://www.legislation.gov.uk/ukpga/1989/5/section/1.

48. U.K. Ministry of Justice, Freedom of Information Guidance: Exemptions Guidance Section 23: Information Supplied by, or Relating to, Bodies Dealing with Security Matters 3 (Mar. 2012), http:// www.justice.gov.uk/downloads/information-access-rights/foi/foi-exemption-s23.pdf.

49. Info. Comm'r's Office, Security Bodies (Section 23) Freedom of Information Act, *supra* note 45.

50. Info. Comm'r's Office, Safeguarding National Security (Section 24) Freedom of Information Act, *supra* note 46.

51. *Id.*

52. U.K. MINISTRY OF JUSTICE, *supra* note 48, at 6.

53. Info. Comm'r's Office, Security Bodies (Section 23) Freedom of Information Act, *supra* note 45.

54. Freedom of Information Act sec 19, Publication Schemes, http://www.legislation.gov.uk/ukpga /2000/36/section/19.

55. Adam Tomkins, Right2Information, Regional Consultation on National Security and the Right to Information, National Questionnaire, Country Analyzed: United Kingdom, http://www.right2info. org/resources/publications/national-security-page/european-questionnaires/united-kingdom-adam -tomkins, at 2.

56. Robert Booth, *UK Took Three Weeks to Act Over Data at New York Times, Says Guardian,* GUARDIAN, Aug. 30, 2013, http://www.theguardian.com/world/2013/aug/30/david-miranda-police -powers-data.

57. U.K. Home Office, Nationality Instructions, Procedures section, The Official Secrets Act of 1989, https://www.gov.uk/government/uploads/system/uploads/attachment_data/file/264795/officalsecretsact.pdf.

58. Official Secrets Act § 5(3), http://www.legislation.gov.uk/ukpga/1989/6/contents.

59. GUYER & PETERSON, *supra* note 33, at 12.

60. http://www.legislation.gov.uk/ukpga/1998/23/section/1.

61. TLT, Whistleblowing Update, http://www.tltsolicitors.com/resources/publications/employment/whistleblowing_update_apr_13/.

62. *Id.*

63. KIRSTINE DREW, UNICORN, WHISTLEBLOWING AND CORRUPTION: AN INITIAL AND COMPARATIVE REVIEW 33 (Jan. 2003), http://www.againstcorruption.org/reportindex.asp.

64. GUYER & PETERSON, *supra* note 33, at 14.

65. *Id.*

66. DREW, *supra* note 63.

67. Information drawn from EMI MACLEAN ET AL., ANNEX D, TSHWANE PRINCIPLES: PENALTIES FOR UNAUTHORIZED DISCLOSURE: COMPARATIVE LAW AND PRACTICE (2013).

68. DREW, *supra* note 63, at 35.

69. Royal Courts of Justice, In the High Court of Justice Divisional Court, Approved Judgment in Case No: CO/11732/2013, Miranda v. Sec'y of State for the Home Dep't, 2014 EWHC 255, Feb. 19, 2014, http://www.judiciary.gov.uk/Resources/JCO/Documents/Judgments/miranda-v-sofshd.pdf; Alan Travis, Matthew Taylor & Patrick Wintour, *David Miranda Detention at Heathrow Airport was Lawful, High Court Rules*, GUARDIAN, Feb. 19, 2014, http://www.theguardian.com/world/2014/feb/19/david-miranda-detention-lawful-court-glenn-greenwald.

70. Alan Travis, Matthew Taylor & Patrick Wintour, *David Miranda Detention at Heathrow Airport was Lawful, High Court Rules*, Guardian, Feb. 19, 2014, http://www.theguardian.com/world/2014/feb/19/david-miranda-detention-lawful-court-glenn-greenwald.

71. *Id.*

72. *Id.*

73. Testimony of Sandra Coliver, *supra* note 6. Coliver is the senior legal officer for freedom of information and expression at the Open Society Justice Initiative. Previous positions include director of the San Francisco-based Center for Justice and Accountability, Law Programme director of Article 19, the Global Campaign for Freedom of Expression, and two decades of work on international law reform, human rights and rule of programs with the United Nations, the Organization for Security and Cooperation in Europe, the International Crisis Group, and IFES.

74. *Id.*

75. Open Soc'y Justice Initiative, Understanding the Tshwane Principles, http://www.opensocietyfoundations.org/briefing-papers/understanding-tshwane-principles.

76. The full text of the draft principles may be viewed at http://www.transparency.org/files/content/activity/2009_PrinciplesForWhistleblowingLegislation_EN.pdf.

77. Open Government Partnership, http://www.opengovpartnership.org.

Law Enforcement Investigations Involving Journalists

10

Jack Lerner and Rom Bar-Nissim

I. INTRODUCTION

How is the government able to investigate former National Security Agency employee Thomas A. Drake and former Central Intelligence Agency (CIA) employee Jeffrey Alexander Sterling for their leaks to journalists? What legal tools can federal law enforcement use to obtain the identity of a leaker and reveal information about the leak? What constitutional and statutory safeguards exist to protect media recipients of the leak, like the reporters James Risen of *The New York Times* and James Rosen of Fox News? Do internal guidelines at the Department of Justice shape its behavior? This chapter answers these questions.

The legal tools available to the government to investigate leaks of classified information can be divided into three overarching categories:

1. Compelling the recipient of the leak to disclose information about the whistleblower and the leak through a conventional search warrant or subpoena;

2. Obtaining information about the whistleblower and the leak through contemporaneous surveillance as authorized by laws such as the Wiretap Act and the Electronic Communications Privacy Act;

3. Retrieving information from third parties about the whistleblower and the leak through subpoenas, search warrants, and court orders authorized by laws such as the Stored Communications Act.

These investigatory powers are limited, of course, by the First and Fourth Amendments. In addition, Congress and state legislatures often pass legislation extending legal protections to journalists when the Supreme Court refuses to recognize Fourth Amendment protections or First Amendment safeguards. Where legislation has been enacted, however, the power of both the government's investigatory tools and protections for journalists can vary tremendously from one jurisdiction to another.[1]

II. GOING AFTER THE SOURCE: COMPELLING DISCLOSURE THROUGH WARRANTS AND SUBPOENAS

A. Seizure of Work Product: Search Warrants

When the government executes a search warrant against the media, it is generally looking for a journalist's work product. A journalist's notes or pictures may provide valuable information about a whistleblower and the leak. Consequently, the friction between the legitimate objectives of law enforcement and constitutional protections against unreasonable search and seizure and guarantees of a free press are most apparent when a search warrant is directed at the media.

The Fourth Amendment to the Constitution protects the public against "unreasonable searches and seizures" by the government. It states that "[t]he right of the people to be secure in their persons, houses, papers, and effects, against unreasonable searches and seizures, shall not be violated."[2] The Supreme Court ruled in *Katz v. United States* that warrantless searches into legally protected areas are presumptively invalid.[3]

In his influential concurrence in *Katz*, Justice John M. Harlan said the government violated the Fourth Amendment because it conducted a warrantless search where the individual maintained a "reasonable expectation of privacy." He stated that, in order for an individual to have "a reasonable expectation of privacy," the person's belief must be objectively and subjectively reasonable.[4] An individual has no objective expectation of privacy if society in general would not recognize it as such—as with, for example, an easily overhead conversation held in the middle of Grand Central Station, even if the conversants intended the conversation to be private. A person has no subjective expectation of privacy if he or she doesn't actually think the conversation will be private—as with a conversation conducted in one's home, when the person knows that his or her conversant intends to repeat it to others.

A valid search warrant must meet certain constitutional requirements. The Fourth Amendment requires warrants (1) to be issued by a judge, (2) to be based on probable cause, (3) to be supported by oath or affirmation, and (4) to describe with particularity (a) the location to be searched and (b) the items to be seized.[5]

In *Zurcher v. Stanford Daily*,[6] the Supreme Court addressed the inherent friction between the First Amendment's guarantee of a free press and law enforcement's ability to search newsrooms and journalists for evidence of criminal activity. *The Stanford Daily* covered a violent campus demonstration at which demonstrators assaulted policemen. The police executed a valid search warrant at *The Stanford Daily*'s headquarters seeking unpublished photos that could identify the assailants.[7] The Supreme Court rejected the newspaper's argument that the First Amendment restricted, if not prevented, executing a search warrant against the press,[8] reasoning that the warrant requirements of the Fourth Amendment were sufficient to safeguard against any potential "chilling effect" from executing search warrants against the press.[9]

In response, Congress passed the Privacy Protection Act of 1980 (PPA).[10] The PPA protects the press and others from searches of any work product by law enforcement for purposes of a criminal investigation. The PPA applies when the individual in possession of the material is "reasonably believed" to have the material in order to "disseminate [it] to the public [in] a newspaper, book, broadcast, or other similar form of public communication."[11]

There are substantial limitations to the scope of the PPA. First, it does not apply when there is probable cause that the media recipient is subject to a criminal investigation. While the crime cannot be merely "receiving, possessing, communicating or withholding the materials," the statute creates exceptions for crimes involving classified information.[12] Therefore, a court may consider a disclosed leak containing national security and classified information as a crime and, as such, outside the PPA's protection.[13] Second, the PPA does not apply if authorities have "reason to believe that the immediate seizure of such materials is necessary to prevent the death of, or serious bodily injury to, a human being."[14]

B. Compelled Disclosure of Sources: Subpoenas and the Reporter's Privilege

During a criminal investigation, the government may compel disclosure of information about the whistleblower and the leak by subpoenaing the recipient.[15] Again, since the recipients of the leak tend to be the press, the issue arises whether the recipient can exercise a "reporter's privilege" to preserve the whistleblower's anonymity.

The Supreme Court addressed whether a reporter must divulge the identity of a confidential source pursuant to a grand jury subpoena in *Branzburg v. Hayes*.[16] Paul Branzburg was a reporter for *The Courier-Journal* in Louisville, Kentucky, who wrote two articles on marijuana use; his sources conditioned their participation on Branzburg protecting their anonymity. Branzburg was subpoenaed to reveal the identity of his sources before a grand jury investigating the criminal activity in the article. Branzburg refused and claimed that the First Amendment provides a "reporter's privilege" protecting him from revealing the identity of his confidential sources.[17]

In a plurality opinion by Justice Byron White, the Supreme Court rejected Branzburg's argument and held that the First Amendment does not protect a reporter's right to conceal criminal conduct by refusing to answer a grand jury's questions, and consequently the First Amendment does not establish an unqualified reporter's privilege, at least not in the context of a grand jury investigation.[18]

Far more influential was Justice Lewis Powell's concurring opinion.[19] His objective was to address the concern raised in Stewart's dissent that *Branzburg* would turn the press into the "investigative arm of the government."[20] While he agreed that there was no unqualified reporter's privilege, he rejected the notion that the government had unfettered discretion to subpoena reporters. Powell stated that, while a reporter cannot challenge the government's general authority to issue a subpoena against the press,[21] the reporter could file a motion to quash if "the grand jury investigation is not conducted in good faith," such as when the questions directed to the reporter are only remotely related to the subject of the investigation, or when revealing the confidential source would not advance legitimate law enforcement goals.[22] In such scenarios, the judge would have discretion on a case-by-case basis to "balance the competing interests" between freedom of the press and the requirement that citizens testify with respect to criminal conduct.[23]

Branzburg and the reporter's privilege remains a hotly contested issue to this day. Federal and state courts interpreting *Branzburg* have come to vastly different conclusions about whether a reporter's privilege exists outside a grand jury context. In 2013, the U.S. Court of Appeals for the Fourth Circuit refused to recognize a reporter's privilege when *New York Times* reporter James Risen refused to testify in Jeffrey Sterling's trial for crimes related to the disclosure of classified documents.[24] In January 2014, Risen petitioned the Supreme Court to hear the case.[25] In June 2014, the Supreme Court rejected Risen's petition.

In jurisdictions that do recognize a reporter's privilege, the legal treatment varies tremendously in terms of who is covered, what is covered, and the type of proceeding in question. A full discussion of the various treatments of the reporter's privilege is beyond the scope of this chapter.[26]

As of 2014, 31 states and the District of Columbia have reporter shield statutes.[27] Congress, however, has attempted and failed to pass reporter's shield legislation on more than 100 occasions.[28] After the 2013 disclosures by former National Security Agency (NSA) contractor Edward Snowden regarding the NSA's surveillance practices, Congress once again considered the issue.[29]

III. SURVEILLANCE: CONTEMPORANEOUS INTERCEPTION OF INFORMATION

When leaks occur, the government may engage in surveillance of both the whistleblower and recipient in order to gain information for a criminal investigation into the leak.

The Electronic Communications Privacy Act of 1986 (ECPA),[30] which amended the older Wiretap Act[31] and included the Pen Register Act[32] and Stored Communications Act,[33] articulates the procedures and circumstances under which the government may engage in telephone surveillance and electronic surveillance, or retrieve information involving telephone or electronic communications. ECPA and these other acts cover a wide range of electronic communications, including phone calls, e-mails, text messages, voicemails, instant messages, and any other form of electronic communication.[34] The statutes thus directly affect websites offering e-mail and cloud storage services such as Google, Microsoft, and Apple, as well as telecommunication companies such as Verizon and AT&T, because law enforcement agencies use ECPA and the other statutes to order such services to assist them with interception or retrieval.

A. Interception of Communications

ECPA prohibits interception of communications without court authorization. The statute defines "intercept" as the "aural or other acquisition of the contents" of various kinds of communications by means of "electronic, mechanical or other devices."[35] ECPA sets forth strict requirements that must be met in order to obtain a warrant to intercept electronic communications and phone calls. First, the application must include a full and complete statement of the particulars of the investigation, communication sought, and necessity for the wiretap.[36] Second, the judge must determine:

1. Is there probable cause to believe that the subject of the wiretap committed, or is about to commit, one of the enumerated offense in the statute?
2. Is there probable cause to believe that information concerning the crime will be obtained by the interception?
3. Are alternative investigative procedures ineffective, unlikely to succeed, or too dangerous?
4. Is there probable cause that the location of the wiretap will yield the sought-for communication?[37]

Under the act, the government only needs to notify the target of the surveillance 90 days after the surveillance has commenced.[38]

B. Interception of Location and Movement: Tracking Devices and United States v. Jones

If the recipient and the whistleblower decide to communicate only in person, tracking devices enable law enforcement to follow the recipient to the whistle-blower. The search warrant issued against Fox News reporter James Rosen states that the Federal Bureau of Investigation (FBI) used security access card information to determine that Rosen and State Department security advisor Stephen Jin-Woo Kim met face-to-face. Because an individual's movements in public are in plain view for all to see, the government can track a person's movements by physically following them in public. However, once the government employs remote tracking devices, a search warrant may be required.

In 1983, the Supreme Court held in *United States v. Knotts* that placing a tracking device in a container with the owner's consent, prior to the defendant taking possession, did not violate the Fourth Amendment.[39] In 2012, however, the U.S. Supreme Court held in *United States v. Jones* that placing a GPS tracking device underneath a person's car without a warrant or the person's consent does violate the Fourth Amendment.[40] The Court distinguished its holding from *Knotts* by noting that the tracking device in *Knotts* was originally placed in the container with the previous owner's consent, while in *Jones* the tracking device was placed without anyone's consent; the latter, the Court held, amounts to an unreasonable search. The fact the car was in plain view of the public did not make placing the tracking device on the car any more reasonable, given the vast amounts of personal information a tracking device can collect.[41]

IV. RETRIEVING INFORMATION FROM OTHERS: SUBPOENAS DIRECTED AT THIRD PARTIES

A. Retrieval of Telephone Records: The Pen Register Act

The term "pen register" refers to a device or process that collects the numbers of all outgoing telephone calls,[42] while a trap and trace device collects the numbers of all incoming calls. The contents of the conversation are not obtained with either technology.[43]

During a criminal investigation, retrieval of a person's phone records may provide insight into a person's relationships. In the context of leaks, the government may place a pen register and a trap and trace device (collectively referred to as "pen registers") to establish a connection between the whistleblower and the recipient of the leak. For example, the Rosen search warrant used information from a pen register to establish the connection between Rosen and Kim to support probable cause.[44]

As discussed above, a person might have a reasonable expectation of privacy in the content of one's communications, like a phone call.[45] In *Smith v. Maryland*, however, the Supreme Court held that the warrantless use of pen registers does not violate the Fourth Amendment because "a person has no legitimate expectation of privacy in information he voluntarily turns over to third parties."[46] Under this "third-party doctrine," once the subscriber dials the phone number, he or she discloses the number to a third party—the telephone company. Once it is disclosed, the telephone subscriber loses his "reasonable expectation of privacy" in his phone records, and therefore a search warrant is not required.[47]

Congress responded by enacting the Pen Register Act. The Pen Register Act applies to both federal and state law enforcement[48] and sets forth the requirements for installing pen registers or trap and trace devices.[49] The legal standard for granting a pen register application is significantly lower than a search warrant, which requires probable cause. To obtain an order requiring a telecommunications company to install a pen register, the government only needs to show that the information is "relevant to an ongoing criminal investigation being conducted by that agency."[50] Granted requests are valid for 60 days and can be extended only upon renewing the application.[51] The government may request that the target of the surveillance not be notified,[52] and frequently does so.

B. Retrieval of Electronic Communications: The Stored Communications Act

Digital communications create analytic problems under the Fourth Amendment. As discussed above, the third-party doctrine states that "a person has no legitimate expectation of privacy in information he voluntarily turns over to third parties."[53] This means that in the digital realm, individuals may lose Fourth Amendment protection for their digital communications because they are sent and stored through third-party service providers.

The Stored Communications Act (SCA) governs when the government may obtain a court order requiring an electronic communications service provider (such as an e-mail service, website, or telecommunications company) to disclose the contents of the communication or the subscriber's records.[54] The SCA is regularly used to investigate leaks. In Thomas A. Drake's indictment, the government used the SCA to obtain e-mails between Drake and a reporter to support charges that Drake retained confidential materials.[55] Along similar lines, the Rosen search warrant was aimed at retrieving Rosen's e-mails to show that Kim illegally disclosed confidential information.[56] And Jeffrey Sterling's e-mails to James Risen were retrieved pursuant to the SCA and used as evidence to prove Sterling violated the Espionage Act.[57]

In light of the third-party doctrine, the government's ability to avail itself of the SCA is significantly easier than obtaining a search warrant, depending on whether the communications have been in storage for more than 180 days. For communications less than 180 days old, the government must obtain a search warrant pursuant to the procedures articulated by the jurisdiction in order to compel providers to supply the content of wire or electronic communications.[58] For communications older than 180 days, however, the government only needs to state "specific and articulable facts" that provide "reasonable grounds" that the information sought is "relevant and material to an ongoing criminal investigation."[59] The government's authority under the SCA is limited to aiding criminal investigations, not civil actions.[60]

In addition, the SCA alters the notice requirement for court orders issued pursuant to the SCA.[61] If the government obtains judicial authorization to retrieve the communication under the SCA, the SCA provides that the government may delay notification for up to 90 days,[62] or not notify the target at all.[63] In availing itself of either provision, the government must show that disclosure will cause an "adverse result."[64] Adverse results are defined as either (1) endangering the life or physical safety of an individual, (2) flight from prosecution, (3) destruction of or tampering with evidence, (4) intimidation of potential witnesses, or (5) otherwise seriously jeopardizing an investigation or unduly delaying trial.[65] Furthermore, the government may renew a request to delay notice if an "adverse result" still exists.[66]

The SCA also authorizes the government to obtain a court order directing the service provider to disclose the subscriber's records. Such information can include the subscriber's name, contact information, payment information, and usage history.[67] Importantly, the government does not need to notify the subscriber when solely requesting subscriber records.[68]

V. A BRIEF DISCUSSION OF FISA AND USA PATRIOT ACT

A discussion of the government's investigation techniques would be incomplete without mentioning the Foreign Intelligence Surveillance Act (FISA)[69] and the Uniting and Strengthening America by Providing Appropriate Tools Required to Intercept and Obstruct Terrorism Act—USA PATRIOT Act.[70] While a detailed discussion is beyond the scope of this chapter, it is worth mentioning how FISA and the USA PATRIOT Act have been used for domestic surveillance activities.

The USA PATRIOT Act and two other statutes authorize the National Security Administration, FBI, and other federal agencies to issue National Security Letters, and obtain information without a court order if the information is "relevant to an authorized investigation to protect against international terrorism or clandestine intelligence activities."[71] The service provider cannot notify the subscriber of the NSL.[72] While the service provider may petition to modify or set aside an NSL, a court will only grant a request upon the service provider showing that there is "no reason to believe that disclosure may endanger the national security of the United States" or a criminal investigation.[73] If the FBI or the Department of Justice certifies that disclosure would endanger national security or interfere with an investigation, the certification is "conclusive unless the court finds that the certification was made in bad faith."[74]

Section 215 of the USA PATRIOT ACT, commonly referred to as the "business records" provision, authorizes the government to obtain "tangible things" from U.S. persons under strict secrecy if "presumptively relevant to an authorized investigation" to obtain "foreign intelligence information" or "to protect against international terrorism or clandestine intelligence activities."[75] The FISA court's interpretation of "tangible things" goes beyond "books, records, papers, documents, and other items" to encompass phone records, also known as telephony metadata.[76] It was pursuant to this provision that NSA has been able to obtain broad orders for metadata from major telephone companies.

FISA requires a nexus between the surveillance activity and national security. FISA authorizes the attorney general and the director of national intelligence to monitor electronic communications containing "foreign intelligence information" and gives the government broad leeway in defining what constitutes "foreign intelligence information."[77] However, FISA does require a showing of probable cause that the target is "a foreign power or an agent of a foreign power" and that the facilities at which surveillance is directed are being used or about to be used by "a foreign power or an agent of a foreign power."[78]

Despite the nexus requirement, the National Security Administration has used its FISA authority to engage in wide-ranging domestic surveillance activity. Most notably, the NSA ordered Verizon to hand over all its subscribers' telephone records.[79] While there is no evidence that NSA surveillance was used to target journalists, the documents obtained by Snowden and published, in part, in *The Washington Post* and *The Guardian* did reveal a program to target and discredit "radicalizers" by gathering records of online sexual activity and visits to pornographic websites.[80]

In addition, a leaked copy of the Internal Revenue Service's agent manual revealed that since at least 2005, the Drug Enforcement Administration has provided information obtained from NSA surveillance to the IRS and other agencies.[81] In addition, the manual directs agents to alter the investigative trail to conceal use of NSA surveillance.[82]

VI. THE DEPARTMENT OF JUSTICE'S POLICY REGARDING OBTAINING INFORMATION FROM THE PRESS

The Department of Justice (DoJ) has established guidelines on obtaining information from the news media that set forth internal procedural requirements that the DoJ must follow, including under what circumstances it can seek information from the press or pursue a criminal investigation against a reporter. Violation of the guidelines does not give rise to a cause of action or legal remedy.

The guidelines have undergone recent changes due to two disclosures in May 2013 revealing the DoJ's aggressive tactics in obtaining information from the press. On May 13, 2013, the Associated Press (AP) reported that the DoJ obtained the phone records of AP journalists.[83] The DoJ gave no official reason why it made the request.[84] On May 23, 2013, *The Washington Post* published online the DoJ's search warrant application for Rosen of Fox News' e-mails.[85] The request was made during the DoJ's investigation into whether Kim, the State Department contractor, violated the Espionage Act when he leaked classified information about North Korea to Rosen.[86]

On May 23, 2013, responding to intense criticism, President Barack Obama ordered the DoJ to review its guidelines toward journalists.[87] On July 12, 2013, the DoJ produced a report on proposed changes regarding its policy toward the press.[88] On February 21, 2014, the DoJ released new guidelines on how the DoJ will seek information from the press.[89]

The guidelines begin with the statement that "[The DoJ]'s policy is intended to provide protection to members of the news media from certain law enforcement tools, whether criminal or civil, that might unreasonably impair ordinary newsgathering activities."[90]

In order to pursue a criminal investigation against a journalist for an act done within the scope of a journalist's activities, the DoJ must get express authorization from the Office of Public Affairs and the attorney general.[91]

In determining whether to obtain information from the press, the DoJ must "strike the proper balance" between (1) protecting national security, (2) ensuring public safety, (3) promoting effective law enforcement and the fair administration of justice, and (4) safeguarding the essential role of the free press in fostering government accountability and an open society.[92]

The DoJ's new policy toward seeking any type of court orders to obtain information from the press is that such orders should be used only as "extraordinary measures, not standard investigatory practices."[93] In a criminal investigation, each tool employed by the government must meet the following standard: (1) there should be reasonable grounds to believe, based on public information, or information from nonmedia sources, that a crime has been committed, (2) that the information sought is essential to the successful investigation or prosecution of that crime, and (3) the request should not be used to obtain peripheral, nonessential, or speculative information.[94]

Under the new rules, the attorney general must personally authorize any application for a court order that is directed toward the press.[95] There are two exceptions to this requirement. The first is when the journalist agrees to turn over the information if she is officially subpoenaed.[96] The second—under exigent circumstances involving national security or harm to an individual, the deputy assistant attorney general for the Criminal Division can authorize an application for a court order, "if there is reason to believe that the immediate seizure of the materials at issue is necessary to prevent the death of, or serious bodily injury to, a human being."[97]

One of the major policy changes advanced in Attorney General Eric Holder's report was to eliminate the presumption that the media not be notified of a court order. His recommendation was that there be a presumption in favor of advanced notice. The presumption would only be overcome when the attorney general determines there is a "compelling reason" that advance notice would pose either (1) a clear and substantial threat to the integrity of an investigation, (2) risk grave harm to national security, or (3) present an imminent risk of death or serious bodily harm." Delay created by notice, negotiations, or potential judicial review would not be considered "compelling reasons."[98]

Holder's statement became part of DoJ's new guidelines.[99] Under the section, the DoJ must give the press "reasonable and timely notice" prior to seeking a court order, unless there is a "compelling reason."[100] When the attorney general determines there is a "compelling reason" not to give notice, he must give notice 45 days after the court order has been issued. The period can be renewed only once, and "[n]o further delays may be sought beyond the ninety-day period."[101]

NOTES

1. The Whistleblower Protection Act protects whistleblowers that disclose information to the government from prosecution, but it does not protect those who disclose to third parties. 10 U.S.C. § 1034(a–b). As for the press, the Supreme Court has clearly indicated in cases such as the Pentagon Papers case, *N.Y. Times Co. v. United States*, 403 U.S. 713 (1971), and *Bartnicki v. Vopper*, 532 U.S. 514 (2001), that the government cannot prevent journalists from publishing truthful information that they have obtained lawfully.

2. U.S. CONST. amend. IV.

3. 389 U.S. 347 (1967).

4. *Id.* at 361.

5. U.S. CONST. amend. IV.

6. 436 U.S. 547 (1978).

7. *Id.* at 550–51.

8. *Id.* at 553–54.

9. *Id.* at 563–67.

10. 42 U.S.C. § 2000aa.

11. *Id.*

12. *Id.* § 2000aa(a)(1), (b)(1).

13. *Id. See, e.g.*, Sennett v. United States, 667 F.3d 531 (4th Cir. 2012); Binion v. City of St. Paul, 788 F. Supp. 2d 935 (D. Minn. 2011).

14. *Id.* § 2000aa(a)(2), (b)(2).

15. *See* FED. R. CIV. P. 45; FED. R. CRIM. P. 41. *See, e.g., In re* Grand Jury Subpoena, Judith Miller, 397 F.3d 964 (D.C. Cir. 2005) (upholding district court's contempt order against New York Times journalist who refused to name Scooter Libby as the source of the leak that revealed Valarie Plame was a CIA agent).

16. 408 U.S. 665 (1972).

17. *Id.* at 667–68.

18. *Id.* at 692.

19. *Id.* at 709–10.

20. *Id.* at 725. It is worth noting that Justice Stewart himself leaked information about the inner workings of the Supreme Court to Bob Woodward in *The Brethren.*

21. *Id.* at 710 n.*.

22. *Id.* at 709–10.

23. *Id.* at 710 n.*.

24. United States v. Sterling, 724 F.3d 482 (4th Cir. 2013).

25. Petition for writ of certiorari, Risen v. United States, http://www.fas.org/sgp/jud/sterling /011314-petition.pdf.

26. For more information on the reporter's privilege, see Reporter's Committee for Freedom of the Press, The Reporter's Privilege, http://www.rcfp.org/reporters-privilege.

27. RCFP, The Reporter's Privilege Compendium: An Introduction, http://www.rcfp.org/browse -media-law-resources/guides/reporters-privilege/introduction.

28. MARK A. FRANKLIN, DAVID A. ANDERSON & LYRISSA BARNETT LIDSKY, MASS MEDIA LAW: CASES AND MATERIALS 465 (8th ed. 2011).

29. The Free Flow of Information Act of 2013, S. 987, 113th Cong. (2013).

30. Pub. L. No. 99-508, 100 Stat. 1848 (1986).

31. 18 U.S.C. §§ 2510–2522.

32. *Id.* §§ 3121–3127.

33. *Id.* §§ 2701–2712.

34. *Id.* § 2510.

35. *Id.* § 2510(4). There is considerable uncertainty as to the scope of the definition. *See* CHARLES DOYLE, CONG. RES. SERV., R41733, PRIVACY: AN OVERVIEW OF THE ELECTRONIC COMMUNICA-TIONS PRIVACY ACT (2012), https://www.fas.org/sgp/crs/misc/R41733.pdf.

36. 18 U.S.C. § 2818(1).

37. *Id.* § 2518(3). The statute also contains an "emergency situation" exception, among many others, that allows the government to engage in surveillance 48 hours prior to obtaining a warrant. An "emergency situation" is when law enforcement "reasonably determines" that (1) there are grounds to issue the warrant and (2) either (a) there is an immediate danger of death or serious injury to a person or (b) involve conspiratorial activities that either (i) threaten national security or (ii) are characteristic of organized crime. *Id.* § 2518(7).

38. *Id.* § 2518(8)(d).

39. 460 U.S. 276, 278–82 (1983).

40. 132 S. Ct. 945, 948 (2012).

41. *Id.* at 951–53.

42. 18 U.S.C. § 3127(3).

43. *Id.* § 3127(4). The Supreme Court's decision in *Riley v. California* (S. Ct. No. 13-132 June 2014) also emphasized the protection of content stored on cellphones, smart phones, and tablets. According to the Court, before American law enforcement officers may search a device for digital content they must first secure a warrant establishing probable cause to believe that a crime has been committed and that evidence of the crime can be found on the device.

44. Ryan Lizza, *The D.O.J. versus James Rosen,* NEW YORKER (May 20, 2013), http://www.new yorker.com/online/blogs/newsdesk/2013/05/the-doj-versus-journalist-gmail.html.

45. United States v. Katz, 389 U.S. 347 (1967).

46. 442 U.S. 735, 743–44 (1979).

47. *Id.* at 744–45.

48. 18 U.S.C. § 3123(a)(2).

49. *Id.* § 3123.

Notes

50. *Id.* § 3123(a)(1).
51. *Id.* § 3123(a)(c).
52. *Id.* § 3123(d).
53. Smith v. Maryland, 442 U.S. 735, 744–45 (1979).
54. 18 U.S.C. § 2703.
55. Indictment, United States v. Drake, http://www.fas.org/sgp/news/2010/04/drake-indict.pdf.
56. Lizza, *supra* note 44.
57. United States v. Sterling, 724 F.3d 482, 488 (4th Cir. 2013).
58. 18 U.S.C. § 2703(a)–(b).
59. *Id.* § 2703(d).
60. *Id.*; *see also* Fed. Trade Comm'n v. Netscape Commc'ns Corp., 196 F.R.D. 559, 561 (N.D. Cal. 2000); Flagg v. City of Detroit, 252 F.R.D. 346, 350 (E.D. Mich. 2008); *In re* Subpoena Duces Tecum to AOL, LLC, 550 F. Supp. 2d 606, 611 (E.D. Va. 2008).
61. 18 U.S.C. § 2705.
62. *Id.* § 2705(a)(1).
63. *Id.* § 2705(b).
64. *Id.* §§ 2705(a)(1–2) & 2705(b).
65. *Id.* §§ 2705(a)(5)(B) & 2705(b).
66. *Id.* § 2705(a)(4).
67. *Id.* § 2703(c)(2).
68. *Id.* § 2703(c)(3).
69. 50 U.S.C. § 1801 *et seq.*
70. Pub. L. No. 107-56, 115 Stat. 272.
71. 18 U.S.C. § 2709(a)–(b).
72. *Id.* § 2709(c)(1).
73. *Id.* § 3511(b)(2).
74. *Id.* § 3511(b)(2).
75. 50 U.S.C. § 1861(b)(2).
76. *See Verizon Forced to Hand over Telephone Data—Full Court Order*, GUARDIAN, June 5, 2013, http://www.guardian.co.uk/world/interactive/2013/jun/06/verizon-telephone-data-court-order [hereinafter *Verizon Court Order*]. The term "metadata" generally refers to data that "does not contain personal or content-specific details, but rather transactional information about the user, the device and activities taking place." *A Guardian Guide to Your Metadata*, GUARDIAN, June 12, 2013, http://www.theguardian.com/technology/interactive/2013/jun/12/what-is-metadata-nsa-surveillance#meta=1000000. Metadata regarding an e-mail includes the sender's and recipients name, e-mail and IP addresses, and the subject of the e-mail. *Id.*
77. 50 U.S.C. § 1801(e).
78. *Id.* § 1805(a), (h)(1).
79. *Verizon Court Order, supra* note 76.
80. *Top-Secret Document Reveals NSA Spied on Porn Habits as Part of Plan to Discredit "Radicalizers,"* HUFFINGTON POST, Nov. 26, 2013, http://www.huffingtonpost.com/2013/11/26/nsa-porn-muslims_n_4346128.html.
81. John Shiffman & David Ingram, *Exclusive: IRS Manual Detailed DEA's Use of Hidden Intel Evidence*, REUTERS, Aug. 7, 2013, http://www.reuters.com/article/2013/08/07/us-dea-irs-idUSBRE9761AZ20130807.
82. *Id.*
83. Mark Sherman, *Gov't Obtains Wide AP Phone Records in Probe*, ASSOCIATED PRESS, May 13, 2013, http://bigstory.ap.org/article/govt-obtains-wide-ap-phone-records-probe.
84. *Id.* However, the article did note that U.S. officials previously stated it was conducting a criminal investigation into a 2012 AP article revealing details on a CIA operation that foiled an al-Qaeda plot in Yemen.

85. Lizza, *supra* note 44.

86. Josh Gerstein, *Stephen Kim Pleads Guilty in Fox News Leak Case*, POLITICO, Feb. 7, 2014, http://www.politico.com/story/2014/02/stephen-kim-james-risen-state-department-fox-news -103265.html?utm_source=dlvr.it&utm_medium=twitter. The request also said that Rosen was Kim's "co-conspirator." Subsequent news reports stated Attorney General Eric Holder personally approved the warrant. *DOJ Confirms Holder OK'd Search Warrant for Fox News Reporter's Emails*, NBCNEWS.COM, May 23, 2013, http://investigations.nbcnews.com/_news/2013/05/23/18451142-doj -confirms-holder-okd-search-warrant-for-fox-news-reporters-emails?lite.

87. Aamer Madhani, *Obama Orders Justice to Review Media Leak Guidelines*, USA TODAY, May 23, 2013, http://www.usatoday.com/story/news/2013/05/23/obama-orders-media-leak-review /2355459/.

88. DEP'T OF JUSTICE, REPORT ON REVIEW OF NEWS MEDIA POLICIES (2013), http://www.justice .gov/iso/opa/resources/2202013712162851796893.pdf [hereinafter DoJ REPORT].

89. 28 C.F.R. § 50.10 (2014); Pete Yost, *Justice Dept. Revises Rules for Obtaining Media Records in Leak Investigations*, WASH. POST (Feb. 22, 2014), http://www.washingtonpost.com/world/national -security/justice-dept-revises-rules-for-obtaining-media-records-in-leak-investigations/2014/02/21 /a6484a14-9b64-11e3-ad71-e03637a299c0_story.html.

90. 28 C.F.R. § 50.10(a)(1).

91. *Id.* § 50.10(f)(1) ("No member of the Department shall subject a member of the news media to questioning as to any offense that he or she is suspected of having committed in the course of, or arising out of, the coverage or investigation of news, or while engaged in the performance of duties undertaken as a member of the news media.").

92. *Id.* § 50.10(a)(2).

93. *Id.* § 50.10(a)(3).

94. *Id.* § 50.10(c)(5)(i)(A) (explicitly discussing subpoenas and requests under the Wiretap Act and Pen Register Act, and alluding to the Stored Communications Act); *id.* § 50.10(d)(3) (incorporating the aforementioned standard in warrants to search a journalist or media outlet's premises). However, the DoJ's policy does not cover numerous crimes associated with espionage and terrorism. *Id.* § 50.10(b)(1)(ii).

95. *Id.* § 50.10(c)(1). Furthermore, a U.S. attorney or assistant attorney general responsible for the matter must endorse the application prior to submission to the attorney general. *Id.* § 50.10(d)(2).

96. *Id.* § 50.10(c)(3)(A).

97. *Id.* § 50.10(f)(1–2).

98. DoJ REPORT, *supra* note 88.

99. 28 C.F.R. § 50.10(e).

100. *Id.* § 50.10(e)(1)(i).

101. *Id.* § 50.10(e)(2).

RESOURCES

Charles Doyle, Cong. Research Serv., Privacy: An Overview of the Electronic Communications Privacy Act (2012), https://www.fas.org/sgp/crs/misc/R41733 .pdf.

Electronic Privacy Information Center, Electronic Communications Privacy Act (ECPA), http://epic.org/privacy/ecpa/.

Orin S. Kerr, *A User's Guide to the Stored Communications Act, and a Legislator's Guide to Amending It*, 72 GEO. WASH. L. REV. 1208 (2004).

Reporter's Committee for Freedom of the Press, The Reporter's Privilege, http://www.rcfp.org/reporters-privilege.

DANIEL J. SOLOVE & PAUL SCHWARTZ, PRIVACY AND THE MEDIA (2008).

DANIEL J. SOLOVE & PAUL SCHWARTZ, PRIVACY LAW FUNDAMENTALS (2d ed. 2013).

GINA STEVENS & CHARLES DOYLE, CONG. RESEARCH SERV., PRIVACY: AN ABBREVIATED OUTLINE OF FEDERAL STATUTES GOVERNING WIRETAPPING AND ELECTRONIC EAVESDROPPING (2012), http://www.fas.org/sgp/crs/intel/98-327.pdf.

Testimony of Deirdre Mulligan, Center for Democracy and Technology, to the House Committee on the Judiciary (Mar. 26, 1998), https://cdt.org/insight/testimony-of-deirdre-mulligan/.

Keeping Secrets: How the Government and the Press Adapt in a World Awash in Information

11

Dina Temple-Raston and Harvey Rishikof

Back in the spring of 2011, Julian Assange, the head of the anti-secrecy organization WikiLeaks, began informing his media contacts that he had documents providing "never-before-revealed" details about detainees in the military prison at Guantanamo Bay, Cuba. At the time, the public knew little about the men held at the detention center—aside from the fact that they were accused of having some sort of link to terrorism or al-Qaeda. So the trove of documents, which were, essentially, dossiers on more than 700 Guantanamo detainees, appeared to have real news value.

Assange permitted just a handful of news organizations to have early access to the files, though he assiduously excluded two outlets—*The New York Times* and *The Guardian* newspaper of the United Kingdom. The editors of those papers were in a long-standing feud with Assange over differences about what constituted the responsible release of classified documents. The WikiLeaks founder retaliated by providing documents to the competition. In the end, *The New York Times* and *The Guardian* were able to acquire the Guantanamo files from a third source, frustrating Assange's efforts. It was an ironic twist: given the nature of data, even Assange could not control who had access to the WikiLeaks files.

What came to be known as the "Guantanamo Tranche" were documents from the Pentagon's Joint Task Force at Guantanamo. Most of the records were marked "secret" and "noforn," meaning the information was not to be shared with representatives from other countries. And while the pages provided interesting details about the prisoners, they did not contain Abu Ghraib-like photos or anything that could be described as a smoking "memo." Instead, the files were copies of assessments, interviews, and internal correspondence meant to determine who the detainees actually were, how they might be connected to terrorism, and whether they posed a future threat to the United States and its allies.

The documents, once published on the WikiLeaks site, allowed the public to connect names and faces to the people Secretary of Defense Donald Rumsfeld called "the worst of the worst." The orange jumpsuit that had become synonymous with the island prison took on a more human shape and form—and a nationality and a name.

The Guantanamo files are important because they are a good starting point from which to look at just how much the world of secrets (and information) has changed. Organizations like WikiLeaks and Glenn Greenwald's new website, The Intercept, have become forces because they have come of age at a time when the world is at a tipping point on two fronts. The first is a revolution in data—the way it is generated, received, downloaded, stored, and searched; the second is a post- 9/11 shift in the way the intelligence community both handles and processes sensitive information. These two developments have significantly complicated the task of keeping secrets.

For the past several years, the buzzword for this explosion of information has been "Big Data." Cognoscenti data mavens have refined the concept and are beginning to call it "Smart Data." Smart Data is data that can be readily searched with a computer algorithm to extract precise pieces of information from mountains or "haystacks" of files. For journalists, this means that millions of WikiLeaks leaked documents can be mined for information in minutes instead of days. For the government, it means that the secrets that officials thought might be buried in blizzards of paper are now readily found with the right word search.

A consequence of the post-9/11 directives to share secret information across the intelligence community gave a young military analyst in Iraq named Bradley Manning access to classified documents that he (now she) had no reason to review. Manning was able to download a huge number of those files onto a CD he marked "Lady Gaga," and pass them to WikiLeaks without detection. While people disagree about why Manning did what he did, it is clear that Manning would have been unlikely to have had access such a variety of classified files before the 9/11 attacks. After the attacks the intelligence community disseminated information differently, and more widely—"need to know" doctrines were replaced by "need to share" directives.

How journalists work with WikiLeaks documents is part of this new paradigm. Documents in the "cloud" allow multiple reporters to simultaneously (and independently) sift through the classified trove and, thanks to encryption, it is difficult for the government to know who is accessing them. For a reporter, it was hard to know where to start; there was so much data from which to choose. So most reporters did what any of us would do: they just started typing random terms into a search engine, essentially hoping that they would hit pay dirt and a document on the topic would pop up.

The Guantanamo papers from WikiLeaks came to light at a time when the Arab Spring uprisings had just started in Libya. Typing "Libya" into the search box yielded a number of hits, including the name of a former detainee who had led a Libyan Islamic Fighting Group, Sufian bin Qumu. According to the documents, he had been a driver for Osama bin Laden and was thought to be an active member of al-Qaeda. Qumu had been transferred to Libyan custody and was subsequently released. (One of the stories both NPR and *The New York Times* ended up independently producing from the Guantanamo papers looked at Qumu and whether he might be playing a role in the uprising against Libyan strongman Mohammar Ghadafi. His name came up again in 2014 when officials began to investigate whether he might have played a role in the deadly attack on the U.S. embassy in Benghazi in 2012, which ended with the death of Ambassador Christopher Smith and three other Americans.[1])

Sources who are working with the Snowden documents will not say how reporters are accessing the information (whether it is cloud-based or on memory sticks or on a database, for example). They will admit, however, that reporters are using the same hit-or-miss search engine method—on a grander scale—to try to find stories in the Snowden files. This is how reporters seem to have been able to publish stories about National Security Agency programs skillfully pegged to news of the day.

Type in "G-20" as a search term, and you will find documents that show that foreign politicians and officials who took part in two G-20 summit meetings in London in 2009 had their computers monitored and their phone calls intercepted. The story came out in *The Guardian* in June of 2013—just days before Britain was set to host another summit for the G-8 nations.

Representative Mike Rogers, chairman of the House Intelligence Committee, said at the time that the Defense Intelligence Agency estimated the number of Snowden documents that concern "vital operations of the U.S. Army, Navy, Marine Corps and Air Force" at approximately 1.7 million."[2] Some say that number is absurdly high and the 1.7 million figure comes under the assumption that Snowden took everything that he touched in the servers. Eventually the true number will be revealed.

The processes involved in Big Data reporting, however—sifting through enormous quantities of information to find a story—are not new. Investigative reporters, and particularly business reporters, have been sitting in the basements of courthouses and regulatory agencies for years hoping that by combing through stacks of paper records, they might find irregularities (and stories). Databases and search engines have made the process infinitely easier and faster.

In the summer of 2012, Bloomberg News reporters in China and Hong Kong produced a series of stories laying out the financial gains relatives of high-ranking Chinese leaders had amassed while their kin were in power. What the reporters uncovered was so specific and so closely tied to legal documents, it made it difficult for Chinese leaders to deny the allegations. According to Bloomberg reports, the family of Chinese President Xi Jinping had investments in companies with total assets of $376 million, including stakes in rare-earth and technology companies, and owned a $31.5 million hillside villa in Repulse Bay, an upscale area of Hong Kong.[3]

It was not just the specificity with which the Bloomberg reporters were able to draw up the president's family assets that boggled the mind. The other lesson was how much of that information was public. Bloomberg reported it came up with its Chinese leadership expose by "using public and business records, interviews with Xi family acquaintances and Hong Kong and Chinese identity card numbers."[4] Reporters only had to know where to look. Family members even took on pseudonyms, but reporters were able to match specific relatives to various assets and identity card numbers.

This access to public information, the recording of facts by private citizens, and then the posting of the information to searchable public databases (such as YouTube) is making it harder and harder to hide issues from the public.

Some companies have made trolling the web for stories their bread and butter. A digital news start-up called Vocativ mines the Internet for exclusive news and other content using data collection software. The president of MSNBC, Phil Griffin, who works with Vocativ, contends the company had found a way to marry Big Data with conventional reporting. In 2014, NewsCorp bought Storyful, a company that finds news and verifies it from sources like YouTube, Twitter, and Instagram. Dataminr uses a Twitter-based tool to help reporters at CNN spot developing news.[5]

Some journalists have gone a step further, creating their own data: they gather information using sensors, creating an entirely new field known as "sensor journalism." In one of the early forays into this kind of reporting, journalists from the Associated Press worked with the Spatial Information Design Lab at Columbia University to connect microprocessors and sensors to the web to independently measure the air quality at the 2008 Beijing Olympics. The group did an end run around the Chinese government by using bicycles and mobile phone apps to take independent air quality readings on which they subsequently reported.[6]

Other journalists have used cameras on balloons and drones and other sensors to observe a number of news events, from the BP spill in the Gulf of Mexico in 2010 to cicadas in New York. RadioLab, a show on *WNYC*, NPR's New York affiliate, created a "Cicada Tracker"[7] by asking listeners to build their own sensors and take soil temperature readings. The idea: to monitor and forecast when the next brood would emerge.

Ordinary citizens are starting to do the same thing in China. In January 2014, a few hundred employees of a Chinese digital payments company called Alibaba were asked to take inexpensive water testing kits to their villages during the Chinese Lunar New Year. They sampled the water in their villages and uploaded their findings via smartphone to an environmental mapping website called Danger Maps. Employees measured water quality in 28 different provinces.

Now Alibaba has asked its 500 million customers to purchase their own water kits for about $10 and do the same. The idea? To help Alibaba's founder, Jack Ma, work with local environmental authorities and nongovernmental organizations, NGOs, to fix China's polluted water system.[8]

The point to all these efforts, as James Fahn explains in his review of sensor journalism in the *Columbia Journalism Review*, is that new technology is eradicating "data deserts" where there is strong reluctance by countries or agencies to share data or information.[9] Now journalists and ordinary citizens can gather the facts on their own, analyze the data, and report or upload the story—bypassing the traditional sources of information. In order to do this new sensor journalism, Fahn recommends—"Get to know a statistician." In fact having a statistician as a friend is becoming the mantra not just for journalists, but for the government as well as it becomes increasingly important for officials to interpret data on the fly.

I. SMART DATA AND GOVERNANCE

In the spring of 1982, two Harvard University social scientists, James Q. Wilson and George L. Kelling, published an article in *The Atlantic Monthly* looking at whether a neighborhood's decline could be correlated with its crime. The seminal article was called "Broken Windows: The police and neighborhood safety," and it set in motion a whole new philosophy in urban governance and policing. Cataloguing "physical disorder" in a neighborhood—from abandoned cars to graffiti to broken windows—appeared to be one way to predict where crime might rise in the future.[10]

Not long after "Broken Windows" caught the imagination of urban planners, the New York Police Department (NYPD) adopted a program called Compstat, a computer application that maps crime, giving a visual picture of where it is happening and when. The idea was to deploy officers to those problem areas. Compstat generated charts that showed the time of day and day of the week crimes happened. It broke the crimes down by type and logged who was arrested and exactly where they were arrested. Compstat, still a key weapon in the NYPD's arsenal, has helped bring crime down a whopping 74 percent since its introduction 20 years ago. Compstat was an early local government application of Big Data.

Boston is trying something even more ambitious by not just tracking crime, but also trying to chronicle neighborhood dysfunction over time. Their source of information: the city's various helplines. The Boston Area Research Initiative (BARI) is a Harvard University-based collaborative of academics and city officials who are mining information from Boston's constituent relationship management (CRM) operation.

Boston's CRM includes a hotline, website, and mobile app that allows Bostonians to report everything from rat problems to abandoned bicycles. The information has allowed researchers to create a nearly real-time atlas of what is ailing the city and track urban development. "The best way to predict something is to go back in time," said BARI research director Daniel O'Brien, who trained as an evolutionary biologist.[11] "I think this is the first time, to our knowledge, that people sat down and tried to figure out how to measure neighborhood conditions over time."

What surprised O'Brien was all the other information researchers were able to glean from the data set. For example, about 80 percent of the people who used the CRM system didn't call about a problem that was more than two blocks from where they lived. Homeowners tended to be the most frequent callers. Immigrants and college students rarely picked up the phone. Crunch the numbers some more and O'Brien could predict how likely residents on any given block would be to report a problem.

He also sees the Boston project as an opportunity to figure out, problem by problem, how neighborhood decay develops. He has set up 28 categories of physical disorder that allow him to track what is going on behind closed doors: everything from mice and rat infestations to bedbugs and asbestos. Traditional surveys, door-to-door questioners, can only see so much from the front stoop. The Smart Data from CRM goes deeper.

II. SMART DATA AND MICROTARGETING

Dan Wagner, the chief analytics officer for the 2012 Obama campaign, wanted to test what would happen if the campaign went for a deeper dive. He was convinced that using Smart Data (in other words, lots of publicly available voter information and an algorithm), he could literally reconstruct the list of 64 million voters who had cast a ballot for Barack Obama in his first presidential run in 2008; and more importantly, in the run-up to Obama's reelection, Wagner thought he could find more people like them. His plan was as audacious as it was simple: he wanted to reassemble the 2008 victory vote by vote.[12]

The Obama administration's analytics team used statistical models to sort the electorate. They started with information the campaign had gathered the first time around. At that time, Obama campaign targeters had assigned every voter in the country a pair of scores based on two things: the probability that the individual would cast a ballot and the odds that that vote would be for Obama. Building on that information, programmers wrote algorithms that trawled for patterns that might reveal similar people. (The campaign eventually came to refer to the algorithms as their "nuclear codes.")

The campaign had short-form questionnaires and longer opinion polls that allowed them to build a statistical picture of every voter. It allowed them not just to target, but *micro*target, potential supporters. This was not based not on sampling (as they did in days of old), but on real, up-to-date information. In a sense, Wagner and his team were actually profiling voters.

In addition to the DNC's 180 million voter lists, the campaign used commercial data warehouse information to refine their analysis. Then, the Obama team sorted through the names of voting-age adults, for example, and compared those names with registration rolls. The ability to get down to the "level of the sidewalks" with this data made it possible for the campaign not only to find undecided voters but also to test various messages that might convince them to cast a ballot for Obama.

What's more, eventually the algorithms helped determine how much a supporter should be asked to contribute to the campaign based on previous solicitations. With this microscopic approach, Wagner and his team were able to see movements too small for traditional polls to pick up.

This story is important because the Obama campaign's use of data is very much what the intelligence community is hoping Smart Data can help them do in the fight against terrorism. They hope masses of data and smart analytics will allow them to see movements that are imperceptible to most people, but might indicate that someone was planning an attack or prone to use violence.

As a cornerstone of its research and development, the intelligence community hopes to discover and purchase new technologies that use data to identify (or microtarget) dangerous individuals. Part of the business of the intelligence community is forecasting the future, to avoid strategic surprise and, in the same vein, understanding the intention of adversaries is critical to good intelligence. Now the community is exploring whether tapping into publicly available data—Twitter and news feeds and blogs, among other things—can help them do that faster and more precisely.

III. PREDICTING THE FUTURE

In 2010, the CIA's investment arm—In-Q-Tel—and Google Ideas invested in a company called Recorded Future. The company was developing algorithms that sort through volumes of information to find relationships between people and organizations. Then its visualization software spits out that information in the form of a giant searchable timeline.[13]

"What we're trying to do here at Recorded Future is figure out a cool way that we can observe the world," cofounder Christopher Ahlberg told NPR in an October 2012 interview. "We're trying to find new ways of generating data that tell us what's going on in the world . . . what did happen, what will happen. We're not going to get 100 percent in terms of outcome, but we can pull things together in a way that no one else can."[14]

The idea is to give users an ability to see events or relationships in sequence to make it easier to find patterns and relationships that traditional Big Data programs might miss. (This is the kind of thing Daniel O'Brien in Boston is working with as well.) Hedge funds already use Recorded Future to invest. The intelligence community would want to use it, among other things, to help predict seminal events before they happen.

As Ahlberg sees it, there are hints about the future everywhere. Governments release economic projections; newspapers report on upcoming events; Twitter can provide a pretty good idea of what people are talking about. In 2013, organizers in Egypt used Twitter and social media to rally protesters. If intelligence analysts had had a systematic way to track those posts, it might have helped them predict just how violent the backlash against Egyptian President Hosni Mubarak was going to be. That kind of tool might have helped forecast the coup that lead to the ouster of his successor, Mohammed Morsi.

This isn't an entirely new idea. There already have been efforts to try to tap into what is simmering below the surface by tracking things like Google searches. Researchers at West Point's Combating Terrorism Center and Princeton University tracked Google searches in Egypt starting in January 2011 and found that there were more searches about events in Tunisia and its protests than for Egyptian pop stars.[15] Politics was taking preference among the public over entertainment.

Recorded Future builds publicly available intelligence—just as Dana Priest did and Dan O'Brien is doing in his neighborhoods project in Boston. Ahlberg says an event might be a world leader traveling from one city to another, a government official making a statement, or a country doing some sort of military maneuver. Recorded Future captures those activities and organizes the data in a way that can help analysts ask the right questions.[16]

In January 2010, Recorded Future predicted in a roster of blog posts that Yemen was headed for disaster. It predicted that a combination of floods, famine and Islamic terrorists were conspiring to wreak havoc. The company used Twitter feeds, blogs, U.N. food program data and news sources to come up with their forecast. Six months later, Yemen appeared on the cover of *The New York Times Magazine* under the headline "Is Yemen the New Afghanistan?"[17] Indeed, Yemen is now home to what the U.S. considers the most dangerous al-Qaeda affiliate, Al-Qaeda in the Arabian Peninsula, or AQAP.

Even so, when it comes to computers predicting the future, there are plenty of skeptics. Gary King, a professor from Harvard University and the director of the Institute for Quantitative Social Science, is one of them. "We need to know if you are getting the right answer randomly or you're getting the right answer because of something you're doing," he cautioned.[18] Recorded Future's Yemen prediction is a start, he says. But it is not enough. There are one billion new social media posts every two and a half days. And while that's an enormous amount of information to mine, it's easy to draw the wrong lessons from all that data.

Part of the problem, and one of the reasons why U.S. intelligence agencies want to gather and store so much information, is that terrorist attacks are rare events and so, as a result, are hard to anticipate. Rare event prediction is difficult for two reasons. First, popular statistical procedures, such as logistic regression, tend to underestimate the probability of rare events. And second, commonly used data collection strategies are not good at trying to analyze rare events data.[19]

Black Swan events, which have a low probability of happening but sometimes take place anyway, are even tougher to see coming. Who could have forecast the Holocaust Museum shooting by a lone gunman in 2009, or the Boston Marathon bombing in 2013, which involved two brothers thought to be planning the event on their own?

One of the experiments in rare event prediction has involved exploding manholes in New York City. There are a few hundred "manhole events" in New York City every year and five years ago, Con Edison, the utility that provides Manhattan with its electricity, asked a handful of Columbia University professors to find a way to predict which manholes were likely to blow. It was a complex problem that involved 94,000 miles of underground cables, 51,000 manholes and service boxes, and countless neighborhoods.[20]

ConEd asked the university mathematicians to comb through more than 100 years of utility records to find some sort of pattern to explain why explosions happened when they did. As a general matter, manholes shoot skyward in response to a series of relatively unpredictable events. The electricity cables in New York carry about 13,000 volts of electricity and when the cables fray or fail, the wires begin to overheat and melt the insulation that covers them. It is the insulation that catches fire, releases gases, and creates such pressure underground that the only release is through a manhole. That's why they shoot up like rockets.

The Columbia professors looked at handwritten maintenance logs and safety reports and hoped they could find a way to put them into a database and analyze them. Basically the utility was asking the Columbia team to use algorithms and computers—"machine learning"—to do rare event prediction. Looking at literally hundreds of thousands of variables, the algorithm was supposed to find patterns to predict something that happened, at most, a couple hundred times a year. (Terrorism events happen less often than that.)

The Columbia University team did manage to write an algorithm that learned from past manhole event records to predict the likelihood that a particular manhole with particular characteristics might flare up. The algorithm actually ranked manholes in the city based on the danger they presented. The top 2 percent of manholes tagged as vulnerable included 11 percent of the manholes that had recently had a fire or explosion. Now Con Edison is using the algorithm's ranking to prioritize manhole maintenance, and other cities have adopted New York's algorithm so they can save infrastructure dollars by doing maintenance just on those manholes that have a good possibility of blowing up.

Officials are hoping that rare event predictive analytics like those used in New York can resolve that issue by taking vast quantities of information—say, hypothetically, all the telephone and Internet metadata in the world—and somehow find specific patterns to reveal the handful of people who might be preparing to launch an attack. But the difference is that manhole explosion prediction is based on a correlation of variables, not a classic causality analysis.

Predicting human manholes requires more specific causality because human emotion, free will, and society are involved. A manhole cover cannot decide when to explode, but a human can. The problem is that correlations for human activity get intelligence officials part way toward predicting violence, but is not yet sufficient for divining human behavior.

IV.   EXCUSE ME—YOUR METADATA IS SHOWING

One ideology driving the online world is the idea that information in sufficiently large quantity somehow automatically becomes "Truth." The question no one has been able to answer is, What if more information is just that, just more information? And more troubling, what if that information ends up implicating the wrong people while unnecessarily invading the privacy of others?

This notion of privacy and what one can do with information is the crux of the discussion surrounding the Snowden documents. The public discussion today about Big Data and Smart Data has actually been part of the government's strategic advantage for the last few decades as technological tools improved. Part of what has changed is how much of that "advantage" has shifted to ordinary people. If someone is determined to find a piece of information, a lot of it can be pieced together from the web—as the *Washington Post*'s Dana Priest and sensor journalism, more generally, demonstrate.

In its broadest sense, metadata is data about other data. In the case of e-mails, it would be the TO: and FROM: lines and perhaps the date an e-mail was sent. While on the surface that might appear to be innocuous information, network analysis software can wring a great deal of information out of those few lines of text. The logic is that metadata is like pen register information or the information on the outside of an envelope. The question is whether this analogy in the world of storage and algorithms still holds.

The Supreme Court went part way toward answering that question in *Smith v. Maryland.*[21] The basic facts of the case are interesting. In 1976, a woman named Patricia McDonough was robbed in Baltimore, Maryland. She gave the police a description of the robber and details about what she thought was his car, a 1975 Monte Carlo. Shortly after the robbery she started receiving threatening and obscene phone calls from someone who claimed to be her assailant. At one point, the caller asked her to go out to the front of her house. When she did so, a Monte Carlo slowly drove by.

The license plate was eventually traced to a man named Michael Lee Smith, and the police asked the telephone company to trace numbers called from Smith's home phone. The phone company agreed and Smith called Patricia McDonough again. Police secured a warrant and when they searched Smith's house, they found a telephone book with a dog-eared page with McDonough's number on it. Smith was put in a line-up and McDonough identified him.

The case was appealed to the Supreme Court and the justices held that individuals had no expectation of privacy when it came to their phone data because recording the numbers with a pen register—which basically recorded the initiating and receiving phone numbers in a call—was not a search under the Fourth Amendment. "Given a pen register's limited capabilities, therefore, petitioner's argument that its installation and use constituted a 'search' necessarily rests upon a claim that he had a legitimate expectation of privacy" regarding the numbers he dialed on his phone," the majority opinion reasoned. But, the opinion continued:

This claim must be rejected. First, we doubt that people in general entertain any actual expectation of privacy in the numbers they dial. All telephone users realize that they must "convey" phone numbers to the telephone company, since it is through telephone company switching equipment that their calls are completed. All subscribers realize, moreover, that the phone company has facilities for making permanent records of the numbers they dial, for they see a list of their long-distance (toll) calls on their monthly bills. In fact, pen registers and similar devices are routinely used by telephone companies "for the purposes of checking billing operations, detecting fraud, and preventing violations of law."[22]

At issue now is whether metadata from electronic communications is the same as pen registers. The National Security Agency (NSA) has argued that it is. Civil liberties groups say today's metadata is much more revealing. Currently two U.S. district courts have disagreed as to whether *Smith v. Maryland* is good law.[23] The Supreme Court may have to revisit the issue.

Cesar Hidalgo and a team of research students at MIT's Media Lab have been studying metadata for years, and, as Hidalgo understands it, the NSA's metadata programs are simply "catching up to what a fringe group of academics have been working on since 2004 and 2005."[24]

Working with a handful of graduate students, Hidalgo wrote a social network analysis program called Immersion, which ingests e-mail metadata and provides a visual representation of the network and connections gleaned from the information. It provides an atlas of connections that would allow an analyst to make a fairly sound and educated guess about an e-mail sender's relationships to other people.

For some time now, the intelligence community has been trying to see if network theory can be used to thwart, or at least identify, terrorists before they strike. The theory holds that if officials have identified one terrorist, link analysis could help them find others. In other words, the intelligence community hopes to eventually turn e-mail metadata into a high-stakes version of the Kevin Bacon game.[25]

Similarly, network theory is about connecting dots. Stanley Milgram, a social psychologist who studied social networks in the late 1960s, found that people in the United States on average seemed to be connected by three friendship links. (Milgram never studied or speculated on global links and never actually used the term "six degrees of separation," though it is often attributed to him.) He eventually published his "small world" findings in *Psychology Today* in 1968[26] and it wasn't until Columbia University reenacted his experiment in 2003 that they confirmed six degrees of separation.[27]

After the September 11 attacks, Valdis Krebs, a Cleveland consultant who does social network mapping for corporate and nonprofit clients, decided to analyze the e-mail exchanges between the 9/11 hijackers. He wanted to look for patterns or red flags that investigators and the intelligence community might have missed before the attacks.[28] He began with two of the hijackers—Khalid al-Midhar and Nawaf al-Hazmi—and used information from press accounts to pull together addresses, phone numbers, and frequent flier information to see if he could build a visual representation of their network.

According to his analysis, all of the 19 hijackers were tied to each other by just a few links. He had created a Kevin Bacon game of terrorists. Nearly all of the hijackers, Krebs discovered, were communicating with one man in particular: Mohamed Atta, the man believed to have led the attacks in the United States.[29]

In 2002, the intelligence community tried to mine large volumes of data for hidden connections in a program called Total Information Awareness, a program established by the Defense Advanced Research Projects Agency. The idea was to bring together a number of surveillance and technology information programs to monitor terrorists.[30]

Total Information Awareness monitored metadata of phone calls and e-mail to see who was communicating with terrorists. But, in the end, it generated so many false positives the Defense Department eventually abandoned the program. And herein lies the dilemma: Big Data, or even Smart Data, may be more probabilistic than precise. That's fine if you are trying to keep a lid on "manhole events" or moving cops to a different beat. But if you are looking at potential terrorism suspects, the mere probability that someone might attack is not good enough under our constitutional framework to put them under surveillance. So a big part of the question is how to balance privacy, prediction, correlation, data storage, and analytical algorithm searches with the need to protect our citizens. What is the standard for appropriate "reasonable articulable suspicion" in the age of metadata?

Sandy Pentland, the head of MIT's Human Dynamics Laboratory, and Nathan Eagle have been involved in a blend of sociology and data mining that they call "reality mining." Pentland believes mobile phones can be used to measure population flows into cities and map how people move during emergencies. The duo processed huge amounts of data from mobile phones to make predictions about human behavior. In one study, by analyzing movements and call patterns, they were able to successfully identify people who had contracted the SARS virus before the people themselves knew they were sick.[31]

"Revolutionary new measurement tools provided by mobile telephones and other digital infrastructures are providing us with a God's eye view of ourselves," Pentland wrote in a technology report for the 2009 World Economic Forum. "For the first time we can precisely map the behavior of large numbers of people as they go about their daily lives."[32]

India claims that the vast majority of its captured terrorists have been identified through mobile phone transactions.[33] The CIA, President Obama, and members of Congress have all said NSA spying programs that scan phone and e-mail metadata have thwarted more than 50 terrorist plots.[34] But since that initial claim was made, officials have dramatically whittled down the number of attacks they say the program helped prevent in the United States.

A potential problem with the NSA's metadata program—aside from concerns about privacy—may be too much information, not too little. Eight years ago, the Army launched a project called Able Danger that sought to identify al-Qaeda members by looking for the patterns in the e-mails they sent. The analysis is supposed to begin with a known suspect and then look at the web of communications links around him. The problem with the Able Danger program is that it produced charts that were 20 feet long.[35]

It was impossible to tell who actually was a threat. Army intelligence analysts admitted to the information overload, but seemed sure that new software would eventually be able to identify individuals who were connected not just by e-mails but similar activity or patterns of behavior—essentially taking the Milgram and Pentland experiments one step further.

For example, research shows that when want-to-be jihadis were getting ready to leave the United States for al-Qaeda training camps, they would apply for a a number of of credit cards and then run up the charges to their limit.[36] Why? Because they assumed they would not be coming back to the United States and so wouldn't have to pay the bills. Could a number of e-mails to credit card companies from suspects provide that kind of clue? And could metadata programs find it?

The main problem researchers have encountered is that the techniques one might use to discover fraud or a stolen credit card aren't the same as those that might discover a terrorist. There is a long history of signature behaviors for fraud, but jihadi terrorism is so infrequent and relatively new that it doesn't provide such reliable patterns. Again, a correlation relation but not a causal one.

Researchers thought they might be able to look at e-mail network hubs to try to discover terrorists. They used algorithms to map out both logistical and hierarchical relationships. The programs looked for strong and weak ties. Strong ties would be someone e-mailing his or her family. Weak ties would be someone who is in a distantly related social network.

MIT unveiled a new tool in July 2013 that uses Gmail or Outlook metadata to build a visual map of someone's strong and weak ties. The researchers at MIT say the program, called Immersion, looks at the history of someone's e-mail life and creates a visualization of what someone has put on the web. Deepak Jagdish, at a 2014 Big Data conference in Cambridge, explained that it is a way to see "who your top collaborators are, and which are the clusters of people who are relevant in your e-mail life at any point in time from past to present."[37]

The Immersion program collects the metadata of an inbox in a particular e-mail account and archives and produces a graphic representation of e-mail interactions. The program can differentiate between real people and other sources of e-mail, like mailing lists or machine-sent e-mails, because if the e-mail account holder receives 50 e-mails from one address but hasn't replied to any of them, it won't show up as a node in the network.

Immersion also allows analysts to move through time, which permits them to see how a person's e-mail habits have changed and when new people come into that person's life. Colors are used to emphasize different groups of people connected to a particular person. Patterns reveal who might be family—the strong ties—and who might be a more distant associate, such as a coworker.

The software plots each of these connections—MIT researchers call them "collaborators"—on a map. A circle connects the e-mail account holder to others based on group e-mails and connections. Bigger circles show higher volumes of e-mails, smaller ones indicate less contact. But could it help find terrorists, as the intelligence community hopes social network analysis will eventually? So far, it will not. This kind of high-level link analysis is something that has been studied for decades and has proved elusive.

V.   A TENTATIVE CONCLUSION

In 1993, Jeff Jonas built the first NORA (Non-Obvious Relationship Awareness) system for a casino looking to identify cheaters (or groups of cheaters) at the gambling tables. He has since concluded that while he could zero in on card sharks, massive phone or e-mail metadata won't help find incriminating evidence against terrorists intelligence officials don't already know about.[38]

"For the record, in my opinion, at least in relation to programs designed to target specific people, predicting which people should be targeted for additional scrutiny or action should *not* be based on machine-discovered patterns when so little historical data exists," said Jeff Jonas, who was named an IBM Fellow last year. "However, this method does become useful when first starting with qualified predicates (e.g., subjects who attended terrorist training camps). This can materially assistant organizations/governments focus these finite investigatory resources."[39]

In other words, if the intelligence community has a specific person in mind, Big Data (and even Smart Data) can help find them and their cohorts. But it can't identify terrorists out of thin air. But what if an algorithm could be written that increases the odds of finding a terrorist by just three percentage points? Would that make it worthwhile? After all, if you can get close to predicting when a manhole will blow, why not a young jihadi?

Part of the problem officials and scientists are struggling with is that predicting manhole explosions is an algorithm of correlation, not causality. A jihadi, on the other hand, is a conscious being. There are patterns and practices that are linked to those prone to violence but they aren't definitive or 100 percent predictive. You could have people ready to blow themselves up, only to change their minds at the last minute. Manhole covers never change their minds.

So where does that leaves us with our approach to the press and the government with regard to Smart Data? Certainly, Big Data and ways to exploit it have arrived, but with some unexpected (and sometimes glossed over) caveats. When, for example, are correlations sufficient and, at other times, is causality required? So much depends on context and the purpose of the data exploitation. Both the press and the state are interested for their own institutional purposes in exploiting these technologies. The state wants to stop bad behavior and understand our adversaries' intentions while maintaining its actions beneath a cloak of secrecy. The press wants to pursue stories that will provide new information and reveal potential government activity it deems worthy of publication, exposure, and discussion. Our legal framework is struggling to provide rules and safeguards that reflect the new technological realties while balancing the historic functions of the press and government.

Individuals, for their part, are caught in the middle. Increasingly, they can neither hide from the press—the family of Xi Jinping can attest to that—nor from the government as it lawfully vacuums up more data than ever before. As this story unfolds, all eyes will be on the courts, which will have to decide how privacy is constitutionally protected in the age of Smart Data. In the end, the answer will turn on legal frameworks and the evolving accountability rules—when does the modern democratic state protect anonymity and when does that anonymity no longer apply? All that remains to be seen. As the ABA workshop on "No More Secrets" noted in 2011, technological vulnerabilities makes keeping information secret for both the private and public sectors increasingly a challenge."[40]

One fact is for certain, however, that the keeping of secrets—whether from individuals, governments, or the media—will be increasingly difficult. You may think you are having a good day, but be careful, your data may be showing.

NOTES

1. David D. Kirkpatrick, *US to List Libyan Groups and Militant Tied to Benghazi Attack as Terrorists*, N.Y. TIMES, Jan. 8, 2014.

2. HPSCI Chairman Mike Rogers, US House of Representatives Permanent Select Committee on Intelligence release, January 9, 2014.

3. Michael Forsythe et al., *Xi Jinping Millionaire Relations Reveal Fortunes of Elite*, BLOOMBERG NEWS, June 29, 2012.

4. *Id.*

5. Leslie Kaufman, *Seeking a Lead on News, Network Turns to Data-Mining Media Group*, N.Y. TIMES, Feb. 23, 2014.

6. James Fahn, *Feel Me?: The Promise and Perils of Sensor-Based Journalism*, COLUM. JOURNALISM REV., Nov. 1, 2013.

7. *Mapping Swarmageddon*, RADIOLAB, http://project.wnyc.org/cicadas/.

8. Ethan Zuckerman, *Water Monitoring in China, and the Changing Role of Citizenship*, MY HEART'S IN ACCRA, Apr. 20, 2014.

9. Fahn, *supra* note 7.

10. James Q. Wilson, *Broken Windows*, ATL. MONTHLY, Mar. 1, 1982, at 3.

11. Author interview with Daniel O'Brien, Nov. 2013.

12. Sasha Issenberg, *How President Obama's Campaign Used Big Data to Rally Individual Voters*, TECH. REV., Dec. 19, 2012.

13. Dina Temple-Raston, *Predicting the Future: Fantasy or a Good Algorithm?*, NPR NEWS, Oct. 8, 2012.

14. *Id.*

15. Dina Temple-Raston, *Google: A New Tool for US Intelligence?*, NPR NEWS, Mar. 25, 2011.

16. Temple-Raston, *supra* note 14.

17. Robert Worth, *Is Yemen the Next Afghanistan?*, N.Y. TIMES MAG., July 6, 2010.

18. Temple-Raston, *supra* note 14.

19. Gary King, Logistic Regression in Rare Events Data (Ctr. for Basic Research in Soc. Scis., Harvard Univ., 2001).

20. Cynthia Rudin et al., *Machine Learning for the New York City Power Grid*, 34(2) IEEE TRANS. PATTERN ANALYSIS & MACH. INTELLIGENCE 328 (Feb. 2012). Her work is also cited in MAYER-SCHONBERGER, VIKTOR AND KENNETH CUKIER, BIG DATA: A REVOLUTION THAT WILL TRANSFORM HOW WE LIVE, WORK AND THINK (Mar. 2013).

21. 442 U.S. 735 (1979).

22. *Id.* at 774–75 (citing United States v. N.Y. Tel. Co., 434 U.S. 159, 174–75 (1977)).

23. The interpretation of *Smith v. Maryland* has generated much legal commentary. One school argues that the lack of expectation of privacy for information with third parties has not been changed with technology, while the other school contends new technology has transformed dramatically what can be done with data and raises fundamental constitutional privacy concerns. Compare Judge Richard J. Leon, *Klayman v. Obama*, D.D.C 2013 (finding an unconstitutional expansion of Smith for government surveillance under the 4th Amendment) and Judge William H. Pauley III, *ACLU v. Clapper*, S.D.N.Y. 2013 (upholding the government's use of Smith as constitutional under the 4th Amendment for its surveillance programs).

24. Cesar Hidalgo interview, IDEAS MAGAZINE, June 2013.

25. Author interview with intelligence officials talking about link analysis and terrorism (Aug. 2013); Andrew Fildes, *How Kevin Bacon Cured Cancer: The Power of Six Degrees*, METRO MAG., 2008.

26. Stanley Milgram, *The Small World Problem*, 1(2) PSYCHOL. TODAY 60 (1967).

27. Peter Dodds, Roby Muhamad & Duncan Watts. *Small World Project*, 301 Sci. J. 827 (Aug. 8, 2003).

28. Valdis Krebs, *Uncloaking Terrorist Networks*, 7(4) First Monday, Apr. 2002, http://journals .uic.edu/ojs/index.php/fm/article/view/941/863.

29. Valdis Krebs, *Connecting the Dots: Tracking Two Identified Terrorists*, ORGNET.COM (2007), http://www.orgnet.com/prevent.html.

30. Jeffrey Rosen, *Total Information Awareness*, N.Y. Times Mag., Dec. 15, 2002.

31. Alex Pentland, Reality Mining of Mobile Communications: Toward a New Deal on Data, World Economic Forum's Global Information Technology Report 2008–2009.

32. *Id.* at 80.

33. Mumbai Terrorist Attacks November 26–29, 2008, FAS.org/irp/eprint/Mumbai.pdf.

34. Disclosure of National Security Agency Surveillance Programs: Hearing Before the House Permanent Select Committee on Intelligence, 113th Congress (2013) (statement of General Keith Alexander, director of National Security Agency).

35. Rosen, *supra* note 31.

36. Dina Temple-Raston, *The Jihad Next Door: The Lackawanna Six and Rough Justice in the Age of Terror*, Pub. Affairs, Sept. 2007.

37. Deepak Jagsih, remarks at an ACTIVATE conference, November 2013.

38. Jeff Jonas, Non-Obvious Relationship Awareness, Emerging Tech. Conference, Mar. 27, 2007.

39. *Id.*

40. *See* ABA Standing Comm. on Law & Nat'l Sec., No More Secrets: National Security Strategies for a Transparent World (Mar. 2011), http://www.americanbar.org/content/dam/aba /administrative/law_national_security/no_more_secrets2.authcheckdam.pdf.

Holding Leakers Accountable: Considering a Comprehensive Leaks Approach

12

W. George Jameson

I agree that unauthorized disclosures can be extraordinarily harmful to United States national interests and that far too many such disclosures occur. . . . Unauthorized disclosures damage our intelligence relationships abroad, compromise intelligence gathering, jeopardize lives, and increase the threat of terrorism. . . .

To the extent that existing sanctions have proven insufficient to address and deter unauthorized disclosures, they should be strengthened. What is in dispute is not the gravity of the problem, but the best way to respond to it.

> President Bill Clinton, November 4, 2000
> (Veto Statement of the President H.R. 4392, The
> Intelligence Authorization Act for Fiscal Year 2001)

I. INTRODUCTION

The theft of classified material relating to foreign intelligence collection activities of the National Security Agency and the resulting revelations and speculation—not always accurate but most certainly titillating—have triggered debate over the legal and policy implications of these programs for U.S. counterterrorism capabilities, foreign relations, and privacy interests in the

United States and abroad. They also have raised concerns about the impact from the inability to keep secrets and hold someone accountable.

What to do about the unauthorized disclosure of sensitive information has long been a seemingly intractable problem. This chapter focuses on one aspect of the leaks dilemma: the need to review both the adequacy and appropriate use of the existing laws and, as necessary, recommend changes that would be more effective at holding leakers properly accountable for their actions. A review of the laws would consider the value in enacting comprehensive leaks legislation to strengthen accountability while respecting both national secrets and civil liberties interests.

The chapter includes a brief look at the leaks dilemma—that is, the need to weigh both legitimate secrecy and free speech issues—and presents discussion points for consideration in determining a possible framework for action, including both criminal and civil remedies. It draws in part from remarks this author delivered at an American Bar Association panel more than a decade ago in discussing the effort at that time to "solve" the leaks problem.[1]

The chapter assumes the following basic premises:

- Those who leak classified information violate their nondisclosure agreements, the public's trust, and the law.
- Reliance on existing espionage statutes to sanction leakers who are not spies warrants serious reconsideration.
- National security and free speech interests are core to the United States and must be reconciled, but respect for free speech principles does not immunize the press from being questioned or held accountable for certain actions that damage national security.
- Leaks legislation alone will not solve the leaks problem.

Finally, the chapter briefly considers possible steps to engage policymakers and the public, including media, academia, and the legal community, in attempting to seek a national consensus on leaks, without which it will be difficult if not impossible to develop any meaningful course of action.

II. SETTING THE STAGE: THE LEAKS DILEMMA

Much of the attention surrounding the public disclosures of information provided to the press by former National Security Agency (NSA) contractor Edward Snowden has centered on the propriety of NSA's intelligence collection programs, the scope of existing legal authorities, and whether changes in the law are needed to curtail or clarify those intelligence collection authorities. Less attention, at least publicly, has been given to determining how to protect classified information, deter unauthorized public disclosures and determining whether and how to hold someone accountable for the leaks, as the unauthorized disclosures of classified information to the media tend to be called.

Leaks and related calls to stop them and punish leakers are not a new phenomenon. The most recent disclosures merely highlight once again the challenges in attempting to reconcile two important interests when seeking to hold people accountable for disclosing classified information without the authority to do so: the need to protect secrets important to the security of the nation and the need to protect free speech interests that are at the core of America's persona in an open society.

The compromises of classified intelligence programs—programs approved to varying degrees not only by the executive branch but also by the legislative and judicial branches—have raised security concerns because of the increasing frequency, nature, and, in a new phenomenon, relative ease with which massive amounts of harmful disclosures of sensitive information have been made public through the courtesy of modern technology.

The threats to national security from insider threats such as these have been called "critical" by the director of national intelligence[2] and "potentially the most massive and most damaging theft of intelligence information in our history."[3] The public debates about this aspect of the problem have included calls for a variety of actions that would, for example, impose or enhance security requirements to protect information more effectively, establish limits on an individual's access to information, hold leakers accountable as traitors or at least lawbreakers, take away their pensions, and prosecute those who actually publish the classified information.[4]

Some commentators and government officials have argued that the current laws are sufficient. They point to the government's successful reliance upon statutes that already criminalize espionage and other unauthorized disclosures of defense information, disclosure of diplomatic codes or communication, unauthorized disclosures of covert agent identities, and theft of government property. Others have argued that those laws are inadequate to fully identify, investigate, and prosecute leakers.

As difficult as it might be to identify and prosecute leakers, the related issues arising from involvement of the press can be even more daunting. Decisions by the government to investigate or question journalists to identify the sources of the leaks serve as proof to some that legislative steps must be taken to constrain government conduct. They seek to expand whistleblower laws or to enact shield laws to insulate the media organizations that published the classified information while attempting to limit government investigations that seek to identify the leakers, labeling them inappropriate if not illegal.

Others, however, including influential members of Congress, have asked if members of the media themselves should be held accountable as guilty of crimes for their roles in publishing the information.

In a *New York Times* article published February 5, 2014, the chairman of the House Permanent Select Committee on Intelligence, Representative Mike Rogers of Michigan, is quoted as saying during a committee hearing that the journalists who wrote articles based on classified documents provided to them by Snowden were, in effect, "fencing stolen material" and should be prosecuted under criminal law.

209

According to the *Times* article:

> At the Intelligence Committee hearing, Mr. Rogers—who has repeatedly speculated that Mr. Snowden may be an agent of the Russian spy service, without offering any evidence to support that charge—led the director of the Federal Bureau of Investigation, James B. Comey, in a colloquy about journalism and criminality.
>
> "So if I'm a newspaper reporter for—fill in the blank—and I sell stolen material, is that legal because I'm a newspaper reporter?" Mr. Rogers asked. "If I'm hawking stolen, classified material that I'm not legally in possession of for personal gain and profit, is that not a crime?"
>
> Mr. Comey responded cautiously. He said that if a reporter was "hawking stolen jewelry," it would be a crime, but that publishing classified information was a more complicated issue because of constitutional protections for press freedom.[5]

This exchange is illustrative of the leaks dilemma today, but is by no means novel. Whether or not existing legal authorities that address such situations are adequate, sufficient, or lacking as measures to identify and prosecute leakers for such unauthorized disclosures has been a matter of frustration and debate for many years. At the heart of the problem has been an inability to fully reconcile national security and free speech interests.

III. CHARACTERIZING LEAKS, THEIR NATURE, AND IMPACT

There are many types of leaks and leakers, and motives and intent may differ for persons in each category.[6] This chapter focuses in particular on situations when the offending activities, regardless of motive, do not fall within what would generally be considered traditional espionage—that is, clandestine spying on behalf of a foreign power. Unlike the actions of spies, such disclosures are intended to be made public, although the source of the leak might not be obvious or known. Leaks can reach the public through disclosures in books, newspapers, or other publications by identified or often unidentified current or former government officials or contractors. In some cases those persons may have had authorized access to the information in question, or they might have gained access to it without authority. The leaks might be by persons who claim whistleblower status, or who otherwise claim the public has a right to know the information, which in some cases might be known by congressional overseers as in the Snowden matter. Still other public disclosures of classified information might be the result of activity by media or other persons who have, in whole or in part, independently and through lawful or unlawful investigative means, obtained and published or threatened to publish classified information.

A common element for all these disclosures is that the government asserts disclosure has damaged or will damage the national security of the United States. Although the reasons for government classification decisions are sometimes less than fully transparent or understood, the disclosure of properly classified government secrets have compromised intelligence collection efforts and resulted in severe and, in some cases, irreparable harm to U.S. national security interests.[7]

The theft and unauthorized revelations by Edward Snowden when he was a contractor at the National Security Agency of agency activities approved by the president and judges on the Foreign Intelligence Surveillance Act court based upon articulated statutory authority have been discussed by President Barack Obama as follows:

And given the fact of an open investigation, I'm not going to dwell on Mr. Snowden's actions or his motivations; I will say that our nation's defense depends in part on the fidelity of those entrusted with our nation's secrets. If any individual who objects to government policy can take it into their own hands to publicly disclose classified information, then we will not be able to keep our people safe, or conduct foreign policy. Moreover, the sensational way in which these disclosures have come out has often shed more heat than light, while revealing methods to our adversaries that could impact our operations in ways that we may not fully understand for years to come.[8]

The Snowden disclosures have stimulated debate about who should be considered a whistleblower, what steps whistleblowers should follow, and whether legitimate whistleblowers should, nevertheless, face legal consequences when damage results. Interestingly, no less a personality than former Central Intelligence Agency (CIA) officer Frank Snepp, who forfeited the royalties from his 1977 book *Decent Interval* for failing to abide by his prepublication review obligations, has criticized Snowden on this score in no uncertain terms:

Granting Edward Snowden clemency, as many have urged, would send a terrible message to other potential whistle-blowers. Yes, he may have sparked an important national privacy debate, but he did so through reprehensible actions that harmed national security. . . .

Yet, for all that I suffered personally, I never ran or tried to hide. And when the time came to face the music, I never bargained for mercy. I simply took my lumps, accepting them as the price we pay in a democracy for the right to speak out.[9]

The Commission on the Intelligence Capabilities of the United States Regarding Weapons of Mass Destruction, known as the WMD Commission, in 2005 expressed concern about the damage and counterintelligence implications caused by leaks, including financial costs, but could not reach a consensus in attempting to determine a way to craft legislation to identify leakers and protect the press's

First Amendment rights in the process. The commission instead recommended steps such as better coordination of leaks investigations, vigorous application of administrative authorities, better education and training, and other changes that could help identify leakers. It further highlighted what it saw as the government's continuing helplessness in dealing with leaks:

> The government's impotence in dealing effectively with this problem was well characterized by then-Deputy Assistant Attorney General Richard K. Willard, in 1982: In summary, past practices with leaks investigations has been largely unsuccessful and uniformly frustrating for all concerned. . . . The whole system has been so ineffectual as to perpetuate the notion that the Government can do nothing to stop the leaks."[10]

In addition, the latest revelations have triggered an interesting national debate about even how to characterize Snowden's actions. *Washington Post* columnist Richard Cohen, for example, described the dilemma it this way: "Snowden is something new under the sun. He defies categorization. He is not a spy and not a conventional traitor. The old remedies and punishments do not fit."[11]

Similarly, more than 60 years ago, a U.S. president expressed concern about the labels attributed to leakers when the public disclosure of classified information in the press provides foreign powers access to the information and damages national interests. As President Harry Truman stated in 1951:

> Whether it is treason or not, it does the United States just as much harm for military secrets to be made known to potential enemies through open publication, as it does for military secrets to be given to an enemy through the clandestine operation of spies. . . .

The question now is how to address the adequacy and appropriateness of remedies for holding transgressors accountable while reconciling them with countervailing interests such as First Amendment and whistleblower considerations.

IV. BASIC LEGAL CONSIDERATIONS IN THE LEAKS DEBATES

A. Protecting National Security Information

A need for government secrecy is recognized in the Constitution itself. Article I, section 5 provides that "Each House shall keep a Journal of its Proceedings, and from time to time publish the same, excepting such Parts as may in their Judgment require Secrecy." Also, few people should be surprised at the significant value afforded to secrecy by the early leaders of the nation:

> The necessity of procuring good Intelligence is apparent & need not be further urged—all that remains for me to add, is, that you keep the whole

212

matter as secret as possible. For upon Secrecy, Success depends in most Enterprises of the kind, and for want of it, they are generally defeated, however well planned and promising a favourable issue.[12]

More recently in U.S. history, the importance of secrecy regarding foreign intelligence, for example, has been reflected in the National Security Act of 1947, as amended. The director of national intelligence, as was the predecessor director of central intelligence, is responsible by law to protect intelligence sources and methods from unauthorized disclosure.

Congress has taken steps to protect intelligence information in many ways since the initial enactment of the 1947 Act. Openness legislation was designed to increase government transparency and make information in the possession of the government more readily available to the public. Nevertheless, these laws have included various national security and other exemptions followed by other legislation to limit or restrict access to, and thus to protect, intelligence and other information affecting the national defense and foreign relations of the United States; that is, national security information.

- The Freedom of Information Act (FOIA) and Privacy Act include provisions to exempt classified information and information protected by statute (e.g., intelligence sources and methods) from disclosure.
- The CIA Information Act (1980) exempts the CIA's operational files from the search and review provisions of the FOIA. Comparable provisions establish similar protections for the National Security Agency, the Defense Intelligence Agency, the National Reconnaissance Agency, and the National Geospatial-Intelligence Agency.[13]
- The Classified Information and Procedures Act (1980) enables a court to balance the needs of a defendant to have access to classified information in order to mount a defense, and permits withdrawal of charges and dismissal of a case if proceeding would jeopardize national security.
- A series of executive orders going back decades have governed the classification and protection of defense, foreign policy, intelligence, and other sensitive information based on the president's constitutional authorities.[14]

The legislation and executive directives resulting from demands to improve information sharing following the scathing critiques of information-sharing failures cited by the 9/11 and WMD Commissions altered the long-standing default stance of the government from one of protection and "need to know" to one of "responsibility to share." The changes enacted after 9/11 recognized that secrecy taken to the extreme also can damage national security interests, but the resulting increased sharing has been decried by some, including critics of the new policies, who assert these changes have proven that the changes resulted in greater risk that the information can be obtained by unauthorized persons to the detriment of the United States ability to counter terrorist and other national security threats.

Of course, these provisions speak to how the government may prevent having to disclose information in its possession. More relevant to the ability to hold leakers accountable are other statutes that address what the government may do when information has been compromised and the government seeks to identify and fire, prosecute, or otherwise sanction the offenders.

B. Holding Leakers Accountable

There is no single, comprehensive statute that governs the handling of leaks. Several statutes, some dating back to the Espionage Act of 1917, are instead cited by prosecutors and others as an adequate legal basis to prosecute those who obtain and reveal information. Some statutes generally criminalize the unauthorized disclosure of national defense information (e.g., the espionage laws). Other statutes criminalize unauthorized disclosures of certain types of information, such as classified communications and activities, names of undercover intelligence officers and covert agents, atomic energy data, and diplomatic codes.

These criminal provisions, taken together, have been cited as adequate authority, and to varying degrees have been used, for the successful prosecution of persons who have made unauthorized disclosures of classified information. Examples include:

- Government prosecutors filed a criminal complaint against Edward Snowden, citing Title 18, sections 641 (theft of government property), 793(d) (unauthorized communication of national defense information), and 798(a)(3) (willful disclosure of communications intelligence). The last two provisions are espionage charges.
- Prosecution of former CIA officer John Kiriakou led to a guilty plea for revelation of the identity of undercover personnel to a member of the press. The actions did not include traditional spying, and the case affirmed the viability of the Intelligence Identities Protection Act as an important tool in protecting intelligence agents and officers.
- An Associated Press story on May 7, 2012, about a bombing plot and secret U.S. counterterrorism operation to penetrate terrorist groups in Yemen highlighted damage that can result to intelligence sources and methods from unauthorized disclosures. Premature revelations in this matter led to concerns about a source's life, required premature removal of the agent from both the operation and the country, and termination of the operation.[15]
- The successful prosecution of intelligence analyst Samuel Loring Morison for disclosure of classified imagery to a foreign media organization supports use of the espionage laws as well as the statute regarding theft of property for unauthorized disclosures to the press even in the absence of traditional "spying"[16] Later, at the end of the Clinton administration, the defendant received a presidential pardon, much to the chagrin of intelligence agencies.

Despite assertions of damage and calls to identify and prosecute leakers, government actions in attempting to do so have led media and other free speech advocates to criticize government efforts to identify the source of a leak by investigating news media that published the leaked information.

- In investigating the Yemen leak, the Department of Justice without notice subpoenaed and obtained telephone records of journalists working for the Associated Press.[17]
- In another matter, the Department tracked Fox News reporter James Rosen's activities including phone calls and e-mails to identify the leaker of classified information regarding North Korea's nuclear capabilities. The warrants labeled Rosen a "co-conspirator" and enabled investigators to avoid giving prior notice and opportunity to challenge the actions.[18] These actions led to calls for shield laws and a change to Justice Department policies.

U.S. Laws Applicable to Leakers—Summary

Espionage Laws

- Title 18, section 793 of the U.S. Criminal Code is the primary statute making espionage, or spying, a criminal offense, with particular reference to defense information and not other national security information.
- Section 793(a) provides that a person who obtains information "respecting" the national defense—defense information—with the intent or reason to believe the information is to be used to the injury of the United States or the advantage of any foreign nation, may be subject to a fine, imprisonment, or both, as well as loss of proceeds from the actions.
- Section 793(d) further provides such penalties for anyone who has lawful possession or access to certain material (such as photos or codes) "relating to the national defense" or to "information relating to the national which information the possessor has reason to believe could be used to the injury of the United States or to the advantage of any foreign nation" and who willfully communicates it to any person not entitled to receive it." The section further enables prosecution of persons who fail to return such information to the government when called upon to do so.
- Section 793(e) covers those who have unauthorized possession of or access to such information and who transmit or communicate the information to other unauthorized persons.
- Section 793(f) provides penalties for persons with authorized access who evidence gross negligence resulting removal of the information or loss or delivery to someone in a violation of trust.

(continued)

- Title 18, section 794 criminalizes the communication of national defense information to any foreign government with the intent or reason to believe that it will be used to the injury of the United States or to the benefit of a foreign nation.
- Title 18, sections 795 and 797 prohibit the unauthorized creation, publication, sale, or transfer of photographs or sketches of vital defense installations or equipment.
- Title 50, section 783 makes it unlawful for an employee of the government or of any corporation "the stock of which is owned in whole or in major part" by the United States to communicate, without authority, information that employee knows or has reason to know is classified to any person the employee knows or has reason to believe is an agent of any foreign government.

Classified/Communications Information

- Title 18, section 798 criminalizes acts of anyone who knowingly and willfully communicates or otherwise makes available to an unauthorized person, "or publishes, or uses in any manner prejudicial to the safety or interest of the United States or for the benefit of any foreign government to the detriment of the United States" any classified information. As defined, the information is that relating to the cryptographic or communications intelligence systems or activities, including the product of collection of the United States, or of a foreign government.

Undercover Intelligence Officers, Agents, Informants, and Sources

- Title 50, section 421 (Intelligence Identities and Protection Act of 1982) provides criminal penalties regarding the disclosure of the identity of an undercover intelligence officer or covert U.S. intelligence agent, knowing the government is taking steps to conceal the identity or relationship to the government. The Act establishes three distinct categories, designed to address disclosures by persons:
  (a) with authorized access to the information in question;
  (b) with authorized access to other classified information who obtain access to the identities of covert agents; and, as the basis for the statute was the public revelation of the identity of a CIA officer in Greece;
  (c) who engage in a "pattern of activities intended to identify and expose covert agents and with reason to believe that such activities would impair or impede the foreign intelligence activities of the United States, discloses any information" to a person not authorized to receive classified information.

Theft of Government Property

- Title 18, section 641 does not by its terms speak of classified information, but it has been used to prosecute leakers for the theft or conversion, for personal or other use, of government records or other property, classified or not, or for receipt or retention of such property for one's own or gain knowing that it has been stolen or converted.

Miscellaneous Provisions

- The Atomic Energy Act prohibits government employees and contractors from knowingly communicating Restricted Data to persons not authorized to receive it, and prohibits anyone with possession, access, or control over Restricted Data from disclosing it with the intent to injure the United States or to benefit a foreign nation. (See Title 42, United States Code, sections 2277 and 2274.)
- Title 18, section 1924, (Unauthorized Removal and Retention of Classified Documents or Material)—Makes it an offense for any government employee, contractor, or consultant who, by virtue of his employment or position obtains classified material, knowingly removes it without authority with the intent to retain it.

Revelations in manuscripts by government personnel raise different aspects of the leaks problem, and provide noncriminal remedies, either when employees or former employees fail to submit their material for prior review (as with Frank Snepp's failure to submit his book about government actions in Vietnam, *Decent Interval*) or fail to abide by decisions about what may not be published. In 2011, a U.S. district court ruled that former CIA officer Ishmael Jones (not his true name) violated his obligation to go through CIA's publication review process properly before publishing his book in 2008 about his work at CIA. In such cases, civil actions are available for breach of the secrecy agreement and can result in loss of proceeds from publication.

Notwithstanding the availability of these laws, there are hurdles for prosecutors who, along with the lawyers of the agencies that originated the classified information, are concerned with the risks associated with having to confirm or reveal classified information in order to present the most effective case. As recently stated:

Putting former NSA contractor Edward Snowden on trial for leaking U.S. surveillance information could be an awkward public spectacle for the Obama administration. More classified material could be at risk and jurors might see him as a whistle-blower exposing government overreach. . . . Administration officials say the possibility of a public

217

spectacle wherein Snowden tries to reveal even more classified information to make his case has not lessened the Justice Department's intent to prosecute him . . . .[19]

Use of the Classified Information Procedures Act offers some protections for classified information through redactions and substitutions approved by the court, but these risks can involve sharing sensitive information (such as Foreign Intelligence Surveillance Act applications) with defense counsel,[20] and to other situations where the harm from disclosure might be too great.[21] It remains to be seen to what extent the government will seek to avoid these problems by, for example, limiting its case to charges that do not implicate whistleblower claims or the most sensitive information.

Other questions also remain: whether these statutes are actually sufficient to enable the government to identify and prosecute leakers; whether new laws are needed when leakers are not traditional spies and an espionage label could be seen as inappropriate; and how to deal with the involvement of the news media.

C. Executive and Congressional Efforts to Solve the Leaks Problems

Several past efforts to deal with leaks included recommendations for changes internal to the executive branch. Others sought legislation to impose strict liability for transgressions, some provided affirmative defenses to permit, for example, disclosures to courts or to Congress without fear of prosecution, and others required proof of actual damage. Most have been directed only at government employees and others with authorized access to classified information.

A review of several efforts to enact leaks legislation suggests that drafters have recognized the difficulty in identifying leakers, indicated a reluctance to establish a process that would require the government to reveal or confirm classified information in order to proceed with a case, and recognized that overly broad bills could be seen to violate free speech, due process, and rights to counsel, for example. These efforts have included:

- *Efforts to clarify or enhance the authority of the director of central intelligence (DCI)* to protect intelligence sources and methods date to the CIA's early history. (Note that with enactment of legislative reform in 2004, the DCI was eliminated and the responsibilities migrated to a director of national intelligence). As the CIA by statute could have no law enforcement powers, DCI and CIA authority to investigate leaks was constrained. Questions about how to deal with this problem arose from early in CIA's history, and through the 1960s CIA and the Department of Justice discussed proposals to identify a category of sources and methods for legislative change to the espionage laws to provide broader protections for intelligence sources and methods.

- *Report of the Interdepartmental Group on Unauthorized Disclosures of Classified Information, the so-called Willard Report (March 31, 1982)*—This report recommended several executive branch actions to improve the protection of information, require secrecy agreements and prepublication review, appropriate policies for dealing with the media, expanded use of the polygraph, and strengthening legislation. National Security Decision Directive 84 directed implementation of many of the recommendations.

- *Proposed Legislation, Unauthorized Disclosures of Classified Information, in several Intelligence Authorization Bills over the following decade (for fiscal years 1984, 1986, 1987, and 1993)*—To varying degrees these unsuccessful legislative efforts took a simple per se approach to punish officers or employees of the United States or persons with authorized access to classified information who willfully disclose classified information to a person who is not an officer or employee and not authorized to receive it; they sometimes required certification that the information was properly classified, and provided for in camera, ex parte judicial review of the propriety of the classification, which raised Sixth Amendment concerns. Some more narrowly criminalized the disclosure of covered information marked Top Secret and information concerning certain technical information provided to persons not authorized to receive it.

- *Proposed legislation, Prohibition on Unauthorized Disclosure of Classified Information*, passed by both the House and Senate in the Intelligence Authorization Act for Fiscal Year 2001 with the support of the attorney general, the DCI, and the director of the Federal Bureau of Investigation (FBI), but vetoed by President Bill Clinton as "badly flawed" and "overbroad." The measure would have taken a simple and limited approach and criminalized the knowing and willful disclosure by anyone with past or present authorized access to classified information to a person who was not an officer or employee of the United States and who was not authorized access to the classified information, where the information was clearly marked as classified or the offender knew or had reason to believe it was classified.

- *Report to the Speaker of the House of Representatives in Compliance with Section 310 of the Intelligence Authorization Act for Fiscal Year 2002 (Ashcroft Report) (October 15, 2002)*—Following the president's veto and in response to statutory requirements to report to Congress on measures to prevent and deter leaks, the report recommended numerous internal measures to improve chances of identifying leakers, enable agencies to investigate certain leaks without awaiting FBI involvement, enhance internal security protections, and review to make changes to the existing Executive orders, directives, to amend secrecy agreements to include liquidated damages provisions, and more.

- Attorney General John Ashcroft concluded that "current statutes provide a legal basis to prosecute those who engage in unauthorized disclosures, if they can be identified. It may be that carefully drafted legislation specifically tailored to unauthorized disclosures of classified information generally, rather than to espionage, could enhance our investigative efforts. The extent to which such a provision would yield any practical additional benefits to the government in terms of improving our ability to identify those who engage in unauthorized disclosures of classified information or deterring such activity is unclear, however."
- Upon the strong urging of DCI George Tenet, the attorney general further concluded: "We should continue to explore what additional specific steps are needed to strengthen the ability of the United States government to combat unauthorized disclosures of classified information, to include continued consideration of various legislative options."
- *The House Permanent Select Committee on Intelligence in 2005* attempted to tackle the problem and held hearings on leaks and how such disclosures harm national security. The Committee sought specific examples of both intentional and unintentional disclosures of classified information and the impact they have had on the intelligence community's ability to perform its missions.[22]
- *Legislation approved by the Senate Select Intelligence Committee in 2012*—Triggered by leaks to reporters concerning cyberattacks on Iran and counterterrorist activities in Yemen, the bill proposed to reduce the number of people in intelligence agencies authorized to speak to reporters on "background" or on the condition of anonymity; require notice to Congress of "authorized" disclosures of classified information; and permit loss of a leaker's pension. Objections to the bill's breadth and its applicability only to agencies in the intelligence community resulted in a much reduced anti-leak law in the Intelligence Authorization Act for Fiscal Year 2013.[23]
- *Department of Defense approval of a Strategic Plan to prevent and deter the unauthorized disclosure of classified information*—It directed numerous actions aimed at enhancing and clarifying internal authorities and controls, security obligations, investigatory roles, education and training, and accountability.[24]
- *Department of Justice "Report on Review of News Media Policies" (July 12, 2013)*—Attorney General Eric Holder in this report responded to criticism of U.S. actions to determine the source of a leak by investigating Associated Press reporter James Rosen. With some exceptions permitted, Justice policy was amended to limit its investigative efforts directed at the press by:
  - Providing advance notice to the news media when seeking news records related to news gathering; elevating approval processes; clarifying that its policies apply to seeking news media information held by third parties; and

220

- Seeking news records under the "suspect exception" to the Privacy Protection Act of 1980 (42 U.S.C. § 2000aa) in limited circumstances. That Act generally prohibits search or seizure of materials held by persons with a purpose of disseminating information to the public. The exception applies when there is probable cause to believe the person possessing materials is suspected of a crime to which the materials relate, including unauthorized disclosure laws. Justice will apply that exception only when the member of the media is the criminal focus "for conduct not connected to ordinary newsgathering activities," and Justice will not seek search warrants under the exception "if the sole purpose is the investigation of a person other than the member of the news media."

The attorney general's statement reiterated his and the Obama administration's support for efforts within Congress to enact a media shield law.

D. Reconciling Conflicting Interests

Government efforts to limit disclosures or to enact legislation to sanction government employees or others for revealing classified information must be assessed in light of the First Amendment strictures. How to deter unauthorized disclosures without improperly "chilling" legitimate speech has long been a challenge.

Legal scholars and practitioners seeking solutions to recent and other leaks disclosures may look to the debates about civil liberties implications of the much discredited Alien and Sedition Acts (1798) and existing espionage laws (1917) to find that disagreements about how to respond to the unauthorized publication of government secrets are not new. Americans have historically engaged in heated debates over implications for free speech and a free press when the government seeks to investigate and prosecute transgressors, particularly when the press is involved. Similarly, Americans today debate the extent to which the WikiLeaks and Snowden disclosures are evidence of freedom of speech and the press, criminal acts, or both.

Government officers and others who obtain classified information sign secrecy agreements as a precondition of access to classified information, and courts have confirmed that persons with access to classified information must fulfill their obligations, whether explicit or even implicit, not to reveal classified information and to submit to removal of certain sensitive material they obtained in the course of their access and that they seek to publish. Failure to observe these obligations can result in a loss of proceeds from book sales as well as loss of security clearances and future access to classified information, as well, of course, as prosecution if they reveal information to unauthorized persons.[25]

More recently, the prepublication review and related requirements have been upheld in an action for the "breach of contract and fiduciary duty" as reflected by a former employee's release of classified information after failing to observe CIA's prepublication review requirements.[26]

Much of the current debate reflected in the media assumes a broad privilege for the press to publish government information and, in some arguments, to be immune from inquiry into the source of the information that has been made public without authority. That is not entirely correct under the law. A reluctance to proceed against the press, even to obtain information only about the sources of leaks, appears to be more policy-based, reflecting perhaps a kind of cultural reluctance to proceed in the face of what are undoubtedly constitutional issues for fear that the odds of success are slim. This also could reflect a principled concern among legal experts inside and outside government that, perhaps, no good is likely to come from assaults on First Amendment principles.

A recent work on the subject addresses leaker motivations, government motivations and impediments that, if not encourage, at least permit leakers to go unpunished, and implications for government secrecy:

> [T]he courts have indicated that while the government has expansive legal authority to prosecute employees who leak, it has minimal authority to stop reporters who receive leaks from broadcasting what they learn, either through ex post penalties or prior restraints. In all cases, it seems, the government would have to prove a reporter's actions threatened grave, immediate harm to national security interests. (It is hard to be sure because the government has never indicted one.). . . . The First Amendment has been understood to provide so little protection for the leaker and yet so much protection for the journalist who knowingly publishes the fruits of the leaker's illicit conduct and thereby enables the very harm—revelation of sensitive information to the public and to foreign adversaries—that the leak laws were designed to combat. In other areas of criminal law, downstream users of illegally obtained material are not similarly insulated from liability.
>
> As a descriptive or diagnostic matter, the literature has pointed to several factors to explain the existence of these features. The leak laws are so rarely enforced, it is said, because the Justice Department finds it so difficult, at the investigatory stage, to identify culprits and so difficult, at the adjudicatory stage, to bring successful cases without divulging additional sensitive information. Courts and prosecutors have privileged journalists over leakers, it is said, because of the former's special First Amendment status and the latter's consent to nondisclosure as a condition of employment. Throughout these discussions, the comparison is often drawn to the United Kingdom's notorious Official Secrets Act. Whatever else might be true of our legal and political regime for regulating leaks, virtually everyone agrees the United States would never abide such a sweeping criminal prohibition.[27]

The Supreme Court, nevertheless, has stated that the freedom to speak and of the press are not absolute and that there "is no constitutional right to publish a fact merely because it is true." While recognizing freedom of the press in rejecting a prior restraint on publication, the Court stated also:

> When a nation is at war, many things that might be said in time of peace are such a hindrance to its effort that their utterance will not be endured so long as men fight, and that no Court could regard them as protected by any constitutional right. *Schenck v. United States*, 249 U.S. 47, 52. No one would question but that a government might prevent actual obstruction to its recruiting service or the publication of the sailing dates of transports or the number and location of troops.[28]

Further, the Supreme Court has held that a journalist generally has no privilege based on the First Amendment to withhold the identity of a confidential source from a good-faith grand jury criminal inquiry.[29] The Court has stated that the right to speak and publish "does not carry with it the unrestrained right to gather information,"[30] and further recognized that the press is not immune from newsroom searches,[31] although government policies have curtailed such actions.

In more recent cases, the courts have declined to recognize a common law reporter's privilege to allow a journalist not to testify. The delegation to a special prosecutor of the attorney general's authority for investigation of the leak involving undercover CIA officer Valerie Plame led to a relaxing of the limiting policies and issuance of subpoenas for telephone records and other information in 2005 from *New York Times* reporter Judith Miller. Her refusal to cooperate led to her spending 85 days in jail, after which she agreed to testify before the grand jury. Citing the *Miller* case, the U.S. Court of Appeals for the Fourth Circuit partially reversed a district court's finding of a privilege claim asserted by *New York Times* reporter James Risen in a case brought against a former CIA employee where the government sought Risen's testimony to confirm the identity of his source. In *United States v. Sterling*, the court stated:

> There is no First Amendment testimonial privilege, absolute or qualified, that protects a reporter from being compelled to testify by the prosecution or the defense in criminal proceedings about criminal conduct that the reporter personally witnessed or participated in, absent a showing of bad faith, harassment, or other such non-legitimate motive, even though the reporter promised confidentiality to his source. In *Branzburg v. Hayes*, 408 U.S. 665 (1972), the Supreme Court "in no uncertain terms rejected the existence of such a privilege." *In re Grand Jury Subpoena, Judith Miller*, 438 F. 3d 1141, 1146 (D.C. Cir. 2006).[32]

In addressing the reporter's arguments, the court noted by way of contrast that, in a civil setting, courts seeking to compel press testimony should indeed, as had been urged for the criminal case, look at relevance, whether the information can be obtained by alternative means, and whether there is a compelling interest in the information. In the criminal context, however, these factors have little impact, any "chilling" effort on newsgathering notwithstanding. Accordingly, Risen can be compelled to identify a source who was accused of disclosing classified information relating to CIA knowledge of and alleged activities relating to Iran's nuclear program. In June 2014, the Supreme Court declined to review this ruling.

It may be that efforts to identify a solution for addressing the rights of the media in leaks cases might also be informed by case law outside the realm of national security and criminal law. In a famous case involving defamation allegations, the Supreme Court highlighted the conflicting principles at stake in finding First Amendment protections. On the one hand, the Court cited ample precedent in expressing strong support for the First Amendment and the flow of information:

> The general proposition that freedom of expression upon public questions is secured by the First Amendment has long been settled by our decisions. The constitutional safeguard, we have said, "was fashioned to assure unfettered interchange of ideas for the bringing about of political and social changes desired by the people."[33]

The Court addressed allegations that defamatory statements caused damage to a public official, and concluded that the First and Fourteenth Amendments would not permit the per se award of damages to a public official for defamatory falsehood relating to his official conduct. The justices instead ruled in the landmark *New York Times Co. v. Sullivan* that the offended official must prove "actual malice"—that is, that the statement was made with knowledge of its falsity or with reckless disregard of whether it was true or false.[34]

The ruling indicates, therefore, that under the right circumstances litigation may proceed against the press for what it publishes. The important lessons of all these cases is that the freedom to speak does not always provide absolute immunity from inquiry or even liability, although the burden on those who would be seen to threaten constitutional safeguards is a heavy one.

E.   When Is a Spy Not a Spy?

All spies are leakers; but not all leakers are spies. Successful application of the espionage and other laws suggests to some, as it did to Attorney General John Ashcroft in 2002, that the laws are adequate. However, the most relevant provisions on the books today to prosecute leakers are contained in the espionage acts. Although technically available for use in the face of many leaks of information, the reality is that public support for the use of espionage laws to prosecute leaks cases is not unconditional. As the recent debates over whether Snowden is a traitor or a hero—whether he violated the public trust or provided a public service—make clear, it may be difficult to generate enthusiasm for investigating and prosecuting leakers who are not spies, or to stave off legislative efforts to curtail the government's ability to do. This is so at least in part because leaks of information are not seen as espionage when the information is not obtained directly by or for a foreign agent, however similar and damaging the results may be. Moreover, although reliance on statutes that authorize prosecution for theft of government property can be adequate, prosecutions for "mere" theft of property can suggest government pursuit of sanctions for actions of a trivial nature.

Carefully drafted laws and regulations that both empower and appropriately constrain government investigators by providing a realistic ability to identify and prosecute leakers who are not spies are important. The leakers have violated their promises not to reveal classified information without authority to do so. In simple terms: a leaker has broken the law, but the leaker also has entered into a contract and then violated the terms of that contract.

F. Practical Challenges in Considering Possible Leaks Remedies

One option is to consider enactment of new laws that are not espionage acts; that is, that do not require an unauthorized recipient of information to be an agent of a foreign power or require prosecutors to show the leaker's intent to damage the United States or benefit to foreign powers. Such legislation would not require the government to confirm or unnecessarily reveal secrets publicly in order to sanction an employee who has intentionally revealed classified information without authority and in violation of the public trust. These factors can dampen the enthusiasm of even the most eager investigators, as well as energize leakers. A prosecution can be even more difficult in a "blended case"—that is, if the leaker has revealed damaging national security information but also can legitimately be seen as a whistleblower who has spotlighted illegal, immoral, or other improper conduct.

Some opposed to leaks legislation to criminalize disclosure of classified information point out that the government classifies too much information and that this leads well-intentioned persons to violate their oaths of secrecy as the only way to bring classified information to light. This should not be the determining factor in the case of persons who have publicly disclosed information they agreed to protect. Laws such as the Whistleblower Protection Act of 1989, augmented by a provision in the Intelligence Authorization Act of 1999 with the enactment of the Whistleblower Protection Act of 1999 to cover intelligence community personnel, and the more recent Whistleblower Protection Enhancement Act (which does not apply to the intelligence community) offer avenues as well as protection from reprisal for employees to report government wrongdoing. Moreover President Obama has taken additional steps to provide reporting avenues and shield personnel in the intelligence community from retaliation for reporting fraud, waste, and abuse.[35] Neither the laws nor the directive, not surprisingly, contemplate that approved avenues for whistleblowers include unauthorized disclosures of classified information to the public.

225

Still others argue that leaks can and do benefit the public by opening up to public debate and challenge important information about proposed or ongoing operations about which the public should be made aware. Jack Goldsmith, a former Justice Department official, was quoted in *The Washington Post*, saying, "Leaks can serve a really important role . . . in helping to correct government malfeasance, to encourage government to be careful about what it does in secret and to preserve democratic processes."[36]

The public, however, is not just the American people, but includes foreign powers, criminals, and, terrorists, and others who think less about the public good in America than might the leaker. If classified information is leaked, the damage is done, limiting its dissemination will be impossible, and it could years for lost capabilities to be replaced. These are the competing national interests against which assertions that leaks benefit the public, and whether the public should be seen to include more than just the U.S. public, will be gauged.

G. Protecting Free Flow of Ideas as Well as Sources and Methods: Who Decides?

A difficulty in seeking an appropriate legislative solution is in attempting to impose criminal penalties for conduct so closely tied to what some have described as the free flow of ideas. This may be a core element of the policy and legal debates seeking to control or communicate information the government has classified. The strong language in *New York Times Co. v. Sullivan* supports this point, but opposing viewpoints ask what public interest would demand the need to reveal the existence of a lawful government operation that relies upon secrecy to be effective and protects national security interests. On one hand, discussion of what information a source has provided and the government's analysis, as opposed to the identity of the source, arguably can further public debate and accommodate the exercise of constitutional rights. On the other, disclosure of the content also can reveal or impede the sources and methods of its collection.

Another challenge to address is that of secrecy and classification decisions. Information leaked and discussed publicly may often appear innocuous to those outside government, and even to the official who is the leaker, but it could be damaging nevertheless either directly or indirectly; for example, if it identifies a source out of the knowledge that the source is not personally in danger, but neglects to consider that the source may have relatives in a foreign country placed at risk. If there are concerns of fraud, waste, abuse, or illegality, adherence to whistleblower laws and oversight avenues could offer an appropriate course for those who would seek to challenge government conduct or to instigate or facilitate meaningful debate.

Examples that show that the government's claims of national security damage are sometimes overblown certainly highlight the need to improve government practices, but the criticisms also help obscure an important question: Who should be allowed to make the disclosure decisions?

Should it be left to persons who steal or lawfully obtain the information but then reveal it in violation of their secrecy obligations? The current mechanism for protection of government secrets contemplates that officials who are elected or appointed to public office are given the legal framework for their classification and declassification decisions, which are subject, as appropriate, to subsequent judicial review. The lukewarm reaction to assertions of ongoing oversight by both Congress and the judiciary regarding the NSA programs, however, raises in the minds of some critics the question of whether the public trust in existing mechanisms is justified when matters of public interest are at stake.

When it is the press that publishes government secrets, it also is legitimate to ask who should make release decisions. Some have asserted that the press should not be investigated for simply "doing their jobs" when they report or publish leaked information. A *New York Times* article discussed *Times* editor Jill Abramson's handling of a government request not to publish classified information: "Holding a story entirely is a 'very rare thing,' [Abramson] said. 'The more usual situation is to withhold a level of detail, and those decisions are excruciating.' . . . Ms. Abramson said editors must apply a 'balancing test,' weighing newsworthiness and the public's right to know against a potential danger to an individual or harm to national security."[37]

That might sound like an appealing First Amendment argument, and proponents argue it has some degree of support, in principle, in the Privacy Protection Act of 1980.[38] That view, however, does not take into account existing statutes that suggest that publication may constitute a crime or address how the publisher might have obtained the information. In some cases, there might be an underlying crime (e.g., theft) as a basis for prosecution. In situations involving the "pattern or practice" of revealing the identities of covert intelligence agents, even press conduct could be contrary to statute.[39]

To combat terrorists, protect critical infrastructure, and serve other important national security interests, U.S. defense, diplomatic, law enforcement, and intelligence agencies must collect, analyze, and communicate information in a timely, meaningful fashion, and secretly. Unauthorized disclosures can hamper those efforts. Policymakers nevertheless have an obligation to keep the American people appropriately informed of information that affects their health, safety, and welfare. The press and others have First Amendment rights that certainly help ensure a free and open democratic society.

The central challenge is how to balance important competing interests— national security and free speech. Courts have indicated that there may be no right to reveal the movement of troops during wartime, or to shout "fire" in a crowded theater. When a whistleblower situation exists or the information held by the press is critical to determining the culpability of a government employee or other public interest, free speech arguments tend to be louder and evoke more sympathy. A more "complicated" challenge is how to clearly distinguish situations involving more direct press complicity in illegal conduct, particularly if a clear public interest is present. Attempting to hold leakers and the press accountable is not and should not be taken lightly, and in enacting leaks remedies to address actions of government officials and others who reveal classified information, the government should consider a number of options to protect information and deter leaks in a way that would not challenge First Amendment rights.

V. CONSIDERATIONS FOR THOSE REVIEWING LEAKS OPTIONS

The Willard and Ashcroft reports, among others, recognized the need for a comprehensive approach to dealing with leaks that would include actions to improve the government's internal processes and practices. Certainly the government must improve how it classifies and protects its information, and within the Department of Defense, intelligence community, and elsewhere in the executive branch efforts are underway. Defense, for example, has taken steps to: improve security and counterintelligence practices to protect information from inadvertent as well as intentional compromise; identify vulnerabilities; and train and better educate personnel to improve information classification and handling practices.

Additional steps could include reviewing and clarifying current policies, authorities, and practices; ensuring transparent processes for dealing with violations; enforcing accountability; making better use of analytic and investigative capabilities and technology to track information and deter leaks; ensuring greater consistency in handling information classification, security, and related practices across government; and, on the theory that unreasonable requirements can lead to ignoring them, facilitating compliance through an approach that is reasonable. Such measures will be an important precondition to enacting legislation.[40]

Supporters of leaks laws have not been effective in making the case that leaking classified information is a violation of trust as well as a crime that should invite penalties like other criminal conduct. As the government seeks to get its own house in order regarding the proper classification and protection of classified information as well as imposition of administrative sanctions, those who would consider legislative measures should not stand idle.

A. *Possible Leaks Framework for Discussion and Consideration*

The following is a framework for exploring options for comprehensive leaks legislation that could apply different degrees of criminal liability, civil liability, or both, as well as provide defenses to unauthorized disclosures in certain circumstances:

- Recognize that unauthorized disclosures by government employees, former employees, and others who promised to protect that information are a violation of their contractual obligations, the public's trust, and a violation of law.

- Consider whether it is a good idea to decriminalize certain leaks.
- Distinguish the crimes of leakers whose actions would be subject to leaks laws from those of spies subject to the espionage laws.
  - Spies would continue to be prosecuted under espionage laws, which might be left intact or modified for such purposes as well, for example, as to clarify the implications of spying for terrorist or other international organizations.
- Adopt a simple, per se approach (such as that vetoed by Clinton) to address the willful disclosure of classified information, by persons entrusted with that information, to persons not authorized to receive it, if the person has reason to believe that the information is classified.
  - There would be no need for the government to prove damage to national security when the information is clearly marked classified or the person has reason to know that the government considers it classified.
  - Unlike the espionage laws, such legislation would not require either an intent to harm the government or benefit a foreign country, nor be linked to "defense" information, as that category may be unduly narrow.
  - Consider, also, any need for legislation that has a focus on a particular category of sensitive information, such as certain technical data.
- Sanctions for violations by those with authorized access could include loss of position, debarment from future government work, loss of profits from publication, restitution to the extent of the government's financial loss, and criminal sanction.
- Enact legislation that would apply to disclosures by those not previously having authorized access to classified information. Similar to the statute governing disclosure of the identities of covert agents, such an approach could encompass persons who had authorized access to some classified information but exceeded their authority, as well as to others outside the government who engage in a "pattern and practice" of disclosing classified information.
  - This will require drafters to assess the need to distinguish who is and who is not a member of the press in light of First Amendment considerations—major "traditional" media versus bloggers versus those revealing secrets who seek protections under the guise of the press.
  - This also, however, will require an assessment of who is a journalist or otherwise may possess free speech rights protected by the First Amendment when technology allows anyone to publish to the Internet.
- Consider whether and if so under what circumstances it is more appropriate that leaks legislation should apply civil rather than criminal

liability for disclosure of classified information, with consideration to be given to enabling third-party actions by those whose privacy or other interests might have been affected by the theft of classified information about them.

- Explore a legislative option that applies to those—including the news media—who have received and revealed classified information with a willful, gross, or reckless disregard of the damage that the disclosures would cause, including financial costs of replacing expensive technology rendered less effective by the leaks.
  - Similar at least in theory to defamation actions, such an approach could bring civil rather than criminal liability.
  - With respect to the press and others whose disclosures do not derive from their access to classified documents but, instead, from legitimate investigative reporting unsupported by leakers, discussion should explore mitigating factors that would provide affirmative defenses and even absolute immunity in some situations.
    - It remains to be seen whether this *New York Times v. Sullivan* inspired option might be applied by analogy as a basis for recovery in a civil action for the publication of false information about classified government operations—for example, that agencies spy on Americans when they do not—or of classified information where the publication was made with knowledge or a reckless disregard of its falsity or with a knowledge or a reckless disregard of whether its disclosures about sophisticated and highly effective government programs would damage the national security.
  - Such an approach could require the government to show damage from the publication in order to satisfy free speech principles as well as ensure fundamental fairness.
- Enhance the ability of investigators to identify leakers and to obtain access to relevant information.
  - This could include clarification regarding efforts to obtain evidence from or about employees through the use of administrative subpoenas.
  - This also could ensure clarity about the authority to obtain evidence from the media about targets who might have leaked the information to them.
  - Legislation could establish criteria to govern when information gathered from the media may be not used against that media organization or person.
  - One approach could provide that the evidence gathered from the press in certain circumstances would be limited to use in administrative proceedings against the leaker; for example, where the goal is to find the leaker and stop further damage without the necessity for public trial.

- Strengthen the ability of the government to obtain the return of unpublished classified information from the leakers, the press, or others. This could include civil actions for the return of the stolen property.
- Enable third parties who might be the subject of the classified information to seek the return or destruction of information that violates their privacy or other interests.
- Consider whistleblower laws that offer avenues other than a public forum for all government employees and contractors, as well perhaps as for the media, with legitimate public interest motivation involving protected categories.
  - Identify appropriate whistleblower defenses for those who have gone public after their efforts have been improperly stymied despite their good-faith efforts to follow lawful procedures.
  - Identify sanctions for those who retaliate or hinder whistleblowers, but explore options for penalizing "bad faith" whistleblowers as well.
  - Address legitimate needs to share classified information with appropriate oversight committees of Congress as well as the courts.
  - Consider expansion of other oversight mechanisms.
- Address the parameters of current legal obligations including separation of powers between Congress and the executive branch.
- Take internal actions to address better prevent and deter leaks, in addition to tightening security measures and use of technology to protect information as well as identify leakers. Such steps could include exploring the actual impact of current policy constraints or authorities in attempting to identify leakers, conducting research into the motivations of leakers, compiling data regarding whether overclassification plays a significant role in leaking, and the like.
- Respect constitutional principles in preserving both national security and civil liberties, and do not be deterred by the enormity of the task.

B. Need for a National Debate and Consensus

One approach for addressing comprehensively and reconciling the legitimate public interests of both national security secrecy and free speech is through a series of public discourses, perhaps under the auspices of the American Bar Association, to address the adequacy of U.S. laws and policies and options for change. An ostensible reason for Clinton's veto of the leaks provision in 2000 was the absence of full and meaningful discussion and debate of its issues and merits. Such events could convene experts from across several relevant interest groups to discuss their perspectives. Events could consist of panels or focus groups from the intelligence, defense, foreign policy, and law enforcement agencies, congressional committees, current and former judges, the private sector, academia, civil liberties groups, the media, and foreign allied countries that face similar leaks problems. In addition, Congress should hold hearings to help determine an appropriate course that is the product of a transparent and deliberative process.

VI. CONCLUSION

Unauthorized disclosures of classified information are a violation of trust, a violation of law, and damaging to national security. The most recent massive and related, continuing disclosures have highlighted once again the need to consider a variety of ways to prevent and deter leaks. A framework for this should be comprehensive, and it should include both a thorough internal government review of its own practices and appropriate changes to existing laws, especially to ensure or clarify the ability to identify and sanction leakers who are not traditional spies.

Any efforts to affect the press that publishes classified information will face an uphill battle. This is both inevitable and appropriate, whether actions seek to obtain information from them or to hold the press—however defined—accountable when they publish damaging information knowingly or recklessly. As a nation, we value public discussion of government operations, policies, and practices, and we value freedom of speech as a matter of law and principle. We also value our national security and condemn actions that threaten that security.

These issues are complicated, and this chapter is intended to stimulate thinking and debate and not to profess a single solution. The notional framework presented should be seen as the beginning, not the end, of an exploration of both the need for and proper approach to considering leaks options.

NOTES

1. W. George Jameson, *Safeguarding National Security Information: Dealing with Unauthorized Disclosures of Classified Information*, Conference Reports, *National Security Law in a Changed World: The Twelfth Annual Review of the Field*, 25(1) Nat'l Sec. L. Rep. (ABA) (May 2003).

2. Testimony, Senate Select Comm. on Intelligence, *World Wide Threat Assessment*, Jan. 29, 2014.

3. *See* Kimberly Dozier & Stephen Braun, *U.S. Official: Snowden Leaks Lead to Pentagon Change*, Associated Press, Feb. 4, 2014.

4. At the same time, public calls for solutions have not been uniform. Unlike many of the debates surrounding the publication of information the government asserts is damaging to national interests, the recent disclosures about NSA surveillance activities have highlighted what some see as the benefits of such disclosures. Vocal elements from both the left and the right sides of the political spectrum have applauded the leaks as important contributions to greater transparency and public debate about the propriety of classified government programs that can affect civil liberties. Some have called for less classification of information and greater transparency into the operations of government, and

they have praised the leakers as heroic whistleblowers who are performing a public service by stimulating policy and legal debates about government operations they see as questionable at the least. Indeed, the release of previously classified documents about these programs and the president's decision to curtail certain programs tends to support at least some of these views. *See* Remarks by the President on Review of Signals Intelligence, Jan. 17, 2014.

5. *See* Charlie Savage, *Republicans Spar on Leaks and Surveillance, Underscoring Partisan Shake-Up*, N.Y. TIMES, Feb. 5, 2014.

6. A comprehensive discussion about motives of leaks can be found at GARY ROSS, WHO WATCHES THE WATCHMEN: THE CONFLICT BETWEEN NATIONAL SECURITY AND FREEDOM OF THE PRESS (2011).

7. *See generally* James B. Bruce, *Laws and Leaks of Classified Intelligence: The Consequences of Permissive Neglect*, 47(1) STUD. IN INTELLIGENCE 39 (Mar. 2003); James B. Bruce, *How Leaks of Classified Intelligence Help U.S. Adversaries: Implications for Laws and Secrecy, in* INTELLIGENCE AND THE NATIONAL SECURITY STRATEGIST (Roger George & Roger Kline eds., 2004).

8. Remarks by the President on Review of Signals Intelligence (Jan. 17, 2014).

9. Frank Snepp, *Edward Snowden's Weasel Ways*, L.A. TIMES.COM, Jan. 31, 2014.

10. COMM'N ON THE INTELLIGENCE CAPABILITIES OF THE UNITED STATES REGARDING WEAPONS OF MASS DESTRUCTION, REPORT TO THE PRESIDENT OF THE UNITED STATES 382 (2005). A more recent discussion has addressed the need to change the "culture of permissiveness" within government that is a logical consequence of this frustration identified by the Commission. Measures could include training and education, clarification of responsibilities and obligations, and in particular taking aggressive, transparent, and reasonable steps to hold those who violate their secrecy obligations appropriately accountable for their actions. JAMES B. BRUCE & W. GEORGE JAMESON, RAND NATIONAL DEFENSE RESEARCH INST., FIXING LEAKS: ASSESSING THE DEPARTMENT OF DEFENSE'S APPROACH TO PREVENTING AND DETERRING UNAUTHORIZED DISCLOSURES (2013).

11. Richard Cohen, *Let Snowden Come in from the Cold*, WASH. POST, Jan. 7, 2014.

12. George Washington to Elias Dayton, July 26, 1777.

13. In addition, section 408 of the FY 2010 Intelligence Authorization provided for the protection of certain records provided to the Office of the DNI from exempted operational files of other intelligence community elements (section 706, 50 U.S.C. § 432d).

14. Exec. Order 13,526, Classified National Security Information, Dec. 29, 2009.

15. Ken Dilanian, *Counterterrorism Leak Compromised an Informant, Sources Say*, L.A. TIMES, May 16, 2013.

16. United States v. Morison, 844 F.2d 1057 (4th Cir. 1988).

17. *Verizon Wireless Secretly Passed AP Reporter's Phone Records to Feds*, N.Y. TIMES, May 14, 2013.

18. *A Rare Peek into a Justice Department Leak Probe*, WASH. POST, May 19, 2013.

19. Kimberly Dozier, *Snowden Trial Could Be Awkward for US*, ASSOCIATED PRESS, Jan. 22, 2014.

20. David H. Laufman, *The Snowden Effect and NSA Snooping*, WASH. TIMES, Feb. 4, 2014.

21. David H. Laufman, *Prosecuting Leaks of Classified Information*, HUFFINGTONPOST.COM, June 12, 2012.

22. *See* Letter to Director of National Intelligence from Chairman Pete Hoekstra and Ranking Democrat Jane Harman (Aug. 15, 2005).

23. Scott Shane, *Inquiry of Leaks Is Casting Chill over Coverage*, N.Y. TIMES, Aug. 2, 2012.

24. *See* Memorandum of the Sec'y of Def., Deterring and Preventing Unauthorized Disclosures of Classified Information (Oct. 18, 2012).

25. Snepp v. United States, 444 U.S. 507 (1980) ("The government has a compelling interest in protecting both the secrecy of information important to our national security and the appearance of confidentiality so essential to the effective operation of our foreign intelligence service."); United States v. Marchetti, 466 F.2d 1309 (4th Cir. 1972).

26. *See* United States v. Jones, No. 1:12-cr-00127-001 (E.D. Va. Apr. 18, 2012).

27. David E. Pozen, The Leaky Leviathan: Why the Government Condemns and Condones Unlawful Disclosures of Information (Columbia Law Sch.: Pub. Law & Legal Theory Research Paper No. 13-341, Mar. 12, 2013).

28. Near v. Minnesota, 283 U.S. 697 (1931).

29. Branzburg v. Hayes, 408 U.S. 665 (1972).

30. Zemel v. Rusk, 381 U.S. 1 (1964).

31. Zurcher v. Stanford Daily, 436 U.S. 547 (1978).

32. 724 F.3d 482 (4th Cir. 2013).

33. Sullivan quoting Roth v. United States, 354 U.S. 476, 484.

34. N.Y. Times Co. v. Sullivan, 376 U.S. 354, 265–92 (1964).

35. Presidential Policy Directive 19, Protecting Whistleblowers with Access to Classified Information, Oct. 12, 2012.

36. Leonard Downie, Jr., *Why We Don't Need Another Law against Intelligence Leaks*, WASHINGTON POST.COM, Dec. 6, 2012.

37. Margaret Sullivan, *A Missing Spy and the Right to Know,* N.Y. TIMES, Dec. 22, 2013, at SR12.

38. 42 U.S.C. § 2000aa.

39. *See* 50 U.S.C. § 42.

40. BRUCE & JAMESON, *supra* note 10.

The Consequences of Leaks: The Erosion of Security

13

Jill D. Rhodes

"Potentially the most massive and most damaging theft of intelligence information in our history."[1] These are the words that Director of National Intelligence James Clapper used to describe the impact of the compromise of more than 1.7 million classified files by former National Security Agency (NSA) contractor Edward Snowden. He was presenting the Worldwide Threat Assessment to the Senate Select Committee on Intelligence, where he declared that leaks such as those caused by Snowden, as well as cyberthreats, are of greater risk to the national security interests of the United States than terrorism.[2]

Much of the media is eager to print such intelligence leaks. On May 29, 2012, *The New York Times* revealed that President Barack Obama personally approves every drone strike on individuals and cited a list of 15 al-Qaeda suspects in Yemen with links to the United States, with descriptions of each individual.[3] On June 1, 2012, *The New York Times* also revealed that an alleged U.S. intelligence community secret program called Stuxnet attacked Iran's main nuclear enrichment facility, Natanz.[4] The story discussed details about a meeting in the White House Situation Room with the president, vice president, and director of the CIA. It also mentioned details of the program that it admitted were "highly classified"[5] and included the names of potential U.S. agencies and allies involved with the program. This information educates U.S. adversaries as much, if not more, than the general public, critics warn.

While the DNI in his Senate testimony described the damage caused by the Snowden compromise of more than 1.7 million files and the resulting leaks, there is no quantifiable way to assess the damage caused by leaks. This leaves room for significant debate as to whether the value brought by making this information public outweighs the risk and cost of protecting our security interests.

It is difficult to understand the impact of leaks because the issue is not just damage resulting from a leak, but also measuring the benefit of critical information remaining classified and secured. Unlike law enforcement, which focuses on the prosecution of incidents after they occur, intelligence collection and the secrecy surrounding it strives to prevent terrorist and related incidents. In addition, much intelligence collection is related to risks and potential future threats. There are limited ways to affirm that because a leak occurred, an incident also occurred. That said, as will be discussed, U.S. adversaries pay close attention to these leaks and respond accordingly by changing their tactics. While there's no assurance that an incident will occur, the threat is there and increases with additional leaks. As the well-known World War II phrase "loose lips sink ships" so aptly describes, one can only surmise what may have occurred had information been or not been exposed. Finally, due to the classified nature of much of the information collected, it is even more complicated, if not impossible, to discuss incidents that were thwarted.

Since the development of the intelligence services, there has been a struggle to balance the amount of information that should remain in a classified environment and that which should be provided to the public. There is a predictive expectation that is placed upon the intelligence community, or IC, by the public that it will keep the public safe. This is complicated with the expectation that the information gleaned through intelligence collection should also be subject to oversight by the public or its representatives. Under the current American system of governance, this balance is met legally through hearings with congressional committees (including classified hearings), as well as separate executive branch and judiciary oversight. Yet this tension remains and is only accentuated by leaks. There may be questions as to the type and amount of information that is identified as classified and its classification level; these are questions for open discussion through lawful means.

In the end, the discussion proves valuable to the U.S. democracy but does not justify leaks. While some short-term damage may be assessed from leaks, such as exposure of methods and sources, names of assets, and strategies, long-term damage about what type of information is no longer available because of leaks is much more difficult to ascertain. Adversaries may change their modus operandi due to leaked information, including stopping methods or tactics they previously used because a leak exposed the U.S. government knowledge of the methods. This result directly impacts the expectation that the U.S. intelligence community will be able to thwart future threats and protect national security interests.

This chapter will assess the damage caused by leaks. It begins with a basic understanding of why it is critical to collect intelligence in a classified manner, and to what extent our adversaries will go to steal that information. It then takes an historical perspective, discussing the World War II Ultra program and potential consequences had that crucial signals intelligence, or SIGINT, program been leaked. The chapter then turns to current affairs, damages caused by leaks brought about by Private First Class Bradley (now Chelsea) Manning and WikiLeaks, as well as leaks by Snowden. Finally, it will touch on the role of the media in this process, and specifically how the media might assess value versus detriment with potential leaks. Leaks have often led to strong debates; from Watergate to the Church and Pike Commissions, and currently the extensive debate that has come out of the Snowden leaks. In the end, though, leaks such as those brought about by Snowden have created more of a threat and harm to U.S. national security than a benefit. U.S. adversaries are leveraging this divulged information, using it to identify U.S. vulnerabilities and change their own behavior.

I. WHY COLLECT INTELLIGENCE?

Perhaps the second oldest profession, spying has been a means for nations to understand the intentions of others in the world around them in order to protect themselves. During the American Revolution, George Washington, along with others such as Benjamin Franklin and John Jay, ran networks of agents and double agents, leveraged sabotage operations and used codes to defeat British troops. Understanding British intentions and then countering them critically helped the United States became independent.

Intelligence collection has been and continues to be critical not only for offensive purposes, that is, for understanding the intentions and desires of the world around us, but also to counteract and defend against those attempting to harm U.S. national interests. While the end of the Cold War eased some of the global tensions, it did not remove all barriers between the United States and its potential nation state adversaries, such as Russia and China, as the recent conflict in Crimea amply demonstrates. In its 2011 Unclassified Report to Congress, the National Counterintelligence Executive stated that Russian intelligence services continue to use a range of activities to conduct economic espionage, including economic information and technology from U.S. targets.[6]

The report also cited Chinese actors as the world's most active and persistent perpetrators of economic espionage.[7] In fact, the Justice Department on May 19, 2014, announced the indictment of five members of the Chinese People's Liberation Army for allegedly hacking into the networks of several major U.S. companies, including United States Steel Corporation. It was a largely symbolic move because China is unlikely to turn over those indicted.

In 2013, Mandiant, a leading cyber security firm, released its intelligence report, *APT1: Exposing China's Cyber Espionage Units*, which established a direct link between the Chinese government and cyber and economic espionage.

"APT1 is a single organization of operators that has conducted a cyber espionage campaign against a broad range of victims since at least 2006. . . . It is one of the most prolific cyber espionage groups in terms of the sheer quantity of information stolen."[8] The report said that amount of information stolen by this Chinese government-sanctioned organization totals close to 120 terabytes of data from more than 20 industries. Of the 141 APT1 victims Mandiant assessed, 87 percent of them are headquartered in countries where English is the native language.[9]

Aside from state actors, the United States is continuously threatened by non-state actors. From the 1998 bombings of embassies in Africa, to the September 11, 2001, terrorist attack on the United States, to more recent efforts to attack the United States within its borders like the Boston Marathon bombing, nonstate actors continue to rise as an even greater threat to national security interests. The director of national intelligence's threat assessment described above declared that terrorist organizations are seeking ways to develop offensive cyber capabilities. They continue to use cyberspace for propaganda and influence operations, financial activities, and personnel recruitment.[10] Clapper also identified homegrown violent extremists and al-Qaeda in the Arabian Peninsula as two groups eager to attack the United States and threaten our national security interests.[11]

Intelligence collection is critical for securing the nation against these threats. When leaks occur, the threats only increase. In a 2006 *New York Times* op-ed piece, then-CIA Director Porter Goss wrote about national security leaks, specifically related to the search for Osama bin Laden:

> I noticed renewed debate in the news media over press reports in 1998 that Osama bin Laden's satellite phone was being tracked by United States intelligence officials. In the recent debate, it was taken for granted that the original reports did not hurt our national security efforts, and any suggestions that they did cause damage were dismissed as urban myth. But the reality is that the revelation of the phone tracking was, without question, one of the most egregious examples of an unauthorized criminal disclosure of classified national defense information in recent years. It served no public interest. Ultimately, the bin Laden phone went silent.[12]

Goss also spoke about the detrimental effect that leaks had on relations with foreign intelligence counterparts. He commented that close counterparts have openly informed the CIA that they are "reconsidering" their participation in key antiterrorism ventures for fear that "exposure of their cooperation could subject their citizens to terrorist retaliation."[13]

The threat today is real. The U.S. must continue to collect information through clandestine means in order to understand and respond to these types of threats. Every leak reduces the ability to do this. As a result, the potential benefit of leaks must always be weighed against the vulnerability created by the exposure.

II. ULTRA—WHAT IF IT HAD BEEN LEAKED?

It would be easy to focus on current events in discussing the effect of leaks on national security. But to better understand how leaks can bring risk to the national security interest of the United States, perhaps it would be easier to look at a historical situation in which, had a leak occurred, the damage created would likely have changed the course of history. Prior to World War II, the Poles developed a deciphering technique that decrypted high-level codes sent by the Germans to their global network. The tool essentially created a copy of the German encryption technique that then allowed the Poles to read SIGINT sent among the Germans. The German encryption technology was called Enigma. As the Germans hardened their technology, the Poles had difficulty decrypting new codes and in 1939, the Poles provided their decryption technology to the British, who improved upon it and began to crack German codes in April 1940.

The British gave the technology the name Ultra because the methods and information garnered from it were more highly classified than any in the past. The British then shared Ultra with their American counterparts. During World War II, Ultra intercepted and later decoded radio and cable messages sent by the Nazis to their clandestine networks in Europe and South America.[14] Ultra was used to pinpoint and neutralize Nazi spy rings and intelligence activities in the Western Hemisphere. It led to the elimination of Nazi spy rings in Argentina and other countries throughout the region.[15]

British Prime Minister Winston Churchill was a significant advocate for the use of Ultra and supported the establishment of a unit of more than 10,000 people to work on deciphering German SIGINT.[16] An exhibit in 2003 on "Secret War" at the Imperial War Museum in London quoted Churchill telling King George VI: "It was thanks to Ultra that we won the war."[17] President Dwight D. Eisenhower called the use of Ultra "decisive" in leading to victory in WWII.[18] In fact, when the U505 German submarine, including two Enigma machines, was captured on June 5, 1944, the United States did not inform the International Red Cross about its prisoners of war as was required.[19] This ensured that the Germans did not learn about the exposure of the U505, its crew, and the Enigma machines. Had the Germans learned about the capture of the U505, they certainly would have modified the Enigma and initiated alternative means of communicating.

It is easy to see the harm that would have been caused had the Germans learned from a leak that the British had this capability to decrypt their communications. Sir Harry Hinsley, official historian of British Intelligence in World War II, stated that Ultra "shortened the war by not less than two years and probably by four years—that is the war in the Atlantic, the Mediterranean and Europe."[20] According to this assessment, had the program either not existed, or had it been compromised, the war would have continued for additional years and the Nazis might even have prevailed.

III. THE U.S. INTELLIGENCE COMMUNITY

To understand how leaks affect national security, it is useful to understand the structure and oversight of the U.S. intelligence community. Media articles stemming from leaks often portray the U.S. government as Big Brother, watching over its citizens and resident aliens. While there is understandably a concern about how much power a government may have over its citizenry, it is important to understand the depth of the commitment of the IC to protect U.S. national security to get a greater understanding of the detriment of leaks.

The U.S. intelligence community consists of 16 agencies and the Office of the Director of National Intelligence. Some of these agencies are components of larger departments, such as the Federal Bureau of Investigation within the Department of Justice or the State Department's Bureau of Intelligence and Research. These agencies are made up of committed individuals, many of whom have dedicated their lives to support the enhanced national security of the United States. There are thousands of people who work within the community. They come from a variety of backgrounds, socioeconomic classes, races, religions, and political affiliations. Most, if not all, members of the community hold some level of security clearance, many at the Top Secret level and others with a required polygraph examination to detect deception and commitment to the United States.

These public employees are sworn to secrecy. While the press can easily write about the intelligence community and publish leaked information, members of the IC cannot respond. Except for a few of the most senior leaders, intelligence employees are forbidden from discussing their business with the press. This is especially limiting when the media either accidentally or intentionally misrepresents leaked intelligence information or does not place it in the correct context. Even more limiting, while classified information may be published in the media, under Executive Order 13,256, it remains classified, despite its disclosure. That means that anyone who comments on disclosures without going through proper channels would be subject to reprimand for discussing classified information in public. As a result, the IC essentially has its hands tied when it comes to responding to leaks and other types of disclosures.

Many have argued that leaks are necessary to ensure the public has an ability to learn about the workings of the IC. The premise of this argument is that the government is not representative of the public. All three branches of government provide significant oversight over the IC. Congress is given regular briefings about the work of intelligence agencies. Both the House of Representatives and the Senate have Select Committees on Intelligence, which are regularly briefed in classified hearings. The House and Senate Appropriations Committees provide funding for the IC, and therefore have access to the details of their budgets. Those agencies that work with the Department of Defense are also subject to hearings before the Senate and House Armed Services Committees as well as other committees providing oversight of the defense budget. In addition, intelligence officials brief dozens of other committees on their activities.

With respect to the courts, the IC is required to obtain approval from the Foreign Intelligence Surveillance Court (FISC) for specific kinds of foreign intelligence activities, including much electronic surveillance. There are significant processes required before the FISC will review any request from the intelligence community such as a sign-off on the request by the attorney general, deputy attorney general, and/or the assistant attorney general for national security, depending upon the request. In each case, there is a regulatory process that must be followed.

Finally, the executive branch also provides oversight. The National Security Council sets the strategic priorities for the intelligence agencies. Agency inspectors general and agency privacy officers are responsible for internal oversight. The president receives daily briefings on national security and intelligence matters and must authorize any covert action that is taken by the intelligence community.

When leaks related to the intelligence occur, the public should understand that many of their publicly elected representatives have known about whatever is being leaked, although there have been exceptions. But the programs and action taken have not occurred in a vacuum.

The desire of the media to expose the workings of the secret national security world, combined with the inability of the intelligence community to speak, can lead to very skewed portrayals of the information that is leaked and even more damage. Hollywood's portrayal of intelligence workers through characters like James Bond or Jason Bourne tends to obscure the true nature of its work.

IV. LEAKS IN THE NEWS

With that background we can now turn to an examination of two recent leaks of classified information and the damage potentially caused as a result. With each of these, damage can only be surmised. In both cases, senior government officials have stated publicly that the damage was significant to U.S. security and government interests.

As a preliminary matter, it bears noting that WikiLeaks and the Snowden leaks are categorically different from the important historical exposures that led to the Church and Pike Commissions and significant reforms that stemmed from each of these. The leaks leading to those commissions focused specifically on illegal collection against U.S. citizens. As described below, the leaks from Manning predominantly concerned collection sources and methods of a global focus, with a minority of the classified information stolen linked back to U.S. persons, and activities that were authorized pursuant to law. Snowden's leaks also had a large foreign focus although they also disclosed NSA programs that collected metadata on millions of Americans.

V. WIKILEAKS

On August 20, 2013, a military judge sentenced Manning to 35 years in prison for the theft of hundreds of thousands of files from the Department of Defense and State Department.[21] He was found guilty under the Espionage Act for copying and disseminating classified military field reports, State Department cables, and assessments of detainees held at Guantanamo Bay, Cuba. In his statement to the public about why he leaked the material, Manning said that he "started to question the morality" of U.S. policy.[22]

Manning had been assigned to an Army intelligence unit in Iraq in 2009. In 2010 he began to leak classified documents to the nongovernmental organization WikiLeaks and its founder, Julian Assange. The materials leaked included videos of a 2007 Baghdad airstrike, more than 250,000 classified and unclassified State Department cables, and approximately 500,000 Army reports related to the wars in Iraq and Afghanistan. The material was published by WikiLeaks or its media partners between April and November 2010. At the time, this series of leaks was considered the largest theft of classified information in U.S. history.

While the Manning's defense argued that no harm was actually caused by Manning's release of classified documents, the documents contained information such as operations conducted by CIA and high-level discussions between U.S. diplomats and their international counterparts.[23] In addition, then Chairman of the Joint Chiefs of Staff Admiral Michael Mullen warned about the threat to Afghan assets who were providing information to the United States and were named in the WikiLeaks documents. No one may know the depth of the harm caused by Manning, or if an asset was killed as a result of being identified by WikiLeaks. What is apparent is that adversaries of the United States were given the opportunity to review all of these materials and learn about the thinking, sources, and methods used by the United States when conducting its military and political affairs.

The leaks also had a chilling effect on the relationship of the United States with its foreign counterparts. In diplomatic relations, sensitive information is often shared between allies and liaison partners with an understanding that the information will remain closely held. When these WikiLeaks exposures occurred, that trust was broken. As a result, the ability of U.S. diplomats to conduct general business and enter into strong relations that would lead to foreign policy decisions was hindered.[24] Goss, the former CIA director, said one could surmise that future potential assets and sources will think twice if collaborating with the United States as it could lead to harm to themselves and/or their families.[25]

VI. SNOWDEN

In June 2013, Glenn Greenwald of *The Guardian* and Barton Gellman of *The Washington Post* began to publish classified documents and information that Snowden had taken while a contractor working at NSA. Snowden was in Hong Kong when he started to release information about how the NSA collects information about U.S. persons and foreigners. Over the course of the following months, even during the writing of this chapter, the media has continued to publish articles about how the government is spying on people's phone calls, e-mails, and gathering other similar information.[26]

The outcry from these revelations has led to extensive debate about the role and oversight of the intelligence community, signals collection in particular, as well as the FISC. Obama appointed a Review Group on Intelligence and Communications Technologies to look at intelligence collection practices. The Review Group issued a report with significant recommendations, many of which are still under review. On January 17, 2014, Obama signed Presidential Policy Directive 28 on Signal Intelligence Collection in which he required modifications to the way intelligence is collected and stored. This directive addressed some of the revelations that were leaked by Snowden and ultimately, will provide additional oversight of intelligence practices. In addition, these leaks also led to revelations and then changes with respect to how the U.S. government collects information on its own citizens.

While these outcomes are ultimately positive, the number of press articles written about how the government is monitoring U.S. and foreign e-mails and phone calls dwarfs the number of articles about the potential damage that these leaks have caused. There have been a few insights into the damage, which then needs to be weighed against the benefits achieved through these leaks.

As mentioned above, at a Senate committee hearing Clapper called the security breaches caused by Snowden "potentially the most massive and most damaging theft of intelligence information in our history." When asked to elaborate on this damage, Senator Dianne Feinstein of California, who is chairwoman of the Senate Select Committee on Intelligence, stopped the questioning, stating that any additional discussion would need to be held in a classified environment.[27]

It has been estimated by government officials that of the more than 1.7 million files compromised, less than 10 percent related to domestic matters. More than 90 percent of the files were not. At least some of that 90 percent included information about sources of intelligence and intelligence collection methods, as well as names of assets, names of intelligence community personnel, and other such information.[28]

At the same hearing in which Clapper testified, General Michael Flynn, director of the Defense Intelligence Agency, commented that Snowden took details of how the military tracks terrorists, of enemies' vulnerabilities, and of American defenses against improvised explosive devices.[29]

Snowden stole classified documents while being employed in positions over several years that allowed him access to sensitive information. He systematically removed files, and then flew to Hong Kong with these files, where he was extensively questioned by the Chinese. He then was granted temporary asylum in Russia and provided a lawyer who works closely with Russian President Vladimir Putin.

Recall that two of the greatest economic espionage and cyberthreats to the United States come from China and Russia.[30] Snowden has spent time with the intelligence services of both of these nations. While he has declared that he did not bring any of these files to Russia, it is quite easy to place files in a cloud environment and retrieve them from any location in the world. While less than 10 percent of the files were actually about domestic collection matters, one can assume that the Russians and Chinese intelligence services have had access to all of this information including U.S. cyber collection methodology, priorities, and potentially sources.

On February 7, 2014, the Associated Press (AP) published an article about "unintentional" disclosures in the media while printing information leaked by Snowden.[31] It cites at least six intelligence officers who have been named publicly. "On one occasion, the *Guardian* newspaper published an NSA document that appeared to identify an American intelligence target living abroad. Before the newspaper could fix its mistake, a curious software engineer, Ron Garret of Emerald Hills, Calif., tried to contact the man at his office. 'I figured someone ought to give him the heads up,' Garret told the Associated Press."[32] Glenn Greenwald, one of the two reporters who wrote about the information Snowden provided them, commented that these disclosures were minor errors made by technical staff and quickly corrected.[33] That said, in its research for the article, AP was able to find the addresses of all six intelligence community employees as well as other information about them and their families. One has to question the true value to the public and/or the media in naming civil servants in the name of transparency. This type of disclosure places the lives of these individuals and their families at risk.

As part of the preparation for the article, AP counted at least eight "accidental disclosures" due to "carelessness by some television broadcasters, sloppy digital redactions applied to copies of documents and, in the Guardian's case, an incomplete understanding of what information might be revealing."[34] One of the exposures included the fact that a Muslim terrorist group had a preference for a certain type of smartphone. Given this, there is a strong likelihood that these cellphones are no longer in use, removing that access to intelligence collection.

These disclosures seem to touch the surface of the type of information that Snowden collected. According to official of the Department of Defense, as well as high-level officials of U.S. allies, the Snowden theft and leaks have had significant impact on their ability to collect intelligence and protect their nations. As Joel Brenner so aptly describes in his recent article about the impact of the Snowden leaks:

If you tell the Russians that NSA collects their diplomatic communications, for example, they conclude immediately NSA has either stolen or broken their codes. That kind of operation can take ten years to pull off. It probably took the Russians twenty minutes to shut it down.[35]

While there is no question that public debate about the role and oversight of the intelligence community is important in a democratic society, it is also critical to understand the cost.

VII. CONCLUSION

The media has an ability to effectively inform the American public while keeping the nation safe. Too often, discussions between the media and representatives of the intelligence community (or other members of the executive branch) are so adversarial that a clear view and neutral position are hard for a reader to obtain. In the case of the Snowden leaks, for example, there have been thousands of articles discussing the documents and information exposed by Snowden. This number dwarfs the amount and types of media articles written about the damage caused by these leaks. In a podcast interview, the Office of the Director of National Intelligence general counsel, Robert Litt, discussed the fact that U.S. adversaries are reading the information from the Snowden leaks and learning how the IC is potentially tracking their communications. He commented that, due to the leaks and potential changes of those adversaries' means of communication, "we don't know what communications we are not seeing anymore and we don't know what the impact is going to be due to the failure to see those communications."[36]

There is no quantifiable means to measure the results of a leak. Ultimately, it would be the cost of the exposure, combined with the loss of the benefit from the information, had it not been exposed. This requires a degree of prediction and assessment of counterfactual situations (i.e., what would have happened without the leak), which make an accurate assessment difficult. Without such an assessment, one must refer to examples and consequences that can lead to a better understanding of the risk and threat caused by leaks such as those described herein.

The intelligence community's job of protecting the nation requires that much of its activities be conducted in secret. The role of the media in holding the government accountable for its action is critical in a democratic society, but the media must always weigh "exposing the government" against an assessment of the impact of that disclosure on public safety and security. The media bears a public trust and must be conscious of that role in determining whether or not to compromise classified material.

NOTES

1. Nick Simeone, *Clapper: Snowden Caused "Massive, Historic" Security Damage,* Am. Forces Press Serv., Jan. 29, 2014, http://www.defense.gov/news/newsarticle.aspx?id=121564.

2. *Id.*

3. Jo Becker & Scott Shane, *Secret Kill List Proves a Test for Obama's Principles and Will,* N.Y. Times, May 29, 2012, http://www.nytimes.com/2012/05/29/world/obamas-leadership-in-war-on-al-qaeda.html.

4. David E. Sanger, *Obama Order Sped Up Wave of Cyberattacks against Iran,* N.Y. Times, June 1, 2012, http://www.nytimes.com/2012/06/01/world/middleeast /obama-ordered-wave-of-cyberattacks-against-iran.html.

5. *Id.*

6. Office of the Nat'l Counterintelligence Exec., Foreign Spies Stealing US Economic Secrets in Cyberspace: Report to Congress on Foreign Economic Collection and Industrial Espionage 2009–2011 (Oct. 2011), http://www.ncix.gov/publications/reports/fecie_all /Foreign_Economic_Collection_2011.pdf.

7. *Id.*

8. Mandiant, APT1: Exposing One of China's Cyber Espionage Units (2013). http://intelreport .mandiant.com/Mandiant_APT1_Report.pdf.

9. *Id.*

10. *Statement for the Record, U.S. Intelligence Community, Worldwide Threat Assessment,* Jan. 29, 2014, at 2, http://www.dni.gov/files/documents/Intelligence%20Reports/2014%20WWTA%20%20 SFR_SSCI_29_Jan.pdf.

11. *Id.* at 4.

12. Porter Goss, Op-Ed Contributor, *Loose Lips Sink Spies,* N.Y. Times, Feb. 10, 2006, https://www .cia.gov/news-information/press-releases-statements/press-release-archive-2006/LooseLipsSinkSpies .pdf.

13. *Id.*

14. Fed. Bureau of Investigation, A Byte Out of History: A Most Helpful Ostrich: Using Ultra Intelligence in World War II, Oct. 6, 2011, http://www.fbi.gov/news/stories/2011/october/intelligence _100611/intelligence_100611 [hereinafter A Most Helpful Ostrich].

15. *Id.*

16. Harold C. Deutsch, *The Influence of Ultra on World War II,* 8(4) Parameters 7 (1978).

17. *See* Ultra, http://www.history.co.uk/study-topics/history-of-ww2/code-breaking.

18. *See* A Most Helpful Ostrich, *supra* note 14.

19. These prisoners were released after the end of the war.

20. Sir Harry Hensley, The Influence of ULTRA in the Second World War, lecture at Univ. of Portsmouth, UK, Nov. 26, 1996, http://www.cdpa.co.uk/UoP/HoC/Lectures/HoC_08e.PDF.

21. Julie Tate, *Judge Sentences Bradley Manning to 35 Years,* Wash. Post, Aug. 21, 2013, http:// www.washingtonpost.com/world/national-security/judge-to-sentence-bradley-manning-today/2013/08 /20/85bee184-09d0-11e3-b87c-476db8ac34cd_story.html.

22. *Id.*

23. *See* Spencer Ackerman, *WikiLeaks Publishes Mundane CIA Thought Experiment,* Wired, Aug. 25, 2010, http://www.wired.com/dangerroom/2010/08/wikileaks-publishes-mundane-cia-thought -experiment/.

24. *See* Tom Ramstack, *WikiLeaks Case Harms U.S. Diplomacy, Manning Sentencing Told,* Reuters, Aug. 5, 2013, http://www.reuters.com/article/2013/08/05/us-usa-wikileaks-manning-id USBRE97403K20130805.

25. *See* Goss, *supra* note 12.

26. While some of the information may be true, at least an equal amount has been misstated, uninformed, and inadequately portrayed.

27. *See* Simeone, *supra* note 1.

28. Kimberly Dozier & Stephen Braun, *US Official: Snowden Leaks Lead to Pentagon Change*, ASSOCIATED PRESS, Feb. 4, 2014, http://news.yahoo.com/us-official-snowden-leaks-lead-pentagon -change-162958727.html.

29. *Id.*

30. *See supra* section I, Why Collect Intelligence?

31. Ralph Satter, *Media Sometimes Try, Fail to Keep NSA's Secrets*, ASSOCIATED PRESS, Feb. 7, 2014, http://in.finance.yahoo.com/news/media-sometimes-try-fail-keep-133516279.html.

32. *Id.*

33. *Id.*

34. *Id.*

35. Joel Brenner, *N.S.A. Not So Secret Anymore*, LAWFARE, Dec. 3, 2013, http://www.lawfareblog .com/2013/12/n-s-a-not-so-secret-anymore/.

36. Benjamin Wittes, *Lawfare Podcast Episode #60: Wherein We Talk to DNI General Counsel Robert Litt,* Feb. 1, 2014, http://www.lawfareblog.com/2014/02/lawfare-podcast-episode-60-wherein -we-talk-to-dni-general-counsel-robert-litt/.

The Consequences of Leaks: Greater Transparency

14

Sophia Cope

I. EXCESSIVE GOVERNMENT SECRECY IS ANTITHETICAL TO A FREE AND DEMOCRATIC SOCIETY

Edward Snowden, the National Security Agency (NSA) contractor who divulged the agency's mass domestic surveillance operations, the scope of which was previously unknown and is arguably beyond the bounds of statutory and constitutional law, told *The Washington Post*, "All I wanted was for the public to be able to have a say in how they are governed."[1] The press plays a central role in informing citizens so they can be engaged participants in the grand experiment that is American self-government. As the Snowden affair shows, sometimes the role of the press in informing citizens involves publishing information that those in government (or private institutions) want to keep secret.

Like it or not, reporting based on unauthorized disclosures or "leaked" information is an important component of American democracy. Journalists act as a safety valve for democracy when information citizens arguably *should* know cannot become public any other way. While the Constitution creates a system of checks and balances between the three branches of government, the press as the "Fourth Estate" serves as an external check on government power. As Bart Gellman, one of the reporters who broke the NSA story, said, "The biggest stakes . . . have to do with, ultimately, the balance of power between government and its citizens."[2]

Excessive government secrecy can lead to abuses of government power and a subsequent loss of liberty or even loss of life. Patrick Henry, whose *Common Sense* was widely read at the time of the American Revolution, understood this when he said in 1788, "The liberties of a people never were, nor ever will be, secure, when the transactions of their rulers may be concealed from them. The most iniquitous plots may be carried on against their liberty and happiness."[3]

In the quintessential leak case—the 1971 Pentagon Papers case—the Supreme Court ruled that *The New York Times* and *The Washington Post* could not, consistent with the First Amendment, be enjoined from publishing the classified documents. In support of the ruling, Justice Hugo Black wrote, "The press was protected so that it could bare the secrets of government and inform the people. Only a free and unrestrained press can effectively expose deception in government."[4]

Black believed that "far from deserving condemnation for their courageous reporting, *The New York Times*, *The Washington Post*, and other newspapers should be commended for serving the purpose that the Founding Fathers saw so clearly. In revealing the workings of government that led to the Vietnam war, the newspapers nobly did precisely that which the Founders hoped and trusted they would do."[5]

While reporting based on leaks can lead to a better-informed citizenry, how the government responds to the issue of leaks can advance the cause of transparency—and thus democracy—or hold it back.

II. THE GOVERNMENT SHOULD ENGAGE MORE OFTEN WITH THE PUBLIC AND THE PRESS

Although a proponent of government transparency, Patrick Henry understood that there could be value in government secrecy. He said, "I am not an advocate for divulging indiscriminately all the operations of government."[6] He understood the inherent tension between the need for occasional government secrecy and the need for an informed citizenry that flows from government transparency. There are actions the government can take to promote transparency and an informed citizenry while preempting leaks or minimizing the harm to national security that might flow from unauthorized disclosures of government information.

A. Some Leaks to the News Media Can Be Preempted by Proactive Disclosures

President Barack Obama has called his "the most transparent administration in history."[7] On his first day in office, Obama issued a transparency and open government memo to all department and agency heads, declaring his adminis-tration's commitment "to creating an unprecedented level of openness in Gov-ernment."[8] The memo stated, "Government should be transparent. Transparency promotes accountability and provides information for citizens about what their Government is doing. . . . My Administration will take appropriate action, consis-tent with law and policy, to disclose information rapidly in forms that the public can readily find and use."[9]

After the Snowden leaks, Obama said, "I welcome this debate and I think it's healthy for our democracy."[10] However, the president's statement, while consis-tent with his administration's guiding principle of transparency, seemed inconsis-tent with his administration's actions. Obama and his subordinates did not intend to disclose what the NSA had been doing domestically (i.e., collecting telephone metadata in bulk and searching the communications content of Americans without a warrant),[11] even as other political leaders like Senator Ron Wyden of Oregon, a Democratic member of the Senate Select Committee on Intelligence, repeatedly warned in cryptic terms (so as to avoid disclosing classified information), "I want to deliver a warning this afternoon: When the American people find out how their government has secretly interpreted the Patriot Act, they will be stunned and they will be angry."[12]

Wyden said three years later on NBC's *Meet the Press* when asked about Snowden, "The bottom line is this is a debate that shouldn't have started that way. It should have been started with the intelligence leadership."[13] Critics of the Obama administration argue that had the president and others in the executive branch initially come to the American people, explained their goals and chal-lenges in combatting terrorism at home and abroad, and set forth their program proposals and where they thought they lacked legal authority, perhaps Snowden would not have been in a place to leak information about the NSA's vast domestic surveillance programs—perhaps because they would not have existed or because the American public already would have known about them.

Ironically, the Snowden leaks have spurred greater government transpar-ency. A positive consequence of what Snowden did, other than forcing an over-due debate about domestic surveillance post-9/11, is that Director of National Intelligence James Clapper declassified scores of intelligence documents.[14] An intelligence community that has historically eschewed transparency and engaging with the public and the press has determined, due to public pressure following the Snowden leaks, that disclosing some intelligence information might be beneficial.

As Siobhan Gorman, a *Wall Street Journal* reporter who has long covered the NSA, said in reference to the intelligence agencies, "You can't operate in this country in complete secrecy forever and still maintain your legitimacy."[15] Clapper seemed to understand this fact when he testified before the Senate Select Commit-tee on Intelligence in January 2014: "The major takeaway for us, certainly for me, from the past several months is that we must lean in the direction of transparency, wherever and whenever we can."[16]

Two months later, Clapper issued a new "media contacts" policy with the ostensible purpose of putting his testimony into action.[17] In the policy, Clapper asserted that the intelligence community "is committed to sharing information responsibly with the public via the media to further government openness and transparency and to build public understanding of the [intelligence community] and its programs, consistent with the protection of intelligence sources and methods."[18] Clapper also wrote that "appropriate . . . engagement with the media is encouraged."[19]

However, the substance of the policy seems to contradict the stated goal. The policy prohibits intelligence community employees from talking to the media about both classified and unclassified "intelligence-related information, including intelligence sources, methods, activities, and judgments" without official authorization or designation.[20] Members of the intelligence community must also report any "unplanned or unintentional contact with the media on covered matters."[21] The news media are concerned that the policy, by incorporating unclassified information and "activities" and "judgments," is exceedingly broad.[22] It goes beyond Clapper's oft-stated goal of preventing leaks of *classified* information and beyond the policy's own stated focus on protecting intelligence sources and methods.

Members of the news media fear that the policy will be implemented strictly, by infrequently authorizing media contact or by limiting such authorization to the agency heads or public affairs officers; rather than implemented liberally, by frequently authorizing subject-matter experts to speak to journalists. If implemented strictly, journalists are concerned that intelligence information that is of vital public interest—including unclassified information about the "activities" and "judgments" of U.S. intelligence officials—will be more difficult to obtain. There will be less understanding among the public, potentially affecting the intelligence community's legitimacy, and policy debates about national security and foreign affairs will be less informed.

How Clapper implements the policy is critical, as the written words alone may create a climate of fear and a significant chilling effect among intelligence agency employees, in contravention of his stated intention of "leaning in the direction of transparency." Someone who violates the policy—for example, by discussing unclassified information with a journalist without prior authorization or by neglecting to report an unplanned conversation with a journalist—could face revocation of his or her security clearance or termination of employment.

The Office of the Director of National Intelligence issued a second policy that prohibits current and former members of the intelligence community (both employees and contractors) from, among other things, citing to leaked information.[23] The fear is that they will "confirm the validity of an unauthorized disclosure."[24] The information need not be classified—it could just be an unauthorized disclosure of "sensitive" intelligence information. Prohibiting former members of the intelligence community from discussing information in the public domain (regardless of how it became public) seems like a constitutionally suspect prior restraint. At the very least, this policy will hamper the ability of former intelligence officials to provide valuable insight during national security and foreign affairs policy debates.

B. The Government Should Engage with the Press and the Press Should Act Responsibly

Even if the government does make strides in proactively disclosing more information to the American public, leaks to the news media will still occur and those in government must deal with this reality. Government officials must be more willing to engage with the press and, in return, the press must act responsibly when publishing government secrets.

In 2003, following a summit attended by top members of the news media and then-Attorney General John Ashcroft, the Aspen Institute published a seminal report with principles that were intended to "serve as important first steps on a path to resolving potential conflicts between journalism and the government in the post-9/11 world."[25] Those principles are

1. Journalists not only have the duty to serve the public interest by reporting and informing, but also the responsibility to consider the consequences of their reporting, including the potential that publication might directly damage the nation's security and the public safety.
2. Journalists have a responsibility to consider the government's position if it objects to publication or asks for a delay.
3. Journalists should give serious consideration to the risk of compromising ongoing investigations and sensitive operations.
4. Before news is reported, a responsible editor or news executive should know the bona fides (the knowledge, expertise, credibility, and interest) of critical confidential sources and be prepared to ascertain their identities.
5. Journalists have a duty to their audience to be transparent about agreements they make with the government and to reveal them when they report the news story itself.

Although some argue that the news media have made mistakes in national security reporting,[26] there are numerous examples of the press acting responsibly. When *The New York Times*, for example, reported on the Iraq and Afghanistan "war logs" leaked to the website WikiLeaks in 2010, Bill Keller, the newspaper's executive editor at the time, said afterward, "[W]e felt an enormous moral and ethical obligation to use the material responsibly."[27]

Keller further explained the paper's approach:

From the beginning, we agreed that in our articles and in any documents we published from the secret archive, we would excise material that could put lives at risk. Guided by reporters with extensive experience in the field, we redacted the names of ordinary citizens, local officials, activists, academics and others who had spoken to American soldiers or diplomats. We edited out any details that might reveal ongoing intelligence-gathering operations, military tactics or locations of material that could be used to fashion terrorist weapons.[28]

The press, however, cannot always act responsibly on its own. The government must also be willing to constructively engage with the news media.[29] Although evidence suggests that the two sides can work together, government officials often engage reluctantly. Later in 2010, for example, when *The New York Times* intended to publish articles based on State Department cables leaked to WikiLeaks, Keller explained that the paper had reached out to the White House before publication because, due to "the range of the material and the very nature of diplomacy, the embassy cables were bound to be more explosive than the War Logs."[30] According to Keller, three *New York Times* staffers "were invited to a windowless room at the State Department, where they encountered an unsmiling crowd. . . . The meeting was off the record, but it is fair to say the mood was tense." Relations eventually improved. As Keller explained:

Subsequent meetings, which soon gave way to daily conference calls, were more businesslike. Before each discussion, our Washington bureau sent over a batch of specific cables that we intended to use in the coming days. They were circulated to regional specialists, who funneled their reactions to a small group at State, who came to our daily conversations with a list of priorities and arguments to back them up. We relayed the government's concerns, and our own decisions regarding them, to the other news outlets.[31]

Another example of constructive engagement between the press and government is the 2005 article by *Washington Post* reporter Dana Priest in which she revealed a network of secret Central Intelligence Agency (CIA) prisons or "black sites" operating in "Thailand, Afghanistan and several democracies in Eastern Europe" as part of the extraordinary rendition program. Priest did not name the participating Eastern European countries and explained why in the story: "*The Washington Post* is not publishing the names of the Eastern European countries involved in the covert program, at the request of senior U.S. officials. They argued that the disclosure might disrupt counterterrorism efforts in those countries and elsewhere and could make them targets of possible terrorist retaliation."[32]

Bart Gellman also actively reaches out to government officials and willingly listens to their concerns before publishing his *Washington Post* stories on the Snowden leaks. "There are times when you have a sufficient relationship of trust, or when everyone realizes the stakes are high enough that you have to try to trust even if it's not all the way there, that they will tell you things that you don't know in order to explain why they hope you won't publish something that you do know. And those can be quite persuasive," he said.[33] While reporting on the NSA, Gellman said, he had conversations with government officials and agreed not to publish certain information based on the national security concerns they expressed.[34] After he won the Pulitzer Prize in 2014, Gellman further explained, "We consulted with the responsible officials on every story and held back operational details. But we were not prepared to withhold the secret policy decisions the government is making for us and the surveillance it's directing against us. The public gets to have a say on those things."[35]

But sometimes engagement can go awry when the government does not make its interest clear. In the case of an Associated Press (AP) article about how the CIA had foiled the second attempted underwear bombing of a U.S.-bound airliner, the AP reached out to the Obama administration before publication. "We held that story until the government assured us that the national security concerns had passed. Indeed, the White House was preparing to publicly announce that the bomb plot had been foiled," explained AP President and CEO Gary Pruitt.[36] However, the Department of Justice (DoJ) later secretly subpoenaed the phone records of the Associated Press in search of the leaker (as discussed in section III below), claiming that the "story did grave harm to national security and that the Department had only informed the AP that concerns over the physical safety of the source had been alleviated prior to the publication."[37]

Constructive engagement between the press and the government is critical to the future of a free and democratic society. By keeping the lines of communication open and communicating in good faith, journalists and government officials will preserve the press's role in informing citizens about government actions and the government's role in keeping the United States secure.

III. THE GOVERNMENT SHOULD RESPECT THE REPORTER-SOURCE RELATIONSHIP

To promote government transparency and an informed citizenry, the government must respect the fact that journalists sometimes rely on confidential sources to do their jobs. Although some people believe that news outlets can be too accommodating to those who want to remain confidential,[38] the rule of thumb is not to use unnamed sources. The Society of Professional Journalists Code of Ethics states, "Identify sources whenever feasible. The public is entitled to as much information as possible on sources' reliability."[39] However, in exchange for providing information or commentary that is newsworthy and in the public interest, there are times when sources will ask not to be identified in a story because they have a legitimate fear of retaliation of some kind, such as being ostracized from the community, losing a job, going to prison, or even being killed.

Sometimes stories that cite confidential sources are also based on leaks of classified or other secret government information from those sources. Once stories based on unauthorized disclosures are published, federal investigators and prosecutors try to enforce the criminal laws. They seek to identify the leaker and thus the potential defendant, often by attempting to force the reporter to testify or to obtain the reporter's communications records, especially in high-profile leak cases. However, as recent cases show, this seemingly logical investigative or prosecutorial tactic has grave implications for freedom of the press and the public's right to know.

In May 2013, the DoJ informed the Associated Press that it had secretly subpoenaed two months' worth of phone records, from April and May 2012. The DoJ was investigating the source of a May 7, 2012, article by the AP about how the CIA had foiled the second attempted underwear bombing of a U.S.-bound airliner.[40] The story was based on a leak of classified information and, according to the department, violated the Espionage Act.[41] The call and text messaging logs affected more than 100 journalists and covered more than 20 numbers including home and cell phones, the AP office in the U.S. House of Representatives press gallery, and AP offices in New York, Hartford, and Washington, even though just two AP reporters were on the byline of the single article. The DoJ did not give advance notice to the AP, so the company did not have an opportunity to negotiate with the department or challenge the subpoenas in court.[42]

In his letter to Attorney General Eric Holder, Gary Pruitt, the AP president and CEO, wrote, "There can be no possible justification for such an overbroad collection of the telephone communications of The Associated Press and its reporters. These records potentially reveal communications with confidential sources across all of the newsgathering activities undertaken by the AP during a two-month period, provide a road map to AP's newsgathering operations, and disclose information about AP's activities and operations that the government has no conceivable right to know."[43]

The DoJ explained why prior notice was not given:

There are a number of reasons—depending on the circumstances of a given case—that may lead the Department to refrain from negotiating with a media organization before seeking a subpoena for telephone toll records. For example, through the negotiation process, the potential target (the leaker) could become aware of the investigation, its focus, and its scope, and seek to destroy evidence, create a false narrative as a defense, or otherwise obstruct the investigation.[44]

The problem in the AP case, however, was that it was publicly known at the time that the government was investigating the leak, and thus presumably the leaker was aware of the investigation as well.[45]

This sort of government overreach has a predictable effect. When sources lack confidence that their identities can be protected, they are less likely to come forward and share valuable information with journalists. Just a few short weeks after the revelation about the DoJ's secret subpoenas, Pruitt said, "Some of our long-trusted sources have become nervous and anxious about talking to us—even on stories that aren't about national security. In some cases, government employees that we once checked in with regularly will no longer speak to us by phone and some are reluctant to meet in person."[46]

The AP's experience is consistent with a 2006 newsroom survey that confirmed that high-profile attempts to uncover confidential sources create a very real chilling effect. Many news outlets reported "a discernable shift in source relationships in the wake of the spurt of cases, with more individuals disinclined to speak on condition of confidentiality, even for general background information."[47]

IV. EFFORTS ARE UNDERWAY TO STRENGTHEN LAWS TO PROTECT CONFIDENTIAL SOURCES

When reporters are subpoenaed to testify in state court, they have laws to rely on when they fear a confidential source could be compromised. Forty-eight states[48] and the District of Columbia provide some legal protection, found in statutes or state judicial precedent, for journalists and their sources.[49] The state laws vary; some provide absolute protection for confidential sources while others create a qualified privilege. Some also protect journalism work product such as unpublished notes and outtakes.

However, there is no comparable protection at the federal level. In a June 2008 letter to the Senate Judiciary Committee expressing support for a federal shield law, 41 state attorneys general noted, "The federal courts are divided on the existence and scope of a reporter's privilege, producing inconsistency and uncertainty for reporters and the confidential sources upon whom they rely."[50] Speaking from experience, the attorneys general said that "recognition of such a privilege does not unduly impair the task of law enforcement or unnecessarily interfere with the truth-seeking function of the courts."[51] They concluded, "Reporter shield laws . . . must now be viewed as a policy experiment that has been thoroughly validated through successful implementation at the state level."[52]

A. *The First Amendment and Federal Common Law Provide Little Protection for Confidential Sources*

The lack of strong legal protection for confidential sources in federal court stems from the 1972 Supreme Court case *Branzburg v. Hayes*.[53] The court ruled that there is no First Amendment-based reporter's privilege to protect a confidential source when a reporter is subpoenaed by a grand jury, absent a showing of bad faith on the part of the government, particularly proof of "official harassment of the press undertaken not for purposes of law enforcement but to disrupt a reporter's relationship with his news sources."[54] Justice Lewis Powell wrote an enigmatic concurrence suggesting that there might in fact be a stronger reporter's privilege under the First Amendment. He said that the judge should apply a balancing test and consider the importance of both "freedom of the press and the obligation of all citizens to give relevant testimony with respect to criminal conduct."[55] But the federal circuits have since inconsistently applied the *Branzburg* interpretation of the First Amendment, particularly in criminal cases.

Some federal courts have flirted with the notion of a federal common law testimonial privilege similar to the doctor-patient and attorney-client privileges. Judge David Tatel of the U.S. Court of Appeals for the District of Columbia Circuit, for example, believes that such a privilege exists. In 2005, the D.C. appeals court considered *New York Times* reporter Judy Miller's motion to dismiss a grand jury subpoena that sought the name of her confidential White House source. The grand jury was attempting to uncover who illegally leaked the name of CIA agent Valerie Plame in retaliation for her diplomat husband questioning the Bush administration's justifications for invading Iraq.[56]

Although Tatel concurred in the judgment against Miller because he believed that "the balance in this case, which involves the alleged exposure of a covert agent, favors compelling the reporters' testimony," he wrote separately to explain why he believed a qualified reporter's privilege exists under federal common law.[57] He noted that virtually all states have a reporter's privilege and that journalists, like other professionals, "depend upon an atmosphere of confidence and trust."[58] Therefore, "denial of the federal privilege would frustrate the purposes of the state legislation by exposing confidences protected under state law to discovery in federal courts."[59] Although he recognized that the "suppression of some leaks is surely desirable," he understood that "the public harm that would flow from undermining all source relationships would be immense."[60] Thus, given the Supreme Court's First Amendment decision in *Branzburg* and that Tatel's common law view has not garnered much support in federal courts, journalists and their confidential sources have only a weak set of protections in federal cases.

More recently, *New York Times* reporter James Risen, in his 2006 book *State of War*, discussed Operation Merlin, a failed CIA plan to disrupt Iran's nuclear program that may have actually given the Iranians valuable nuclear technology.[61] Risen's reporting was based on classified information given to him by a confidential CIA source. The DoJ investigated the leak and eventually filed criminal charges under the Espionage Act against former CIA employee Jeffrey Sterling.

Although the DoJ had significant evidence against Sterling, including communications evidence, the federal prosecutor nevertheless subpoenaed Risen to testify at trial about his confidential source for the book (after two previous grand jury subpoenas). Risen filed a motion to dismiss the subpoena and in 2011 the district court agreed that Risen should be able to protect his confidential source.[62] However, the U.S. Court of Appeals for the Fourth Circuit reversed the trial judge, rejecting both a First Amendment and common law reporter's privilege in criminal cases in its 2013 opinion.[63]

Risen filed an appeal with the Supreme Court in January 2014, asking it to resolve the conflict among the circuits about whether a reporter's privilege exists under the First Amendment and federal common law.[64] However, the Supreme Court denied Risen's petition for certiorari in June 2014, allowing the Fourth Circuit decision to stand.[65]

B. A Federal Shield Law Would Protect Confidential Sources in Federal Court

Given the weak state of judicial precedent in protecting confidential sources in federal court, those in the media and journalism community have been urging Congress to enact a federal statute for the past several years. They argue that passing a federal shield law is crucial because reporters often cannot predict when the work they do will implicate a state or federal case (although reporting based on leaks of classified information will almost always spur a federal investigation).

Following the revelation in May 2013 that the DoJ secretly subpoenaed the phone records of the Associated Press, the Obama administration immediately called on Congress to reintroduce legislation from the 111th Congress.[66] Senators Chuck Schumer, a Democrat, and Lindsey Graham, a Republican, along with a bipartisan group of senators, introduced a bill in the 113th Congress, the Free Flow of Information Act.[67] Graham said, "A free press remains essential to our democracy. The media shield law tries to bring balance between those who report the news all the while protecting our national security."[68] The Senate Judiciary Committee approved the Act in September 2013 on a bipartisan 13–5 vote. As of the writing of this chapter, the bill has not come before the full Senate for consideration.

The Free Flow of Information Act would create a qualified privilege for reporters to protect their confidential sources in federal court. It would provide judges with clear and reasonable standards for reviewing a motion to dismiss a subpoena or other compulsory process that seeks to identify a confidential source or other information obtained by the journalist in confidence. In a criminal case, for example, to compel a journalist to testify the judge would have to conclude that

1. The government exhausted all reasonable alternatives sources of the information;
2. There are reasonable grounds to believe that a crime has occurred;
3. There are reasonable grounds to believe that the information is essential to the investigation or prosecution or to the defense against the prosecution;

4. If the subpoenaing party is the DoJ, the attorney general has certified that the subpoena complies with the Department's internal guidelines (discussed in more detail below); and

5. The journalist has *not* shown by clear and convincing evidence that disclosing the identity of the confidential source would be contrary to the public interest.[69]

The heart of the privilege analysis is the fifth element, where the judge would have to apply a balancing test and consider the public interest in gathering and disseminating the information or news at issue in the case and, generally, maintaining the free flow of information, as well as the public interest in knowing the identity of the confidential source. Thus, although the burden would be on the journalist to establish the need to maintain confidentiality, the journalist would also have legal grounds to argue before the judge that the public interest demands that the confidential source's identity be protected in a particular case.[70]

In a criminal leak case, however, a journalist would have to testify if knowing the name of the confidential source "would materially assist the federal government in *preventing or mitigating* an act of terrorism or other acts that are reasonably likely to cause significant and articulable harm to national security."[71] Thus, although the privilege would have to yield to national security concerns under certain circumstances, an important limiting characteristic of the national security exception in leak cases, specifically, is that the government would be limited to proving that compelling the journalist to testify is vital to preventing *future* harm to national security. And, importantly, the risk of further unauthorized disclosures from the unknown source would not, alone, be sufficient future risk to national security for this exception to apply.[72] If the judge finds that this exception applies, the judge would not be permitted to apply a balancing test and consider the journalist's countervailing argument as to why protecting the confidential source's identity is in the public interest.[73] The Free Flow of Information Act provides other exceptions to the privilege.[74]

Finally, the Senate bill would define "covered journalist" for purposes of applying the testimonial privilege, which would encompass the vast majority of people who use confidential sources in newsgathering. The person invoking the shield law as protection must have had the primary intent to gather news or information and disseminate it to the public. The person must also have (or had when engaging with the confidential source) some working relationship with a news entity or have a track record of doing freelance journalism, regardless of the medium of distribution; the definition is meant to be technology neutral. Monetary compensation is not an express requirement. Importantly, the bill includes a safety valve, giving federal judges the discretion to protect the source of someone who does not fit precisely into the definition of "covered journalist" if the judge finds that doing so would be in the interest of justice.[75]

Contrary to what some have argued, defining "covered journalist" for the narrow purpose of creating a testimonial privilege does not run afoul of the First

Amendment. Although the First Amendment generally guarantees all individuals the right to speak and publish, not all citizens may resist an otherwise valid subpoena to testify. The law recognizes that the private nature of certain professional relationships (such as attorney-client and doctor-patient) is worth protecting to ensure frankness and quality professional work even if evidence from those relationships would be beneficial to a case. The journalist-source relationship is no different, and Congress is free to specify the legal contours of such a privilege. In fact, the Supreme Court in *Branzburg* expressly invited Congress to craft a statutory reporter's privilege: "Congress has freedom to determine whether a statutory newsman's privilege is necessary and desirable and to fashion standards and rules as narrow or broad as deemed necessary to deal with the evil discerned and, equally important, to refashion those rules as experience from time to time may dictate."[76] Moreover, making some accommodation for journalists in statutory law is not new. The Freedom of Information Act, for example, defines "news media" for the purpose of granting fee waivers when obtaining federal government records.[77]

C. The DoJ Wrote Meaningful Revisions to Its News Media Guidelines

Following the revelation of the subpoenas for the AP's phone records, the DoJ announced that it would be reviewing its news media guidelines, which had not been revised since 1980.[78] In July 2013, the DoJ sent proposed revisions to the president.[79] The final rule was published in the *Federal Register* in February 2014.[80] Many media organizations applauded the department's effort but expressed the view that a federal shield statute was still needed.[81]

Although the policy "does not create any right or benefit,"[82] the guidelines are intended to ensure that the DoJ strikes the proper balance between "protecting national security, ensuring public safety, promoting effective law enforcement and the fair administration of justice, and safeguarding the essential role of the free press in fostering government accountability and an open society."[83]

1. The New Policy Applies More Broadly and Includes New Accountability Mechanisms

The guidelines set forth specific standards. The primary benefit of the guidelines is that they generally require the attorney general to approve ("personally endorse") information requests by DoJ prosecutors and investigators related to members of the "news media,"[84] whether to journalists themselves or to third-party businesses.[85] (The new guidelines contain significant exceptions whose practical applications are unclear: attorney general approval is not required for "members of the news media who may be perpetrators or victims of or witnesses to, crimes or other events, when such status . . . is not based on, or within the scope of, ordinary newsgathering activities"[86] and in "exigent circumstances."[87])

In all cases, the government should make all reasonable attempts to obtain information from alternative sources before seeking evidence from a journalist (often called the "exhaustion" requirement).[88] In criminal cases (applicable to leak cases), "there should be reasonable grounds to believe, based on public information, or information from non-media sources, that a crime has occurred, and that the information sought is essential to a successful investigation or prosecution."[89]

The new guidelines apply to more forms of compulsory process: not only subpoenas issued to journalists or third parties in civil and criminal cases, but also warrants to search the premises of a member of the news media or to obtain the content of communications messages pursuant to the Electronic Communications Privacy Act (ECPA) (discussed in section D below), and court orders issued pursuant to 18 U.S.C. § 2703(d) of ECPA ("d orders") or 18 U.S.C. § 3123 for a pen register (to record outgoing numbers dialed) or trap and trace device (to obtain the number of an incoming call).[90]

The new guidelines also broadly apply to all DoJ requests for "communications records" and "business records" about members of the news media held by third parties. "Communications records" include both the content of messages and certain noncontent account information or metadata (like the call logs obtained in the AP case) obtainable pursuant to ECPA: "source and destination information associated with communications, such as email transaction logs and local and long distance telephone connection records, stored or transmitted by a third-party communication service provider with which the member of the news media has a contractual relationship."[91]

"Business records" encompass "records of the activities, including the financial transactions, of a member of the news media related to the coverage, investigation, or reporting of news, which records are generated or maintained by a third party with which the member of the news media has a contractual relationship"— and such records are specifically "limited to those that could provide information about the newsgathering techniques or sources of a member of the news media."[92] Adding business records is critical given that a journalist's credit card transactions or travel itineraries could lead the government to a confidential source.

Perhaps the most important update to the guidelines was the creation of a presumption of advance notice to members of the news media when the DoJ seeks their records from a third-party business. The final rule states, "The changes to the policy also strengthen the presumption that Department attorneys will negotiate with, and provide advance notice to, affected members of the news media when investigators seek to obtain from third parties communications records or business records related to ordinary newsgathering activities."[93]

Specifically, the new guidelines provide that "the affected member of the news media *shall* be given reasonably and timely notice . . . *unless* the Attorney General determines that, for compelling reasons, such notice would pose a clear and substantial threat to the integrity of the investigation, risk grave harm to national security, or present an imminent risk of death or serious bodily harm" (this language is very similar to that in section 6 of the federal shield bill, discussed in section D below).[94] Importantly, that advance notice and potential judicial review might delay the investigation is not a compelling reason to delay notice to the journalist.[95] Notice to the journalist or media outlet that the DoJ obtained the journalist's communications or business records held by a third party may be delayed for an initial 45-day period; the attorney general must conduct a new "compelling reasons analysis" before authorizing one additional 45-day delay.[96]

The new guidelines also require that searches of journalists' third-party records be circumscribed: "search protocols [should be] designed to minimize intrusion into potentially protected materials or newsgathering activities unrelated to the investigation, including but not limited to keyword searches (for electronic searches) and filter teams (reviewing teams separate from the prosecution and investigative teams)."[97]

Additionally, in leaks cases, the new guidelines authorize information requests to members of the news media or third parties following a certification by the director of national intelligence of "the significance of the harm raised by the unauthorized disclosure and that the information disclosed was properly classified and . . . the intelligence community's continued support for the investigation and prosecution."[98] According to the July 2013 report, this certification is intended to be an additional check on DoJ actions in leak cases: "This change will ensure that the Department's investigative efforts are consistent with the harm assessment of the relevant intelligence agency prior to employing investigative tools involving members of the news media."[99]

Other accountability mechanisms include the creation of an internal News Media Review Committee to advise the attorney general when federal prosecutors conduct leak investigations, seek journalists' records without prior notice, or seek information that would compromise a confidential source.[100] The DoJ also created an external News Media Dialogue Group "to assess the impact of the Department's revised news media policies and to maintain a dialogue with the news media."[101]

Finally, the DoJ will enhance its reporting requirements:

Department attorneys will be required to report . . . whether an approved subpoena, court order or search warrant was issued, served, or executed, and whether the affected member of the news media or recipient . . . complied with or challenged the subpoena, court order, or search warrant, and the outcome of any such challenge. From this information, the Department will make public, on an annual basis, statistical data regarding the use of media-related process.[102]

2. The New Policy Makes Clear That Investigative Journalists Are Not Criminals

Not only can sources be chilled by government actions in response to leaks, so can the journalists themselves. In May 2013, in addition to the subpoenas for the AP's phone records, it came to light that the DoJ had used a warrant to seize e-mails from Fox News reporter James Rosen's Gmail account in 2010. In the warrant application, the DoJ argued that there was probable cause to believe that Rosen was an "an aider and abettor and/or co-conspirator" to a violation of the Espionage Act.[103] The government believed that Rosen received without authorization classified information from State Department official Stephen Jin-Woo Kim[104] and used it as the basis for a story about how North Korea planned to respond to a pending UN resolution "condemning the communist country for its recent nuclear and ballistic missile tests" with another nuclear test.[105]

In order to get around the Privacy Protection Act (PPA), the DoJ alleged that Rosen had committed a crime. The PPA generally prohibits the government from executing search warrants to seize work-product materials and other documents about members of the news media *unless* the journalist is suspected of having committed a crime, including violating the Espionage Act.[106] The media community was outraged that the DoJ would allege that an investigative reporter violated the Espionage Act in the course of doing his job. In response, the new guidelines state that the "suspect exception" to the PPA may be invoked to obtain a search warrant only "when the member of the news media is a focus of a criminal investigation for conduct not based on, or within the scope of, ordinary newsgathering activities" and not "if the sole purpose is to further the investigation of a person *other than* the member of the news media."[107]

Therefore, it appears that the DoJ in a leak investigation will no longer use an allegation of violating the Espionage Act as a reason to execute a search warrant against a member of the news media in an attempt to uncover the identity of the leaker. (The Free Flow of Information Act, if adopted, would partially preempt the "suspect exception" to the Privacy Protection Act by permitting a covered journalist to challenge any compulsory process seeking information that could implicate confidential sources even if the journalist may have technically violated the Espionage Act.[108])

Additionally, in response to the outcry over the Rosen warrant, the DoJ wrote in the preamble to its July 2013 report, "It bears emphasis that it has been and remains the Department's policy that members of the news media will not be subject to prosecution based solely on newsgathering activities."[109] In May 2014, Attorney General Eric Holder held the first meeting of the News Media Dialogue Group, during which he said, "As long as I'm attorney general, no reporter who is doing his job is going to go to jail. As long as I'm attorney general, someone

264

who is doing their job is not going to get prosecuted."[110] Although these statement are not binding on future administrations, the public nature of these statements was significant, especially given that some members of Congress have called for the prosecution of members of the press or otherwise alluded to their criminal culpability.[111]

Although improvements to the DoJ's news media guidelines are a positive development in response to a leak case, it is important to understand that they do not have the full force and effect of law and so cannot be a guaranteed check on government overreach.[112] Also, unlike the Free Flow of Information Act, they apply only to DoJ prosecutors and investigators, not to other parties who may seek information from journalists in federal court, such as special prosecutors, criminal defendants, and civil litigants.

D. Statutory Changes Would Better Protect Journalists' Communications Records

The AP revelation was so shocking to the media community because the DoJ was able to obtain the phone records in secret, without advance notice to the company or the journalists. Although the government did not obtain the contents of the reporters' conversations with sources, transactional information or "metadata" can be just as revealing. Yet current law does little to protect communications content and metadata held by third parties.

There is no doubt that the Fourth Amendment protects a person's private documents stored at home or at the office, whether in paper or electronic format. However, there is an outstanding legal question as to whether the Fourth Amendment protects records held by third-party businesses. This is a critical question for communications records in particular given that journalists routinely use web-based e-mail, land lines and cell phones, voicemails, text messaging, chat or instant messaging, nonpublic social media messaging, and cloud-based storage services. In 2010, the U.S. Court of Appeals for the Sixth Circuit ruled that the Fourth Amendment does apply to the *content* of stored e-mails and that the government, therefore, must obtain from a judge a warrant based on probable cause before seizing the records.[113] Unfortunately, other courts have concluded the opposite, relying on the "third-party doctrine" that citizens have no reasonable expectation of privacy, and thus no Fourth Amendment rights, in information they have voluntarily given to a third party.[114]

In the absence of a judicial consensus on the applicability of the Fourth Amendment, the applicable law for communications records is the Electronic Communications Privacy Act (ECPA) (specifically, the Stored Communications Act, which is part of ECPA), which Congress passed in 1986 seeking to create some statutory contours around this important question.[115] Under ECPA, the government may obtain *messaging content* that is 180 days old or less or unopened, *only* using a warrant based on probable cause; that is, there must be probable cause to believe that the new or unopened messages include evidence of a crime, committed by the account holder or someone else. Notice of the warrant need not be given to the account holder. If messages are older than 180 days or opened, the government may simply use a subpoena based on a standard of relevance to the investigation to obtain the content. (Note that if the account holder is a journalist and the government seeks to use a warrant, the government is bound by the Privacy Protection Act, as in the case of James Rosen of Fox News.) When using a subpoena for messaging content, the government must provide advance notice to the account holder. However, notice may be and is often delayed.[116]

Nonmessaging content stored in the cloud, such as a journalist's interview notes or draft articles stored using a service such as Dropbox, Google Docs, or Microsoft's OneDrive, also may be obtained with a subpoena and delayed notice.

To obtain *noncontent* account information, a warrant is never required under ECPA, nor is advance notice, as in the case of the AP phone records (though the revised DoJ guidelines are supposed to trump ECPA with the new presumption of advance notice). The government may use a subpoena based on a standard of relevance to obtain basic subscriber information, which includes the phone numbers a journalist called and was called by, the times and durations of those calls, and the journalist's IP address.

To seize other noncontent account information, such as the e-mail addresses of people the journalist sent e-mails to and received e-mails from, the IP addresses of other computers the journalist communicated with, and the addresses of web pages the journalist visited, the government must obtain a "d order" from a judge. To issue a "d order," a judge must conclude that the government presented "specific and articulable facts showing that there are reasonable grounds to believe that . . . the records or other information sought are relevant and material to an ongoing criminal investigation."[117]

To obtain location information generated by a mobile device (also referred to as stored or historic cell site information), some courts have required a warrant based on probable cause while others have permitted a "d order."[118]

Thus, it is quite easy for the government to seize a journalist's (or other account holder's) communications records, whether content or metadata, held by a third-party service provider. The ease with which the government can obtain this information about a journalist reflects how easy it is for the government to compromise confidential sources, often without the journalist's knowledge. Given the absence of universal Fourth Amendment protection for communications records, a diverse group of organizations known as the Digital Due Process coalition has been advocating for an amendment to ECPA that would require the government

266

to obtain a warrant based on probable cause for *all content* stored by third-party service providers, as well as location information generated by mobile devices.[119] Several bills were introduced in the 113th Congress to codify these principles.[120]

Additionally, section 6 of the Free Flow of Information Act would preempt ECPA's notice provisions, applying a presumption of advance notice in *all cases* where the government seeks information from a journalist's communications service provider or other third-party business. Delayed notice would be permitted for no longer than 90 days if the judge concludes based on clear and convincing evidence (for each 45-day period) that advance notice to the journalist "would pose a clear and substantial threat to the integrity of the criminal investigation, would risk grave harm to national security, or would present an imminent risk of death or serious bodily harm."[121]

By giving journalists and their sources meaningful protections, these new laws and policies would enable journalists to do their jobs with confidence. Laws and policies should respect the important role that the press plays in informing the public and promoting government transparency and public accountability.

V. CONCLUSION

The government can advance the cause of transparency by respecting the role of the press in a democracy, which includes respecting the reporter-source relationship. To ensure an informed citizenry that flows from government transparency, the legal system must better protect journalists' confidential sources and their confidential newsgathering communications. The government must also constructively respond to the issue of unauthorized disclosures of government secrets. Many leaks can surely be preempted with more proactive disclosures to the public. But leaks to the news media will still happen. Together, the press must act responsibly and the government must be willing to engage journalists in good-faith dialogues, to ensure that citizens know what the government is doing in their name and to minimize harm to individuals or national security from the publication of leaked information.

NOTES

1. Barton Gellman, *Edward Snowden, after Months of NSA Revelations, Says His Mission's Accomplished*, WASH. POST, Dec. 23, 2013, http://www.washingtonpost.com/world/national -security/edward-snowden-after-months-of-nsa-revelations-says-his-missions-accomplished /2013/12/23/49fc36de-6c1c-11e3-a523-fe73f0ff6b8d_story.html.

2. Bart Gellman, remarks at "National Security versus Freedom of the Press," American Forum panel discussion hosted by American University and the Newseum Institute (Nov. 6, 2013), http:// www.newseum.org/programs/2013/1106-american-forum/national-security-versus-freedom-of-the -press.html.

3. Patrick Henry, Speech on the Expediency of Adopting the Federal Constitution, Delivered in the Convention of Virginia (June 9, 1788), http://www.thefederalistpapers.org/category/founders /patrick-henry.

4. N.Y. Times Co. v. United States, 403 U.S. 713 (1971) (Black, J. concurring), http://www.law .cornell.edu/supremecourt/text/403/713#writing-USSC_CR_0403_0713_ZC.

5. *Id.*

6. Henry, *supra* note 3.

7. Jonathan Easley, *Obama Says His Is "Most Transparent Administration" Ever*, THE HILL, Feb. 14, 2013, http://thehill.com/blogs/blog-briefing-room/news/283335-obama-this-is-the-most-transparent -administration-in-history.

8. President Barack Obama, Transparency and Open Government; Memorandum for the Heads of Executive Departments and Agencies (Jan. 21, 2009), 74 Fed. Reg. 4685, Jan. 26, 2009, https://www .federalregister.gov/articles/2009/01/26/E9-1777/transparency-and-open-government.

9. *Id.*

10. Ezra Klein, *Was President Obama the Leaker?*, WASH. POST, June 7, 2013, http://www.wash ingtonpost.com/blogs/wonkblog/wp/2013/06/07/was-president-obama-the-leaker/.

11. *See* Spencer Ackerman, *NSA Performed Warrantless Searches on Americans' Calls and Emails—Clapper*, GUARDIAN, Apr. 1, 2014, http://www.theguardian.com/world/2014/apr/01/nsa -surveillance-loophole-americans-data.

12. Charlie Savage, *Senators Say Patriot Act Is Being Misinterpreted*, N.Y. TIMES, May 26, 2011, http://www.nytimes.com/2011/05/27/us/27patriot.html?_r=0.

13. *Meet the Press*, Mar. 30, 2014, http://www.nbcnews.com/meet-the-press/meet-press-transcript -march-30-2014-n67356.

14. IC on the Record, Declassified, http://icontherecord.tumblr.com/tagged/declassified.

15. Siobhan Gorman remarks at event hosted by Medill National Security Journalism Initiative and the Reporters Committee for Freedom of the Press on President Obama's Review Group on Intel- ligence and Communications Technologies (Jan. 24, 2014), http://nationalsecurityzone.org/site /national-security-privacy-rights-discussed-at-panel-of-journalists-and-lawyers-friday/.

16. Director of National Intelligence James R. Clapper, Remarks on Worldwide Threat Assessment, delivered to the Senate Select Comm. on Intelligence (Jan. 29, 2014), http://www.dni.gov/files/documents /WWTA%20Opening%20Remarks%20as%20Delivered%20to%20SSCI_29_Jan_2014.pdf.

17. Office of the Dir. of Nat'l Intelligence, Intelligence Community Directive 119 (Mar. 20, 2014), http://www.fas.org/irp/dni/icd/icd-119.pdf.

18. *Id.*

19. *Id.*

20. *Id.*

21. *Id.*

22. Editorial Board, *Clapper's U.S. intelligence directive is the opposite of trust-building*, DALLAS MORNING NEWS (May 4, 2014), http://www.dallasnews.com/opinion/editorials/20140504-editorial -clappers-u.s.-intelligence-directive-is-the-opposite-of-trust-building.ece; Editorial Board, *The U.S. intelligence chief's gag order does not stir trust*, WASH. POST (April 23, 2014), http://www .washingtonpost.com/opinions/the-us-intelligence-chiefs-gag-order-does-not-stir-trust/2014/04/23 /c7660e18-ca29-11e3-93eb-6c0037dde2ad_story.html; Matt Sledge, *James Clapper Bans Intelligence Community From 'Unauthorized' Media Contacts*, HUFFINGTON POST (April 21, 2014), http://www .huffingtonpost.com/2014/04/21/james-clapper-unauthorized-media_n_5186921.html.

23. Office of the Dir. of Nat'l Intelligence, From the PAO: Updates to ODNI Pre-Publication Review Policy, http://www.fas.org/irp/dni/prepub-pao.pdf.

24. Office of the Dir. of Nat'l Intelligence, Instruction 80.04, ODNI Pre-Publication Review of Information to be Publicly Released (Apr. 8, 2014), http://www.fas.org/irp/dni/prepub.pdf.

25. Adam Clymer, *Journalism, Security and the Public Interest: Best Practices for Reporting in Unpredictable Times*, ASPEN INST. (2003), http://www.aspeninstitute.org/atf/cf/%7BDEB6F227 -659B-4EC8-8F84-8DF23CA704F5%7D/JOURNSECRTY.(64PAGE)72.PDF.

26. *See, e.g.*, Byron Calame, Public Editor's Journal, *Keller Letter on Banking Data Elicits Intense Reader Reaction*, N.Y. TIMES, June 26, 2006 (discussing reader reaction to the article disclosing the government's monitoring of terrorist financial transactions under the Swift program), http:// publiceditor.blogs.nytimes.com/2006/06/26/keller-letter-on-banking-data-elicits-intense-reader -reaction/?_php=true&_type=blogs&_r=0.

27. Bill Keller, *Dealing with Assange and the WikiLeaks Secrets*, N.Y. TIMES MAG., Jan. 26, 2011, http://www.nytimes.com/2011/01/30/magazine/30Wikileaks-t.html.

28. *Id.*

29. *See* Rick Blum, *Stop Trying to Stop Leaks. Engage the Press Instead*, ROLL CALL, Sept. 16, 2013, http://www.rollcall.com/news/stop_trying_to_stop_leaks_engage_the_press_instead_commentary -227621-1.html.

30. Keller, *supra* note 27.

31. *Id.*

32. Dana Priest, *CIA Holds Terror Suspects in Secret Prisons*, WASH. POST, Nov. 2, 2005, http:// www.washingtonpost.com/wp-dyn/content/article/2005/11/01/AR2005110101644.html.

33. Gellman, *supra* note 2.

34. *Id.*

35. Paul Farhi, *Washington Post Wins Pulitzer Prize for Public Service, Shared with Guardian*, WASH. POST, Apr. 14, 2014, http://www.washingtonpost.com/politics/washington-post-wins-pulitzer-prize-for -public-service-shared-with-guardian/2014/04/14/bc7c4cc6-c3fb-11e3-bcec-b71ee10e9bc3_story .html?hpid=z1.

36. Statement by Gary Pruitt, president and CEO of the Associated Press (May 14, 2013), http:// blog.ap.org/2013/05/13/ap-responds-to-intrusive-doj-seizure-of-journalists-phone-records/.

37. S. REP. NO. 113-118 (Nov. 6, 2013), Senate Judiciary Comm. Report on the Free Flow of Infor- mation Act, S. 987, 113th Cong., at 6, http://beta.congress.gov/113/crpt/srpt118/CRPT-113srpt118 .pdf.

38. *See, e.g.*, Margaret Sullivan, Public Editor's Journal, *Introducing "AnonyWatch": Tracking Nameless Quotations in The Times*, N.Y. TIMES, Mar. 18, 2014, http://publiceditor.blogs.nytimes .com/2014/03/18/introducing-anonywatch-tracking-nameless-quotations-in-the-times/.

39. Society of Professional Journalists Code of Ethics (1996), http://www.spj.org/ethicscode.asp.

40. Adam Goldman & Matt Apuzzo, *CIA Derails Plot with Al-Qaida Underwear Bomb*, ASSOCI- ATED PRESS, May 7, 2012, http://seattletimes.com/html/nationworld/2018160830_apusairlineplot .html.

41. Donald John Sachtleben pled guilty in September 2013. Sari Horwitz, *Former FBI Agent to Plead Guilty in Leak to AP*, WASH. POST, Sept. 23, 2013, http://www.washingtonpost.com/world /national-security/ex-fbi-agent-to-plead-guilty-in-leak-to-ap/2013/09/23/4a17a3ce-2491-11e3-b3e9 -d97fb087acd6_story.html.

42. S. REP. NO. 113-118, *supra* note 37, at 5.

43. Letter from Gary Pruitt to Eric Holder (May 13, 2013), http://www.ap.org/Images/Letter-to -Eric-Holder_tcm28-12896.pdf.

44. S. REP. NO. 113-118, *supra* note 37, at 5 (citing letter from Principal Deputy Att'y Gen. Peter J. Kadzik to Hon. Bob Goodlatte (June 4, 2013)).

45. Michael Schmidt, *F.B.I. Chief Says Leak on Qaeda Plot Is Being Investigated*, N.Y. TIMES, May 16, 2012, http://www.nytimes.com/2012/05/17/world/middleeast/fbi-chief-says-leak-on-qaeda-plot -is-under-investigation.html?_r=0.

46. Lindy Royce-Bartlett, *Leak Probe Has Chilled Sources, AP Exec Says*, CNN, June 19, 2013, http://www.cnn.com/2013/06/19/politics/ap-leak-probe/index.html.

47. RonNell Andersen Jones, *Media Subpoenas: Impact, Perception, and Legal Protection in the Changing World of American Journalism*, 84 WASH. U. L. REV. 317, 369 (Aug. 2009), https:// digital.lib.washington.edu/dspace-law/bitstream/handle/1773.1/170/Jones_Article_Aug2009 .pdf?sequence=1.

48. Hawaii and Wyoming are outliers. The Hawaii legislature passed a media shield law in 2008, but it expired in June 2013.

49. Reporter's Comm. for Freedom of the Press, The Reporter's Privilege, http://www.rcfp.org /reporters-privilege.

50. Letter from the Nat'l Ass'n of Att'ys Gen. to Sens. Harry Reid and Mitch McConnell (June 23, 2008), http://www.rcfp.org/newsitems/docs/20080625_naag_letter.pdf.

51. *Id.*

52. *Id.*

53. Branzburg v. Hayes, 408 U.S. 665 (1972), http://www.law.cornell.edu/supremecourt/text/408/665.

54. *Id.* at 707–08.

55. *Id.* at 710.

56. *See* Joseph C. Wilson IV, *What I Didn't Find in Africa*, N.Y. TIMES, July 6, 2003, http://www .nytimes.com/2003/07/06/opinion/what-i-didn-t-find-in-africa.html.

57. *In re* Grand Jury Subpoena, Judith Miller, 438 F.3d 1141 (D.C. Cir. 2006) (Tatel, J., concurring), http://www.cadc.uscourts.gov/internet/opinions.nsf/AB27667DC06A22658525742B0054AE9B/$f ile/04-3138a.pdf.

58. *Id.* at 1168.

59. *Id.* at 1170.

60. *Id.* at 1168.

61. JAMES RISEN, STATE OF WAR (2006). An excerpt from the book appeared in *The Guardian*, Jan. 4, 2006, http://www.theguardian.com/environment/2006/jan/05/energy.g2.

62. United States v. Sterling, 818 F. Supp. 2d 945 (E.D. Va. 2011), http://www.documentcloud.org /documents/229733-judge-leonie-brinkemas-ruling-dismissing-subpoena.html.

63. United States v. Sterling, 724 F.3d 482 (4th Cir. 2013), http://www.ca4.uscourts.gov/Opinions /Published/115028.P.pdf.

64. Petition for Writ of Certiorari, Risen v. United States, No. 13-1009 (4th Cir. Jan. 13, 2014), http://images.politico.com/global/2014/01/13/risen_petition.html.

65. U.S. Supreme Court, Order List for June 2, 2014, http://www.supremecourt.gov/orders/court orders/060214zor_m6hn.pdf; *see also* Adam Liptak, *Supreme Court Rejects Appeal from Reporter over Identity of Source*, N.Y. TIMES, June 2, 2014, http://www.nytimes.com/2014/06/03/us/james -risen-faces-jail-time-for-refusing-to-identify-a-confidential-source.html?emc=edit_na_20140602 &nlid=63518611&_r=0.

66. Charlie Savage, *Criticized on Seizure of Records, White House Pushes News Media Shield Law*, N.Y. TIMES, May 15, 2013, http://www.nytimes.com/2013/05/16/us/politics/under-fire-white-house -pushes-to-revive-media-shield-bill.html?_r=0.

67. Free Flow of Information Act of 2013, S. 987, 113th Cong., http://beta.congress.gov/bill/113th -congress/senate-bill/987. A similar bill was introduced in the House of Representatives (H.R. 1962).

68. Sen. Charles Schumer, Press Release, Schumer, Graham, Bipartisan Group Push New Media Shield Law (July 17, 2013), http://www.schumer.senate.gov/Newsroom/record.cfm?id =345352&&&search_field=free%20flow%20of%20information%20act.

69. Free Flow of Information Act § 2(a)(2)(A).

70. The Free Flow of Information Act also applies to subpoenas issued to journalists in federal civil cases. *Id.* § 2(a)(2)(B).

71. *Id.* § 5(a)(2)(A) (emphasis added).

72. *Id.* § 5(d).

73. In other criminal, nonleak investigations and prosecutions that implicate national security, a journalist would have to testify if knowing the name of the confidential source "would materially assist the federal government in preventing, mitigating, or identifying the perpetrator of an act of terrorism or other acts that have caused or are reasonably likely to cause significant and articulable harm to national security." Thus, in nonleak cases, the judge could consider both prospective and retrospective harm to national security. Free Flow of Information Act § 5(a)(2)(B).

74. A journalist would have to testify about a confidential source if the journalist was an eyewitness to a crime or the journalist engaged in criminal conduct. Importantly, this exception does not apply in leak cases; that is, when the criminal conduct was the act of communicating the leaked documents (which is in direct reference to the Espionage Act). Free Flow of Information Act § 3. Other exceptions to the privilege include when knowing the name of the confidential source is reasonably necessary to prevent or mitigate a specific case of death, kidnapping, substantial bodily harm, sex crimes against children, or the destruction of critical infrastructure. *Id.* § 4.

75. *Id.* § 11(1).

76. Branzburg v. Hayes, 408 U.S. 665, 706 (1972), http://www.law.cornell.edu/supremecourt/text /408/665.

77. 5 U.S.C. § 552(a)(4)(A)(ii).

78. 28 C.F.R. § 50.10, Order No. 916-80, 45 Fed. Reg. 76,436 (Nov. 19, 1980).

79. Dep't of Justice, Report on Review of News Media Policies (July 12, 2013), http://www .justice.gov/iso/opa/resources/2202013712162851796893.pdf.

80. Policy Regarding Obtaining Information from, or Records of, Members of the News Media; and Regarding Questioning, Arresting, or Charging Members of the News Media, Order No. 3420-2014, 79 Fed. Reg. 10,989 (Feb. 27, 2014), https://federalregister.gov/a/2014-04239.

81. *See, e.g.*, Newspaper Ass'n of Am., Press Release, NAA Supports Revisions to Justice Department Regulations; Continues Call for Federal Shield Law (July 12, 2013), http://www.naa.org/News -and-Media/Press-Center/Archives/2013/NAA-Supports-Revisions-to-DOJ-Regulations.aspx.

82. 28 C.F.R. § 50.10(i).

83. *Id.* § 50.10(a)(2).

84. Unlike the Free Flow of Information Act, the guidelines do not define "news media," though they do expressly exclude individuals linked to terrorism or foreign powers. *Id.* § 50.10(b)(1).

85. *Id.* § 50.10(c), (d).

86. *Id.* § 50.10(c)(3)(ii)(C).

87. *Id.* § 50.10(g).

88. *Id.* § 50.10(c)(4)(ii), (c)(5)(ii), (d)(3).

89. *Id.* § 50.10(c)(4)(i)(A), (c)(5)(i)(A), (d)(3).

90. *Id.* § 50.10(b)(2).

91. *Id.* § 50.10(b)(3)(i)(A). "Communications records" do *not* include the name and address of the journalist; the length of service (including start date) and the types of service utilized; the telephone or instrument number or other subscriber number or identity, including any temporarily assigned network address; or the means and source of payment for such service (including any credit card or bank account number). Thus the DOJ could obtain this information without complying with the guidelines, specifically the advance notice requirement. *Id.* § 50.10(b)(3)(i)(B) (citing 18 U.S.C. § 2703(c)(2)(A), (B), (D), (E), (F)).

92. 28 C.F.R. § 50.10(b)(3)(iii)(A). The guidelines do *not* apply to "records unrelated to ordinary newsgathering activities, such as those related to the purely commercial, financial, administrative, or technical operations of a news entity." *Id.* § 50.10(b)(3)(iii)(B).

93. 79 Fed. Reg. 10,989–90.
94. 28 C.F.R. § 50.10(c)(5)(iii)(A), (e)(1)(i) (emphasis added).
95. *Id.* § 50.10(e)(1)(ii).
96. *Id.* § 50.10(e)(2).
97. *Id.* § 50.10(c)(5)(vi), (d)(7).
98. *Id.* § 50.10(c)(4)(v), (5)(iv).
99. DEP'T OF JUSTICE, *supra* note 79, at 5.
100. *Id.* at 4.
101. *Id.* at 6.
102. *Id.* at 4.
103. Application for Search Warrant of Gmail Account, Case No. 10-291-M-01 (D.D.C. May 28, 2010), http://apps.washingtonpost.com/g/page/local/affidavit-for-search-warrant/162/.
104. Stephen Jin-Woo Kim pled guilty in February 2014. Josh Gerstein, *Stephen Kim Pleads Guilty in Fox News Leak Case*, POLITICO, Feb. 7, 2014, http://www.politico.com/story/2014/02/stephen-kim-james-risen-state-department-fox-news-103265.html.
105. James Rosen, *North Korea Intends to Match U.N. Resolution with New Nuclear Test*, FOX NEWS, June 11, 2009, http://www.foxnews.com/politics/2009/06/11/north-korea-intends-match-resolution-new-nuclear-test/.
106. 42 U.S.C. § 2000aa.
107. 28 C.F.R. § 50.10(d)(4), (5) (emphasis added).
108. S. REP. NO. 113-118, *supra* note 37, at n.30 (referring to section 3(b) of the bill).
109. DEP'T OF JUSTICE, *supra* note 79, at 1.
110. Charlie Savage, *Holder Hints Reporter May Be Spared Jail in Leak*, N.Y. TIMES (May 27, 2014), http://www.nytimes.com/2014/05/28/us/holder-hints-reporter-may-be-spared-jail-in-leak.html.
111. *See, e.g., FBI Director Comey Discusses Legality of Reporters, Stolen Snowden Documents* (video and transcript), WASH. POST, Feb. 4, 2014, http://www.washingtonpost.com/world/national-security/fbi-director-comey-discusses-legality-of-reporters-stolen-snowden-documents/2014/02/04/e39a67bc-8dbd-11e3-833c-33098f9e5267_story.html; Braden Goyette, *Rep. Peter King: Reporters Should Be Prosecuted for Publishing Leaked Classified Information*, HUFFINGTON POST, June 11, 2013, http://www.huffingtonpost.com/2013/06/11/peter-king-reporters-prosecuted_n_3424541.html; Walter Pincus, *Prosecution of Journalists Is Possible in NSA Leaks*, WASH. POST, May 22, 2006, http://www.washingtonpost.com/wp-dyn/content/article/2006/05/21/AR2006052100348.html.
112. The guidelines provide a vague and weak explanation of consequences: "Failure to obtain the prior approval of the Attorney General . . . may constitute grounds for an administrative reprimand or other appropriate disciplinary action." 28 C.F.R. § 50.10(h). Also, "This policy is not intended to, and does not, create any right or benefit, substantive or procedural, enforceable at law or in equity by any party against the United States, its departments, agencies, or entities, its officers, employees, or agents, or any other person." *Id.* § 50.10(i).
113. United States v. Warshak, 631 F.3d 266 (6th Cir. 2010), http://caselaw.findlaw.com/us-6th-circuit/1548071.html.
114. Smith v. Maryland, 442 U.S. 735 (1979), http://www.law.cornell.edu/supremecourt/text/442/735.
115. 18 U.S.C. § 2703.
116. *Id.* § 2705.
117. *Id.* § 2703(d).
118. *U.S. v. Davis*, 2014 U.S. App. LEXIS 10854 (11th Cir. 2014) (requiring a warrant based on probable cause), http://caselaw.findlaw.com/us-11th-circuit/1669503.html; *In re Application of the United States of America for an Order Directing a Provider of Electronic Communication Service to Disclose Records to the Government*, 620 F.3d 304 (3d Cir. 2010) (holding that a magistrate judge may require a warrant based on probable cause, but "it is an option to be used sparingly because

Congress also included the option of a § 2703(d) order"), http://caselaw.findlaw.com/us-3rd-circuit/1537433.html; *In re Application of the United States of America for Historical Cell Cite Data*, 724 F.3d 600 (5th Cir. 2013) (holding that "d orders" for historic cell site information are not "per se unconstitutional"), http://caselaw.findlaw.com/us-5th-circuit/1640605.html.

119 Digital Due Process, http://www.digitaldueprocess.org.

120. Electronic Communications Privacy Act Amendments Act (S. 607, H.R. 1847); Email Privacy Act (H.R. 1852); Online Communications and Geolocation Protection Act (H.R. 983); Geolocation Privacy and Surveillance Act (GPS Act) (S. 639, H.R. 1312); Reasonable Expectation of American Privacy Act (REAP Act) (H.R. 3557).

121. Free Flow of Information Act § 6(c).

About the Editors

Timothy J. McNulty is a veteran journalist whose career in national and foreign news coverage includes roles as both a war correspondent and White House correspondent. He is a Lecturer at Northwestern University's Medill School of Journalism, Media, Integrated Marketing Communications and Co-Director of the school's National Security Journalism Initiative. McNulty was the *Chicago Tribune*'s Public Editor and, earlier, Associate Managing Editor for Foreign News. During a long career at the newspaper, including posts as National Editor and Foreign Editor, McNulty helped direct the newspaper's coverage of the September 11 tragedy, the American strike into Afghanistan, and the invasion of Iraq. Earlier, he was a national correspondent based in Atlanta. Following the reestablishment of diplomatic relations with China, McNulty was one of the first eight American journalists allowed to reside in and report from Beijing. Later as a foreign correspondent, he worked in Beirut and Jerusalem and reported throughout the Middle East.

In Washington for more than a decade, McNulty focused on social and political policymaking, including five years as White House correspondent. In 1992, McNulty won the White House Correspondents Association award for journalistic excellence for a series on the impact of satellite television on presidential decision making and diplomacy. McNulty was the National Reporter for the *Tribune*'s 1985 series on the emergence of an urban underclass, which won the Robert F. Kennedy Journalism Award and the Sidney Hillman Foundation Award. He won the *Tribune*'s Beck Award three times: for his contribution to reporting on Tiananmen Square, for his coverage of the Israeli siege of Beirut, and for distinguished reporting on the suicide/killing of more than 900 cult followers in Guyana. McNulty holds a bachelor's degree from Wayne State University in Detroit and a master's degree from Georgetown University. Along with co-editors Rosenzweig and Shearer, McNulty also co-edited the first volume in this series, *National Security Law in the News: A Guide for Journalists, Scholars, and Policymakers.*

Paul Rosenzweig is the founder of Red Branch Consulting PLLC, a homeland security consulting company, and a Senior Advisor to the Chertoff Group. Rosenzweig formerly served as Deputy Assistant Secretary for Policy and twice as Acting Assistant Secretary for International Affairs in the Department of Homeland Security, where his responsibilities ranged from aviation security, border control, and visa policy to international data sharing, biological threats, and international relations. He is currently a Distinguished Visiting Fellow at the Homeland Security Studies and Analysis Institute, a federally funded research and development center. Rosenzweig also serves as a Professorial Lecturer in Law at George Washington University, where he teaches a class on cybersecurity law and policy. He is a Senior Editor of the *Journal of National Security Law & Policy* and a Visiting Fellow at the Heritage Foundation. In 2011 he was a Carnegie Fellow in National Security Journalism at the Medill School of Journalism at Northwestern University, where he now serves as an Adjunct Lecturer. He is also a member of the Advisory Committee to the American Bar Association Standing Committee on Law and National Security and a senior contributor to the *Lawfare* blog.

Rosenzweig is a cum laude graduate of the University of Chicago Law School, has a master of science degree in chemical oceanography from the Scripps Institution of Oceanography, University of California at San Diego, and a bachelor's degree from Haverford College. Following graduation from law school he served as a law clerk to Judge R. Lanier Anderson III of the U.S. Court of Appeals for the Eleventh Circuit. He is the co-author (with James Jay Carafano) of the book *Winning the Long War: Lessons from the Cold War for Defeating Terrorism and Preserving Freedom* and author of *Cyberwarfare: How Conflicts in Cyberspace Are Challenging America and Changing the World.*

Ellen Shearer is the William F. Thomas Professor in the Medill School of Journalism, Media, Integrated Marketing Communications at Northwestern University and Director of the school's Washington Program. She also is Co-Director of the school's National Security Journalism initiative. She is a member of the board of advisors of the Defense Information School Foundation and is a Past President of the Washington Press Club Foundation. She was a leader in the News21 project on privacy and civil liberties post-9/11; those stories won a special National Press Foundation citation and were picked up by hundreds of newspapers and TV stations. Prior to the start of the war in Iraq, she created, with funding from the Robert R. McCormick Foundation, a course titled Covering Conflicts, Terrorism and National Security, which educated graduate students as well as working journalists on military strategy, conflicts, crimes of war, and terrorism—it was the precursor to the National Security Journalism Initiative.

Shearer was the conference coordinator for the Reuters Foundation/Medill Washington Conference, which addressed the quality of information Americans receive from the U.S. news media concerning Russia; she was curator for the Mongerson Prize for Investigative Reporting on the News and is the Medill liaison with the Crimes of War Project and Military Reporters and Editors. She regularly serves as an accreditor for the Accrediting Council on Education in Journalism and Mass Communications. Since 1999 she has coordinated judging for the White House Correspondents' Association's annual awards. She is co-author of the book *Nonvoters: America's No-Shows*, and has contributed chapters to six other books. Before joining the Medill faculty, Shearer, who has more than 20 years of experience in the news industry, was a senior editor at *New York Newsday*, a consulting editor at Newhouse News Service, and a marketing executive at Reuters, and held positions as senior executive, bureau chief, and reporter at United Press International.

About the Contributors

Rom Bar-Nissim is a California attorney who focuses on Internet, media, and entertainment issues. A 2013 graduate of the University of Southern California Gould School of Law, he received the Norma Zarky Memorial Award for Excellence in Entertainment Law. After graduating, Bar-Nissam worked with Professor Jack Lerner and the USC Intellectual Property and Technology Law Clinic on copyright, First Amendment, and privacy issues. He co-authored an amicus brief on behalf of the International Documentary Association and Film Independent in the Court of Appeals for the Ninth Circuit case *Garcia v. Google*. In addition, he co-authored a public comment on behalf of the visual art social networking platform deviantART to the Department of Commerce's green paper, "Copyright Policy, Creativity, and Innovation in the Digital Economy." Prior to entering the law, Bar-Nissam was an English teacher in Israel and the West Bank. He received his BFA in theater from Florida Atlantic University in 2002 and later served as artistic director of the film and theater production company Walking Man Productions.

Judith K. Boyd serves as the Northeast Regional Privacy Officer within the Department of Homeland Security U.S. Citizenship and Immigration Service (DHS/USCIS) Office of Privacy. Her responsibilities include promoting compliance with federal privacy laws, regulations, and policies through education and awareness training, policy development, and incorporating appropriate privacy protections into USCIS technology systems. She is also a Senior Fellow and Adjunct Professor with Long Island University's Homeland Security Management Institute, where she teaches and engages in research about constitutional issues related to homeland security. Previous positions held include Chief Counsel for the Minority, U.S. House of Representatives Permanent Select Committee on Intelligence; Deputy Associate General Counsel for Intelligence in the Office of General Counsel, Department of Homeland Security; and more than 16 years as an Active Duty and Reserve Army Judge Advocate and Military Intelligence Officer. Boyd earned a MA in Security Studies from the Naval Postgraduate

School's Center for Homeland Defense and Security, a JD from the University of North Carolina School of Law, and dual BA degrees in history and English from North Carolina Wesleyan College.

Sophia Cope is the Director of Government Affairs and Legislative Counsel at the Newspaper Association of America. She is responsible for all federal legislative and regulatory issues related to the First Amendment, open government/ freedom of information, privacy, intellectual property, and digital media. Prior to joining the Newspaper Association, Cope was the inaugural Ron Plesser Fellow at the Center for Democracy & Technology and worked on legal and policy issues related to civil liberties and technology. Prior to that, she worked at the First Amendment Project litigating cases relating to free speech. Cope is a graduate of the University of California, Hastings College of the Law and Santa Clara University.

Thomas M. Devine is legal director of the Government Accountability Project, where he has worked since January 1979. GAP is a nonprofit, nonpartisan public interest organization that champions the rights of whistleblowers, those employees who exercise freedom of speech to challenge abuses of power that betray the public trust. During his 35 years at GAP he has represented or informally helped more than 7,000 whistleblowers to defend themselves against retaliation or make a difference. He has been a leader in campaigns to pass or defend 28 domestic or international whistleblower laws—from the Whistleblower Protection Act of 1989 to the Whistleblower Protection Enhancement Act in 2012 for federal employees. Devine has been an "Ambassador of Whistleblowing" for the State Department in more than a dozen nations. He has authored or co-authored numerous books, including *Courage without Martyrdom: The Whistleblower's Survival Guide, The Art of Anonymous Activism*, and *The Corporate Whistleblower Survival Guide: A Handbook for Committing the Truth*, as well as law review articles and newspaper op-ed articles. He has received the Hugh Hefner First Amendment Award and the Fund for Constitutional Government's Defender of the Constitution Award.

Andrew D. Fausett is an attorney-advisor at the Department of Homeland Security. Prior to joining DHS, Fausett was an associate in the litigation department at Sidley Austin LLP and a law clerk for Judge Reggie B. Walton of the U.S. District Court for the District of Columbia, and Judge S. Martin Teel, Jr. of the United States Bankruptcy Court for the District of Columbia. Fausett earned his Bachelor of Arts degree with honors in religious studies from the University of Florida and his Juris Doctor degree summa cum laude from American University's Washington College of Law.

Emily Grannis is the 2013–14 Jack Nelson Legal Fellow at the Reporters Committee for Freedom of the Press. Grannis handles freedom of information issues for the Reporters Committee. She graduated from Case Western Reserve

University School of Law in May 2013. During law school, she worked as a legal intern representing clients through the Milton A. Kramer Civil Litigation Clinic at Case and the Federal Defender's Office for the Northern District of Ohio. She also reported on legal cases in New York and Cleveland for Bloomberg News. Grannis previously interned at *Legal Times* and the U.S. Supreme Court. She has a bachelor's degree in journalism from Ohio University.

W. George Jameson is a lawyer and consultant whose firm, Jameson Consulting, advises on national security matters, operations, and governance. He also is Chairman and President of the Council on Intelligence Issues, a nonprofit organization that educates the public about intelligence and national security issues and provides legal resources for intelligence officers who may need assistance. His lectures and writing on intelligence and other national security matters have included co-authorship of *Fixing Leaks* (RAND, 2013) and authorship of "Intelligence and the Law," in *The Law of Counterterrorism* (ABA, 2011). He is an Adjunct Staff member at the RAND Corporation.

Jameson served more than 33 years in the CIA and the U.S. intelligence community, most as an attorney and manager in the CIA's Office of General Counsel. He also managed legislative affairs at the CIA and the Office of the Director of National Intelligence, and was the Director of the CIA's policy and coordination office. His responsibilities have included reviewing the legality and propriety of operations including covert action, counterterrorism, and counterintelligence operations; war crimes matters; foreign relationships; information and privacy; security; and matters relating to formulation and implementation of intelligence community policies and reform. Jameson headed the CIA's litigation unit and served briefly as a Special Assistant U.S. Attorney in the District of Columbia and as Assistant White House Counsel. Jameson advises the Advisory Committee for the American Bar Association's Standing Committee on Law and National Security; he is a member of the Steering Group for the Bar Association of D.C.'s Committee on National Security Law, Policy & Practice; and he is a member of the ABA's Section on Administrative Law and Regulatory Practice. He is a graduate of Harvard College and William & Mary Law School.

Steven L. Katz has a professional background in law, national security, and the First Amendment. From 1986 to 1989 he worked to advocate for the passage of the Whistleblower Protection Act as Legislative Counsel to People for the American Way; then served as Chief Counsel to the Senate Subcommittee on Government Information and Regulation from 1989 to 1991. He also served as Counsel to the Senate Committee on Governmental Affairs overseeing the implementation of the WPA, working with individual whistleblowers and related federal agencies from 1991 to 1993. Katz was Chief Counsel to the Chairman of the U.S. Merit Systems Protection Board assisting in the adjudication of whistleblower cases brought by the Office of Special Counsel and as affirmative defenses by individual plaintiffs. Related government responsibilities included coordinating the Senate's

1991 hearings and oversight of the Pentagon's Press Restrictions in the Persian Gulf War; assisting in the development and promulgation of the President John F. Kennedy Assassination Records Collection Act of 1992; serving in the Executive Office of the President in the Clinton White House on the selection and nomination of inspectors general; and, serving as Senior Advisor to the Comptroller General of the United States. Katz left government service in 2000 and serves as a consultant to government agencies and nongovernmental organizations. He is the author of *Intelligence and the Law*.

Jack Lerner is Assistant Clinical Professor of Law at the UC Irvine School of Law. Prior to 2014, he was Clinical Associate Professor of Law at the University of Southern California Gould School of Law and the USC Annenberg School of Journalism. Lerner was also a Faculty Fellow at the USC Center on Communication Leadership and Policy. He served on the Legal Advisory Boards for the Code of Best Practices in Fair Use for Scholarly Research in Communication and the Statement of Principles in Fair Use for Journalists. He was also a member of the Carnegie Media Law for Journalism Schools Task Force. Lerner received a BA, with distinction, in English from the University of Kansas and a JD from Harvard Law School. He clerked for Judge Fred I. Parker on the U.S. Court of Appeals for the Second Circuit and Judge G. Thomas Van Bebber in the U.S. District Court for the District of Kansas. He practiced with Wilson Sonsini Goodrich & Rosati, P.C. in Palo Alto, CA, and had fellowships at Harvard Law School and the UC Berkeley School of Law.

Gregg P. Leslie is the Legal Defense Director for the Reporters Committee for Freedom of the Press. He has been with the Committee since 1994 and director of legal defense since 2000. He supervises the Committee's amicus brief writing efforts and journalism hotline services and is regularly interviewed by journalists on media law topics. He also serves as Editor of the Reporters Committee's news publications and guides. Leslie has served as a member of the American Bar Association's Fair Trial and Free Press Task Force, as chairman of the D.C. Bar's Media Law Committee, and as a member of the bar's Arts, Entertainment, Media, and Sports Law Section. Before and during law school, he worked as a journalist and research director for the Washington business and political magazine *Regardie's*.

Edward R. McNicholas is a global coordinator of Sidley Austin's Privacy, Data Security, and Information Law practice. His practice focuses on clients facing complex information technology, constitutional, and privacy issues in civil and white-collar criminal matters. McNicholas has significant experience with a wide range of complex Internet and information law matters involving privacy and data protection, electronic surveillance, cybersecurity, cloud computing, trade secrets, online advertising, "big data," and national security. His internal investigation and litigation matters frequently involve complex, multijurisdictional, and multinational litigation issues, particularly federal court jurisdictional and constitutional concerns, especially related to the First and Fourth Amendments. His practice has been recognized by numerous rankings including *Chambers USA* (since 2008), *Chambers Global* (since 2011), and the *US Legal 500*. He has participated in more than a dozen cases before the Supreme Court. Prior to joining Sidley, McNicholas served as an Associate Counsel to President Bill Clinton, advising senior White House staff regarding various independent counsel, congressional, and grand jury investigations. McNicholas received his JD (cum laude) from Harvard Law School, where he was an editor of the *Harvard Law Review*. He received his AB (summa cum laude) from Princeton University, and served as a clerk for Judge Paul Niemeyer on the U.S. Court of Appeals for the Fourth Circuit.

Gene Policinski is chief operating officer of the Newseum Institute and senior vice president of the Institute's First Amendment Center. He has been writing and commenting on First Amendment issues for more than 20 years, and is co-author of the weekly national column "Inside the First Amendment." A veteran journalist, Policinski joined the Freedom Forum, principal funder of the Newseum Institute and of the Newseum, in 1996 from *USA Today*, where in 1982 he was one of its founding editors. He also has hosted, produced, and directed television and radio news operations, including "Newseum Radio" on NPR Worldwide; and helped direct *USA Today*'s early online ventures. He is the occasional host of "Freedom Sings," a "live" multimedia stage production of the First Amendment Center. A trustee of the National Academy of Television Arts and Sciences and of the Association for Opinion Journalists Foundation, Policinski is an adjunct faculty member at Winthrop University in South Carolina, and is a member of the Board of Advisors for the Institute for Media, Culture, and Ethics at Bellarmine University, Louisville. He is a former trustee of the Watkins College of Art and Design, in Nashville; and of the United States Sports Academy, in Daphne, Alabama. A graduate of Ball State University, he attended the Nashville School of Law. In 2011, he received a special lifetime achievement Emmy Award for his work as executive producer of the public television series *Speaking Freely*.

S. Elisa Poteat is an attorney with the National Security Division of the United States Department of Justice and a member of the Division's Counterterrorism Section, the Antiterrorism Council, and the National Security Cyber Network. Before handling complex national security cases, she was an assistant U.S. attorney for the District of Columbia where her focus was prosecuting organized crime and white-collar cases. Poteat is also a former Public Defender for Los Angeles County and, earlier, clerked with the American Civil Liberties Union of Southern California. She is a dedicated bicycle commuter and the author of a weekly bicycling news blog for bicycling advocates and humorists. She also blogs on the environment and sustainability issues.

Jill D. Rhodes is Vice President and Chief Information Security Officer for Trustmark Companies. Previously, Rhodes spent 20 years working in and with the federal government. She joined the Office of the Director of National Intelligence in 2007. In her last position, she supported the intelligence community integration of data and security into the IC's Cloud Environment for the IC Chief Information Office. Prior to that, Rhodes was on detail to the CIA, where she worked with data management, foreign language, and training matters, addressing issues such as data security and exploitation. She has edited or published two books, including the recent *American Bar Association Cybersecurity Handbook: A Resource for Attorneys, Law Firms, and Business Professionals.* Rhodes holds a bachelor's degree from the University of Illinois, a JD from the University of Cincinnati College of Law, and an LLM from the George Washington Law School. She is a Certified Information Privacy Professional and Project Management Professional.

Harvey Rishikof is professor of cybersecurity at Drexel University School of Law and College of Computer Informatics. He is the chair of the advisory board for the ABA Standing Committee on Law and National Security, outside director of the Chicago Bridge and Iron, board of visitors member at National Intelligence University, former senior policy advisor to the director of National Counterintelligence Executive, and previous chair of the American Bar Association Standing Committee on Law and National Security. He is a lifetime member of the American Law Institute and the Council on Foreign Relations. Rishikof was a federal law clerk in the U.S. Court of Appeals for the Third Circuit for Judge Leonard I. Garth, a social studies tutor at Harvard University, attorney at Hale and Dorr, administrative assistant to the Chief Justice of the United States, legal counsel for the deputy director of the FBI, and dean of the Roger Williams School of Law in Rhode Island.

Steven G. Stransky currently serves as an Attorney-Advisor in the Intelligence Law Division at the Department of Homeland Security. As part of his responsibilities, Stransky provides legal advice and counsel regarding the Department's ability to collect, exploit, retain, analyze, and disseminate information and intelligence. From 2009 to 2011, he served as a Senior Policy Advisor in DHS, Office of Counterterrorism Policy, and assisted in the development of a wide range of national security policies and strategies. He also served as a DHS representative on the 2009 Guantanamo Bay Detainee Task Force and the 2009 Detention Policy Task Force, respectively. From 2008 to 2009, Stransky served as a Foreign Affairs Officer at the Department of State, Office of Iraq Affairs. He received an LLM in National Security Law from Georgetown University Law Center, a JD from the University of Akron, C. Blake McDowell Law Center, and a BA from the Ohio State University.

Dina Temple-Raston is the counterterrorism correspondent for National Public Radio and has just finished a year studying the intersection of Big Data and the intelligence community as a Nieman Fellow at Harvard University. Temple-Raston was the first Murrey Marder Nieman Fellow in Watchdog Journalism. Temple-Raston joined NPR in March 2007 and her reporting can be heard on NPR's newsmagazines. Prior to NPR, Temple-Raston was a longtime foreign correspondent for Bloomberg News in Asia. She opened Bloomberg's Shanghai and Hong Kong offices and worked for Bloomberg's financial wire and radio operations. She served as Bloomberg News' White House correspondent during the Clinton administration and covered financial markets and economics for both *USA Today* and CNNfn. Her first book concerning race in America, *A Death in Texas*, won the Barnes and Noble Discover Award and was chosen as one of *The Washington Post*'s Best Books of 2002. Her second book, *Justice on the Grass*, on the role Radio Mille Collines played in fomenting the Rwandan genocide, was a *Foreign Affairs* magazine bestseller. Her more recent two books relate to civil liberties and national security. The first, *In Defense of Our America*, co-authored with Anthony D. Romero, the executive director of the ACLU, looks at civil liberties in post-9/11 America. The other, *The Jihad Next Door*, explores America's first so-called "sleeper cell." Temple-Raston holds a bachelor's degree from Northwestern University and a master's degree from the Columbia University School of Journalism. She has an honorary doctorate from Manhattanville College. She was born in Belgium and French was her first language. She also speaks Mandarin Chinese and some Arabic.

Stephen I. Vladeck is a Professor of Law and the Associate Dean for Scholarship at American University Washington College of Law. A nationally recognized expert on the role of the federal courts in the war on terrorism, he is a co-editor of Aspen Publishers' leading national security and counterterrorism law casebooks, and has authored reports on related topics for a wide range of organizations, including the First Amendment Center, the Constitution Project, and the ABA's Standing Committee on Law and National Security. Vladeck has won awards for his teaching, his scholarship, and his service to the law school. He is a member of the American Law Institute, co-editor-in-chief of the *Just Security* blog, a senior editor of the peer-reviewed *Journal of National Security Law and Policy*, a senior contributor to the *Lawfare* blog, the Supreme Court Fellow at the Constitution Project, and a fellow at the Center on National Security at Fordham University School of Law. A 2004 graduate of Yale Law School, Vladeck clerked for Judge Marsha S. Berzon on the U.S. Court of Appeals for the Ninth Circuit, and Judge Rosemary Barkett on the U.S. Court of Appeals for the Eleventh Circuit. He earned a BA summa cum laude with Highest Distinction in history and mathematics from Amherst College in 2001.

Index

Index

Index

INDEX

Index